RETURN TO AZTLAN

STUDIES IN DEMOGRAPHY

General Editors

Eugene A. Hammel
Ronald D. Lee
Kenneth W. Wachter

RETURN TO AZTLAN

The Social Process of International
Migration from Western Mexico

Douglas S. Massey
Rafael Alarcón
Jorge Durand
Humberto González

UNIVERSITY OF CALIFORNIA PRESS
Berkeley   Los Angeles   London

University of California Press
Berkeley and Los Angeles, California

University of California Press, Ltd.
London, England

Copyright © 1987 by The Regents of the University of California
First Paperback Printing 1990

Library of Congress Cataloging in Publication Data

Return to Aztlan.
Vol. 1 in Studies in Demography

  Bibliography: p.
  1. Mexico—Emigration and immigration—Case studies.   2. United States—
Emigration and immigration—Case studies.   3. Mexicans—United States.
4. Return migration—Mexico. I. Massey, Douglas S.
JV7401.R47   1987   325.72'0926   87–5913
ISBN 0-520-06970-6 (alk. paper)

Printed in the United States of America

1 2 3 4 5 6 7 8 9

Contents

Preface

This book is a collaborative, binational effort by an interdisciplinary team of researchers. It does not present the views of any single author, but represents the consensus view of the entire research team. Every finding was considered and discussed in detail by all four authors, and results were not included in the book unless they met with the general approval of everyone. The findings reported here have been checked against qualitative data gathered through anthropological fieldwork as well as quantitative data garnered through sample surveys, and findings are not presented unless they are consistent with both sources of information. The book is not written from either a Mexican or an American viewpoint, and it does not adopt an approach that is only anthropological, sociological, or demographic. It is an amalgam of all these perspectives.

The preparation of the book was truly a team effort. Each author had primary responsibility for writing certain sections of the book, but the outline and approach to be followed in each chapter were decided by the team in advance, and each draft was subjected to a lengthy process of review, criticism, and modification by all four authors. The first draft was written in both Spanish and English. In subsequent drafts, Spanish portions of the text were translated into English and edited by the first author, and the final manuscript was prepared in English. The work reflects the effort all together and none individually.

Many people and institutions made this book possible. The research was supported by a grant from the National Institute of Child Health and Human Development in the United States, administered through its Center for Population Research, and the authors thank the institute and its staff for their support. Joshua Reichert was instrumental in preparing the original proposal for the research and in arranging initial contact between the collaborators. Guillermo de la Peña actually brought the research team together and provided administrative and moral support throughout the project.

The project could not have been carried out without the support of the faculty, staff, and students of the Centro de Estudios Antropológicos at the Colegio de Michoacán and the Population Studies Center at the University of Pennsylvania, to whom the authors extend their sincere thanks. In Mexico, special thanks go to Patricia Arias, Margarita Calleja, Macrina Cárdenas, Gloria Fernández, Luis González, Margarita González, Salvador González Villa, Elena de la Paz, María Sánchez de Tagle, Catalina S. de Spada, and Gustavo Verduzco. In the United States, special thanks are owed to Paul Allison, Christopher Colletti, Felipe García España, Nancy Denton, Eugene Hammel, Jacqueline Litt, Brendan Mullan, Miranda Tanfer, Millicent Minnick, Elsie Pamuk, and Bryan Roberts. Most of all, the authors thank the people of Altamira, Chamitlán, Santiago, and San Marcos for allowing us into their lives and sharing their experiences with us. Through them we have been able to see the process of international migration as the complex and deeply human process that it is. If this book is dedicated to anyone, it must be them.

Philadelphia, Pennsylvania   D. M.
November 24, 1986   R. A.
                                                             J. D.
                                                             H. G.

1

Introduction

If you drive up the Harbor Freeway from San Pedro to Los Angeles and take the exit for the University of Southern California, you will come to an intersection at the bottom of the ramp. Turn left, and you enter an all-American world of college fraternities and sororities. Turn right, and you enter Mexico. Except for the houses themselves, which are modest, pre–World War II wood frame bungalows, the neighborhood is much the same as any working-class neighborhood of Guadalajara. Parked cars and vans dot the curbsides, and children run through the streets chattering excitedly to one another in rapid Spanish. In the early evening young men gather on street corners to banter and to flirt with the young women taking their evening *paseos* (walks, strolls) around the block. Men sit quietly on porches, talking about the latest news from Mexico, drinking beer, and watching the dusk settle in, while their wives gather in front of the television sets to watch the latest episode of a popular Mexican soap opera.

A few blocks away lies an Anglo-American world of fast-food restaurants, video stores, and designer boutiques, but here the world is decidedly Mexican. A statue or picture of the Virgin of Guadalupe graces the front of most houses. The mom-and-pop store on the corner, the one with the sign that says *"Tienda de Abarrotes"* (grocery store) flashes *"Cerveza Bud"* (Budweiser beer) in red neon light through the window onto the sidewalk, and the larger market down the street advertises itself as a *Supermercado Mexicano* (Mexican supermarket) in big green, white, and red letters. Not far away is a *Carnicería* (meat market), where a butcher prepares *chorizo* (sausage) spicy enough to suit the most discriminating Mexican palate, and next door is *Novias* (sweethearts) *"Lupita,"* where young girls gather to admire the frilly white communion dresses. All down the street, the signs present a litany of Mexican culture, history, and geography: *Farmacia* (pharmacy) *"El Águila," Refacciones* (repairs) *"Lázaro Cárdenas,"* and *Restaurante "Birria de Chapala."*

Now imagine that it is December, just before Christmas, and you are driving along a highway in the Mexican state of Jalisco just before dusk on a Sunday evening. Judging by the traffic, you wonder whether you haven't taken a wrong turn out of Guadalajara and driven into California. Every other vehicle that passes has license plates from that state, and now and again one from Texas or Illinois goes past. Turning off the main highway onto a cobbled road, you see a small farm town in the valley below. Over the red tile roofs a thicket of television antennas sprouts, ensuring that few homes in this community will miss an episode of "Dallas."

As you pull into town, late-model cars, trucks, and vans with American license plates line the narrow streets where not long ago donkey carts and cattle were the only traffic. The main plaza is mobbed with people of all generations, standing, sitting, and circling in a welter of animated conversation. An out-of-tune brass band plays in the gazebo, and above the din a multitude of vendors hawk their wares, selling tacos, tortillas, ears of roasted corn, sweets, lottery tickets, balloons, confetti, and trinkets.

There is a palpable excitement in the air. At last the *califas* (Californians) have returned from *el Norte,* and people who haven't seen each other for many months are together again: mothers and sons, wives and husbands, children and fathers. Young unmarried women, especially, savor the few weeks that lie ahead, with their promise of romance, courtship, and perhaps, marriage. A party atmosphere prevails, as families, friends, and lovers try to pack a year's worth of life into the short time that lies before them. Soon the men will be called back by work and wages in the North, but for now the plaza is full of frenetic exuberance.

Evidence of the migrants' return is everywhere. In front of the church, young *cholos* ("cool" young men; "blades") stand listening to salsa music from a tape deck, wearing black tapered pants, plaid shirts, and nets over their perfectly sculpted hair. Behind dark glasses they watch lines of pretty young women walk slowly around the plaza in new designer jeans. Young wives cling tightly to the arms of husbands bronzed by the California sun. A group of men cluster on a bench listening and laughing while a migrant from Los Angeles regales them with stories of life in el Norte, salting his tales with English words to give them a ring of authenticity and sophistication. Children scramble through the plaza calling out to one another in English, telling of a childhood spent in Oakland, Los Angeles, or Bakersfield.

All over the plaza, people are spending money—buying drinks for friends, cakes for wives, balloons for children, or trinkets for sweethearts. The migrants, in particular, are free and easy with their cash. For a little while, they have both time and money to spare, and they want to enjoy both to the fullest. Many will pass the next few weeks relaxing in homes newly outfitted with color televisions, tape decks, video cassette recorders, stereos, refrigerators, and washing machines brought from the United States. Others will get right to work building a new home or fixing an old one, using the dollars they have brought or sent home. Still others will pursue some local investment opportunity: buying land, purchasing cattle, setting up a business, or buying new tools. In the coming weeks, the men will attend to the details of rest, work, or investment, and by February they will begin to disappear again, heading to el Norte.

These two sketches—vignettes of a migrant barrio in the United States and a sending community in Mexico—are common scenes from a way of life prevalent throughout the southwestern United States and western Mexico. During the 1970s, such scenes became increasingly familiar as Mexican migration emerged as a mass phenomenon involving millions of people. To many observers mass migration seemed to develop out of nowhere. Americans wondered where the millions of Spanish-speaking migrants had suddenly come from, and Mexicans fretted over the rapidly increasing influence of Anglo-American culture and the English language. Both became uneasy about the mutually dependent relationship into which they had fallen. Suddenly, after years of quiescence, international migration became a political issue on both sides of the border.

In fact, there was nothing at all sudden about the emergence of mass Mexican migration during the late 1970s. It had been a long time coming, the end result of a dynamic social process set in motion many years before. This social process involves a complex set of changes at the individual, household, and community levels. These changes, which unfold in a predictable, orderly fashion and are remarkably similar across communities, act in unison to cause an increase in international migration over time. In place after place, the social process of migration develops according to a well-defined internal logic. Once the process is set in motion, a powerful, self-sustaining momentum takes hold, culminating in mass migration. This book examines that social process.

MIGRATION AS A SOCIAL PROCESS

We are not the first to recognize that international migration has a social as well as an economic basis. Many studies have explored and documented the social changes that accompany migration, and these changes have received theoretical attention as well. Prior work has considered the social elements of migration in isolation of one another. They have not been viewed as parts of a single, integrated complex of changes acting together to produce a particular outcome.

We argue that international migration is a dynamic, cumulative process whose operation is governed by six basic principles. A major goal of this book is to illustrate and verify these principles, using data that we specially collected in four Mexican communities. These principles can be induced from a judicious review of the existing theoretical and research literature.

Economists typically view migration as a means of allocating workers between areas of low and high wages, which they assume reflect differences in marginal productivity (see, e.g., Lewis 1954; Ranis and Fei 1961; Todaro 1976). The Mexican-American wage gap by itself does a poor job of explaining trends in Mexican migration to the United States (Jenkins 1977; Blejer 1978; Frisbie 1975). Wage differentials cannot explain why poor communities equally distant from the United States send vastly different numbers of migrants or why migration suddenly begins after a wage gap has existed for years (Piore 1979). To explain these findings, one must consider structural relations in society. The first principle of international migration is that migration originates in structural transformation of sending and receiving societies.

In receiving societies, migration stems from economic segmentation, which creates a class of unstable, poorly paid jobs with limited opportunities for advancement (Bohning 1972; Piore 1979). Since natives shun these jobs, employers turn to foreign workers and typically initiate migration streams through recruitment. Mexican workers were actively recruited into the United States at the turn of the century, during World War I, throughout the 1920s, and especially during the Bracero Accord of 1942 to 1964 (Galarza 1964; Craig 1971; Samora 1971; Cardoso 1980).

In sending countries, migration represents an adjustment to inequalities in the distribution of land, labor, and capital that arise in the course of economic development (Furtado 1970; Hewitt de Alcantara 1976). Processes of enclosure and mechanization displace rural workers from agriculture, while capitalization displaces urban operative workers from factories, generating underemployment and unemployment, leading to international migration. Such a process is occurring now in Mexico (Alba 1978; Hewitt de Alcantara 1976; Arizpe 1981) and has occurred in the past in both Mexico (Cardoso 1980) and western Europe (Thomas 1954).

International migration may originate in structural changes within sending and receiving societies; however, the second principle is that, once begun, this migration eventually develops a social infrastructure that enables movement on a mass basis. Over time, the number of social ties between sending and receiving areas grows, creating a social network that progressively reduces the costs of international movement. People from the same community are enmeshed in a web of reciprocal obligations upon which new migrants draw to enter and find work in the receiving society. The range of social contacts in this network expands with the entry of each new migrant; thus encouraging still more migration and ultimately leading to the emergence of international migration as a mass phenomenon (Reichert 1979; Mines 1981, 1984).

The idea that social networks are central to migration is not, of course, new. Research in the 1920s demonstrated a tendency for migrants from particular sending areas to be channeled to specific districts in American cities (Zorbaugh 1929; Gamio 1930). Similarly, Tilly and Brown (1967) refer to the "auspices" of migration, by which they mean "social structures which establish relationships between the migrant and the receiving community before he moves." Others have called these relationships "migration chains" (MacDonald and MacDonald 1974; Graves and Graves 1974; Tilly 1978). Anthropological studies have long underscored the importance of assistance provided to migrants by relatives and friends (Magnin 1959, 1970; Jongkind 1971; Lomnitz 1975; Arizpe 1978; Roberts 1973, 1974, 1978). Economists have also demonstrated the importance of network connections in household migration decisions (Stark and Levhari 1982; Taylor 1984).

The third principle, based on generalization from the research literature, is that as international migration becomes more widely accessible, it is increasingly adopted by families as part of larger strategies for survival, with the timing of migration determined by life cycle changes that affect the relative number of dependents and workers in the household. The importance of life cycle changes in promoting migration has long been documented by sociologists (Rossi 1955; Simmons 1968; Speare 1974; Findley 1977), and recent studies from anthropology (Lomnitz 1975; Roberts 1978; Wood 1981; Pressar 1982) and economics (Stark and Levhari 1982; Stark 1983; Taylor 1984) suggest that households do formulate and implement strategies for survival in a changing economic world. Once networks have developed to the point where a foreign job is within easy reach, international migration becomes a preferred strategy among poor families seeking to alleviate pressing economic needs caused by many dependents and few workers.

The fourth principle is that international migration is strongly disposed to become a self-sustaining social process. The experience of migration itself affects individual motivations, household strategies, and community structures in ways that lead to increased migration. At the individual level, one trip has a way of breeding another, as high wages and living standards change tastes and expectations among people who initially plan only one trip (Bohning, 1972; Piore 1979). Within households, families adapt to the routine of international migration and make it a permanent part of their survival strategies. At the community level, studies show that migration alters social and economic structures in ways that encourage more migration (Randall 1962; Paine 1974; Rhoades 1978, 1979; Reichert 1981, 1982; Mines and de Janvry 1982; Roberts 1984; Wiest 1984).

The fifth principle, based on generalization from the research literature, is that no matter how temporary a migration flow may seem, settlement of some migrants within the receiving society is inevitable. Migrants may begin as seasonal commuters, but over time they acquire social and economic ties that draw them into permanent residence abroad (Gamio 1930, 1931; Taylor 1932; Piore 1979; Mines 1981). These settlers form cohesive daughter communities in the receiving society, which greatly strengthen the networks by providing a firm anchor for social relationships abroad and creating a secure context within which migrants can arrive and adjust.

The sixth principle is that networks are maintained by an ongoing process of return migration, where recurrent migrants regularly go home for varying periods each year and settled migrants return to their communities of origin. It is a sociological truism that every migration stream breeds a counterstream (Ravenstein 1885, 1889), and the process of settlement in the United States is partially countered by a concomitant process of return migration (Cornelius 1978; Mines 1981). Even among those who have lived abroad for a long time, many eventually return to live and work in their home communities (Rhoades 1979). Mexican migrants may be drawn north for economic reasons; however, they retain a strong sentimental attachment to their native culture, which is expressed in a powerful ideology of return migration (Cornelius 1976; Reichert and Massey 1979), a finding that has been observed among migrant groups in a variety of settings (Philpott 1973; Bovenkerk 1974; Bretell 1979; Rubenstein 1979).

These, then, are the six basic principles that shape the ensuing analysis: that migration originates historically in transformations of social and economic structures in sending and receiving societies; that once begun, migrant networks form to support migration on a mass basis; that as international migration becomes widely accessible, families make it part of their survival strategies and use it during stages of the life cycle when dependence is greatest; that individual motivations, household strategies, and community structures are altered by migration in ways that make further migration more likely; that even among temporary migrants, there is an inevitable process of settlement abroad; and that among settlers, there is a process of return migration.

NATURE OF THE STUDY

The study of migration as a dynamic social process requires a research strategy capable of securing valid and reliable data at many points in space and time. The approach we chose borrows from both anthropology and sociology. It combines the techniques of ethnographic fieldwork and representative survey sampling in an intensive study of a carefully chosen community. In this marriage of convenience, called the *ethnosurvey*, ethnographic methods provide historical depth and interpretive richness, whereas survey methods lend quantitative rigor and a firm basis for generalization.

A mix of quantitative and qualitative methods is not original to this project. Indeed, the approach can be traced back to the seminal work of Gamio (1930, 1931) and Taylor (1932, 1933). More recently, various combinations of ethnographic and survey methods have been applied to study migrant communities in several Mexican sending states: Jalisco (Cornelius 1976, 1978; Shadow 1979), Michoacán (Wiest 1973, 1984; Reichert 1979, 1981, 1982; Dinerman 1978, 1982), Guanajuato (Roberts 1982), and Zacatecas (Mines 1981).

This study expands these recent efforts in two important ways. First, it views the migrant community as a binational entity and collects data from migrants on both sides of the border. Sending communities are typically linked to one or more daughter communities through a dense network of interpersonal ties, forming a single continuum of social relationships. With the notable exception of Mines (1981), however, recent field studies have focused attention on only the stem community, ignoring its various branches in the United States. Second, this study considerably extends the amount and detail of quantitative information collected, compared to earlier field investigations, especially by making life histories an integral part of the survey design. In gathering exhaustive histories from migrants on both sides of the border, we emulate a research strategy pioneered by Gamio (1930, 1931) and Taylor (1932, 1933).

In spite of its debt to anthropology, the present study is not an anthropological investigation per se. Rather, it is a specialized study of a particular social phenomenon, made by applying anthropological and other methods. The anthropology of Mexico provides a backdrop to the analysis; however, the subject under investigation is international migration, not Mexican culture or society. A full understanding of Mexican migration cannot be achieved without knowledge of the context within which it occurs; for an appreciation of cultural setting, we rely on the classic studies of Gamio (1922), Redfield (1930), Foster (1942), and Lewis (1951), as well as on later studies by Wolf (1959), Lewis (1960), Nutini (1968), Fromm and Maccoby (1970), Bonfil (1973), and de la Peña (1981). Especially relevant to our investigation are community studies conducted in Michoacán and Jalisco, where our own samples were drawn (Taylor 1933; Beals 1946; Brand 1951, 1960; Foster 1967; Díaz 1966; Belshaw 1967; González 1972).

Although our study rests on a broad tradition of anthropological fieldwork, it is essentially an interdisciplinary analysis of a rather narrow subject: international migration to the United States. Since immigration studies in general, and those of Mexican migration in particular, are typified by a wealth of opinion and a scarcity of facts, the ensuing chapters emphasize the extensive data collected in this study. In telling our story of the social process of migration, we employ two kinds of empirical data: qualitative information gathered by employing ethnographic field techniques and quantitative data obtained through survey sampling methods. No generalization is offered nor any conclusion presented unless it is consistent with both sources of information. Neither kind of data is more valid than the other, but their simultaneous use endows each with a validity that neither would possess alone.

PLAN OF THE BOOK

This book is written for at least three audiences simultaneously, so it is not completely suited to any of them; nonetheless, we hope that it may be read in different ways by different audiences, each for its own purposes. At the most general level, the book was written for an educated lay audience interested in the subject of Mexican migration to the United States. These people will probably want to skip the technical details of the study's design and the more specialized aspects of analysis, which may be done by reading chapter 4, skipping chapter 5, and then reading chapters 6 through 11.

Chapter 4 examines the historical origins of U.S. migration within each of the four communities under study, explaining how and why migration grew from very modest beginnings to become the mass phenomenon it is today. Chapter 6 shows how migrants' social networks develop and grow over time and how they gradually support migration on a continuously widening scale. Chapter 7 analyzes the role that

U.S. migration plays in the household economy, studying how it is manipulated as part of a larger strategy of survival. Chapter 8 considers the impact of U.S. migration on the socioeconomic organization of Mexican communities. Chapter 9 shifts attention north of the border to analyze the process of U.S. settlement in some detail. Finally, chapter 10 summarizes the insights of the prior chapters by estimating four statistical models that measure how different factors determine key events in the migrant career. Chapter 11 briefly recapitulates the findings and makes some concluding remarks.

This book is also written for professional social scientists who are not immigration specialists. In addition to the chapters mentioned in the preceding paragraph, they will want to read chapters 2 and 3, which outline in detail the design of the study. Chapter 2 presents the rationale for the ethnosurvey method, and chapter 3 undertakes a comparative demographic, social, and economic profile of the four sample communities.

Finally, the last group of readers consists of immigration specialists, who will want to read the entire book, even chapter 5, which conducts a detailed analysis of current migration patterns within each sample community. This chapter was written to provide a set of standard statistics against which other studies might be compared and to indicate clearly the extent of current and past U.S. migration from each place.

2
Study Design

Migration between Mexico and the United States is a salient topic that has attracted the attention of social scientists from a variety of disciplines. It has been examined from many angles with the use of widely different data sources and diverse methodological approaches. Anthropologists have analyzed ethnographic information collected in Mexican migrant communities (Gamio 1930; Taylor 1932; Wiest 1973; Shadow 1979; Reichert 1979; Dinerman 1982). Sociologists, economists, and political scientists have studied sending communities from a quantitative perspective (Cornelius 1978; Reichert and Massey 1979, 1980; Mines 1981; Stuart and Kearney 1981; Roberts 1982). Other quantitatively oriented scholars have made productive use of national or subnational surveys to study the characteristics of Mexican migrants (Bustamante 1978; Zazueta and Corona 1979; Seligson and Williams 1981; Ranney and Koussoudji 1983, 1984; Selby and Murphy 1984), and still other investigators have creatively used U.S. and Mexican census data for the same purpose (Conroy et al. 1980; Bean et al. 1984; Passel and Woodrow 1984). One recent study used data on the flow of checks between banks in the United States and Mexico to speculate about the number and regional distribution of Mexican migrants abroad (Díez-Canedo 1980).

A study of Mexican migration to the United States presents special problems because many migrants are undocumented and, therefore, reluctant to reveal information about themselves to outsiders (Cornelius 1982; Rosenthal-Urey 1984). Community studies overcome this reluctance by interviewing migrants in the comparative safety of their home communities, but some migrants do not return home or do so with such infrequency that they will not be contacted even during prolonged fieldwork. Researchers have, therefore, experimented with a variety of approaches for gathering information on undocumented migrants in the United States.

In several studies data were gathered directly from migrants apprehended by the U.S. Immigration and Naturalization Service (INS) on the theory that, once caught, they would have little to lose by cooperating with investigators (e.g., Samora 1971; Dagodag 1975; North and

Houstoun 1976; Villalpando 1977; Avante Systems 1978; Flores and Cardenas 1978; Jones 1982). In other studies deported migrants were interviewed as they were released across the border into Mexico (Bustamante 1977; García y Griego 1979). Several investigators have used kin and friendship networks to locate nonrepresentative samples of undocumented migrants living in U.S. cities (North and Houstoun 1976; Orange County Task Force 1978; Melville 1978; Mines 1981; Simon and DeLey 1984; Browning and Rodriguez 1985). Others have interviewed undocumented workers located at their places of employment in the United States (Maram 1979; Mines and Anzaldua 1982; Morales 1983). Another strategy has been to locate undocumented migrants through churches or social service agencies (Avante Systems 1978; Van Arsdol et al. 1979; Rosenthal-Urey 1984), and in one study the investigators gathered a local sample of undocumented residents by working through birth records (Falasco and Heer 1984).

In spite of the plethora of studies, relatively little is known about the social process of migration. A general picture can be induced after a fashion from the research accumulated from these diverse sources; however, no single study provides enough information for a comprehensive picture of migration as a dynamic social process. A full understanding of the migration process requires information that is historically grounded, ethnographically interpreted, and quantitatively rigorous (reliable data gathered from a large sample of migrants).

Studies based on large sample surveys provide quantitative rigor but lack historical depth and ethnographic richness. Moreover, surveys are seldom designed specifically to study international migration, so information must be adapted from variables collected for other purposes, and often variables central to the migration process are omitted entirely. Even when surveys are designed to study international migration, they tend to be ahistorical and acultural. As cross-sectional instruments, they necessarily preclude the study of migration as a developmental social process.

Sample surveys also have limitations in dealing with the binational character of international migration. A complete picture of the migration process requires data on communities of origin and destination, as well as on the social networks that link the two. Few surveys are equipped to provide this kind of information or—especially—are adept at measuring the kin and friendship connections that constitute the social structure upon which international migration rests.

Anthropological studies avoid many of the problems of survey sampling, but usually at the cost of quantitative rigor and generalizability. Ethnographies are especially effective at capturing the richness and detail of migrants' social networks. Orally obtained histories supplemented with archival work provide historical depth, and the firsthand experience of fieldwork gives insight into the role that migration plays in the real life of the community.

The main drawback of ethnographic research is the relative dearth of quantitative information, which makes it difficult to demonstrate the veracity of findings to other social scientists. Subjective elements of interpretation and selection are more difficult to detect and control. The usual scientific canons of replication and reanalysis are extremely difficult to undertake with ethnographic data. Unless data are in machine-readable form, reanalysis, reconsideration, and replication are very awkward and laborious. One always has the uneasy feeling that were the fieldwork done by someone else or considered from a different point of view, different results might be obtained. [See Redfield (1930) vs. Lewis (1951) for a classic dispute between two ethnographers who reached different conclusions about the nature of community life in a Mexican town.]

The ethnosurvey method provides a means of overcoming these shortcomings. It combines intensive ethnographic study with representative survey sampling to generate precise quantitative information on social processes operating at the community level. Strictly speaking, the ethnosurvey is neither ethnography nor a sample survey, but a marriage of the two. Questionnaire design, sampling, and interviewing are shaped by the ethnographic conventions of anthropological research, while the ethnographies are guided and illuminated by quantitative data from the representative sample survey. In design and analysis the two approaches inform each other, so that one's weaknesses become the other's strengths. In the end, the data that emerge have much greater validity than would be provided by either method alone.

The concept of the ethnosurvey is not original to this project. Ethnographic and survey techniques have been blended in earlier work by Hammel (1969), Scudder and Colson (1980), and others. In Mexico, several researchers (Cornelius 1976; Reichert 1979; Mines 1981) have combined quantitative and qualitative methods to study migrant communities, following a tradition established by Gamio (1930) and Taylor (1933). The present study is unusual in having been conducted from start to finish by an interdisciplinary team of researchers representing anthropology, sociology, and demography. A qualitative ethnographic perspective and a quantitative statistical view were thus brought to bear on all phases of the study.

The ethnosurvey is not, of course, the last word in studying international migration. One is still faced with the issue of generalizability. The ethnosurvey is not a technique for aggregate statistical estimation. Facts and figures computed from ethnosurvey data cannot be easily extrapolated to the rest of Mexico or to the population of Mexican migrants. What the method does provide is a way of understanding and interpreting the social processes that underlie the aggregate statistics. The strength of the ethnosurvey is that it provides hard information so that the social process of international migration can be described to others in a cogent and convincing way.

QUESTIONNAIRE DESIGN AND INTERVIEWING

The design of the ethnosurvey questionnaire represents a compromise between the exigencies of survey research and ethnography. On one hand, a highly structured instrument consisting of a battery of closed questions is inappropriate for studying undocumented migration among rural Mexicans, many of whom are poorly educated or illiterate (Cornelius 1982); on the other hand, some standardization is required for collection of comparable information from each respondent. Basically we sought a design that was informal, nonthreatening, and as unobtrusive as possible, one that allowed the interviewer some discretion about how and when to ask sensitive questions but ultimately yielded a standard set of data.

The form we chose was a semistructured interview schedule. The instrument was laid out in a series of tables with household members listed down the side (entries in leftmost column) and variables across the top (column headings). The interviewer could then solicit the required information in ways that the situation seemed to demand, using judgment as to timing and precise wording, and filling in the table accordingly. Each table corresponded to a different topic, and these were at times separated by questions of a more specialized nature in order to elaborate a particular theme. The questionnaire was designed in Spanish during August 1982, pretested, and modified during September and October of that year. Fieldwork began in November.

The interviews were conducted by three of the authors, all anthropologists, who constituted the field unit of the research team. They were assisted in rural areas by local elementary school teachers and in urban areas by graduate sociology students from a local university. Obviously, in using an ethnographic approach that does not rely on standardized question wording, it is absolutely essential that interviewers understand clearly what information is being sought in each table of the questionnaire. The authors thus spent long hours going over the questionnaire in painstaking detail, making sure that each person had the same understanding of what information was being sought and why. The anthropological fieldworkers, in turn, placed considerable emphasis on training their assistants, repeating the ponderous task of going over the questionnaire line by line. In each community, subsamples of the questionnaires were checked with informants to verify accuracy, and additional checks for internal consistency were later performed with a computer.

The questionnaires were applied in two phases. In the first phase, basic social and demographic data were collected from all people in the household. In the opening question, the head of household was identified, followed by the spouse and living children. If a son or daughter was not currently a member of the sample household but had already established a home elsewhere, this fact was ascertained and recorded. One was considered to be in a separate household if one was married, maintained a separate house or kitchen, and organized expenses separately. Other household members were also identified and their relationship to the household head clarified.

A particularly important task in the first phase of the questionnaire was the identification of people with prior migrant experience in either the United States or Mexico. Each person who had *ever* been to the United States or who had *ever* migrated for work within Mexico was asked a series of questions about the first and last trips (date, duration, state, city, occupation, wage, documentation) and was asked to state the total number of trips taken thus far over the lifetime.

The second phase of the questionnaire compiled a complete life history for household heads with prior migrant experience in the United States. The life history focused on lifetime processes of occupational mobility, migration, resource accumulation, and family formation. If the household head had never been a U.S. migrant but an older son had, an abbreviated life history (mainly a labor history) was taken. Both groups were also asked a series of detailed questions about their experiences on their most recent trip to the United States, focusing on economic and social contacts therein.

SAMPLE DESIGN

The questionnaires were applied to households selected in simple random samples of four communities located in western Mexico, the most important source region for Mexican migration to the United States (Samora 1971; Dagodag 1975; North and Houstoun 1976; Cornelius 1978;

Jones 1982*a*; Ranney and Kossoudji 1983; Morales 1983). Two criteria were employed in selecting the communities. First, we sought towns or cities in which a member of the anthropological research team had prior ethnographic experience. With an established unobtrusive presence in the community and an existing network of trusted informants, the potential level of threat from a study of out-migration was considerably reduced and the validity of data much enhanced. Second, we wanted to select four different kinds of communities in order to give the study a comparative focus. With a few recent exceptions (e.g., Selby and Murphy 1984), prior studies have examined rural agricultural towns, and we sought to include urban industrial communities in order to broaden our base of generalization.

In Mexico, the basic unit of local government is the *municipio*, which is similar in function to a U.S. county, although it is typically much smaller. Each municipio has a town that is the seat of local government called a *cabecera*, which usually bears the name of the municipio. Outlying settlements within the municipio are called *rancherías*. Four communities were selected for study, two rural and two urban.

Altamira[1] is a rural municipio of 6,100 people located in a traditional agricultural region of southern Jalisco. A majority of its families engage in farming for household consumption on small parcels of land. Because Altamira has a relatively small population, it was possible to sample the entire municipio, which consists of 579 dwellings in the cabecera, plus 438 more scattered throughout twelve smaller rancherías. Chamitlán is a somewhat larger cabecera of 9,900 inhabitants located in a rich agricultural region not far from the city of Zamora, Michoacán. The area is characterized by much capital-intensive farming, and most of Chamitlán's families do not farm for household consumption but work as paid laborers in local fields or canneries. Because the relatively large size of the municipio strained our resources, sampling was confined to the cabecera alone.

The first of the two urban communities is Santiago, an industrial town of about 9,400 people located southeast of the metropolis of Guadalajara, in the state of Jalisco. Its main source of employment since the turn of the century has been a textile mill, and its population contains virtually no agricultural workers. As with Chamitlán, the large size of Santiago also required sampling of the cabecera alone. The second urban community is San Marcos, an urban barrio of 4,800 people located in a working-class section of Guadalajara itself, Mexico's second largest city.

---

[1] The community names are fictitious to protect the anonymity of respondents.

Its inhabitants generally work in one of Guadalajara's many crafts industries or in sales or clerical positions within its large service and commercial sectors.

Four very different kinds of communities were chosen, therefore, in order to provide a basis for comparative analysis and broader generalization: a traditional agricultural town, a commercialized agrarian community, an industrial town, and an urban barrio. These communities were *not* selected because they were thought to contain many migrants. Although we knew that all contained *some* U.S. migrants, with the exception of Chamitlán, which we knew had a long migrant tradition, we had no idea whether they contained many or few.

Detailed maps showing the location of dwellings in each community were prepared during August 1982, and from these the sampling frames were constructed. In order to minimize underenumeration, and especially to avoid overlooking migrant households, all buildings that could conceivably be used as dwellings were listed on the frame, even if they appeared to be unoccupied at the time. In all, 1,017 dwellings were enumerated in Altamira, 1,925 in Chamitlán, 1,903 in Santiago, and 831 in San Marcos. The interviews began in November 1982 and ended in February 1983; most were conducted during the months of December and January, the months when most seasonal migrants are home from the United States. Dwellings were selected with reference to a table of random numbers. If a structure was unoccupied throughout the month of December or proved not to be a dwelling, or if the interview was refused, another dwelling was randomly selected. Strictly speaking, then, the sample is representative of dwelling units that were occupied during the month of December 1982 in each of the four communities.

Details of the sampling procedures are summarized in table 2.1. In each community we sought to compile a random sample of 200 households. This number was judged large enough to provide a sufficient number of cases for analysis, yet small enough so that detailed, ethnographically informed interviews could be conducted. Because of refusals and other problems, between 208 and 235 dwellings were selected to achieve the target size of 200. Overall, the refusal rate was relatively modest, ranging from 1.5 percent to 4.8 percent. In Altamira, two questionnaires were discarded because cross-checking with informants revealed systematic misrepresentation among the answers. In Chamitlán, one of the selected dwellings was found to be that of the field investigator and could not be used. Of the eight problematic interviews in Santiago, four were not completed because of difficulties in arranging a meeting time and the other four, because the address could not be

TABLE 2.1
CHARACTERISTICS OF SAMPLES DRAWN IN FOUR MEXICAN COMMUNITIES:
NOVEMBER–FEBRUARY 1982–1983

| | Community | | | |
Characteristic	Altamira	Chamitlán	Santiago	San Marcos
Number of dwellings selected	208	227	221	235
Vacant dwellings	0	20	5	8
Nondwellings	0	3	0	8
Refusals	6	3	8	10
Other problem	2	1	8	9
Number of dwellings surveyed	200	200	200	200
Number of dwellings on frame	1,017	1,925	1,903	831
Sampling fraction	.197	.104	.105	.241
Refusal rate	.038	.015	.038	.048
Standard error				
With P = .50	.032	.033	.033	.031
With P = .40	.031	.033	.033	.030
With P = .30	.029	.031	.031	.028
With P = .20	.025	.027	.027	.025
With P = .10	.019	.020	.020	.018

located. In San Marcos, respondents in six dwellings could not arrange a meeting time and there were three cases of incorrect addresses.

Since the total number of dwellings in each of the four communities ranged from 831 to 1,925, a constant sample size implies a varying sampling fraction. In Chamitlán and Santiago this fraction was about 10 percent, whereas in Altamira and San Marcos it was much higher, about 20 percent and 25 percent, respectively. At the bottom of table 2.1, standard errors are shown for different assumed population proportions. As the relative frequency of the trait under consideration varies from .10 to .50, the standard error changes slightly, varying between .02 and .03. The 95 percent confidence interval thus has a width of between eight and twelve percentage points.

In Santiago, relatively few migrants turned up in early interviews conducted within sample households. In order to guarantee a number of migrants sufficient for detailed analyses, an additional 25 migrant households were located and interviewed from outside the sample. Unless specifically noted, results for Santiago presented in this book exclude these extra cases. (Their exclusion does not markedly change the pattern of results). In all, the four communities yielded a sample of

5,945 people enumerated in 825 households. Of these people, 4,953 were members of sample households and 1,352 were older sons and daughters of the household head who had already left home to form their own households.

Obviously, studies limited to migrants interviewed in their home communities underrepresent, if not exclude, migrants who have settled more permanently in the United States. The four community samples were supplemented by an additional sixty interviews conducted with members of households residing in California during August and September 1983, therefore, using a slightly modified version of the ethnosurvey questionnaire. Representative random sampling was impossible, so migrants were located by using the chain-referral or "snowball" method (Goodman 1961), and both documented and undocumented migrants were included. Twenty households each were selected from Altamira, Chamitlán, and Santiago, yielding a total sample of 367 California-based migrants in sixty households. Of these, 305 were members of the sample households and 62 were sons and daughters living in their own households. A household was eligible for inclusion in the California sample if its head had been in the United States for three continuous years and was born in either Altamira, Chamitlán, or Santiago. Out-migrants from San Marcos were not sought because most were not born there, since they were migrants to Guadalajara from surrounding rural communities.

This sampling design produced four kinds of data that were combined in different ways for different purposes. The fundamental data are the representative community samples, which include members of 200 households selected in each of the four communities. These data are supplemented by information from three other sources: older children of the household head who were no longer part of the household at the time of the survey ("nonhousehold members"); the twenty-five extra migrant households that were surveyed in Santiago to boost the number of migrants in the sample (the "extra Santiago households"); and the sixty permanent out-migrant households that were surveyed in California (the "California sample").

In general, the strict community samples were used by themselves whenever the goal of analysis was to represent the state of affairs in the communities at the time of the survey, as in chapters three, five, and seven. When the purpose of analysis was to examine migrants or their effects in depth and from the Mexican viewpoint, as in chapters four and eight, the strict community samples were supplemented by data gathered from the nonhousehold members and the extra Santiago households. (Tables were prepared with and without these additional data items and inspected to make sure that results were not markedly affected by their inclusion.) Finally, when the goal of analysis was to study migrant processes in both the United States and Mexico, as in chapters six, nine, and ten, the California data were included as well. Throughout the book, notes at the bottom of each table attempt to state clearly the precise sample from which results were derived. In these notes, "all persons" and "all migrants" indicate that nonhousehold members were included in the table, while the term "household members" means that these people were excluded.

Throughout the course of the fieldwork, but especially between the Mexican and U.S. phases of the ethnosurvey (roughly February through July 1983), the anthropological field team conducted a thorough ethnographic study in each of the four communities. The investigators used this time to read historical documents in local archives, construct genealogies of migrant and nonmigrant families, conduct additional in-depth interviews with selected migrants, and compile a series of case studies among migrant families. The study draws not only on quantitative data garnered from the ethnosurvey interviews, therefore, but also on qualitative data gathered through intensive ethnographic fieldwork.

DATA CODING AND FILE CONSTRUCTION

Following the end of the Mexican phase of the ethnosurvey in February 1983, data were transcribed onto specially designed codesheets at the Colegio de Michoacán in Zamora. Coding was done by the field assistants, who were already familiar with the questionnaire through their prior experience as interviewers. Following initial coding in Mexico, the data were shipped for entry onto computer at the University of Pennsylvania. Data were logged directly onto magnetic disk by use of special data entry programs that simultaneously verified and checked the information for clerical errors. After initial entry and screening, all data were subjected to an extensive set of logical checks for internal consistency.

When all the necessary corrections had been made, data were organized into four data files, which together comprise the quantitative data base for the book: PERSFILE contains basic social and demographic data on 6,312 persons enumerated in the 885 sample households, including the 60 California households; HOUSEFILE contains information on the socioeconomic status of the 825 households sampled in Mexico; MIGFILE contains detailed information on the U.S. experiences of 440 migrants on their latest U.S. trip; and LIFEFILE contains the individual life histories of household heads (and a few older sons) who reported U.S. migrant experience. The latter file, LIFEFILE, goes through each respondent's life year by year from the first job onward, recording changes in occupation, marital status, family composition, migrant characteristics, and economic status. It contains more than 22,000 person-years of information.

SUMMARY

This study employs the ethnosurvey approach to gather data on the social process of Mexican migration to the United States. This approach combines survey sampling methods with ethnographic field methods in order to generate valid and reliable data on the social process of migration. Quantitative and qualitative data are compared throughout the study to yield results of greater validity than either an ethnography or a sample survey could provide alone. The method was designed to provide a picture of Mexican-U.S. migration that is historically grounded, ethnographically interpretable, quantitatively accurate, and rooted in receiving as well as sending areas.

Questionnaires were designed in a semistructured format to produce an interview schedule that was flexible, unobtrusive, and nonthreatening. The structure of the questionnaire allowed the interviewer discretion as to when and how to ask sensitive questions. The ethnosurvey data were cross-checked with local informants to ensure their validity, and a separate ethnographic study of the community was conducted to provide an independent base of qualitative information.

Four different kinds of communities were sampled in order to provide a basis for comparative study and generalization: a traditional rural town, a commercialized agricultural community, an industrial town, and an urban barrio. Simple random samples of 200 households were selected from each location, except in the industrial town, where an additional 25 migrant households were chosen. Because the communities were of different sizes, the sampling fraction varied from about 10 percent to 25 percent, yielding standard errors ranging from two to three percentage points. Interviewing occurred during the months of December and January 1982–1983, when most seasonal migrants were at home. This Mexican-based field survey was followed in August and September of 1983 by a nonrandom "snowball" sample of 60 permanent out-migrant households living in California, giving information on a total of 885 households and 6,312 people.

The ethnosurvey data were organized into four files: PERSFILE, containing basic social and demographic data on all persons in the sample; HOUSEFILE, containing data on the socioeconomic status of households; MIGFILE, holding detailed information on migrants' experiences on their last U.S. trip; and LIFEFILE, containing life histories of selected U.S. migrants. These files, together with the separate ethnographic and historical information, provide the data on which this book is based.

3

A Profile of the Four Communities

GEOGRAPHIC SETTING

As mentioned in the last chapter, the four study communities are located in western Mexico, the traditional source region for migration to the United States. This region includes the states of Jalisco, Michoacán, Zacatecas, Colima, Aguascalientes, Nayarit, and Guanajuato (see map, fig. 3.1). Historically, these states have made up an integrated regional economy held together by strong social, economic, and cultural ties centered in Guadalajara. Surveys indicate that between half and three-quarters of all Mexican migrants come from these states and between a quarter and a half come from Michoacán and Jalisco alone (Bustamante 1984; Jones 1984).

Altamira lies in the Valley of Sayula in southern Jalisco. This valley is formed by a ridge of mountains that rises up from a saltwater lagoon in the valley floor to the sierra of Tapalpa above. The municipio extends from the edge of the lagoon to the top of the ridge and occupies about 132 square kilometers. At the shoreline the slope is almost imperceptible, but the land rises quite steeply from the foot of the ridge. The most productive farmland lies in a flat, narrow strip between the lagoon and the base of the mountain. Here fresh water runs in underground streams at a depth of 20 to 120 meters, permitting some irrigation. Irrigated land is scarce, however, and most families farm the hillsides, which are dry, rocky, and unproductive.

Altamira and its rancherías are situated on a moderate slope near the base of the ridge. The adobe and tile houses are shaded by groves of walnut and fruit trees, which grow in small plots around them or in larger orchards outside the settlements. The orchards are fed by springs that flow down from the sierra. The trees provide supplemental food and income for many families, a majority of whom subsist on small-scale farming (González 1981). Historically, the valley of Sayula has been a very traditional area, and the graphic depiction of its way of life by the Mexican writer Juan Rulfo (1953, 1955) has made it well known throughout Mexico.

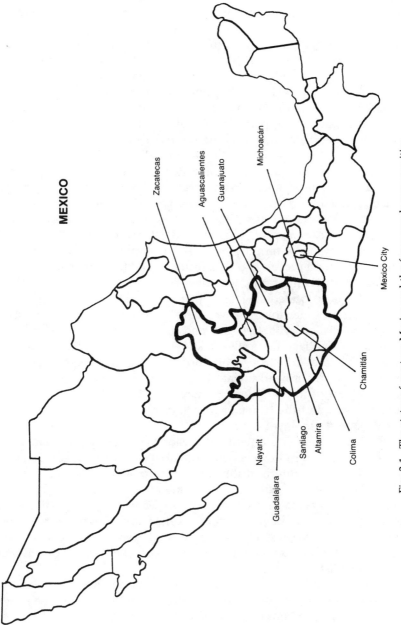

MEXICO

Zacatecas

Aguascalientes

Guanajuato

Michoacán

Nayarit

Guadalajara

Santiago

Altamira

Colima

Chamitlán

Mexico City

Fig. 3.1. The states of western Mexico and the four sample communities.

Chamitlán lies in a basin of rich agricultural land in the highlands of northeastern Michoacán known as the Zamora Valley (González 1978). Since colonial times this valley has been an important center of commercial agriculture, thanks to an abundance of level, moist land, a good part of which is irrigated (Verduzco 1984). The municipio of Chamitlán, in particular, has historically been an important agrarian center, lying in a part of the valley that experienced intensive agricultural development related to the availability of water. The northeastern section of the municipio is part of a federal irrigation district, and although most townspeople own land in the northwestern section, which is dry, some parcels there are irrigated by deep wells.

Because of the abundance of water and rich farmland, the area around Chamitlán has long been attractive to large, heavily capitalized agricultural enterprises. Production is geared largely to national and international markets. Cash crops such as strawberries and sorghum are grown for sale or export, mostly to the United States. This intense commercialization of farming has made the valley a regional center of canning and food processing. As a result, Chamitlán's families rely more on wage labor than farming for self-support.

Santiago is located in Jalisco just southeast of Guadalajara. It is different from other towns in western Mexico, which typically have a strong association with the land and agrarian traditions. In contrast, residents of Santiago have always known an industrial way of life. The town was founded in 1896, when British engineers built a large textile factory alongside a nearby waterfall, which provided a natural source of power. Since its inception, Santiago has been first and foremost a factory town, and the textile factory survives to the present day as the town's largest employer.

With the dynamic economic expansion of nearby Guadalajara during the last two decades, however, an industrial corridor has extended some twenty kilometers south of the city, enveloping the town of Santiago. Within this industrial zone, large multinational firms have built modern factories and plants, with petrochemicals leading the way. Given their long industrial experience, factory workers from Santiago were well poised to take advantage of this expansion. In recent years many townspeople have secured employment outside the textile mill in one of these newly established plants.

Guadalajara itself is, of course, a major metropolis. It is not only the capital of Jalisco; it is also the capital of western Mexico and the second largest city in the country, with a population of around 2.8 million. Located in the geographic center of the region, it has historically been the commercial, industrial, and administrative center of western Mexico. Guadalajara has a highly diversified economy with significant employment in modern industries such as petrochemicals and electronics. It also supports large commercial and service sectors. In spite of its many large, modern factories and offices, however, Guadalajara's industrial structure is dominated by numerous small-scale firms (Arias 1980; Lailson 1980; Alba 1985). In the national division of labor, it specializes in the production of basic consumer goods such as clothing, shoes, and foods, which are often produced clandestinely in small workshops. An extensive "underground economy" supports a large secondary labor market that operates outside the control and regulation of the state (Arias and Durand 1985).

Guadalajara is highly segregated by social class (Walton 1978). Officially, the city is divided into four administrative areas, but in reality it is split in half socially and economically by the Calzada Independencia, a main avenue that follows the old bed of the San Juan River through the center of town. To the east are the Reforma and Libertad sectors, which house the poorer classes, many of whom are migrants from rural areas. To the west are Hidalgo, a fashionable residential sector, and Juárez, an industrial-commercial zone of mixed land use.

In the eastern sections, homes are small and tightly packed, and although they are of diverse styles and construction, they generally reflect working-class tastes and budgets. The streets have few trees, and cars are relatively scarce. On the other hand, children, street vendors, and a myriad of small shops and stalls abound. The few large buildings are typically public institutions such as hospitals, sports complexes, public markets, and transportation terminals. The western sections of Guadalajara, in contrast, have spacious, well-built houses interspersed with many large buildings, such as offices, apartment complexes, banks, and stores. The streets are wide, shaded by tall trees, and lined with many restaurants, cafés, and boutiques. Driving through the western sections, one sees many monuments and fountains, and much automobile traffic, but few children.

The barrio of San Marcos is situated in the eastern Libertad sector, in a zone inhabited by laborers, artisans, office workers, and craft workers. It is a relatively old, well established neighborhood, not one in the process of formation. It is no shantytown of ramshackle dwellings, but an area of permanent adobe or concrete homes. The barrio is served by a full array of urban amenities: water, electricity, sewage, telephones, paved roads, transportation lines, and trash collection. The sample area consists of eighteen square blocks, which includes a commercial zone plus two different residential areas, one built some twenty-five years ago, and one new, more modern area built in recent years by the elite of the working-class stratum.

A DEMOGRAPHIC PROFILE

The ethnosurvey data reveal basic contrasts between the four communities. Table 3.1 compares the demographic characteristics of each community, focusing on measures of mortality, fertility, growth, and population composition. The mortality and fertility measures were estimated indirectly from responses to questions on the number of children ever born, the number of children surviving, and the number of births in the last year, using standard demographic methods (United Nations 1983).

Life expectancy at birth is a key indicator of socioeconomic development. The preservation of life is a universal goal of people everywhere, and life expectancy is very sensitive to differences in variables such as education and income, which are strongly associated with development (Preston 1975). By this measure, Altamira clearly stands out as the least developed of the four communities. Its life expectancy of fifty-eight years is well below the level for Mexico as a whole and eight to nine years below expectancies in the two urban communities (sixty-seven in Santiago and sixty-six in San Marcos). The average length of life is somewhat higher in Chamitlán (roughly sixty-two years) but still below the national average.

The estimates of infant mortality rate (deaths in the first year of life per 1000 births) bring out the contrast even more clearly. The infant mortality rate in Altamira is almost twenty points higher than in Chamitlán, the next highest, and double that in Santiago, the lowest. Of every 1000 children born in Altamira, 80 die before their first birthday, compared to 63 in Chamitlán, 39 in Santiago, and 46 in San Marcos. The national average for Mexico is 69.

During the late 1970s, fertility fell strongly throughout Mexico, on average from 6.5 to about 5.4 births per woman (Rowe 1979; CELADE 1982), and the four communities followed this trend. The population pyramids shown in figure 3.2 give the percentage distribution of men and women by age for each community. In each case there is a pronounced constriction at the base of the pyramid, indicating a recent and marked decline in fertility. The relative deficit of males in the age range from twenty-five to forty in Altamira and Chamitlán illustrates the demographic impact of international migration, but the fact that the deficit

TABLE 3.1
DEMOGRAPHIC CHARACTERISTICS OF FOUR MEXICAN COMMUNITIES, 1982

Characteristic	Community				
	Altamira	Chamitlán	Santiago	San Marcos	Mexico
Mortality					
Life expectancy	57.9	61.5	67.3	65.5	64.1
Infant mortality rate	80.2	63.3	39.2	45.8	69.2
Crude death rate	11.9	10.1	5.8	4.2	7.9
Fertility					
Total fertility rate	5.8	4.6	4.5	3.6	5.4
Crude birth rate	33.0	30.1	31.7	24.7	37.6
Growth					
Rate of natural increase	2.1	2.0	2.6	2.1	2.9
Composition					
Mean age	24.5	25.2	23.0	22.4	21.9
Median age	18.0	18.0	18.0	17.0	17.0
Total dependence ratio	86.0	72.1	82.5	73.1	93.3
Child dependence ratio	75.9	62.9	76.3	70.3	86.4
Elderly dependence ratio	10.1	9.2	6.2	2.8	6.9

Sources: PERSFILE and CELADE (1982); household members enumerated in Mexican community samples.

is not especially pronounced suggests that many seasonal migrants were captured by the December ethnosurvey.

The indirect methods used to compute the fertility rates in table 3.1 assume constant or slowly changing birth rates, and the recent declines in fertility indicate that the estimates are biased upward. Nonetheless, they give a rough indication of the relative standing of each community with respect to family limitation. The total fertility rate is the average number of births a woman can expect over her reproductive lifetime. Again, Altamira is highest, with 5.8 births per woman, with the other communities arrayed in descending order: Chamitlán (4.6), Santiago (4.5), and San Marcos (3.6). All except Altamira are below the national average, and for a rural community, Chamitlán is especially low, roughly the same as Santiago. Chamitlán also happens to have the highest rates of out-migration to the United States. Limited evidence suggests that the separation of spouses through seasonal migration can significantly lower the birthrate in migrant sending communities (Massey and Mullan 1984), and Chamitlán's relatively low fertility rate may well reflect this effect.

Because of the upward bias in the fertility estimates, the rates of natural increase (birth rates minus death rates) are probably too high and should be interpreted with caution. Most likely the rate is at or

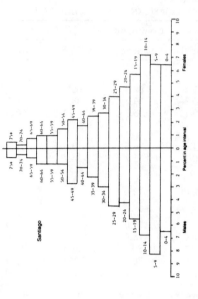

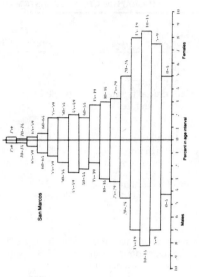

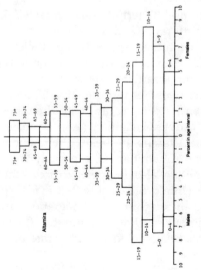

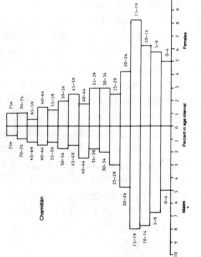

Fig. 3.2. Population pyramids for four Mexican communities, 1982.

below 2 percent in each case. The recent decline in fertility has also produced relatively low ratios of child dependence (the number of persons below age fifteen divided by the population aged fifteen to sixty-four), well below that observed in Mexico as a whole. The number of children per working age adult ranges from sixty-three to seventy-six, compared to a level of eighty-six for Mexico as a whole.

A SOCIOECONOMIC PROFILE

The four communities also display important socioeconomic differences. The educational data shown in table 3.2 reveal a basic rural-urban contrast between the four sample communities. Adults in Altamira have completed an average of 4.2 years in school, and those in Chamitlán have finished only 3.4, compared to 5.5 and 5.2 years in Santiago and San Marcos, respectively. Very few people in any of the communities have attended college. Differences in average education stem from contrasts in the relative number of illiterates and primary-school graduates. Chamitlán stands out particularly in the number of illiterates. Almost 28 percent of its adult population has no formal education, compared to under fifteen percent elsewhere. At the other extreme, a very large share of adults from Santiago (60 percent) have finished primary school, reflecting the educational requirements of factory employment; and about 50 percent of San Marcos's adults have completed grade school, compared to only around 30 percent in the two rural communities.

A very important indicator of social status is occupation. In the raw data files, occupation was coded by using a two-digit classification adapted from the Mexican census. For analytic purposes, the eighty-seven detailed occupations were recoded into six broad categories corresponding to major social groups in the socioeconomic hierarchy. Although six groups make up the occupational structure in each community, the groups are different in rural and urban areas. Both areas contain skilled and unskilled manual workers. In the two rural communities, however, "farmworkers" are subdivided into three separate groups that reflect differences in wealth and access to land—*agricultores, campesinos,* and *jornaleros*—whereas in urban areas "nonmanual workers" are divided into three groups that reflect different levels of education, skill, and income—professional-technical workers, clerical-sales workers, and service workers.

The criteria used to distinguish between categories of Mexican farmworkers require some elaboration. In rural Mexico agricultores are large landholders who generally hire others to work their land. Campesinos

TABLE 3.2
YEARS OF EDUCATION COMPLETED BY PERSONS AGED 20 AND
ABOVE IN FOUR MEXICAN COMMUNITIES, 1982

Years of education	Community			
	Altamira	Chamitlán	Santiago	San Marcos
None (%)	15.3	28.2	12.1	12.0
Primary (%)	70.6	61.9	64.8	64.9
1–3 years (%)	32.7	32.1	16.7	27.3
4–5 years (%)	21.0	12.1	10.9	9.7
6 years (%)	16.9	17.7	37.2	27.9
Secondary (%)	5.7	5.1	11.6	12.3
7–8 years (%)	1.3	1.7	4.8	4.6
9 years (%)	4.4	3.4	6.8	7.7
Preparatory and normal school (%)	6.5	2.4	8.1	7.1
10–11 years (%)	1.5	0.9	3.0	4.2
12–13 years (%)[a]	5.0	1.5	5.1	2.9
University (%)	2.1	2.4	3.2	3.9
13–15 years (%)	1.7	1.5	1.9	1.3
16+ years (%)	0.4	0.9	1.3	2.6
Average years completed	4.2	3.4	5.5	5.2
Total persons aged 20+	544	536	468	549

Source: PERSFILE; household members enumerated in Mexican community samples.

[a] Some normal-school curricula offer a four-year certificate.

are small-scale farmers who work the land in one of three ways: as *medieros,* who are sharecroppers owning no land; as *ejidatarios,* who have the right to use *ejido* land set aside by the government for the use of community members; or as small landowners who rely on household labor to farm a small plot of family-owned land. The third major type of farmworker, *jornaleros* do not farm the land directly but work in the fields for others and live exclusively from their daily wages.

The six occupational groups shown in table 3.3 are arrayed in a rough hierarchy of social prestige. The nature and relative standing of the social groups to which they correspond will become clearer as the book progresses; at present, however, we indicate their ranking according to a common measure of occupational prestige. The standard international prestige scores in column 1 of table 3.3 were obtained by matching each occupational group in the table with the closest comparable category in Treiman (1977: 235–260). These scores give the relative prestige of each occupational group on a scale of 0 to 100 and are based on results culled from international social surveys (Treiman 1975). The

TABLE 3.3
SELECTED SOCIOECONOMIC INDICATORS FOR HOUSEHOLDS CLASSIFIED BY OCCUPATIONAL STATUS OF
HEAD AND RURAL VERSUS URBAN LOCATION: FOUR MEXICAN COMMUNITIES, 1982 [a]

Origin and occupation	(1) Prestige of group	(2) Education of head	(3) Mean household income	(4) Mean no. of goods owned	(5) Mean no. of cars owned	(6) Percent with modern house	(7) Mean hectares of land owned	(8) Mean hectares of private land owned	(9) Head of livestock
Rural areas									
Agricultor	63	4.6	—	5.7	0.11	25.0	20.2	16.3	22.9
Nonmanual	50	3.9	—	4.2	0.09	25.9	1.4	1.1	3.8
Skilled	40	2.6	—	3.6	0.05	22.7	0.0	0.0	1.0
Campesino	35	1.8	—	3.0	0.01	7.4	2.7	0.9	3.8
Unskilled	18	3.4	—	3.5	0.06	14.3	0.4	0.0	1.1
Jornalero	18	2.2	—	3.1	0.00	14.4	0.4	0.1	1.1
Urban areas									
Professional	58	9.9	$3,412	6.1	0.27	76.9	—	—	—
Sales-clerical	41	4.2	$1,374	6.0	0.23	83.1	—	—	—
Skilled	40	4.6	$2,702	5.4	0.14	73.1	—	—	—
Services	27	4.6	$2,990	5.5	0.21	56.3	—	—	—
Unskilled	18	4.2	$2,978	5.6	0.17	61.4	—	—	—
Farmworker	18	2.9	$1,529	4.8	0.26	55.6	—	—	—

Sources: All data from HOUSEFILE except column 1, which is from Treiman (1977) and column 2, which is from PERSFILE; households enumerated in Mexican community samples.

[a] Columns: (1) prestige scores for occupational groups; (2) years of completed schooling; (3) average yearly income of non-U.S. migrants in 1982 U.S. dollars; (4) eight possible consumer goods—stove, refrigerator, washing machine, radio, television, stereo, and telephone; (6) a modern house has concrete walls, concrete or metal roof, and a tile floor; (7) private and ejido land; (8) private land only; (9) livestock including cows and pigs.

prestige of an occupational group reflects the skill, income, and wealth commanded by its incumbents and the extent to which they control scarce resources such as land and capital (Treiman 1977).

Table 3.3 divides households into occupational groups based on the occupation of the household head and then computes selected measures of socioeconomic status for each group. Wage income is not reported in rural areas since it is a very poor indicator of socioeconomic status in the rural context. Many farm families are outside the wage economy, and others send migrants to work for high wages in the United States. In neither of these circumstances would wage income be an accurate indicator of a household's socioeconomic status in the community.

The indicators in table 3.3 are not perfectly consistent with one another; however, they do suggest a rough socioeconomic ranking of the groups, and about the extremes there is little disagreement. In rural areas, jornaleros lie at the bottom of the scale regardless of which measure is considered and agricultores are at the top. Between them in descending order of status are nonmanual workers, skilled workers, campesinos, and unskilled workers. In urban areas, professionals head the socioeconomic hierarchy, whereas farmworkers—who are essentially jornaleros—are at the bottom, with sales and clerical workers, skilled workers, service workers, and unskilled workers lying in between. These occupational groups will be employed throughout the remainder of the book and correspond roughly to basic socioeconomic classes.

Distinctions between the four communities stand out very clearly when their occupational structures are compared in table 3.4. The labor forces of Altamira and Chamitlán are both dominated by agricultural workers, who make up 63 percent and 66 percent of all workers, respectively. In Altamira, however, agrarian workers are much more likely to own and cultivate land. There are twice as many agricultores in Altamira as in Chamitlán and 53 percent more campesinos. The number of landless jornaleros in Chamitlán is nearly twice that in Altamira (42 percent vs. 23 percent), however. The two rural labor forces are both overwhelmingly agrarian, but the nature of the agricultural work is thus entirely different. Altamira is a town of small-subsistence farmers, whereas Chamitlán is dominated by a rural proletariat of landless wage laborers.

There are also distinct differences between the two urban communities. Both localities have trivial numbers of farmworkers, but Santiago is dominated much more by a class of skilled workers than is San Marcos, which specializes more in services and clerical and sales work, reflecting Guadalajara's more diversified economy. While almost 50 percent of San Marcos's workers are employed in nonmanual occupations

TABLE 3.4
OCCUPATIONAL DISTRIBUTION BY RURAL VERSUS URBAN ORIGIN:
FOUR MEXICAN COMMUNITIES, 1982

Origin and occupation	Community		
Rural areas	*Altamira*	*Chamitlán*	*Total*
Agricultor (%)	6.3	2.7	4.6
Nonmanual (%)	19.3	23.7	21.3
Skilled manual (%)	5.3	4.1	4.7
Campesino (%)	33.5	21.9	28.0
Unskilled manual (%)	12.9	5.9	9.6
Jornalero (%)	22.7	41.7	31.7
Number of workers	379	338	717
Urban areas	*Santiago*	*San Marcos*	*Total*
Professional-technical (%)	9.0	6.4	7.5
Clerical-sales (%)	12.6	30.7	23.0
Skilled manual (%)	42.8	34.1	37.8
Services (%)	6.8	9.1	8.1
Unskilled manual (%)	24.8	18.1	21.0
Farmworker (%)	4.0	1.6	2.6
Number of workers	278	375	653

Source: PERSFILE; household members enumerated in Mexican community samples.

(professional-technical, clerical-sales, and services), only 25 percent of Santiago's workers are so employed. Moreover, 43 percent of Santiago's workers are skilled laborers, compared to only 34 percent of those in San Marcos, and most of the unskilled workers in Santiago are in fact semiskilled factory workers, rather than mere laborers. Santiago is thus a blue-collar factory town of skilled crafts and factory workers, whereas San Marcos is an urban barrio providing workers for diversified employment in office, retail, service, and blue-collar vocations.

THE AGRARIAN ECONOMIES OF ALTAMIRA AND CHAMITLÁN

In the two rural communities, socioeconomic structure is critically determined by prevailing systems of land tenure and agricultural production. We have already mentioned the contrast between Altamira and Chamitlán in a general way, stating that the former is a community of farmers and small landowners located in a region of self-sufficient agriculture, while the latter is a town of landless day laborers working in a region of large-scale, market-oriented farming. Table 3.5 undertakes a more

TABLE 3.5
CHARACTERISTICS OF LAND DISTRIBUTION IN
TWO RURAL MEXICAN COMMUNITIES, 1982

Characteristic	Community	
	Altamira	Chamitlán
Percent of households owning land	45.5	18.5
Private (%)	34.5	2.5
Ejido (%)	11.0	16.0
Hectares of land owned	874.4	212.0
By tenure		
Private (%)	82.5	13.7
Ejido (%)	17.5	86.3
By kind of land		
Irrigated (%)	7.6	27.3
Dryland (%)	62.7	68.9
Pasture (%)	24.4	3.8
Orchard (%)	5.3	0.0
Average hectares owned	9.6	5.7
Percent of households share-cropping land	37.5	28.5
Medieros (%)	16.5	1.5
A partido (%)	9.0	0.5
Ecuarero (%)	13.5	25.1
Hectares of land sharecropped	319.2	131.4
Irrigated (%)	8.7	8.4
Dryland (%)	86.7	51.8
Pasture (%)	0.0	39.9
Orchards (%)	4.6	0.0
Average hectares sharecropped	4.3	2.3
Percent of households with access to farmland	71.5	46.5
Percent of farmland under cultivation	85.1	100.0
Hectares under cultivation	832.1	344.0
Corn (%)	70.2	69.0
Sorghum (%)	23.0	30.4
Beans (%)	1.2	0.3
Other (%)	5.6	0.3

Source: HOUSEFILE; households enumerated in Altamira and Chamitlán.

systematic comparison of the two communities for a fuller documentation of this contrast.

These data reveal pronounced differences in both the prevalence of land ownership and the amount of land owned. The vast majority of households (81 percent) in Chamitlán are landless, while nearly half (46 percent) of those in Altamira own farmland, and the total amount of land owned in Altamira (874 hectares) is more than four times that in Chamitlán (212 hectares). The average size of a plot in Altamira is double that in Chamitlán (9.6 hectares vs. 5.7 hectares), although the overall quality of land is somewhat better in Chamitlán, where 27 percent is irrigated, compared to only 7 percent in Altamira.

A second contrast between the towns concerns the tenure of land ownership. In Chamitlán nearly all of the land is part of an ejido, while in Altamira it is mostly private. Ejidos were created after the Mexican Revolution in an effort to redistribute land from large landowners to landless peasants. In order to obtain ejido land, residents of a community band together and petition the government for a land grant from a local estate or hacienda. The land granted comprises the ejido, and rights of use are divided among the petitioners. Rights to use ejido land may be inherited but not rented or resold. Of all the land owned in Chamitlán, 86 percent is part of an ejido, but in Altamira it is the reverse—83 percent is private. Moreover, of landowning families in Chamitlán, 86 percent are ejidatarios, whereas the figure is only 24 percent for Altamira.

Households in Altamira are not only more likely to own land, they are also more likely to rent it through some sharecropping arrangement. Of households in Altamira, 38 percent sharecrop farmland, compared to only 29 percent in Chamitlán, and the quantity of agricultural land sharecropped in the former (319 hectares) is 2.4 times the amount in the latter (131 hectares). Moreover, much of the land sharecropped in Chamitlán (40 percent) is pasture for grazing livestock rather than growing crops, implying that there is less use of labor than in Altamira, where all such land is used for cultivation, and the average size of sharecropped parcels in Altamira is about twice that in Chamitlán.

The two communities differ in the kind of arrangement by which land is most commonly sharecropped. There are four basic arrangements between a landless sharecropper and a landowning patrón (Cardoso 1980; de la Peña 1982). Medieros lease land and seed from the patrón but provide their own labor and tools. In return, the mediero gives half of the harvest to the patrón. Those who lease land a partido bring nothing but their labor to the production process, renting not only seeds and land but tools and draught animals. They not only owe half the harvest but must hand over an additional fifth of the remainder as rental on the tools and animals that they borrow. Finally, ecuareros work unproductive land on the hillsides, giving a negotiable share of their crops to the patrón at harvest, depending on the quality of the land. Since farming on an *ecuaro*, or hillside, is generally not sufficient to support a family, most ecuareros also work as day laborers.

About 26 percent of the households in Altamira sharecrop land either as medieros or a partido, compared to a mere 2 percent in Chamitlán. By far the most prevalent form of sharecropping arrangement in Chamitlán is that of an ecuarero, which is the arrangement for 25 percent of households (89 percent of those who sharecrop). Only 14 percent of households in Altamira lease land as ecuareros (36 percent of those who sharecrop). Between owning and renting, 72 percent of households in Altamira have access to some 980 hectares of farmland (not counting pasture), of which 85 percent is productively used to grow a variety of crops, including the traditional staples corn and beans—which take up 71 percent of all farmland—as well as the cash crop sorghum, which occupies 23 percent of Altamira's farmland. In Chamitlán, fewer families have access to a smaller amount of land, all of which is farmed, and agricultural production is somewhat more heavily specialized on corn and sorghum. Only 47 percent of Chamitlán's families have access to farmland, with 69 percent planted in corn and 30 percent in sorghum.

The last table in this chapter, table 3.6, continues the agricultural profile by listing characteristics of agricultural production in the two communities. The most notable contrast is the share of households engaged in farming in the two places. In Altamira 69 percent of the households engage directly in agricultural production, compared to only 46 percent in Chamitlán. Moreover, households in both communities are about equally likely to raise cash crops, while those in Chamitlán are less likely to grow traditional subsistence crops and tend to use more modern methods and inputs. In three basic farming tasks—clearing, plowing, and sowing—households in Chamitlán are thus more likely to use machinery and less likely to use day laborers than are those in Altamira. They are also more likely to use scientific inputs such as improved seeds, insecticides, and fertilizers. Only in the harvest is this contrast reversed.

SUMMARY

The study is based on data from four communities located in Mexico's western region—an area that includes the states of Jalisco, Michoacán, Zacatecas, Colima, Aguascalientes, Nayarit, and Guanajuato—which together comprise an integrated regional economy centered in Guadalajara. Altamira is located in the Sayula Valley in southern Jalisco, and Chamitlán is situated in the Zamora Valley in Michoacán. Both are

TABLE 3.6
CHARACTERISTICS OF AGRICULTURAL PRODUCTION IN
TWO RURAL MEXICAN COMMUNITIES, 1982

Characteristic	Community	
	Altamira	Chamitlán
Percent of households farming (%)	68.5	45.5
Percent of landed households farming (%)[a]	95.8	97.8
Farming cash crops (%)	33.6	28.0
Farming subsistence crops (%)	88.1	79.6
Percent of farming households using hired day laborers (%)	47.5	49.5
For clearing (%)	16.1	6.7
For plowing (%)	11.0	12.2
For sowing (%)	30.7	23.3
For harvesting (%)	39.4	46.7
Percent of farming households using agricultural machinery (%)	38.0	38.5
For clearing (%)	19.7	37.4
For plowing (%)	12.4	23.1
For sowing (%)	10.2	18.7
For harvesting (%)	32.9	25.3
Percent of farming households using modern inputs (%)	85.4	95.6
Improved seeds (%)	42.3	56.0
Chemical fertilizers (%)	75.2	94.5
Insecticides (%)	71.5	78.0

Source: HOUSEFILE; households enumerated in Altamira and Chamitlán.

[a] Landed households are those that own or sharecrop land. Cash crops include sorghum, alfalfa, wheat, linseed, and strawberries. Subsistence crops include corn, beans, garbanzos, potatoes, tomatoes, pumpkins, and walnuts.

agrarian communities. Santiago is a factory town located in a dynamic industrial zone to the south of Guadalajara, while San Marcos is a stable working class barrio in one of the large popular districts of Guadalajara.

Demographic and socioeconomic indicators show a strong cleavage between rural and urban settings. Altamira and Chamitlán have relatively high birthrates and low life expectancies compared to those in the two urban areas. They also have higher rates of illiteracy, lower mean educational levels, and higher shares of their labor forces engaged in agriculture. The rural and urban communities also differ among themselves. The two urban communities are quite similar demographically and educationally, but their occupational structures are very different. Santiago is dominated by a working class of skilled and semiskilled crafts workers who together constitute the majority of the work force. In contrast, workers are somewhat more evenly distributed among occupational groups in San Marcos, reflecting its more diversified economy.

Among the rural communities, Altamira is the more traditional agrarian setting. Most farmworkers are campesinos or agricultores, and nearly 70 percent of households subsist through farming. In Chamitlán, most farmworkers are landless day laborers and only 46 percent of households actually live by cultivating the soil. Fewer than 20 percent of households in Chamitlán own land, compared to 46 percent in Altamira. Among households that do farm, those in Chamitlán are more likely to use capital-intensive methods and less likely to grow staple crops than are those in Altamira.

In short, the contrasting socioeconomic organizations of the four communities suggests a firm basis for comparative study. They represent four very different ways of life: a traditional agrarian town of small landowners and subsistence farmers, a commercialized farm community of landless day laborers, a factory town of skilled industrial workers, and an urban barrio of diverse working-class occupations. In spite of these apparent socioeconomic differences, similar traditions of international migration ultimately developed in each of the four communities. To understand why, we must understand the historical roots of migration in each place.

4

Historical Development of International Migration

THE MACROHISTORICAL CONTEXT

Today's massive movement between Mexico and the United States has its roots in the late nineteenth century, when political and economic developments in each country produced conditions favorable to international migration. Mexican development policies created a highly mobile mass of impoverished rural workers, and in the United States integration of the southwestern states into the national economy generated a sustained demand for low-wage labor. The connection between these complementary conditions was the railroads, which made economic growth possible and provided an inexpensive, quick, and reliable means for the international transfer of workers.

In 1872 a young general named Porfirio Díaz came to power in Mexico, ending 50 years of political instability and ushering in a long period of economic growth known as the *Porfirian Peace*. Except for a brief period from 1876 to 1880, Díaz autocratically ruled Mexico as president until 1911. Under Díaz, elite Mexican interests were united for the first time since Independence, and with the backing of the military, the clergy, hacienda owners, and merchants, he assumed all powers of government during his reign (Parkes 1950).

In rural areas, the foundation of the Porfirian political economy was the hacienda (Cardoso 1980). Before Díaz, communal ownership of land by peasants had been recognized by successive governments. During the Porfirian era, this ancient system of land tenure was destroyed and virtually all land was brought under the private control of hacienda owners. Mexican peasants were displaced from their lands in massive numbers, and by 1910, 97 percent of rural families were landless (Cardoso 1980, p. 7). One-seventh of the entire country was owned by twenty-nine individuals and companies (Sotelo Inclán 1970).

Through a variety of means, the hacienda system kept Mexican peasants in a state of permanent and abject poverty (Verduzco and Calleja 1982; de la Peña 1977; Cardoso 1980; González 1982). The haciendas themselves operated on a principle of debt peonage. Sharecropping forced workers further into debt each year, and they were compelled to buy overpriced goods on credit from hacienda stores. Debt was accumulated from year to year and generation to generation. Moreover, population growth and the enclosure of communal lands steadily increased the supply of landless workers, while irrigation and mechanization of production steadily reduced demand for day laborers, producing falling wage rates (Russell 1977). As wages fell, the shift from staple to cash crops exerted an upward pressure on food prices. Production was geared to international markets rather than domestic consumption, and between 1877 and 1907, the production of export crops grew by 4 percent annually, while corn production dropped by 0.8 percent per year (Cossío Silva 1965). As a result, the price of corn rose 60 percent between 1890 and 1910 (Cardoso 1980, pp. 10–11).

Porfirian industrial policy was equally harsh, oriented not to internal development and employment but to extraction and export. Foreign investment was encouraged, and most sectors of the nonagrarian economy were controlled by foreign interests (Parkes 1950; Gilly 1971). Strikes were illegal and union activity was suppressed by the police. Factory workers labored twelve- to fourteen-hour days and were often paid in script that could be spent only in company stores. Wages were kept low by the constant influx of displaced peons from the countryside. The urban economy was small and could not begin to absorb the arriving rural migrants. In 1910 there were only 400,000 industrial workers in all of Mexico (Russell 1977).

Porfirian economic development was thus important in creating conditions favorable to migration. Its climax during the early 1900s brought the enclosure of communal lands, falling agricultural wages, rising food prices, a shift to capital-intensive production methods, and decreased opportunity for urban employment. Together, these conditions created a large and growing rural mass of landless peasants with few economic prospects and weak ties to the land.

Meanwhile, between 1880 and 1910 there was rapid economic development of the southwestern United States. This expansion was led by mining and agriculture, which were suddenly made profitable by new rail links with the industrial East. During the 1870s and 1880s rail networks steadily expanded through the southwestern states, and in 1883 the Southern Pacific Railroad completed a transcontinental link through Arizona. Coal and copper mines opened up in Arizona, New Mexico, Colorado, and Oklahoma, and agricultural fields were rapidly brought into production throughout the region. From 1899 to 1909 the amount of land planted in cash crops nearly doubled to more than 14 million acres (Cardoso 1980: 19).

Both mining and agriculture were labor-intensive activities, and the native labor pool of the sparsely populated southwestern states was inadequate to meet the demand. The kind of agriculture practiced in the Southwest was far different from the small family farm typical elsewhere in the United States. Cultivation was carried out on very large tracts of irrigated land and was devoted almost entirely to cash crops destined for Eastern markets. This kind of farming required large quantities of unskilled stoop labor willing to work cheaply and seasonally. Prior to 1880, U.S. employers had turned to Asia for exploitable unskilled workers, but a surge of nativist sentiment after 1880 cut off this source. In 1882 the U.S. Congress passed the Chinese Exclusion Acts, and the 1907 "gentlemen's agreement" with Japan effectively ended labor migration from Asia (Keely 1979).

Given the increasing demand for labor in the southwestern United States and the growing mass of poor, landless workers just across the border, migration was inevitable, and the catalyst that made it happen was the railroads. According to Cardoso (1980: 26) "it was the railroads more than any other single factor that pulled Mexican workers over the border and spread them over the southwest and beyond as a mobile, cheap labor force available for all types of unskilled work." The first railway reached western Mexico in 1885, running through Jalisco and Michoacán on its way from Guadalajara to Mexico City. The United States and Mexico were first connected by rail when the Southern Pacific Railroad met the Mexican International Railroad at Piedras Negras in 1884. This link was quickly followed by other connections at Laredo, Nogales, and Matamorros. By 1890, Mexican rail lines were linked directly or indirectly to all forty-eight U.S. states (Cardoso 1980: 14–17).

The railroads connected areas of labor surplus and shortage. They permitted unemployed Mexican farmworkers and artisans displaced by the wave of Porfirian economic modernization to look outside their native communities for better opportunities. News of higher wages and better jobs spread rapidly, and by the 1890s, rural migrants had begun to leave their homes for work in the United States. Labor contractors representing U.S. farms, mines, and railroads established offices in border cities and developed contacts with Mexican recruiters through whom they drew upon the large pool of displaced peasants coming up from western Mexico (Cardoso 1980).

Railroads were the initial source of employment for Mexican migrants to the United States. They were eagerly recruited to lay tracks, construct roadbeds, and maintain the lines. By 1909, Mexicans made up 17 percent of the maintenance force on the nine most important U.S. railroads (Reisler 1976: 18) and 10 percent of the workshop crews in the southwestern states (Cardoso 1980: 27). As time passed, railroads served more as intermediate employers. Important rail centers such as Los Angeles, San Antonio, El Paso, Kansas City, and Chicago soon began to attract Mexican workers into local industries. From rail crews, Mexicans moved in growing numbers into steel, meat packing, and other industries throughout the industrial Midwest. By 1916, Mexicans had become an important component of the urban industrial labor force in several cities of the industrial North (Gamio 1930; Taylor 1932); however, employment of Mexicans was concentrated in the Southwest.

At the outbreak of the Mexican Revolution in 1910, migration to the United States was well established, numbering about 18,000 persons per year. In the ensuing decade, this annual number rose during periods of revolutionary violence (Hoffman 1974; Cardoso 1980; Hall 1982) and jumped sharply after the United States entered World War I (Taylor 1932; Cardoso 1980). By 1919, the annual number of Mexican immigrants had reached 29,000. When European immigration was closed by restrictive legislation in 1921, employers in the Midwest and Southwest began to recruit Mexican workers to bridge the gap. During the 1920s, a yearly average of 49,000 Mexican immigrants entered the United States, establishing enclaves in cities throughout the Southwest and the industrial Midwest, particularly in Los Angeles, San Antonio, and Chicago.

The onset of the Great Depression in 1929 brought an end to Mexican migration until 1942. Jobs that remained were given preferentially to U.S. citizens, and economic relief was denied to Mexicans. During the 1930s, the U.S. government, in cooperation with state and local authorities, took measures to expel thousands of Mexican workers, and 415,000 were forcibly repatriated, and another 85,000 left voluntarily (Hoffman 1974).

The revolution produced significant changes in Mexico's pattern of socioeconomic development, but its full impact was not felt until the 1930s. The various reform measures decreed by the 1917 Constitution were largely ignored until the regime of President Lázaro Cárdenas (1934–1940), who redistributed over 45 million acres of land to peasants through the *Reparto Agrario*, the federal land redistribution program (Russell 1977: 43). This land reform scheme confiscated hacienda land and set up communal ejidos under the control of local villages. After the Reparto Agrario, the hacienda ceased to be a factor in national economic life. Its place was taken by the government, which became the main promoter of economic development, and by the capitalist firm, through which resources and investment were channeled to promote industrial and agricultural development.

Following the Cárdenas regime, the Reparto Agrario was scaled back, and during the 1940s the share of farmland in ejidos actually declined (Russell 1977). Large agricultural interests began to lease or extort land from poor ejidatarios in order to produce cash crops for sale in national and international markets. Agricultural production was boosted through the investment of capital and by the widespread use of new technologies. The federal government, through its manipulation of credit markets, irrigation projects, and control of agricultural innovation and diffusion, encouraged the exploitation of the richest and most productive agricultural areas of the country by large firms.

This agrarian policy produced an unbalanced development within Mexican agriculture. On one hand, a commercial sector of intensive agriculture registered large gains in productivity through the consolidation of high-quality lands and intensive capital investment. On the other hand, small landholders and ejidatarios, who originally benefited from the Reparto Agrario, increasingly were left with less land of inferior quality. With limited access to credit and resources, they continued to produce at a subsistence level. The proportion of rural families that were landless actually rose from 58 percent in 1940 to 77 percent in 1970 (Cornelius 1978).

The entry of the United States into World War II once again spurred the recruitment of Mexican labor for seasonal agricultural work in the southwestern states. In 1942 the governments of Mexico and the United States established a temporary-worker arrangement known as the *Bracero Accord*, which lasted until 1964 (Craig 1971; Reisler 1976). By the end of the program, some 4.5 million Mexicans had worked as *braceros* in the United States, and at its height in the late 1950s, more than 400,000 workers migrated each year (Cornelius 1978). As in the 1920s, braceros came primarily from western Mexico, and four states—Jalisco, Michoacán, Guanajuato, and Zacatecas—accounted for 45 percent of all bracero migration between 1951 and 1962 (Craig 1971: 133).

The governments of Mexico and the United States ended direct participation in the recruitment and regulation of Mexican migrant workers when the Bracero program expired in 1964. Since then, both legal and undocumented migration have continued to grow. Undocumented migration began to grow rapidly during the 1950s, as the demand for Bracero visas exceeded their supply (Reichert and Massey 1982). Legal migration began to rise in the mid-1960s, when former braceros took advantage of liberal immigration laws in force at that time to acquire residence documents (Cornelius 1978; Mines and Massey 1985). In spite of increasingly restrictive amendments to U.S. immigration law and stronger border enforcement, both legal and undocumented migration have increased in recent years. Between 1960 and 1980, a minimum of

1.1 million undocumented migrants and an equal number of documented migrants entered the United States from Mexico (Massey and Schnabel 1983; Passel and Woodrow 1984).

In summary, migration between Mexico and the United States is ultimately rooted in the structural economic transformation of both countries that occurred around the turn of the century. Economic modernization under Porfirio Díaz created an abundant supply of poor, landless workers, while the integration of the southwestern states into the U.S. national economy generated a demand for their services; the railroads provided the link between supply and demand. These structural causes were encouraged at critical junctures by recruitment from the United States, notably from 1917 through 1929, and again from 1942 through 1964. These macrohistorical developments form the backdrop against which migration developed in each of the four communities examined here.

ALTAMIRA: MICROHISTORY OF A TRADITIONAL TOWN

Before the Reparto Agrario

At the turn of the century, the vast majority of people in Altamira lived by cultivating the soil. Until the beginning of the Reparto Agrario in the late 1930s, however, farmland in Altamira was scarce and highly concentrated. According to the Public Register of Altamira, during the first decade of the century nine families controlled 58 percent of the municipio's farmland, almost all of it land of the highest quality: the watered and level fields near the lagoon. These families also owned most of the municipio's woodlands near the summit of the sierra. The other 42 percent of the cultivable land, most of it on the rocky hillsides, was divided among fifty families in plots ranging from one to fifty hectares.

Many families in Altamira were landless. Those without any land could make a living in several ways. A variety of goods and services was produced in Altamira to meet a steady local demand. The municipio was more or less self-sufficient and supported a variety of nonagricultural trades: masons, tanners, coachbuilders, shoemakers, teachers, butchers, and muleteers. Most of the landless survived meagerly as medieros or jornaleros, however, or, more typically, through some combination of the two roles.

The staple crops grown in Altamira around the turn of the century were corn, beans, squash, and garbanzos. These were mostly planted in dry fields watered by rainfall. Irrigated lands were used to cultivate crops such as sugarcane, grown for refining on a nearby hacienda; small vegetable gardens, which were kept by medieros and agricultores alike; and orchards of walnut, coffee, or citrus trees, which were cultivated by most households. These orchards were typically small groves of less than ten square meters located beside a family's house; however, some landowners and merchants maintained large orchards of up to twelve hectares on the town's perimeter. Since livestock were fed mostly by foraging, cattle raising was generally confined to wealthy landowning families. Most families could afford to raise only small domestic animals for household use, such as chickens or burros.

On the eve of the Mexican Revolution in 1910, the population of the municipio stood at 5,210, but over the next decade it fell by 16 percent to 4,357 in 1921 and by 1930, stood at around 4,338. This dramatic decline and subsequent stagnation of the population reflects several factors: revolutionary violence and its attendant disorder, crop failures, and a 1919 influenza epidemic. These disasters only exacerbated a trend already begun, one that stemmed from the economic transformation that gripped southern Jalisco at the turn of the century.

During the late stages of the Porfirian regime, economic activity in the region was redirected toward newly accessible national and international markets (de la Peña 1977). With the arrival of the railroad in the Sayula Valley in 1901, traditional commercial systems were transformed and workers displaced. Cattle ranching and the cultivation of cash crops such as sugarcane began to spread, bringing the consolidation of land and the restriction of opportunities for subsistence farming. Muleteers also found job opportunities severely curtailed, and many became unemployed, as did the local artisans and merchants who supplied them with products such as saddles, saddlebags, and bridles. Vocations such as hostelry and innkeeping, vestiges of the era of the horse and buggy, also began to disappear.

The new means of transportation favored commodity speculation on national and international markets, and local products became increasingly subject to manipulations by businesspeople from outside the region and country (González 1981; Veerkamp 1981). Activities and crafts that had driven the regional economy during the second half of the nineteenth century were unable to modernize and could no longer compete with factories in other parts of the country and the world, whose products began to arrive with the railroad. Beginning at the turn of the century, this economic reorganization brought about a loss of population throughout all of southern Jalisco, one that was exacerbated by the instability of the revolution.

According to oral histories taken from the oldest people in Altamira, about this time the first migrants left for work outside the municipio. The first out-migrants moved primarily within Mexico, going mainly to Guadalajara and Mexico City, but also to the developing northern states of the republic. Migration to the United States emerged somewhat later, in 1918, following the years of revolutionary violence. Informants state that the first to leave were men who had already worked elsewhere in Mexico. Thereafter migrants bound for the United States always went north in small groups guided by someone with prior U.S. experience. The migrants regarded an experienced guide as essential because the journey was costly, and they could not afford to sacrifice the money that they had invested for the trip. Setbacks based on erroneous information, such as encounters with hucksters or unscrupulous officials, could cause migrants to fail to reach el Norte, requiring them to go hungry until they could earn enough money to return home.

The destination of the first U.S. migrants from Altamira was Arizona, where they worked on the railroads. According to an informant, the work "was very hard, but we were young and used to it. They didn't pay very much, but since we were far away from the nearest town, we didn't spend much and could save." Later on, recruiters began to arrive from steel mills near Chicago, where the pay was better, and a new routine emerged during the 1920s. Migrants would go north, work for a while on a U.S. railroad to save up enough money for the long trip to Chicago, and then secure a job in one of its high-paying steel mills. In the mid-1920s, the first pioneer migrants also began to work in California, where new agricultural fields were opening up and the pay was good.

The goal of most migrants was to work hard for a short time, save money, and return home to spend the money in Altamira. This goal is put into perspective when one considers that the typical salary of a Mexican day laborer in 1923 was about 0.80 pesos per day (about 40 U.S. cents). At the time, the American railroads paid about 0.50 pesos per *hour* (25 U.S. cents), and after five months of work in the United States it was possible to accumulate a sum of money that would be impossible to amass in Mexico without owning cattle or land.

Older migrants report that border-crossing in those days was easy. One could readily obtain a pass to enter the United States, and with it there were no problems from U.S. immigration authorities. During this early phase of migration, the first few migrants began to arrange their papers and settle permanently in the United States. Migration to the steel mills and to California ended in 1929 with the onset of the Great Depression, which made work difficult to find and turned the political climate against Mexicans. Few people left Altamira for the United States during the 1930s.

The ethnosurvey data shed some light on patterns of migration during this early period. Figure 4.1 graphs the absolute number of U.S. and Mexican migrants leaving Altamira on their first trip between 1910 and 1982, and figure 4.2 shows the legal status of U.S. migrants by time period. Obviously, before 1940 only a small number of people made the long trip to el Norte. A few of these people went with legal documents, and some went as contract laborers, but most simply went across without official papers to obtain jobs that were eagerly offered by U.S. employers.

The demographic and social background of early migrants can be seen in tables 4.1 through table 4.3 which present selected characteristics of migrants leaving Altamira on their first trips during three periods: 1910 to 1939, 1940 to 1964, and 1965 to 1982. Mexican migrants and nonmigrants are included as points of comparison.[1] In the first epoch, which roughly corresponds to the time before the Reparto Agrario, there are several important contrasts between the three migrant status groups.

The pioneer U.S. migrants were entirely male, while roughly 14 percent of the first internal migrants and, of course, nearly 50 percent of nonmigrants, were women (table 4.1). Townspeople report that the earliest U.S. migrants were young unmarried men with no dependents. It is difficult to confirm statements about the relative ages of migrants since our information was gathered from survivors still alive in 1982, when any older migrants from that earliest era would be dead. The admittedly incomplete information given in table 4.1 suggests that the earliest U.S. migrants were somewhat older than Mexican migrants and nonmigrants, however.

Work in the United States required a spirit of adventure and motivation that not all men had and, above all, a considerable quantity of money to make the long trip north by rail (between $90 and $100 U.S. in 1923). In those days local moneylenders did not loan to people with-

---

[1] Nonmigrants are people who had not yet migrated by the end of the period in question. For example, nonmigrants during 1940 to 1944 were people who had not yet begun to migrate by 1944. Nonmigrants were identified in successive five-year intervals from 1910 through 1982 (with one odd two-year period at the end). Demographic and socioeconomic distributions were then determined for nonmigrants in each five-year interval and then averaged to give three distributions corresponding to each period shown in tables 4.1 through 4.3. The data thus refer to the average characteristics of nonmigrants over the time period shown, and the totals give the average number of nonmigrants who lived in the period. Nonmigrant characteristics were defined similarly in tables 4.7 through 4.9 and tables 4.11 through 4.13.

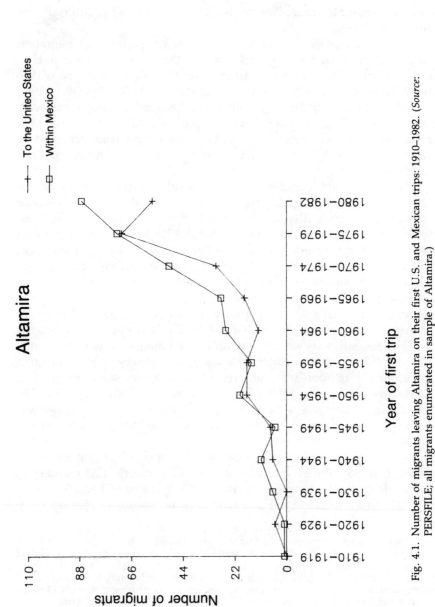

Fig. 4.1. Number of migrants leaving Altamira on their first U.S. and Mexican trips: 1910–1982. (*Source:* PERSFILE; all migrants enumerated in sample of Altamira.)

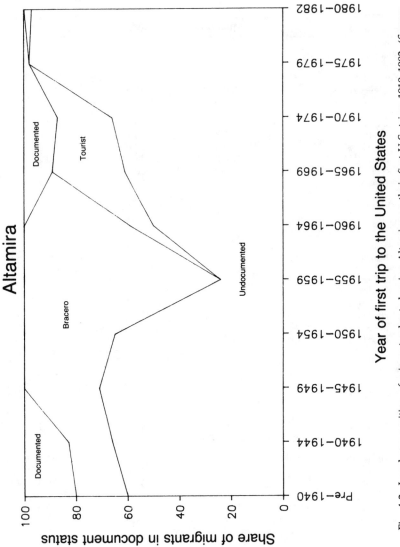

Fig. 4.2. Legal composition of migrant cohorts leaving Altamira on their first U.S. trips: 1910–1982. (*Source:* PERSFILE; all migrants enumerated in sample of Altamira.)

TABLE 4.1

DEMOGRAPHIC CHARACTERISTICS OF MIGRANTS TO THE UNITED STATES,
MIGRANTS WITHIN MEXICO, AND NONMIGRANTS IN THREE PERIODS: ALTAMIRA, JALISCO

Migrant status, sex, and age	Period		
	1910–1939	1940–1964	1965–1982
Migrants to United States			
Sex			
Male (%)	100.0	91.5	81.6
Age			
Under 15 (%)	0.0	5.1	3.3
15–19 (%)	60.0	23.7	32.9
20–34 (%)	40.0	57.6	53.3
35–54 (%)	0.0	13.6	9.2
55+ (%)	0.0	0.0	1.3
Average	21.8	23.9	23.7
Number	5	59	152
Migrants within Mexico			
Sex			
Male (%)	85.7	62.3	61.9
Age			
Under 15 (%)	42.9	31.2	7.4
15–19 (%)	57.1	20.8	40.6
20–34 (%)	0.0	40.3	44.6
35–54 (%)	0.0	7.8	6.4
55+ (%)	0.0	0.0	1.0
Average	12.4	19.3	21.7
Number	7	77	202
Nonmigrants			
Sex			
Male (%)	46.3	44.3	43.1
Age			
Under 15 (%)	79.3	60.4	57.1
15–19 (%)	6.8	10.8	9.1
20–34 (%)	13.1	17.7	16.3
35–54 (%)	0.8	9.9	11.7
55+ (%)	0.0	1.2	5.8
Average	7.7	14.3	18.7
Number	527	2,681	3,977

Source: PERSFILE; all persons enumerated in sample of Altamira.

TABLE 4.2
MEXICAN OCCUPATION OF MIGRANTS TO THE UNITED STATES, MIGRANTS WITHIN
MEXICO, AND NONMIGRANTS IN THREE PERIODS: ALTAMIRA, JALISCO

	1910–1939		1940–1964		1965–1982	
Migrant status and occupation	Occupation in period	Occupation in 1982	Occupation in period	Occupation in 1982	Occupation in period	Occupation in 1982
Migrants to United States						
Agricultor (%)	0.0	100.0	8.0	20.8	7.7	4.8
Nonmanual (%)	0.0	0.0	8.0	11.3	1.9	11.9
Skilled manual (%)	0.0	0.0	2.0	1.9	9.6	7.1
Campesino (%)	40.0	0.0	54.0	43.4	38.5	16.7
Unskilled manual (%)	0.0	0.0	2.0	9.4	5.8	22.2
Jornalero (%)	60.0	0.0	26.0	13.2	36.5	37.3
Number	5	2	50	43	52	126
Migrants within Mexico						
Agricultor (%)	14.3	25.0	0.0	7.5	8.0	0.8
Nonmanual (%)	14.3	25.0	8.0	32.5	4.0	36.1
Skilled manual (%)	0.0	0.0	0.0	5.0	0.0	6.8
Campesino (%)	42.9	50.0	56.0	32.5	44.0	15.0
Unskilled manual (%)	14.3	0.0	8.0	7.5	20.0	27.8
Jornalero (%)	14.3	0.0	28.0	15.0	24.0	13.5
Number	7	4	25	40	25	133
Nonmigrants						
Agricultor (%)	1.5	0.0	6.2	3.7	5.4	3.2
Nonmanual (%)	6.1	19.0	8.8	16.5	11.5	18.5
Skilled manual (%)	0.4	4.8	3.1	4.6	5.8	7.2
Campesino (%)	61.3	47.6	54.4	52.6	47.1	44.7
Unskilled manual (%)	1.3	14.3	4.1	9.0	5.9	10.1
Jornalero (%)	29.4	14.3	23.5	13.4	24.3	16.4
Number	540[a]	42	2,124[a]	454	2,082[a]	665

Source: Occupation in period from LIFEFILE; occupation in 1982 from PERSFILE; all persons enumerated in sample of Altamira.

[a] Number refers to person-years observed rather than number of people.

out property, and very few landless peons were willing to risk the family house in order to obtain credit to go north. Moreover, during the 1920s and 1930s the local economy was beginning to recover from the revolution, and money and manpower were needed increasingly in town.

In terms of social class, therefore, townspeople report that the very first migrants to the United States were drawn predominantly from the property-owning class of agricultores, and principally those with the largest landholdings. The data in table 4.2 are not entirely consistent with these oral reports. In terms of their 1982 occupations, the first migrants indeed show up as agricultores, but back when they first left for the United States they were campesinos or jornaleros. This discrepancy is partially explained by the fact that at least two of these early migrants were young men who had not yet inherited land to become agricultores in their own right. Moreover, the five U.S. migrants represented in the first column of table 4.2 actually left in the 1920s, so they were not the very first U.S. migrants mentioned by townspeople. By the 1920s, villagers report that U.S. migration had spread to include some landless workers.

In contrast to upper-class origins of the first U.S. migrants, migrants within Mexico were drawn from more diverse origins, with many coming from the poorer campesinos. Even among Mexican migrants, there were few jornaleros, however, since they apparently lacked the money even to make the short trip to Guadalajara. The higher social origins of U.S. migrants are also indicated by the educational data presented in table 4.3, which shows them to have more schooling than the other migrant status groups.

Pioneer U.S. migrants were thus a fairly exclusive lot, drawn from a relatively narrow segment of Altamira's socioeconomic hierarchy. They were principally scions of landowning families going north for adventure and some extra money. Although this pattern changed and campesinos became increasingly involved during the 1920s, initially at least, U.S. migrants were not the poorest of the poor.

The Reparto Agrario and the Bracero Era

After a long and sometimes violent struggle, residents of the cabecera in 1936 obtained permission to establish an ejido under the terms of the Reparto Agrario set in motion by President Cárdenas. Before the end of the decade, two other ejidos were also set up in the municipio: one in the second largest ranchería, Tepectl, and another in a smaller ranchería nearby. For two reasons, however, the results of the Reparto Agrario proved disappointing for the ejidatarios.

First, very little land was actually redistributed, and most of that given out was of poor quality. Only the landholdings of a few of the largest landowners were broken up, most of it pasture. Almost all of the highest-quality land—the watered flatlands—was not affected, and even the most productive of the dry lands also remained in private hands. According to records of the Department of Agrarian Affairs, the new ejidatarios received only 30 percent of the arable dry land in the municipio, and 89 percent of the land they did get was pasture. Although pasture can be cultivated, it is unproductive and must lie fallow every other year, and even after redistribution, the landowners con-

TABLE 4.3
YEARS OF EDUCATION AMONG U.S. MIGRANTS, MEXICAN MIGRANTS, AND
NONMIGRANTS AGED 15 AND OVER IN THREE PERIODS: ALTAMIRA, JALISCO

Migrant status and education	Period		
	1910–1939	1940–1964	1965–1982
Migrants to United States			
None (%)	0.0	17.9	3.4
1–3 (%)	80.0	50.0	14.9
4–5 (%)	20.0	32.1	23.1
6 (%)	0.0	0.0	36.7
7–9 (%)	0.0	0.0	14.3
10–11 (%)	0.0	0.0	2.7
12 (%)	0.0	0.0	3.4
13+ (%)	0.0	0.0	1.4
Average	2.2	2.6	5.7
Number	5	56	147
Migrants within Mexico			
None (%)	60.0	22.6	4.3
1–3 (%)	20.0	37.7	18.7
4–5 (%)	0.0	18.9	12.8
6 (%)	20.0	11.3	26.7
7–9 (%)	0.0	3.8	13.9
10–11 (%)	0.0	0.0	6.4
12 (%)	0.0	3.8	11.2
13+ (%)	0.0	1.9	5.9
Average	1.8	3.4	6.8
Number	5	53	187
Nonmigrants			
None (%)	34.9	22.1	14.1
1–3 (%)	53.2	48.3	34.6
4–5 (%)	9.2	21.7	21.9
6 (%)	2.8	5.9	19.1
7–9 (%)	0.0	0.6	4.5
10–11 (%)	0.0	0.1	1.5
12 (%)	0.0	1.2	3.2
13+ (%)	0.0	0.1	1.2
Average	1.8	2.5	4.0
Number	109	1,063	1,793

Source: PERSFILE; all persons enumerated in sample of Altamira.

tinued to control a large part of the municipio's pastureland. The Reparto Agrario thus bestowed relatively small (eight-hectare) parcels of very unproductive farmland on a minority of Altamira's families.

A second problem was that the Reparto Agrario addressed only the issue of land redistribution, not agricultural production. The Reparto provided the land, but not the means, for ejidatarios to engage in farming. Lacking the money to buy seed, tools, and labor, the ejidatarios had to turn around and rent their lands to monopolist granary operators and large property owners. The only favorable condition the campesinos were able to impose was that these people rent their lands as sharecroppers, turning over to them a portion of the crop; however, the percentage they were able to extract was very low because so much ejido land was available. Ejidatarios even began to rent parcels to one another. Those who had been lucky enough to obtain quality parcels, or who had received part of the rich communal woodland, rented land from those who had obtained only poor-quality pasture. Sharecropping, even among the ejidatarios, thus continued to be the principal means by which agricultural work was organized, with the family as the basic unit of production, a situation that characterized agrarian life in Altamira through the 1950s.

Then, as now, most of the arable land in the municipio of Altamira was not irrigated, so variations in seasonal rainfall seriously affected the economic life of the community. The 1940s were years of poor rainfall. Those who lived through the decade mention two periods of extreme drought—1941–1942 and 1948–1949—with generally bad years in between. In 1941 it was impossible to cultivate the fields for lack of water, and desperate campesinos began to leave the municipio in search of work. The next year, the rains were also very scarce, and once again many were forced to leave in search of work. By 1945, the flow of water from the town's springs had fallen so low that it was necessary to construct a dam to store up water during the night so that it could run with enough force to feed the irrigation canals during the day. By 1949, many walnut trees had dried up, and for the first time people from surrounding areas stopped coming to Altamira for the walnut harvest.

Thus conditions during the 1940s once again favored widespread out-migration from Altamira. The Reparto Agrario had not been a great success. It gave a small number of families poor lands but provided no resources to cultivate them, and a series of severe droughts had ruined harvests, producing widespread hunger and unemployment. Opportunities in the United States had dried up with the hostility and unemployment of the Great Depression, so at first townspeople left for Mexican urban areas, such as Tecomán, on the northwestern coast, and Guadalajara. The 1942 Bracero Accord between Mexico and the United States was seen by townspeople as a godsend, however. Even though the Bracero contracts originally lasted for only forty-five days, they meant secure work at wages, which when changed into pesos, seemed like a dream. It didn't matter that they had to pay part of their travel expenses, that they had to leave their families behind, or that there was discrimination against Mexicans in the United States. They needed work, and to el Norte went young and old, male and female, married and single.

The Bracero program significantly widened the road to the United States (see table 4.1). Since there was no work to support a family anyway, the desperate straits of the 1940s allowed both married and unmarried men to go north. Care and education of the children were left to wives, mothers, and sisters. As older family men went north, there was a broadening of the age composition. Also in these years, the first women began to migrate, some in order to settle in the United States with their husbands and others, widows or unwed mothers, who went to work.

Bracero contracts were handed out in special offices within Mexico, and once obtained, transportation was arranged and a U.S. job guaranteed. Thus the financial risk of the earlier years was removed, allowing a much broader participation by townspeople. As table 4.2 shows, the largest single group among migrants leaving between 1940 and 1964 was campesinos. At the same time jornaleros also began to migrate in greater numbers, and the earlier dominance of the agricultores substantially declined. The humbler origins are also indicated by the lower educations of U.S. migrants compared to Mexican migrants and nonmigrants (table 4.3).

Among the campesinos who began to migrate to the United States, the most important group was the ejidatarios. The Reparto Agrario had left them with small plots of poor land but no money to begin farming. The Bracero program provided cash that could be used to start farming, and the campesinos eagerly embraced the idea of U.S. wage labor as a source of investment capital. Through migration, ejidatarios could obtain the animals, inputs, and money necessary to farm their land. Sharecroppers used their U.S. earnings to maintain their families, pay off debts, or buy a house or orchard.

Within a short time, the demand for Bracero contracts outstripped the supply, and migrants began to leave in increasing numbers without documents. As time passed, braceros "learned the ropes" of life in el Norte. Relationships with employers were established, and migrants soon realized that there would be work waiting for anyone who showed up, with no questions asked. Those with prior contacts or experience fared well. Others without these advantages arrived hungry and cold, could not find work, and didn't have enough money to return home. Some of these unfortunate ones were children of twelve or thirteen years who, because of the penury of their families, left for el Norte by themselves in search of work (see table 4.1).

As figure 4.2 shows, the relative number of migrants leaving Altamira without documents swung sharply upward during the late 1940s. The percentage of undocumented migrants fell again in the early 1950s as the number of Bracero contracts available grew by about 100,000 between 1950 and 1951. The number of contracts remained stable for the next three years, however, and by 1954, the number of undocumented migrants had risen to such an extent that public agitation led to "Operation Wetback," a mass deportation program organized by the U.S. Border Patrol (Samora 1971: 51–55). After 1955, the number of Bracero contracts was markedly increased, to peak at over 430,000 annually through the late 1950s. The percentage of undocumented migrants from Altamira thus fell throughout the decade and began to increase only as the Bracero program wound down during the first half of the 1960s.

During the late 1940s and 1950s, various townspeople deported from the United States began to settle in the border cities of Tijuana and Mexicali, which were just beginning a period of sustained growth. These migrants started small businesses selling food from stalls or streetcarts, worked in local cantinas or shops, and drove taxis. Eventually they sent home for their families and settled down to permanent life in these cities. Over the course of the Bracero years, these border communities of townspeople became important nodes in social networks that connected the municipio with employers, friends, and relatives in the United States. Because of its proximity to California, which became increasingly important as a destination, Tijuana began to assume major importance as a safe haven and staging area for crossing the border.

Back in Altamira, migration to the United States lost its novelty and became routine. The period when the first pioneers returned with glowing descriptions about the strange customs, cities, and inventions in the United States was left behind. Now many knew for themselves the hard physical labor of life in el Norte, where "how much you earned depended on how much you sweat," and they felt the profound nostalgia for home and family that went with exile in a foreign land.

Concomitant with U.S. migration there was also movement to other places in Mexico, mainly to large urban areas such as Guadalajara and Mexico City. During the 1940s both cities experienced rapid industrial development with a strong demand for labor. Guadalajara, because of its closeness and its traditional connection with southern Jalisco, attracted the greatest number of migrants from Altamira. In 1949 the first dirt road between passed through Altamira on the way to Manzanillo· from Guadalajara, only ninety-eight kilometers (sixty-one miles) away, reinforcing the link between the municipio and that city. By 1956, this highway was paved, and it suddenly became possible to travel to and from Guadalajara in a morning.

As with U.S. migration, the social base of internal migration broadened considerably during the 1940s and 1950s, as a result of the reduced costs of movement. Over time, people of more diverse ages, occupations, and educations joined the migrant stream, compared to the era before the Reparto Agrario (see tables 4.1 through 4.3). Among them were many young women looking for temporary work as servants, and during the 1940–1964 period females made up 62 percent of all internal Mexican migrants. Before this time, the independent migration of women was rare. Females typically moved only to join their husbands or to accompany their families.

The 1940s and 1950s were also a time of economic recovery in southern Jalisco. In Altamira, the surest sign of a rebounding economy was the growing amount of land under cultivation and, hence, the expansion of opportunities for productive agricultural employment. Between 1950 and 1960, the number of hectares of dry land in production increased by 40 percent and the number of irrigated lands being farmed, by 63 percent (González 1984). On rain-fed fields traditional staple crops were grown as before, but on irrigated lands the cultivation of sugarcane was abandoned. In its place, farmers began growing new cash crops, such as vegetables destined for market in Guadalajara, and alfalfa, sold as fodder to dairy stables located around that city.

This growth in agricultural production was not shared equally by all townspeople, however. Table 4.4 presents the distribution of land in 1950 and 1960 by size of plot and class of soil. Growth in the cultivation of irrigated land was concentrated primarily in the largest plots, those greater than five hectares, which were then still in the hands of the town's largest landlords. Large landowners were able to increase their holdings of irrigated land by drilling new wells on the level fields near the lagoon. The money for these wells was raised through market-oriented farming and cattle raising.

There was also a sharp increase in cultivable dry land among the largest parcels. Of the total increase in arable dry land between 1950 and 1960, 57 percent occurred within plots of five hectares or more. Five hectares is about the minimum required to support a family in Mexico (Stavenhagen 1970). This land was owned mostly by ejidatarios and worked by using family labor or sharecroppers. Money for cultivation was raised through savings from local labor and, importantly, by temporary migration to the United States. International migration during the 1940s and 1950s thus did not separate people from local economic activ-

TABLE 4.4
HECTARES OF LAND AND UNDER CULTIVATION BY CLASS OF LAND, TENANCY,
AND SIZE OF PARCEL: ALTAMIRA, JALISCO, 1950 AND 1960

Class, tenancy, and size	Year	
	1950	1960
Irrigated land	141	230
Private	141	229
Over 5 hectares	109	202
Under 5 hectares	32	27
Ejido	0	1
Humid land	17	14
Private	17	10
Over 5 hectares	16	10
Under 5 hectares	1	0
Ejido	0	4
Dryland	2,948	4,127
Private	2,367	3,362
Over 5 hectares	1,920	2,593
Under 5 hectares	447	769
Ejido	581	765

Source: 1950 and 1960 Censuses of Agriculture and Livestock, State of Jalisco.

ity; rather, it was partly responsible for the notable increase in dryland holdings, as ejidatarios returned with U.S. earnings and tried to bring their marginal farmland into production.

Agricultural Modernization

In the mid-1960s, the continued integration of local agriculture into national and international markets brought profound changes in the way that farmwork was organized, particularly in the mix between labor and capital. During the 1960s, a new cash crop, sorghum, was introduced and spread rapidly through the unirrigated flatlands on the valley floor. This crop, a cattle fodder, had two advantages over traditional staples: it was more resistant to variations in weather and shortages of water and had a higher productivity per hectare, thereby enabling larger and more secure yields than corn, beans, or garbanzos. Since there was ample demand and good prices for both corn and sorghum, farmers naturally chose the crop with the highest yield and the least risk.

The cultivation of another cash crop, alfalfa, also spread rapidly and eventually displaced vegetable gardening from irrigated fields, further restricting the diversity of local crops. Alfalfa was attractive because, unlike vegetables, it had a secure and steady demand at high prices from the dairies becoming established around Guadalajara. The raising of livestock itself declined in Altamira as more pasture was taken up by sorghum cultivation and as animal power ceased to be important in production. Livestock raising became a specialized commercial activity increasingly concentrated in large farms around Guadalajara.

Both sorghum and alfalfa had the advantage of allowing mechanization, which considerably cheapened the costs of production and led to a very rapid substitution of machines for hand labor. Threshing machines arrived in the early 1970s for use in the sorghum fields. Subsequently they were also employed in bean and garbanzo cultivation. Within a few years, tractors were also introduced and by the late 1970s were in general use on level land. At about the same time, large combine threshers also arrived, displacing even more hand labor from the fields.

As the use of agricultural machinery became more general between 1965 and 1980, other new agricultural inputs were also applied: scientifically improved seeds, chemical fertilizers, insecticides, and herbicides. The application of these new inputs brought an increase in production, but they also reduced the demand for agricultural workers. Above all, the use of herbicides replaced the task of hand weeding, which had always required an abundant supply of labor precisely at the phase of the growing cycle when there was no other work.

All of these technical innovations brought escalating absolute costs of production, and all could not share equally in their benefits. Those with access to capital—large landowners and migrant ejidatarios—invested heavily in the drilling of wells, the purchase of machinery, and the application of scientifically improved inputs. Medieros and nonmigrant ejidatarios, on the other hand, continued to rely on corn and beans for family subsistence; however, by the mid-1970s, even these people began to supplement these traditional crops with sorghum cultivation.

Over the course of the 1970s ejidatarios and medieros increasingly invested their limited capital to plant sorghum on the hillsides. New technologies were incorporated wherever terrain and resources permitted, but the new methods were used only with sorghum and alfalfa. Traditional staples were still grown by employing human labor, the cheapest and most plentiful resource. For most households, farming the land still required a heavy investment of labor, and the use of family workers with traditional methods permitted them to undertake most of the tasks of cultivation with little capital. For these households, the family continued to be the primary unit of economic production.

The technological revolution in cultivation brought about a marked change in the social organization of work in Altamira, however. Share-croppers, who had been given the rain-fed flatlands and most of the irrigated vegetable gardens until the mid-1970s, suddenly found themselves without work. Not only was there less good land to sharecrop but those medieros still able to farm could no longer find the supplemental work they needed to survive. Large property owners were using machinery to cultivate sorghum and alfalfa on the best lands and needed jornaleros only sporadically. The ecuareros who cultivated the hillsides also suffered from the contraction of the labor market, although less so than the medieros of the plain, since hillsides did not permit full mechanization.

The decline in opportunities for local day labor meant that many families could no longer afford to farm, since sharecropping alone was not sufficient to provide for the households' needs. Table 4.5 shows a decline in the amount of land under cultivation in Altamira between 1960 and 1970. Most of this decrease was concentrated in the dryland category, which declined by 46 percent during the 1960s, from 4,127 to 2,226 hectares. This decline was centered in the properties of small campesino producers and ejidatarios. Large landholders, who had not been affected by the Reparto Agrario, still had their level lands on the plain and continued channeling their resources toward acquiring more land, obtaining machinery, drilling wells, and paying the costs of industrial inputs and labor.

The 1960s thus witnessed a profound socioeconomic transformation of the community. Subsistence crops were displaced from the most productive land by fodder crops such as alfalfa and sorghum, which provided a better return on investment. This shift was accompanied by new technologies that reduced the costs of production and eliminated many traditional sources of employment. The parallel processes of commercialization and mechanization, in turn, produced a decline in agricultural production. A small increase in the cultivation of cash crops on the richest lands was overshadowed by the progressive disuse of land more marginal to capitalist investment. Corn and beans increasingly had to be bought at higher prices from outside the region, putting additional pressure on the resources of the poor.

The drastic reduction in employment opportunities for ejidatarios, medieros, and jornaleros after 1965 created the conditions for mass migration. Census figures show that the population of Altamira declined by 29 people from 1960 to 1970, from 4,824 to 4,795. During the same period, there were 1,857 births and 565 deaths, for a natural increase of 1,202 people; thus approximately 1,231 people, or a quarter of the

TABLE 4.5
HECTARES OF LAND IN PRODUCTION BY CLASS OF LAND AND YEAR:
ALTAMIRA, JALISCO, 1960 AND 1970

	Year	
Class of land	1960	1970
Cultivable land	4,426	2,536
Irrigated	230	270
Humid	14	2
Dry	4,127	2,226
Orchard	55	38
Pasture	5,119	3,499

Source: 1960 and 1970 Censuses of Agriculture and Livestock, State of Jalisco.

municipio's population, migrated out of the community during the 1960s.

Medieros and jornaleros looked for work wherever they could find it but turned increasingly to the United States. During the Bracero program, migration to the United States had become routine. Job contacts with U.S. employers had been formalized, regular seasonal patterns established, and a good knowledge of life in the United States acquired. By the late 1960s, many people from Altamira had taken out legal documents and settled in U.S. cities, and together with those in Tijuana, formed a social network that facilitated the entry and incorporation of new migrants into the U.S. labor market. When the Bracero program ended in 1964, migrants continued to come by drawing upon the resources of these migrant networks. By the mid-1960s, the official recruitment mechanism of the Bracero program had become utterly dispensable, and rather than ending with its termination, migration to the United States flourished (fig. 4.1), and most of these new migrants were undocumented (fig. 4.2).

The institutionalization of the migrant networks during the Bracero era considerably reduced the costs and risks associated with U.S. migration and made it accessible to everyone, young and old, male and female, poor and rich. Although most migrants leaving Altamira between 1965 and 1982 were aged twenty to thirty-four, fully one-third were teenagers, and 18 percent of these new migrants were women (see table 4.1). The most dramatic shift between the Bracero and contemporary eras was the change in the socioeconomic origins of migrants. Prior to 1940 migrants were mainly sons of landowners and a few campesinos' and migrants; between 1940 and 1965 were mainly ejidatarios. By the most recent period jornaleros had come to predominate, together with a large number of nonagricultural workers. Together these two landless groups comprised a majority of all migrants (table 4.2), and of those migrants who were campesinos, most were medieros rather than ejidatarios.

Concomitant with the rise in U.S. migration after 1965 was an increase in internal migration, primarily to the expanding metropolis of Guadalajara. During the 1960s and 1970s, this city underwent a tremendous expansion of its industrial and service sectors. The composition of the internal migrants thus is quite different from that of the international migrants. Internal migrants are somewhat younger and more likely to be female (table 4.1). They also tend to be drawn from the nonmanual and unskilled occupational groups, reflecting the conditions of demand in Guadalajara. Together these two occupational groups account for most internal migrants leaving Altamira between 1965 and 1982 but a smaller share of international migrants (table 4.2). Accordingly, Mexican migrants are better educated than either U.S. migrants or nonmigrants (table 4.3).

By the late 1970s, therefore, seasonal out-migration for wage labor had become a way of life for people from Altamira. The predominant strategy was still sporadic migration for temporary work abroad, with migrants maintaining strong links to life at home. New patterns of recurrent and settled international migration had also begun to emerge, however, attenuating the social and economic connections between migrants and the community. One consequence has been the deterioration of Altamira's orchards, which require constant grooming and attention, services traditionally provided by young men. By the early 1970s, teenage men were more likely to be found working in the United States than in Altamira, and between 1960 and 1970, the number of hectares of orchards being cultivated fell from fifty-five to thirty-eight hectares. This decline in the orchards symbolizes how Altamira's young men increasingly look to the United States for economic opportunity, rather than to the family or the community.

CHAMITLÁN: MICROHISTORY OF A COMMERCIAL AGRARIAN TOWN

The Era of the Latifundio

In the Porfirian era there were two types of land tenancy in the municipio of Chamitlán: *latifundios* and *ranchos*. Latifundios were large expanses of land owned by absentee landlords and run by hired administrators. Ranchos were smaller properties directly farmed by their own-ers. Archival data from the late 1880s show that the municipio was dominated by three large latifundios, which together controlled 55 per-cent of the cultivable land. The remaining 45 percent was divided among 90 ranchos of small to middling size, and many families were landless.

The latifundios and ranchos of Chamitlán mainly grew staples such as corn, wheat, and garbanzo. Most of the crops were grown for market, especially wheat and garbanzo; however, a large part of the corn crop was consumed in the municipio. Because corn was a basic foodstuff of the Mexican diet, *latifundistas* often used it to pay their workers. Wheat was ground into flour at mills near Zamora and taken by muleteers for sale in various parts of western Mexico, notably Guadalajara, Colima, and the coastal areas of Michoacán.

The latifundistas cultivated their land by employing sharecroppers and hired day laborers. They selected the hardest working and most trustworthy peons to be medieros, who were responsible for all the tasks of cultivation, which were accomplished primarily with unpaid family labor. Jornaleros were only employed sporadically, usually work-ing on special projects such as construction of irrigation canals, water tanks, or fences. During the harvest season, medieros also might hire them. Because of the insecurity of daily wage labor, however, most jornaleros also had to cultivate ecuaros, or marginal hillside plots. Since the latifundistas owned the hillsides as well as the flatlands, these jornalero-ecuareros were obliged to pay a share of their meager harvest as rent. Medieros and jornaleros were used in a conscious strategy of exploitation, enabling the latifundistas to accumulate large profits with a minimum of investment (González 1982). All that was required was land and a little seed. Since work was organized through the family, the social reproduction of the labor force was assured without direct intervention by the landowners.

Apart from medieros and jornaleros, the working class in Chamitlán consisted of a variety of artisans and small merchants who produced and marketed many goods and services for local consumption. In a report entitled "A Note on Commerce, Agriculture, and Mining in 1903," one chronicler observed the following commercial establishments in Chamitlán:

> a deep freeze, a sugar mill, and two tortilla factories, the former two powered by electricity and the latter by steam; a machine to wash and dry hemp, another to wash and dry stockings; eight cigarette factories and two soap factories; three breweries and three factories for making seltzer; two photography studios;

various workshops housing tailors, shawl-makers, carpenters, shoemakers, blacksmiths, tinsmiths, and tanners; an old-style brick factory; a couple of pulque [fermented maguey juice] stills; and two sculptor's studios.

Along with these artisans, Chamitlán housed many muleteers who carried the goods to locations throughout the area.

At the turn of the century, Chamitlán thus was an important economic center in the Zamora Valley. It was endowed with a rich agricultural economy that supported a strong demand for labor in the form of sharecroppers and day laborers. It also housed a variety of small, family-run artisan workshops producing goods and services to satisfy local demand. It was a well-established node in a regional trade network, with a wide radius of influence that provisioned the ranchos and the haciendas of the municipio and other towns visited by its muleteers. Although wages were low, there was generally enough work to go around, unlike the case in many other communities.

All this began to change at the turn of the century, when a wave of modernization reached the Zamora area, bringing with it a host of technological changes—the railroad, electricity, the telegraph, and telephones—which transformed socioeconomic life in the community. The railroad had the most profound effect. With the construction of the town's train depot in 1899, Chamitlán was incorporated into the national rail network, and one of the first effects of the train was the displacement of muleteers from the scene. A few who traded with outlying settlements were able to hang on for a short while, but eventually they, too, succumbed. The railroad also meant that wheat produced in Chamitlán was no longer milled locally but shipped directly to Mexico City, Toluca, and Irapuato, where it was processed more cheaply by large milling companies (Verduzco 1984).

At about the same time, several sections of the municipio's farmland were irrigated, as the result of a Porfirian drive for water and flood control. A report in the Municipal Archives of Zamora, written in 1904, states that the municipio of Chamitlán contained 5,438 hectares of cultivable land. Of this quantity, 24 percent was irrigated, 59 percent was rain-fed, and the remaining 17 percent was pasture. The 1910 Census listed 4,366 inhabitants, of which 2,387 lived in the cabecera, with the remaining 1,979 scattered throughout ten smaller rancherías.

By 1919, the economic picture in Chamitlán had changed considerably. The railroad had rendered the muleteers' jobs redundant and had brought many new city goods into town, displacing traditional handicraft workers. The spread of irrigation and more intense agriculture lessened the demand for hand labor and began to undercut the positions of medieros and jornaleros. In addition to these changes, the Mexican Revolution disrupted normal patterns of trade, and by the end of the decade, economic life in the Zamora Valley had virtually dried up.

There is no indication in townspeople's accounts of anyone migrating to the United States before 1910. Between 1910 and 1939, however, a few pioneer migrants left to escape economic hardships brought on by the revolution. They organized themselves into groups and arranged passage to El Paso, Texas, where they crossed into the United States to work on the railroads. Table 4.6 presents some characteristics of the first U.S. migrants, gathered from oral histories taken from migrants or their descendants. These earliest migrants went to work primarily in midwestern states as construction or maintenance workers for the railroads or as unskilled workers in steel mills around Chicago. Most were young, illiterate men from campesino, jornalero, or artisan families.

From the beginning, migration from Chamitlán was directed principally to the United States, and not to urban areas within Mexico. Figure 4.3 shows the number of townspeople leaving on their first trips to the United States and Mexico by time period from 1910 to 1982, and figure 4.4 classifies U.S. migrant cohorts by documentation. Townspeople re-

TABLE 4.6

AGE AT FIRST TRIP, YEAR OF FIRST TRIP, MEXICAN OCCUPATION, U.S. DESTINATION, AND U.S. OCCUPATION OF PIONEER U.S. MIGRANTS FROM CHAMITLÁN, MICHOACÁN

Age	Year of first trip	Mexican occupation	Destination in United States	First job in United States
32	1912	Jornalero	Chicago, Ill.	Railroad track worker
16	1914	Jornalero	St. Louis, Mo.	Railroad water carrier
21	1915	Fireworks maker	Santa Fe, N. Mex.	Railroad track worker
??	1916	Blacksmith	Petersburg, Okla.	Coal miner
21	1918	Mill worker	Montana	Railroad track worker
17	1917	Jornalero	Gary, Ind.	Foundry worker
18	1918	Jornalero	Chicago, Ill.	Foundry worker
18	1918	Mediero	Austin, Tex.	Railroad track worker
??	1919	Mediero	Parlier, Calif.	Farmworker
26	1920	Mediero	Texas	Railroad track worker

Source: Oral histories of selected townspeople.

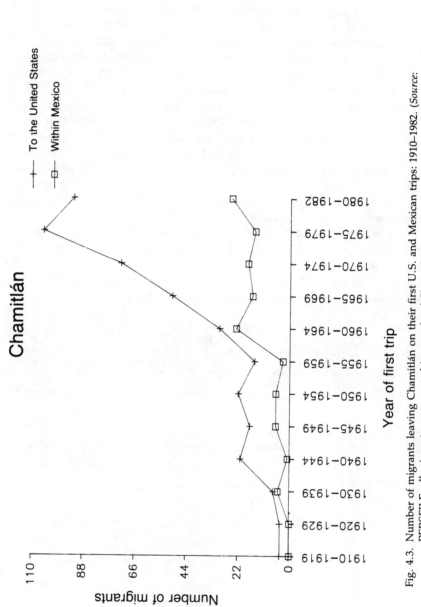

Fig. 4.3. Number of migrants leaving Chamitlán on their first U.S. and Mexican trips: 1910–1982. (*Source:* PERSFILE; all migrants enumerated in sample of Chamitlán.)

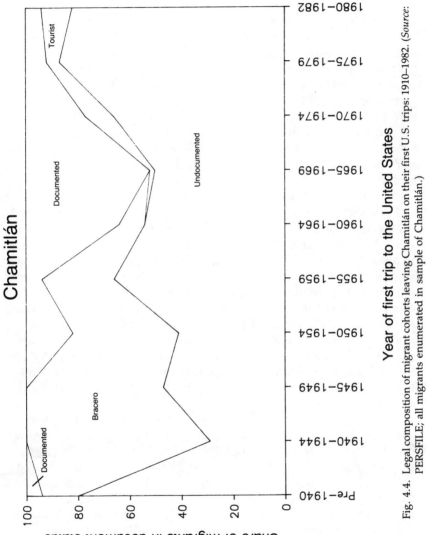

Fig. 4.4. Legal composition of migrant cohorts leaving Chamitlán on their first U.S. trips: 1910–1982. (*Source:* PERSFILE; all migrants enumerated in sample of Chamitlán.)

port no internal migration before 1930, only some temporary displacement stemming from the revolution and from the incursions of local bandits. These reports are confirmed by the ethnosurvey data, which show steady out-migration to the United States from 1910 through 1939, but no internal migration until the 1930s, and very little of it then (fig. 4.3). Most U.S. migrants simply crossed the border without documents, which were not required until 1917. A few entered after obtaining a labor contract through a recruiter, and one person obtained legal papers.

Tables 4.7 through 4.9 present selected characteristics of migrants leaving Chamitlán during three periods. These data are consistent with the oral reports of villagers in suggesting that the earliest U.S. migrants were predominantly young unmarried males (table 4.7) of campesino and jornalero origin (table 4.8). As in Altamira, the earliest migrants were not the poorest of the poor, but were principally medieros and small property owners. Since the vast majority of townspeople who lived through the 1910–1939 period were illiterate, migrants are not very different from others in terms of education (table 4.9).

During the early phases of Mexican migration to the United States, there were three basic types of migrant: legal settlers, temporary workers, and refugees (Hall 1982). Migrants from Chamitlán went mostly as temporary workers seeking to stay for a few years and then return home to invest their savings in land, houses, or livestock. The U.S. government paid little attention to Mexican migrants before 1917, but after its entry into World War I, it supported a contract labor program for Mexican braceros that lasted until 1922 (Kiser and Woody 1979). According to oral histories, six workers from Chamitlán went as wartime contract workers and were subsequently forced to enlist in the U.S. army and sent to France. Government agents told them that "since the United States is helping you, you have to help the United States." Fortunately, all returned unharmed.

In summary, migration to the United States originally developed as a result of the constriction of economic opportunity following Porfirian economic modernization and then the Mexican Revolution. The outflow of young, unmarried men to the United States began in small numbers but increased slowly and steadily from 1910 to 1940. In contrast to other Mexican communities (Reichert and Massey 1980; Mines 1981), U.S. migration continued even through the depression years of the 1930s. When the Bracero program began in 1942, Chamitlán thus had an unusually well developed migrant tradition honed over thirty years of experience, and townspeople were well positioned to take advantage of the return of labor recruitment.

TABLE 4.7

DEMOGRAPHIC CHARACTERISTICS OF MIGRANTS TO THE UNITED STATES, MIGRANTS
WITHIN MEXICO, AND NONMIGRANTS IN THREE PERIODS: CHAMITLÁN, MICHOACÁN

Migrant status, sex, and age	Period		
	1910–1939	1940–1964	1965–1982
Migrants to United States			
Sex			
Male (%)	92.9	89.5	69.5
Age			
Under 15 (%)	21.4	18.1	13.5
15–19 (%)	42.9	30.5	24.1
20–34 (%)	28.6	48.6	47.2
35–54 (%)	7.1	1.9	13.1
55+ (%)	0.0	0.9	2.1
Average	16.7	20.3	23.8
Number	14	105	282
Migrants within Mexico			
Sex			
Male (%)	100.0	87.2	87.5
Age			
Under 15 (%)	20.0	30.8	10.9
15–19 (%)	20.0	25.6	7.8
20–34 (%)	40.0	41.0	57.8
35–54 (%)	20.0	2.6	23.4
55+ (%)	0.0	0.0	0.0
Average	23.0	18.5	26.8
Number	5	39	64
Nonmigrants			
Sex			
Male (%)	48.4	42.5	39.7
Age			
Under 15 (%)	82.2	63.9	51.8
15–19 (%)	8.0	11.3	11.3
20–34 (%)	8.7	17.5	19.8
35–54 (%)	1.0	6.6	13.2
55+ (%)	0.0	0.7	3.9
Average	5.4	13.1	19.4
Number	572	3,146	4,252

Source: PERSFILE; all persons enumerated in sample of Chamitlán.

TABLE 4.8
MEXICAN OCCUPATION OF MIGRANTS TO THE UNITED STATES, MIGRANTS WITHIN
MEXICO, AND NONMIGRANTS IN THREE PERIODS: CHAMITLÁN, MICHOACÁN

Migrant status and occupation	1910–1939		1940–1964		1965–1982	
	Occupation in period	Occupation in 1982	Occupation in period	Occupation in 1982	Occupation in period	Occupation in 1982
Migrants to United States						
Agricultor (%)	0.0	0.0	0.0	1.3	0.0	0.6
Nonmanual (%)	14.3	11.1	0.0	9.1	18.2	17.5
Skilled manual (%)	0.0	0.0	8.2	13.0	2.3	7.6
Campesino (%)	42.9	77.8	34.7	40.3	11.4	11.7
Unskilled manual (%)	0.0	0.0	4.1	7.8	9.1	8.2
Jornalero (%)	42.9	11.1	53.1	28.6	59.1	54.4
Number	7	9	49	77	44	171
Migrants within Mexico						
Agricultor (%)	0.0	50.0	0.0	4.4	0.0	2.0
Nonmanual (%)	20.0	0.0	6.7	43.5	14.3	40.8
Skilled manual (%)	0.0	0.0	6.7	8.7	4.8	16.3
Campesino (%)	40.0	50.0	26.7	17.4	4.8	10.2
Unskilled manual (%)	40.0	0.0	6.7	4.4	9.5	2.0
Jornalero (%)	0.0	0.0	53.3	21.7	66.7	28.6
Number	5	2	15	23	21	49
Nonmigrants						
Agricultor (%)	0.0	2.8	0.5	1.8	2.7	2.7
Nonmanual (%)	7.8	8.3	7.3	30.0	19.7	27.3
Skilled manual (%)	2.5	2.8	4.6	8.5	7.8	6.0
Campesino (%)	33.5	58.3	33.1	22.0	25.0	14.2
Unskilled manual (%)	5.6	0.0	7.3	5.9	6.3	9.2
Jornalero (%)	50.6	27.8	47.3	31.8	38.5	40.6
Number	358[a]	36	1,043[a]	437	1,175[a]	697

Sources: Occupation in period from LIFEFILE; occupation in 1982 from PERSFILE; all persons enumerated in sample of Chamitlán.

[a] Number refers to person-years observed rather than number of people.

The Era of the Moneylenders and the Braceros

The large latifundios of Chamitlán were finally destroyed in the 1930s
with the consolidation of the agrarian movement under the leadership
of Lázaro Cárdenas. Agrarian activism had a long history in Chamitlán.
It arose in the early 1920s on the initiative of a few medieros and
jornaleros, some of whom had become radicalized through eye-opening
proletarian experiences in the United States. Before the large estates
could be broken up, however, many hurdles had to be overcome.

The first difficulty that the agrarian leaders faced was the apathy

TABLE 4.9
YEARS OF EDUCATION AMONG U.S. MIGRANTS, MEXICAN MIGRANTS, AND
NONMIGRANTS AGED 15 AND OVER IN THREE PERIODS: CHAMITLÁN, MICHOACÁN

Migrant status and education	Period		
	1910–1939	1940–1964	1965–1982
Migrants to United States			
None (%)	91.7	34.9	11.5
1–3 (%)	8.3	44.2	30.0
4–5 (%)	0.0	10.5	18.1
6 (%)	0.0	9.3	26.3
7–9 (%)	0.0	1.2	10.3
10–11 (%)	0.0	0.0	1.7
12 (%)	0.0	0.0	0.8
13+ (%)	0.0	0.0	1.2
Average	0.2	2.1	4.4
Number	12	86	243
Migrants within Mexico			
None (%)	75.0	37.0	15.8
1–3 (%)	25.0	33.3	49.1
4–5 (%)	0.0	11.1	10.5
6 (%)	0.0	11.1	8.8
7–9 (%)	0.0	0.0	7.0
10–11 (%)	0.0	0.0	3.5
12 (%)	0.0	3.7	1.8
13+ (%)	0.0	3.7	3.5
Average	0.8	2.8	3.7
Number	4	27	57
Nonmigrants			
None (%)	64.4	41.2	23.0
1–3 (%)	24.8	34.1	34.5
4–5 (%)	2.0	9.4	11.1
6 (%)	8.9	12.4	22.6
7–9 (%)	0.0	1.8	5.3
10–11 (%)	0.0	0.5	1.3
12 (%)	0.0	0.4	1.1
13+ (%)	0.0	0.2	1.0
Average	1.1	2.2	3.5
Number	101	1,131	2,151

Source: PERSFILE; all persons enumerated in sample of Chamitlán.

and fear of the peons, many of whom did not want any part of an agrarian political party. Many of them thought that redistribution of the latifundistas' land was robbery; others felt that life was more secure under the protection of the landowners. A second barrier, of course, was the latifundistas themselves, who actively fought the agrarian movement, in some cases resorting to violence. A third hurdle was the clergy, which generally sided with the latifundistas. Townspeople still speak of a priest who taught that the agrarian movement was immoral. He did his best to instill fear in the hearts of the peons, saying: "Mark my words; it will be a very bad time when the lands of the rich are given to the poor; because those who take them will be the Bolsheviks!"

In spite of barriers placed in their paths, the agrarian reformers of Chamitlán petitioned officially for a land grant under the 1917 Constitution in February 1927. This request required considerable courage, since it occurred during the *Cristero* Rebellion, a popular armed uprising against the government that was encouraged by the Catholic Church (Meyer 1976). Centered in western Mexico, it drew upon the resentment of a deeply religious populace against the anticlerical measures unleashed by the revolution, and in Chamitlán, the Cristeros were violently opposed to agrarian reform.

The event that turned the tide for agrarian reform was the appointment of Lázaro Cárdenas as the governor of Michoacán in 1928. From the moment he took office, he supported and energized the Reparto Agrario in the state. Likewise, the national Reparto Agrario experienced its most intense phase after he was elected president in 1934. In June 1929 he made a provisional grant of 1,114 hectares for the formation of an ejido in Chamitlán, with expropriations from landholdings near the town.

The applicants from the cabecera were not satisfied with this provisional grant, however, which consisted mostly of rocky hillsides. They accused the surveyors of altering the original plans after being bribed by the landowners. The discontent of the campesinos led to a reconsideration of their petition, and in September 1930 President Ortíz Rubio set aside 894 hectares of higher-quality land as an ejido, intended for the use of 163 campesinos and their families. A population register compiled in December 1927 listed 2,064 people and 450 families in the cabecera, implying that only 36 percent of its families received a grant of ejido lands. The fact that only about a third of all families received an allotment partially reflects the reluctance of townspeople to participate in the agrarian struggle.

Over the years, the attitude of people from Chamitlán changed, and the ejido was enlarged three more times (table 4.10); however, the size and quality of ejido parcels generally declined with each successive allotment. Those who received land before the second expansion got four hectares of irrigated land and eight hectares of dry land, whereas those in the third expansion got only two hectares of low-quality dry land. The agrarian leaders also organized committees in the rancherías and neighboring communities, and through their work, land was obtained for the formation of nine more ejidos during the 1930s. At pres-

TABLE 4.10
ORIGINAL ALLOTMENT AND ADDITIONS TO THE EJIDO OF
CHAMITLÁN, MICHOACÁN (IN HECTARES)

| Action initiated | Year | Class of land | | | |
		Irrigated	Dryland	Pasture	Total
Original allotment	1930	38.1	431.2	424.9	894.2
First addition	1936	192.0	704.0	0.0	896.0
Second addition	1962	0.0	218.4	0.0	218.4
Third addition	1966	0.0	84.6	0.0	84.6
Total	1982	230.1	1,438.2	424.9	2,093.2

Source: Archives of the Secretary for Agrarian Reform, Morelia, Michoacán.

ent about 300 ejidatarios live in Chamitlán, plus others from outlying rancherías who have come to live in town.

As in Altamira, after taking possession of their allotments, the new ejidatarios were unable to cultivate their lands because they lacked the necessary animals, tools, seed, and—in general—money. Ejidatarios in Altamira rented lands to their former patrones, whereas those in Chamitlán turned to the rich to rent oxen, borrow money, and obtain seed to begin farming. The five or six wealthy people to whom they turned were not the former latifundistas but small-property owners, merchants, and former hacienda administrators. These people at first refused to give the ejidatarios financial aid on principle. They considered the ejidatarios to be thieves and feared their growing political influence. Nevertheless, the wealthy changed their attitudes when they realized that loaning to the ejidatarios was good business.

In time these moneylenders became important commodity speculators, monopolizing wheat, corn, and garbanzo. They soon widened their operations to neighboring communities, prospered, and eventually became the new patrones of the capital-poor campesinos. As in the time of the haciendas, campesinos had to borrow seed to plant their fields, corn to feed their families until harvest, and cash for other expenses of production. They were required to return double the corn that had been borrowed, together with seed as payment for any cash advances. Frequently campesinos sold the future crop outright. The domination of the moneylenders continued until the 1960s because of the unavailability of credit from the government's rural development bank.

During the 1930s and 1940s, therefore, social relations in Chamitlán were dominated by a small group of moneylender-monopolists who profited by loaning to campesinos while simultaneously exploiting medieros and jornaleros. Most campesinos continued to produce at the subsistence level, and as in the era of the latifundio, corn continued to be the dominant crop. Most of the harvest controlled by the moneylenders was sold outside the region. In 1934 alone, some 1,834 metric tons of corn and 274 tons of fodder were sent out of the Chamitlán train depot (Foglio 1936).

Agricultural production at this time was still quite labor-intensive, with the flatlands worked by animal-drawn plows and the hillsides farmed by hoe. The cultivation of hillsides continued to be a very important activity in the community during these years, providing the means for survival of many poor families, especially those of jornaleros. The only important technological changes emerged during the late 1940s, when tractors were introduced by the richest agricultores, and metal plows pulled by mules or horses were substituted for the old wooden plows pulled by oxen.

During the late 1940s, Chamitlán lost further importance as a commercial center when the highway between Guadalajara and Mexico City opened, passing only four kilometers away. This road linked Chamitlán even more closely with national markets and brought about the final decline of the artisan activities that had previously flourished there. In addition to these dislocations, the agrarian movement began to stagnate, especially during the term of President Miguel Alemán (1946–1952).

These difficulties coincided with establishment and expansion of the Bracero program in the United States, an event that radically transformed the migration process in Chamitlán. This program was tremendously important for all classes of agricultural workers. For ejidatarios, who had land but no money, it provided a ready source of capital with which to finance agricultural production; for medieros, it was a much needed supplement to the meager living that could be eked out by sharecropping; and for jornaleros, it provided wages for day labor far exceeding any that could be had locally.

Seasonal work in the United States was therefore rapidly adopted as a preferred economic strategy by a majority of working-age men in Chamitlán. As figure 4.3 shows, the number of new out-migrants increased considerably during the 1940s and early 1950s. In the first few years of the program, most people went north as braceros, but by the late 1940s the demand for permits far exceeded supply, and undocumented migration began to rise, a trend that continued through the 1980s (see fig. 4.4). After fluctuating at a moderate level from 1940 through the mid-1950s, the total volume of migration increased sharply after 1955 (fig. 4.3).

The social and demographic composition of migrants also shifted during the Bracero period. Between 1940 and 1964 migration shifted to favor older, married family men with dependents; and late in the period the first few women began to migrate, usually accompanying their husbands (table 4.7). The predominance of campesinos among U.S. migrants also lessened (table 4.8). This shift was brought about by the greater participation of skilled and unskilled manual laborers, and especially by landless jornaleros, who, unable (or in some cases unwilling) to petition for an ejido, were forced to subsist by selling their labor to the highest bidder.

Many ejidatarios greatly improved their economic fortunes through migration during the Bracero period. Savings from U.S. wages allowed the purchase or rental of additional land, leading to significant increases in production and the beginnings of capital accumulation. At this time, medieros began to sharecrop not only lands owned by moneylenders and grain monopolists but also those owned by U.S. migrants who were spending an increasing amount of time abroad. As in the time of the latifundio, therefore, much land was cultivated by medieros for absentee landlords, only now the patrones were the moneylenders and the U.S. migrants.

The Bracero period also witnessed the beginnings of a market for ejido lands, something that was quite illegal under the terms of the Reparto Agrario. The sale and rental of ejidos, although common, did not indicate a return to the Porfirian hacienda, however, because the ejido community would not permit their lands to be obtained by the former latifundistas, nor would they allow the monopolization of lands in a few hands. Many of those who benefited from the sale of ejido parcels were migrants who had saved their U.S. earnings.

Over the course of the Bracero years, migration from Chamitlán focused increasingly on California and a growing percentage of migrants acquired legal documents. The majority of people still worked as braceros or without documents; however, during the 1950s and early 1960s a few families began to apply for legal papers and settle permanently in the United States (see fig. 4.4). They established themselves in several California communities and in the Chicago area, where several men had long-standing connections and regular jobs with the U.S. Steel plant in Gary, Indiana.

During the late 1950s townspeople also began to migrate to other regions in Mexico; however, except for one 5-year period, this internal movement was insignificant compared with migration to the United States (fig. 4.3). A few went to Mexico City and Guadalajara to work in the burgeoning service sector, and nearby Zamora attracted a few jornalero families during the growth years of potato cultivation in the 1950s. Migrants from Chamitlán also worked seasonally in several rural areas, and a few families settled permanently out of the municipio. Interestingly, one minor cause of out-migration was not economic at all, but an old-fashioned family feud. After a bitter rivalry left several members of both sides dead, some families left permanently for the United States and other parts of Mexico.

The extent of out-migration during the Bracero period is indicated by census data that show a population loss during the 1940s. Chamitlán's population fell from 7,685 in 1940 to 7,549 in 1950, which, given the positive rate of natural increase that must have prevailed at the time, indicates fairly extensive out-migration, principally to the United States.

In summary, the period from 1940 to 1964 was one in which a wealthy group of moneylender-monopolists dominated social and economic affairs in Chamitlán. The Reparto Agrario had brought an end to the old latifundios, but, as in Altamira, the redistribution of land had left ejidatarios with soil to cultivate but no money to carry it out. They were forced to borrow at usurious rates from local moneylenders, who also acted as landlords to medieros and employers for jornaleros. The advent of the Bracero program offered a way out of this cycle of exploitation, and U.S. migration was quickly taken up by a variety of occupational groups. It was of particular benefit to the ejidatarios, providing them with an outside source of investment capital and giving them independence from the moneylenders. By the end of the Bracero program in 1964, several families had settled in U.S. cities and migration to the United States was rapidly accelerating.

Agricultural Modernization and Recurrent U.S. Migration

During the 1970s agriculture in Chamitlán, as in Altamira, experienced a wave of modernization characterized by the growing use of machinery and modern scientific inputs, a shift from subsistence to cash crops, and the predominance of paid work over unpaid family labor. Accordingly, the social organization of cultivation in Chamitlán underwent a dramatic transformation.

The shift to cash crops was especially marked. Irrigated lands that previously had been sown with wheat were taken over by linseed, sorghum, and strawberries. At the same time, the cultivation of sorghum took over hectares of dry lands that were once planted in corn. Over the course of the 1970s, sorghum production increased whereas that of corn stagnated. In 1974, 250 hectares of corn were planted in the municipio, and 800 hectares were sown in 1976. In contrast, the number of hectares sown in sorghum increased from 2,000 in 1974 to 3,500 in 1976.

The shift to cash crops had a strong impact on patterns of land tenancy. According to 1980 Census data, the municipio of Chamitlán contains 11,515 hectares of land. About 11 percent is irrigated, 43 percent is dry, 42 percent is pasture, and 4 percent is not cultivable. About 73 percent of all land is in ejidos, while some 94 percent of irrigated land is so classified, compared with 63 percent of dry land and 80 percent of hillside land. It appears that most of the municipio's land is taken up in ejidos; however, the picture changes substantially when the private rental of ejido lands is taken into account.

In the mid-1960s the Zamora Valley experienced a boom in the cultivation of strawberries for export to the United States. Production of this luxury crop proved to be extremely lucrative, and the irrigated parcels of land in Chamitlán were increasingly coveted by large agri-businesses based in Zamora. At the same time, large companies sought to rent dry land in order to plant sorghum. The practice of renting ejido parcels thus grew considerably over the course of the 1970s. It is now common practice for many ejidatarios to rent their lands to large growers for a handsome price and then to migrate for work in the United States. The buying and selling of ejido parcels has declined since the mid-1960s, however, mainly because the intense demand for land has made the price too dear for most townspeople.

The changeover to cash crops was accompanied by the emergence of a technological package based on agricultural machinery and modern inputs such as chemical fertilizers and insecticides. These innovations led directly to the unemployment of a large number of jornaleros. With the exception of strawberries, most of the tasks involved in cultivation of cash crops can be accomplished more economically and effectively with machines.

All of these trends were spurred by the growing integration of Chamitlán into national and international markets and were supported by various governmental interventions. The process of agricultural mechanization, in particular, was supported by the federal government's credit policies. The rural development bank, through its loan policies, allotted great quantities of money to large farmers for the purchase of agricultural machinery but little support to small farmers for basic inputs such as seed and fertilizers.

The rise of agricultural companies and governmental institutions eventually brought the eclipse of the moneylenders as a socioeconomic power and led to their retirement from community affairs. Now large agribusinesses have taken the place of the former elites in exploiting

poor campesinos and jornaleros. By renting parcels from migrant ejidatarios and using machinery in conjunction with poorly paid jornaleros
to farm them, companies are able to grow crops at a very high profit.
Sharecropping and family labor have ceased to provide an important
means for organizing production, since the combination of mechanization and cheap labor produces higher profits for the new patrones.

It might seem logical to suppose that jornaleros displaced from
working the best land by mechanization would return to cultivation of
hillsides as a means of surviving. But the cultivation of ecuaros likewise
has declined notably in recent years. Instead, the number of jornaleros
turning to U.S. migrant labor has grown tremendously, and since 1965
this group has come to dominate the process of international migration.
At the same time, Chamitlán has declined in importance as a center of
commerce and crafts, which are now concentrated in Zamora, and the
proportion of nonmanual workers among migrants has also risen.

These trends all occurred after the termination of the Bracero program. The end of the temporary worker program did not bring an end
to migration. On the contrary, migration increased in volume (see fig.
4.3). Most migrants simply went without documents, but those with
prior contacts and experience used their connections to obtain "green
cards" under the relatively liberal immigration laws that prevailed for
Mexicans up until 1968 (see fig. 4.4). In the late 1960s and early 1970s,
newly legalized families from Chamitlán began to settle in California,
and by the late 1970s, there were important concentrations of townspeople in several cities.

These communities provided a solid U.S. anchor for the already
well-developed migratory networks, unleashing a torrent of migration
from Chamitlán. Between the periods 1955–1959 and 1975–1979, the
number of first-time U.S. migrants grew from less than 20 to nearly 110
(fig. 4.3). The composition of migrant cohorts also broadened considerably to include more women and a variety of age groups (table 4.7),
representing virtually all occupational categories (table 4.8) and educational levels (table 4.9). The extent to which migration is increasingly
viewed as the road to advancement is indicated by the reversal of
migration differentials since 1965. Migrants to the United States have
become more educated than other migrant status groups, as better-
educated young people increasingly seek their fortunes in the United
States (table 4.9).

In short, international migration from Chamitlán has become a mass
phenomenon. It began with changes in the social organization of work
spurred by agricultural modernization that affected primarily campesinos and jornaleros, but it eventually expanded to encompass all social

groups when migrant networks developed to put a U.S. job within easy reach of everyone. Chamitlán is now connected to several daughter communities in the United States by well-established networks of social ties. Although some townspeople have settled abroad, the prevailing strategy remains one of temporary migration, and the annual commuting for work in the United States has become a way of life for many families in Chamitlán.

SANTIAGO: MICROHISTORY OF AN INDUSTRIAL TOWN

A Company Town

Just before the end of the nineteenth century, during the rapid economic expansion of Porfirian Mexico, a large, modern textile factory was founded on land belonging to the Hacienda of Santiago in Jalisco. This location was selected for several reasons: closeness to the city of Guadalajara, a natural market only thirty kilometers away; accessibility to rail lines, one of which passed within a few kilometers of the factory; the availability of potable water and hydraulic power from a nearby river and waterfall; the presence of forests, providing fuel to heat cauldrons used in dyeing and bleaching of fabrics; and finally, the ready availability of open land, which belonged to a family of local entrepreneurs who were quite willing to sell. This site gave the factory more than enough space for current and future needs and allowed the company to take advantage of the latest technologies: rail transport for importing raw materials and exporting finished products and hydroelectricity to power the factory's motors and spindles.

At first, the town and the factory were one and the same. Santiago was set up on the model of a "company town" in which the factory, in addition to giving work and organizing production, provided housing and basic services to workers, thereby exercising near total control over the population. The factory was organized as a self-contained compound, and within its confines the owners were the ultimate political, civil, and legal authorities.

The physical plant of the factory was, and remains, impressive. Built in the industrial style of York, England, it has an imposing facade with a monumental portico that encloses several large buildings that provide spacious quarters for the factory's various divisions: spinning, dyeing, bleaching, weaving, and printing. Employee housing within the compound reflects the social stratification prevailing at the time, with one sector of stately homes for owners and administrators (many of whom

were English), another area of large and comfortable houses for technicians and salaried workers, and a zone of some 800 modest homes for
workers and their families. The compound also had a central plaza
containing a fountain and a gazebo, surrounded by company stores, a
post office, a medical dispensary, and a pharmacy. The town also
boasted a chapel, a theater, and later on, various sports facilities; these
buildings were enclosed by a common large wall that restricted access
to a single gate.

Once constructed, the new company town began to recruit skilled
labor from all over Mexico. Initially, the factory demanded trained workers ready to enter immediately into the tasks of spinning, weaving,
dyeing, and printing. Unskilled workers from nearby settlements eventually began to appear at the factory gates seeking work, however,
especially local jornaleros who had helped to build the factory. Textile
workers arrived with their families and were incorporated promptly into
the routine of the factory. In many cases, their wives also worked and
their children generally served as apprentices. By passing jobs from
person to person and generation to generation within families, the
company eventually not only succeeded in reproducing its labor force
but also saved the expense of training new workers and adapting them
to factory life.

Children and relatives of workers had priority in filling new positions in the factory, especially those created when increased demand
obliged an expansion of production to two or three shifts. The peons of
the surrounding hacienda and the neighboring agrarian town of Ixtlán
had little chance of employment in the factory. A few could, if they were
lucky, find work in unspecialized jobs that required no training; however, these made up only about 5 percent of the factory's jobs and were
poorly paid.

Within a few years of its founding, Santiago's factory proved very
lucrative. It soon reached a level of production equivalent to the combined output of its three closest competitors in Guadalajara. According
to archival and census data, in 1907 the factory produced 760 metric tons
of fabric annually and employed about 1,500 workers.

The years that followed the fall of the Porfirian dictatorship were
difficult for the company. It was forced to reduce the number of shifts
and workdays because of falling demand, and although the revolution did not touch the company directly and workers did not actively
participate in the conflict, the factory had to overcome a series of labor
problems that arose out of the social ferment of the times. Poor work
conditions and low wages caused continual friction between labor and
management. Until 1920 the factory compound continued as a walled

company town, within which the factory's British manager remained the highest authority, a status quo that was maintained until the new revolutionary government intervened on the workers' behalf.

Period of Transition

By the early 1920s, the days of the company town were numbered. Until then, the owners had been able to rule within the compound only because the state had specifically ceded broad powers of government to them. Following the revolution, however, shaky federal and state governments were in the process of consolidating power and taking control of many arenas formerly dominated by hacienda owners and industrialists. In Santiago, this meant that the factory's owners were finally forced to surrender the reins of political power to state and local authorities. Although this change was certainly an important advance for the workers, it created new problems because Santiago became politically dependent on the neighboring town of Ixtlán, the cabecera of the municipio, with which it had always maintained a rancorous rivalry.

The new political regime swept in by the revolution brought a new style of government, with federal and state officials trying to serve as mediators in worker-company conflicts. For their part, the workers had also evolved politically, a change exemplified in the proliferation of unions and other worker organizations and the growing participation of these groups in national politics. Eventually, worker organizations, with the help of governmental authorities, brought about important changes in workers' conditions of employment.

In 1921 the workers of Santiago succeeded in forming a union affiliated with the anarchist movement and began to fight for better wages and working conditions. Isolated protests soon became organized strikes, and the union began to achieve important results on the worker's behalf (Durand 1983). The harried industrialists, occasionally assisted by state and local officials, naturally resisted the changes. Several times they responded to workers' demands with lockouts or slowdowns, temporarily closing the factory or reducing its hours. Strikes and labor problems were frequent.

Given that the town depended almost entirely on the company for employment, fluctuations in demand for the factory's products had a profound impact on the town. During boom periods the company could impose a second, or even a third, shift on the workers and their families, and in slack times it could suspend these extra shifts entirely. This was possible because the company was obliged to give permanent work only to those employed on the first shift, and in town there was always a surplus of qualified workers—apprentices, spouses, relatives, and, of course, local jornaleros—who were only too willing to work, even if only temporarily.

Another labor supply regulating mechanism was provided by the workers' organizations themselves. In addition to making demands of owners, workers were battling among themselves, as different factions fought for control of the union organization; in these internal power struggles, a good number of dissident workers were expelled from the factory (Durand 1983). Eventually, these internal struggles were overcome, and a single union faction prevailed. This union faction succeeded in obtaining in its contract with the company a provision that all workers be union members, giving it effective right of veto over hiring and ultimately controlling entry into the factory.

Within this context of factional struggle and political consolidation among unionists, outsiders seeking work in the factory were almost automatically excluded. In order to enter into the factory, it was necessary not only to be from the town and to live there but also to have been active in political life, or at least to profess allegiance to the group in power, circumstances that in Santiago were conducive to a closed atmosphere.

The political situation of Santiago with respect to the rest of the municipio also contributed to its isolation and reinforced the union's influence. The relationship between the town and the cabecera was one of permanent conflict. Residents of Santiago controlled the only source of local employment, while people from Ixtlán had political control of the municipio. They resented their exclusion from the factory and took revenge by imposing an irritating series of sanctions, rules, and requirements on Santiago.

Differences between the two communities went deeper than mere political rivalry, however. In fact, they reflected a fundamental cleavage between two ways of life, two different cultures that, given the political situation, could only lead to antagonisms. The workers of Santiago felt themselves separate and distinct from their neighbors in Ixtlán and vice versa. This sense of separation reached the point of endogamy. People from Santiago tended to marry each other and developed very few family connections with agrarian workers in neighboring towns. Of the 1,000 to 1,500 workers employed in the factory, only a small number, between 50 and 100, lived in the neighboring town of Ixtlán, which was just across the river, and they typically occupied the least desirable jobs. These former campesinos had few opportunities for advancement within either the factory of the union.

Given its industrial history, it is not surprising that Santiago's migration patterns are quite different from those in the two rural communities. From its earliest days, it was a center of in-migration rather than out-migration. Indeed, the town was originally founded with skilled workers who came as migrants from all over Mexico to work in the new textile mill. Since the company was quite paternalistic—providing work, housing, and basic services to its employees—the bulk of the population settled and remained in Santiago for generations. This permanence depended on the capacity of the factory to provide work, and despite its many faults, the company was able to maintain a large, constant work force for many years.

Few migrants left Santiago for destinations either in or out of the country before 1940, therefore. Figure 4.5 shows the number of first-time migrants leaving Santiago by period from 1910 to 1982. During the 1910–1919 decade, the ethnosurvey shows only one person migrating to the United States, and during the 1920s this number rose to four. In the next decade three more people became U.S. migrants, for a total of eight people by 1940. Figure 4.6, which presents the legal status of U.S. migrants, shows that half of these early pioneers went north as legal U.S. immigrants, a quarter as contract workers, and another quarter without documents. The first internal migrant did not leave Santiago until the late 1920s, followed by another three in the 1930s.

Tables 4.11 through 4.13 show characteristics of migrants and nonmigrants in three periods. The eight U.S. migrants leaving before 1940 were all young males (table 4.11) who were, tellingly, drawn from among agricultural laborers rather than factory workers (table 4.12). Those who left were illiterate or marginally schooled, like most people in the sample who were alive at that time (table 4.13). Among the five Mexican migrants there was one woman, but missing data and the small number of cases hampered any further characterization of the first few internal migrants from Santiago.

In general, therefore, the quantitative data suggest that until 1940, the factory acted as a strong magnet holding workers fast to life in Santiago. The few who did leave were primarily farmworkers who had few prospects for factory jobs. This state of affairs depended entirely on the factory's ability to provide employment to workers and their families.

Modernization in a Union Town

The Great Depression of the early 1930s hit the factory hard, leading to widespread unemployment among factory workers. Since the situation was much the same elsewhere in Mexico and the United States, how-

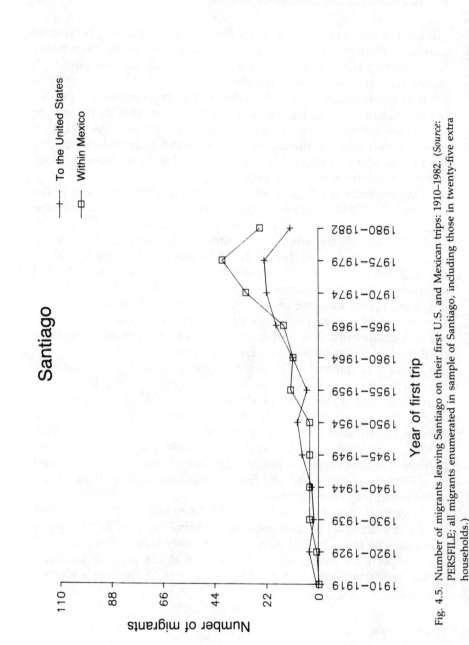

Fig. 4.5. Number of migrants leaving Santiago on their first U.S. and Mexican trips: 1910–1982. (*Source:* PERSFILE; all migrants enumerated in sample of Santiago, including those in twenty-five extra households.)

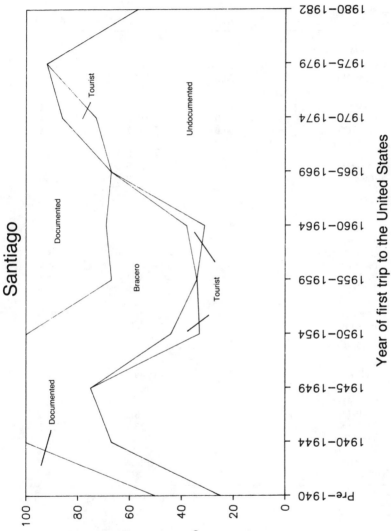

Fig. 4.6. Legal composition of migrant cohorts leaving Santiago on their first U.S. trips: 1910–1982: (*Source:* PERSFILE; all migrants enumerated in sample of Santiago, including those in twenty-five extra households.)

TABLE 4.11
DEMOGRAPHIC CHARACTERISTICS OF MIGRANTS TO THE UNITED STATES, MIGRANTS
WITHIN MEXICO, AND NONMIGRANTS IN THREE PERIODS: SANTIAGO, JALISCO

Migrant status, sex, and age	Period		
	1910–1939	1940–1964	1965–1982
Migrants to United States			
Sex			
Male (%)	100.0	94.9	76.1
Age			
Under 15 (%)	25.0	7.7	7.0
15–19 (%)	25.0	12.8	32.4
20–34 (%)	50.0	66.7	47.9
35–54 (%)	0.0	12.8	8.5
55+ (%)	0.0	0.0	4.2
Average	17.6	24.9	24.5
Number	8	39	71
Migrants within Mexico			
Sex			
Male (%)	80.0	94.3	69.9
Age			
Under 15 (%)	80.0	14.3	8.7
15–19 (%)	20.0	40.0	37.9
20–34 (%)	0.0	31.4	45.6
35–54 (%)	0.0	14.3	7.8
55+ (%)	0.0	0.0	0.0
Average	10.0	21.5	21.4
Number	5	35	103
Nonmigrants			
Sex			
Male (%)	53.1	49.6	46.1
Age			
Under 15 (%)	86.5	71.2	54.8
15–19 (%)	6.7	8.8	11.7
20–34 (%)	5.7	13.9	20.5
35–54 (%)	1.1	5.5	10.2
55+ (%)	0.0	0.6	2.8
Average	6.4	11.8	18.3
Number	525	2,812	4,403

Source: PERSFILE; all persons enumerated in sample of Santiago, including those in twenty-five extra households.

ever, there was little out-migration (see fig. 4.5). After 1935, the economic situation began to improve, but it was World War II that made Santiago a true boomtown. All over Mexico, factories capitalized on the war to unleash a period of industrial prosperity. Santiago's textile factory joined in this dynamic spurt of development. For the first time, goods

TABLE 4.12
MEXICAN OCCUPATION OF MIGRANTS TO THE UNITED STATES, MIGRANTS WITHIN
MEXICO, AND NONMIGRANTS IN THREE PERIODS: SANTIAGO, JALISCO

Migrant status and occupation	1910–1939		1940–1964		1965–1982	
	Occupation in period	Occupation in 1982	Occupation in period	Occupation in 1982	Occupation in period	Occupation in 1982
Migrants to United States						
Professional-technical (%)	0.0	0.0	0.0	0.0	5.4	1.9
Clerical-sales (%)	0.0	0.0	3.0	12.9	18.9	17.3
Skilled manual (%)	14.3	0.0	3.0	38.7	21.6	55.8
Services (%)	0.0	0.0	3.0	9.7	2.7	13.5
Unskilled manual (%)	28.6	0.0	48.5	19.4	32.4	7.7
Farmworker (%)	57.1	100.0	42.4	19.4	18.9	3.9
Number	7	2	33	31	37	52
Migrants within Mexico						
Professional-technical (%)	0.0	—	4.4	6.9	18.2	21.3
Clerical-sales (%)	50.0	—	4.4	17.2	18.2	12.5
Skilled manual (%)	0.0	—	26.1	17.2	22.7	12.5
Services (%)	0.0	—	0.0	37.9	9.1	43.8
Unskilled manual (%)	0.0	—	39.1	17.2	22.7	1.3
Farmer (%)	50.0	—	26.9	3.5	9.1	8.8
Number	2	—	23	29	22	80
Nonmigrants						
Professional-technical (%)	1.5	0.0	3.1	8.0	5.4	12.0
Clerical-sales (%)	5.9	7.1	8.6	21.2	10.4	15.5
Skilled manual (%)	1.5	7.1	10.9	30.1	25.3	46.1
Services (%)	1.5	7.1	4.7	5.1	3.4	3.6
Unskilled manual (%)	42.9	28.6	49.2	30.8	46.7	19.9
Farmworker (%)	46.8	50.0	23.4	4.8	8.8	3.0
Number	342[a]	14	1,225[a]	312	1,361[a]	906

Sources: Occupation in period from LIFEFILE; occupation in 1982 from PERSFILE; all persons enumerated in sample of Santiago, including those in twenty-five extra households.

[a] Number refers to person-years observed rather than number of people.

were produced on a large scale for export abroad. To meet production requirements, workers had to work two, and then three, shifts. During 1940 to 1945 the factory never lacked for work. The old machinery was in constant use, and all production was easily sold as soon as it was made.

Unfortunately, the economic bonanza did not coincide with political tranquillity. The union experienced another series of internal struggles between antagonistic groups vying for political control. Moreover, the traditional conflict with Ixtlán escalated to violence, at a considerable cost in lives. Finally, in 1944 Santiago's political problems were solved when it achieved independence from its neighbor. After many negotia-

TABLE 4.13
YEARS OF EDUCATION AMONG MIGRANTS TO THE UNITED STATES, MIGRANTS WITHIN
MEXICO, AND NONMIGRANTS AGED 15 AND OVER IN THREE PERIODS: SANTIAGO, JALISCO

Migrant status and education	Period		
	1910–1939	1940–1964	1965–1982
Migrants to United States			
None (%)	50.0	27.8	1.5
1–3 (%)	50.0	19.4	15.2
4–5 (%)	0.0	8.3	13.6
6 (%)	0.0	41.7	43.9
7–9 (%)	0.0	2.8	16.7
10–11 (%)	0.0	0.0	1.5
12 (%)	0.0	0.0	4.6
13+ (%)	0.0	0.0	3.0
Average	0.8	3.6	6.3
Number	6	36	66
Migrants within Mexico			
None (%)	0.0	13.3	3.2
1–3 (%)	100.0	36.7	6.5
4–5 (%)	0.0	16.7	4.3
6 (%)	0.0	16.7	40.9
7–9 (%)	0.0	10.0	16.1
10–11 (%)	0.0	0.0	5.4
12 (%)	0.0	3.3	18.3
13+ (%)	0.0	3.3	5.4
Average	2.0	4.4	7.8
Number	1	30	93
Nonmigrants			
None (%)	43.7	20.7	8.5
1–3 (%)	35.2	30.5	17.5
4–5 (%)	11.3	16.4	11.9
6 (%)	7.0	24.6	36.8
7–9 (%)	0.0	3.6	14.9
10–11 (%)	0.0	0.6	3.4
12 (%)	2.8	3.1	4.8
13+ (%)	0.0	0.5	2.2
Average	1.9	3.7	5.7
Number	71	810	2,133

Source: PERSFILE; all persons enumerated in sample of Santiago, including those in twenty-five extra households.

tions and compromises and much ado before the state government, the union at last succeeded in achieving the creation of the Municipio de Santiago. After this date, whichever political group controlled the union also controlled the town and its rancherías; thus the union ceased to be a pressure group. As part of the ruling establishment, it had the economic, legal, and political resources to achieve its goals.

The newly autonomous officials decided the time had come to give the town a new appearance, and the municipio set out to attack several pressing problems: a location for the municipal offices, the suppression of cantinas and brothels that had proliferated with the collusion of prior municipal authorities from Ixtlán, the construction of a cemetery to avoid dependence on the neighboring town, and the building of schools, highways, and water and sewage systems.

Union officials also supported the creation and dedication of several sporting clubs. The workers of Santiago had learned to play soccer from British technicians who had earlier worked in the factory, and they achieved some distinction at it. They were good enough to participate in the soccer draft run by professional leagues at the state level, and many workers, sponsored by the union, were able to get onto professional teams. Santiago's soccer teams were later to play an important role in the social organization of U.S. migration.

The political and sporting conquests of the mid-1940s were not accompanied by continued economic progress, however. The wartime boom had been temporary, and the realization of peace meant an end to the second and third shifts, production for foreign markets, and record profits for the company. Reality returned with all its weight to reveal the true face of the textile industry in Mexico: obsolete machines, antiquated production systems, and production costs incapable of competing on world markets. It had been only a short step from boom to bust, but there was little hope for a return to the bonanza. The factory would have to change, modernize, and—above all—reduce its labor costs and, ultimately, the number of workers.

Ten years passed before the changes were put into effect. There were serious difficulties in obtaining loans to finance the modernization, and it took time to negotiate an agreement with the union about the policy for reducing the work force. The industrialists proposed a personnel cut of 75 percent, consistent with the new technological regimen. One person could manage four of the old spindle machines simultaneously, while the same worker could now operate twelve of the new ones. The union, of course, wanted a smaller cut. In the end, the work force of 1,400 workers was cut by about 70 percent, leaving only 400 employees with permanent jobs.

In implementing these reductions, it was a great advantage for the company to have a strong and authoritative union with which to deal. The task of cutting the work force fell to union bosses, who were able to save the jobs of their friends and relatives. Nevertheless, when the announcement of the personnel reductions was made in 1954, it set off a chain of events outside the union's control, leading to the beginnings of widespread migration to the United States. Nearly 700 willing laborers were left without work, and there simply were no local alternatives for their employment.

In addition, there were few possibilities for working in textile factories in other parts of the country, because all of Mexico was in the same economic situation, facing a necessary but costly process of modernization. Given this bleak outlook, many older workers decided to retire voluntarily and receive their pensions. Some used the firings as an occasion for leaving town and seeing a bit of the world, and others who had not been fired sold their jobs and left in search of adventure. Most displaced workers, especially the young, had no choice but to migrate elsewhere in search of work. For these migrants, the modernization of the textile factory was the start of a long migratory tradition, one that linked Santiago to various locations in Mexico and the United States.

The choice of destination depended on a variety of factors. One was the economic situation of western Mexico in the late 1950s and early 1960s. Although textile jobs were scarce everywhere, this was a relatively good period for employment in other industries, especially in Guadalajara, which was beginning to develop as an important industrial center. Although it was by no means easy to leave town to look for work, people from Santiago had a distinct advantage over other migrants as they had long been accustomed to factory work and knew how to run machines. For some, the firings simply meant a change of jobs, albeit one that also implied a change of residence within Mexico.

Many other migrants left to look for work in el Norte, however. The reasons why they chose the United States are partly personal and idiosyncratic, but they also reflect a systematic, well-defined social phenomenon prevailing at the time. Since the late Porfirian era, the potential labor market for workers from western Mexico had included, within its gamut of possibilities, employment in the United States, a fact that was valid in urban as well as rural areas. By the late 1950s, the tradition of U.S. migration in western Mexico was over fifty years old; and even though few of Santiago's factory workers went north before this time, they could nonetheless make use of an extensive social infrastructure formed by migrants from neighboring towns and villages.

Over the course of five decades, many of the migratory processes had become institutionalized. "Coyotes," or paid guides who smuggled those without documents across the U.S. border, had established themselves and were widely available to any potential migrant. United States migrant communities had developed in many American cities, providing safe houses, legal help, a ready-made Spanish-speaking community, a familiar environment, and a host of job contacts. Moreover, Santiago was never completely divorced from the migration process. Within the municipio, and in the neighboring town of Ixtlán, many migrants of campesino origin had been migrating to the United States for some time. Consequently, many factory workers sought work in specific U.S. cities and factories because they had some relative there, because some friend or neighbor had gone there before, or because news of hirings had arrived from this or that company. The ease of U.S. migration was also facilitated by the Bracero program, which had been recruiting workers for the United States since 1942 and in the late 1950s was expanding rapidly.

Santiago's tradition of migration really began in the period leading up to and following the textile factory's modernization in 1954. The period from 1945 to 1960 witnessed the first sizable wave of out-migration of workers from Santiago (see fig. 4.5). Many of these people worked in the Bracero program, but about a third could not or did not obtain bracero permits and became undocumented migrants. Others simply acquired tourist visas and headed north, and some waited to arrange their legal papers and left to work in the United States with green cards (fig. 4.6).

Before the era of modernization, migrants from Santiago were mostly campesino men going north for jobs as farmworkers. After 1940 the relative number of farmworkers fell as new migrants were increasingly made up of displaced factory workers (table 4.12). Most of these workers had been laid off in the prime of their working lives (table 4.11), and a sizable number had completed primary school (table 4.13). In other words, these were not impoverished, illiterate peons fleeing the harshness of the countryside but skilled workingmen caught in the grip of industrial transformation. The 1940–1954 period also witnessed the beginnings of female migration to the United States (table 4.11), as some displaced workers settled in U.S. cities with their wives. Parallel trends characterized the out-migration of people to Mexican urban areas.

Starting a new migratory process in the 1950s was not always easy for Santiago's factory workers, however. The Korean War had just ended and, competing with returning servicemen, it was often difficult for Mexicans to find jobs in the United States. Migrants from Santiago preferred urban industrial work to farm labor, which made their situations more difficult, since this type of work could more easily be filled by veterans. It was partly in response to political pressure from veterans and labor unions that Operation Wetback was launched in 1954, which expelled more than a million Mexicans from the United States (Morales 1981).

During the late 1940s and 1950s, out-migration from Santiago reached a scale that supported its institutionalization. The process of emigration for work in the United States became commonplace and, ultimately, routine. Personal and kinship networks were established between the town and settled communities in U.S. urban areas, especially Los Angeles. For many families, U.S. migration became another economic strategy they could employ to cope with the problems life had to offer.

Although the laying off of over 1,000 workers implied the exit of many families, it did not diminish the importance of the factory in the municipio. Until the late 1960s it continued to be the only industry in the municipio. The industrial destiny of Santiago didn't end with its textile mill, however. Santiago's strategic location a mere thirty kilometers from Guadalajara, together with its ready access to water, open land, highways, and rail lines, made the municipio a location with considerable potential for development.

Economic Expansion

In the early 1970s an industrial decentralization plan formulated to relieve congestion in Guadalajara created an "industrial corridor" stretching south of the city some ninety kilometers, an area that enveloped the municipio of Santiago (Arias 1983: 40). Within a few years, new and modern factories began to spring up, producing a wide variety of products, such as chemicals, rubber, tools, sweets, and containers. In the late 1970s an "industrial park" was conceived and promoted as an alternative to the corridor concept, and in 1980 it was established in the municipio of Santiago. Many factories are currently under construction, and in recent years, Santiago has led all other municipios of Jalisco in industrial growth, including Guadalajara itself (Soto 1982).

This recent boom in factory employment has brought many new industrial jobs and has generated a host of ancillary positions to provide goods and services to the factory workers. This industrial development has been the principal agent of change in Santiago, and has reinforced the working-class complexion of the community. Workers who were formerly unable to find work in the textile factory have increasingly been able to find jobs in other factories.

Table 4.14 shows the population size and industrial composition of the labor force in Santiago, as reported in the 1950, 1960, and 1970 Censuses. These figures show the stagnation of population growth and the decline in manufacturing that beset the municipio following mod-

TABLE 4.14
ECONOMICALLY ACTIVE POPULATION CLASSIFIED BY INDUSTRY OF EMPLOYMENT
IN THREE CENSUS YEARS: MUNICIPIO OF SANTIAGO

Industry	Year		
	1950	1960	1970
Economically active population			
In agriculture (%)	37.5	49.2	26.0
In manufacturing (%)	44.7	33.1	44.1
In other industry (%)	17.7	17.7	29.9
Total population	8,290	9,014	12,367

Source: Mexican Censuses of 1950, 1960, and 1970.

ernization of the textile factory in 1954, trends that were reversed during the 1960s, when the population increased by a third and the proportion of workers in manufacturing returned to its 1950 level. The relatively large shares in agriculture, compared to the ethnosurvey data in chapter 3, occur because the census covers the entire municipio, which contains several agrarian rancherías.

While out-migration from Santiago has continued to grow steadily since 1965 (see fig. 4.5), the municipio's industrial development has simultaneously made it a center for in-migration. Indeed, many industrial workers from Guadalajara have found jobs in one of the new factories and moved into Santiago to avoid a daily commute. According to the ethnosurvey data, only 64 percent of the town's residents were actually born there; 16 percent are from Guadalajara, 4 percent from Ixtlán, 9 percent from other locations in Jalisco, and 4 percent from other western states, with another 3 percent from states elsewhere in Mexico.

The municipio of Santiago is today a vibrant community of more than 12,000 people. The old walled compound—containing the original plaza, a few buildings, and the workers' quarters—is now only one of several neighborhoods, and the town has spread to take up five times its original area. The recently renovated main plaza contains municipal offices, built in Mexican colonial style; a large church with an impressive nave, tall stone towers, and a large atrium; parochial offices; a bank branch; and various commercial buildings. Unions have their own offices, and the textile workers union also has facilities for social events. The town contains various soccer clubs, and the most important have extensive recreational facilities, including large halls for holding parties and celebrations.

With industrial growth has come material progress, and the town now boasts all the amenities of modern urban life. Streets are paved and publicly illuminated. Houses are served with electricity, telephones, running water, sewage lines, and trash collection. Several transportation lines provide service to Guadalajara, about thirty minutes away, every half hour. Santiago has several movie theaters with daily shows; a variety of restaurants and bars, some of which accept credit cards; a supermarket; pharmacies; newsstands; and numerous commercial and service establishments. A new public market with spacious and modern facilities has been constructed, along with a new plaza surrounded by an arcade that houses many merchants. Because of the concentration of workers, the federal Social Security Administration opened a clinic in town, and several schools provide primary and secondary education.

In spite of the growth in prosperity and employment since 1965, however, out-migration has not stopped. Rather, both internal and international migration grew through the late 1970s and remain important options in the array of economic strategies open to people from Santiago (see fig. 4.6). With the advent of increasingly restrictive immigration policies in the United States and the end of the Bracero program in 1964, however, the vast majority of migrants since 1965 have been undocumented (see fig. 4.6). The relative number of women and teenagers among U.S. migrants also increased after 1965, suggesting the growing prevalence of family migration (table 4.11). In the most recent period, nearly a quarter of all U.S. migrants were female, and 39 percent were under the age of fifteen.

During the most recent period, migrants' socioeconomic origins have also broadened considerably. Migrants in the earliest period were predominantly campesinos, whereas migrants during the period of modernization were manual workers, and since 1965 they have been drawn from all segments of the occupational hierarchy. The occupational data in table 4.12 indicate that skilled and unskilled manual workers, as before, constitute a majority of U.S. migrants, but nearly a fifth of all migrants are sales and clerical workers, and significant shares are also drawn from the ranks of professional and service workers. These recent trends are consonant with the educational data in table 4.13, which indicate that migrants are drawn selectively from among the more educated classes, a trend especially true for internal migrants.

In short, while economic conditions within Santiago were generally quite favorable and were in fact improving through the 1970s, out-migration to the United States and elsewhere continued. Indeed, U.S. migration came to incorporate ever broader segments of society. At present, international migration for wage labor is a common feature of community life.

GUADALAJARA: A DIFFERENT HISTORICAL ROLE

The Postwar Boom

Guadalajara is the socioeconomic capital of western Mexico and the state capital of Jalisco. It is located in the geographic center of the western region and has traditionally been its most important commercial, industrial, and administrative center. The city's political importance dates back to colonial times, when it was given administrative authority over all of western Mexico. Its economic independence was finally achieved at the end of the colonial era with the founding of the *Consulado de Guadalajara* (Consulate of Guadalajara), an institution that grouped local merchants together to resist the financial and commercial dominance of Mexico City (Ramírez Flores 1970).

Following the attainment of Mexican independence in 1821, Guadalajara joined in the development effort propagated by successive republican governments. Factories were established for the manufacture of textiles, paper, soap, and other products. By the end of the nineteenth century, a regional bourgeoisie linked to diverse activities—industry, commerce, agriculture, mining, banking, and construction—had succeeded in consolidating its position within the country and was in a position to profit handsomely from the economic boom of the Porfirian years.

For Guadalajara, the twentieth century really began in 1910, with the outbreak of the Mexican Revolution. Jalisco was enveloped by the rising tide of revolutionary violence and was the scene of several bloody battles. Attack followed counterattack as the city was successively taken and retaken by different factions. The coming of peace after a decade of armed conflict did little to quell the social upheaval. The postrevolutionary years were a time of great political agitation as the new parties attempted to reconstruct the country and consolidate power. Political tranquillity was finally established as the world economy entered the depression years of the 1930s.

Although it was an important regional center, Guadalajara remained a relatively small city until World War II, with an economy based primarily on commerce, finance, and agriculture rather than industry. At the beginning of the 1940s, however, Guadalajara's population began to expand rapidly, initiating a forty-year period of urban growth and development. Beginning with a population of 229,000 in 1940, Guadalajara grew at an annual rate of 5 percent throughout the 1940s, 7 percent during the 1950s, 5 percent in the 1960s, and 8 percent in the 1970s (Walton 1978). By 1980, the urban area of Guadalajara was a major metropolis of nearly 2.8 million people (United Nations 1980). As the city's population grew, so did its physical size, from 1,995 hectares in 1940, to a sprawling 11,000 hectares 30 years later (Vázquez 1985).

This demographic expansion rested on the city's economic development. Following World War II, Guadalajara, like the rest of Mexico, embarked on an ambitious plan of modernization and industrialization. In the ensuing decades, old factories were renovated and many new firms were attracted to the city. The government of Jalisco offered a very attractive promotional package that waived taxes for companies relocating new industrial plants into the Guadalajara area and for firms that agreed to modernize existing factories (Arias 1983). In the three decades from 1940 to 1970, hundreds of companies took advantage of these offers. The extent of the industrial expansion is reflected in Jalisco's rapid industrial growth during the 1950s and 1960s. During the former decade, crude industrial production grew by an annual rate of 7.7 percent and during the latter decade, by 6.3 percent.

Over the course of 30 years, this development program not only expanded the city's industrial plant but also diversified it. Petrochemical industries flourished in the city and its environs, as new plants for making chemicals, rubber, plastics, and other synthetics were built. Large electronics companies also established many new factories. Numerous multinational firms, with names such as Kodak, IBM, Celanese, Purina, and Union Carbide, opened offices and factories in the city. Mexican companies also invested in Guadalajara, above all the large conglomerates from Mexico City and Monterrey. Local entrepreneurs financed a project for construction of an independent iron and steelwork in the city.

Modern Industrial Organization

In spite of this industrial diversification and intensification, Guadalajara has traditionally specialized in producing basic consumer goods on a small scale, and it continues to do so. It is especially well known as a center for the production of nondurable consumer goods such as clothing, shoes, and food. Within the national division of labor, Guadalajara has carved out an important niche with respect to Mexico City and Monterrey, the other large industrial centers. By providing basic items of subsistence to the masses cheaply and efficiently, it contributes importantly to Mexico's reproduction of labor (Arias 1980).

This role is made possible by the proliferation of thousands of small *talleres* (workshops, sweatshops, small factories), which continue to compose a large and very important part of Guadalajara's industrial configuration. These talleres produce a great quantity of shoes, clothing, and foods. They are run by small, independent entrepreneurs and many are "clandestine," operating outside formal government regulation. For this reason, it is difficult to measure the magnitude of this shadow economic sector, but various studies suggest that it is large and of great economic importance (Arias 1980; Lailson 1980; Alba 1985). In a recent survey of 1,153 private business owners in the city, for example, 869, or 75 percent, were in the smallest category (State of Jalisco 1982).

Together, these small firms manufacture literally thousands of pairs of shoes each day, especially for women, along with many tons of clothes, hundreds of styles of furniture, a wide array of leather goods, and an immense variety of foods and sweets. At present there are no reliable figures on the number and productive capacity of these firms. Some experts guess that for every registered factory there are eight or ten clandestine talleres, and in the case of shoe factories, there are said to be more than 2000 small underground workshops (Arias 1980).

These small companies are organized in a variety of different ways. Some talleres use only family labor, others only paid workers, while others employ a combination of the two. Some carry out the entire productive process from start to finish, while others farm out work to individual *maquiladores* (labor-intensive factories) or private homes, where much work is done by wives, mothers, and sisters. No matter how organized, these small factories have a set of productive relations expressed in a series of implicit "rules of the game" that are well understood by workers and owners.

In general, there is little social distance between workers and owners. Most taller owners were at one time workers themselves and may become so again, especially in times of economic stress. The workers are usually relatives, neighbors, friends, or acquaintances, and these relationships help to mitigate labor tensions and forge solidarity in times of economic difficulty, giving the taller great flexibility in dealing with changing economic conditions.

The workers know the situation of the talleres and accept their limitations and possibilities. They know that the level of production and, hence, their pay must be reduced at times; they also know that someday there will be enough work for extra hours and more pay, so they don't complain. Taller owners depend on a core of good and loyal workers and try to keep them on even in bad times. This set of implicit understandings and overlaying social relations labor gives the taller owner an unusual ability to expand or reduce the work force according to economic conditions.

These small factories and workshops are concentrated within Guadalajara's many poor, working-class neighborhoods. They are clandestine in the sense that they are not subject to regulation (and taxation) by the Social Security Administration, the Secretaries of Treasury and Health, and other state and local authorities, and they do not face wage and labor demands from unions. Also, the small industrial sector does not face the problem of external debt. Few firms have ever required formal credit. In many cases, the subject of a bank loan has never been considered. Rather, small entrepreneurs depend on their own resources and perhaps those of family and friends.

The talleres generally rely on old machinery, which has a great capacity for adaptation and modification, giving the shadow sector a certain technological independence. New tools can easily be rigged from available parts and machines, to suit whatever task, and machinery does not have to be imported from abroad. This dependence on old, often discarded machinery has spawned a large number of mechanical talleres that specialize in ad hoc repairs and "rough-and-ready" engineering. These shops make all manner of repairs and design and construct the many different apparatuses, tools, and machines demanded by the small industrial sector.

The talleres also try to maintain flexibility in their lines of supply and distribution. They do not import costly or sophisticated foreign inputs and are not dependent on particular raw materials. Rather, they readily adapt to changes in the national market of raw materials, modifying production to meet conditions of surplus, scarcity, or the appearance of new materials. In marketing their products, the talleres usually try to maintain a stable relation with some merchant or large distributor; however, experience has taught them to avoid the large chains and big companies. Their strategy is to keep informed of markets and cultivate several different avenues for merchandising, even though it may mean fewer sales at a given point in time.

This adaptability and flexibility at all levels—in labor relations, work sites, merchandising, materials, and machinery—is inherent to small-scale production. It is a proven strategy for survival and gives the working classes of Guadalajara a tremendous advantage in facing the uncertainties of economic life. Indeed, the working class of Guadalajara has fared far better during the recent economic crisis than have workers in other Mexican cities (Arias and Durand 1985). The city's informal economic sector also comprises an important node in a network of migrant relations that connects western Mexico to the United States, and U.S. migration plays an important part in the maintenance and development of many talleres.

The Role of U.S. Migration

Guadalajara is different from most U.S. migrant sending communities because in addition to sending migrants abroad, it also attracts rural and urban migrants from all parts of the country. According to recent estimates by the United Nations (1980: 24), a third of Mexico's recent urban growth comes from in-migration, and Guadalajara is no exception. Many of the city's inhabitants are migrants from rural towns and villages, principally in western Mexico, who have come to the city in hopes of sharing its economic progress. According to ethnosurvey data from the barrio of San Marcos, 44 percent of the sample was born outside the city—39 percent in the states of western Mexico. Among household heads, the figure is even higher—78 percent were born outside the city. If we go back another generation, the rural origin of *tapatíos*, as people from Guadalajara are called, becomes even more overwhelming. Only 5 percent of the household heads in the sample had fathers who were born in Guadalajara (55 percent had fathers born in Jalisco, and 24 percent had fathers from another western state).

These facts suggest the important rural heritage of most residents of San Marcos, a fact that is crucial in understanding its patterns and processes of international migration. For although these people may now be urban residents, they maintain strong linkages with the towns and villages from which they or their parents came. Indeed, they are intimately linked to these communities by ties of kinship and friendship and often take an active role in village affairs. The urbanites are thus deeply embedded in a social web emanating from a myriad of towns and villages throughout western Mexico, and these towns and villages form the basis for a strong communal life.

The tradition of U.S. migration originated in the rural environment; however, with the urbanization of Mexico, it, in turn, became urban. As migrants left towns and villages to take up life in Guadalajara, they brought with them their histories of migration to the United States. Rather than being the final point of destination in a rural-to-urban move, migration to Guadalajara was simply one more stage in a larger migratory process. Of those people with U.S. migrant experience enumerated in the ethnosurvey of San Marcos, 76 percent were born outside Guadalajara.

Moreover, Guadalajara has become a principal point of return from the United States. Rural migrants return with savings earned abroad to invest them in the more favorable economic environment of Guadalajara, with its dynamic sector of small businesses. This large shadow sector of small-scale enterprises provides opportunities for profit with very little investment, and U.S. migration provides funds for poor people whose access to capital would otherwise be quite limited. A few years of work in el Norte can provide enough money to found a small taller for making clothes or shoes, a neighborhood grocery store, or a small repair shop. A recent survey of 1,153 firm owners in Guadalajara revealed that 15 percent had prior experience as U.S. migrants (State of Jalisco 1982). When the figures were broken down by size of firm, 17 percent of those in the smallest category had worked in the United States, compared to 7 percent in the largest. In the barrio of San Marcos, 27 percent of family-operated businesses were owned by U.S. migrants and 16 percent were established directly with U.S. earnings.

The city and its inhabitants, especially the working class, are thus well integrated into the international migratory system. In Guadalajara, there are signs of this fact everywhere, particularly in working-class neighborhoods. On street corners one finds *marketas* rather than *mercados* or *tiendas*, with proper Spanish words for "market" or "store" replaced with Hispanified versions of an English word. On the streets one sees many vehicles with U.S. license plates from important destination states—California, Texas, and Illinois—especially in the winter months. Telephones are much in demand to make and receive calls from family members abroad, and merchants are only too willing to exchange dollars or accept U.S. money orders. Banks in these neighborhoods exist almost exclusively to exchange and invest money sent home by U.S. migrants.

Guadalajara is thus woven into a web of social ties that connects western Mexico with towns and cities in the United States. Workers in Guadalajara participate in a single, large binational economy and labor market. In spite of the city's current importance in this international migratory circuit, it is not the principal hub of the network. Rather, the migrant networks predate Guadalajara's incorporation into them. Migratory processes historically developed in the towns and villages, and networks that appear to begin in urban areas such as Guadalajara or Tijuana, in fact usually originate in a myriad of smaller communities in western Mexico. The cities are a recent insertion into these networks, providing yet another node in the social infrastructure supporting U.S. migration.

When migrants go to the United States, therefore, they do not go as tapatíos, but as *paisanos* from their communities of origin. There are no daughter communities of out-migrant tapatíos in the United States. Rather, as migrants, they draw upon social networks based in rural areas. The rural origins of tapatíos are thus crucial to understanding the role of international migration in Guadalajara.

Admittedly, our ethnosurvey sample is only of one barrio, and not of the entire city, and if this barrio is not representative of the rural origins of most tapatíos, it might give a skewed picture of migration processes. Fortunately, we can compare the origins of respondents in our ethnosurvey to a representative sample of Guadalajara drawn from a National Household Survey (Arroyo 1985). As we noted, the vast majority of in-migrants to Guadalajara in our sample are from the states of western Mexico. Table 4.15 compares the state of birth of migrants from western Mexico as enumerated in the ethnosurvey of San Marcos and the National Household Survey. Obviously, the two distributions, although not exactly the same, are remarkably alike. In each case, Jalisco, Zacatecas, and Michoacán are the three largest migrant-sending states, responsible for 85 percent to 90 percent of all in-migrants to Guadalajara. Although the relative sizes of these three contributors are somewhat different in the two samples, the ordering is the same. The San Marcos sample thus seems to provide a fair representation of Guadalajara's population, at least with respect to its rural origins.

Since most adult residents of San Marcos were not born in Guadalajara, and because the barrio does not comprise a discrete spatial entity, it makes little sense to study nonmigrants and internal migrants by time period. Rather, tables 4.16 through 4.18 and figures 4.7 and 4.8 simply present information on U.S. migrants by the date of their first trip. Among current residents of San Marcos, none began to migrate abroad

TABLE 4.15
STATE OF BIRTH OF MIGRANTS FROM WESTERN MEXICO TO GUADALAJARA AS
SHOWN IN THE NATIONAL HOUSEHOLD SURVEY AND THE ETHNOSURVEY

State of birth	National Household Survey	Ethnosurvey
Jalisco (%)	58.6	47.2
Zacatecas (%)	15.8	25.6
Michoacán (%)	11.2	15.8
Nayarit (%)	5.6	2.3
Colima (%)	3.6	4.4
Guanajuato (%)	3.2	2.3
Aguascalientes (%)	2.0	2.3
Total migrants (%)	271,180	386

Sources: National Household Survey from Arroyo (1985) and ethnosurvey from PERSFILE; household members enumerated in sample of San Marcos.

TABLE 4.16
DEMOGRAPHIC CHARACTERISTICS OF MIGRANTS TO THE UNITED STATES IN
TWO PERIODS: SAN MARCOS, GUADALAJARA, JALISCO

Sex and age	Period	
	1940–1964	1965–1982
Sex		
Percent male (%)	95.5	80.0
Age		
Under 15 (%)	13.6	0.0
15–19 (%)	27.3	27.1
20–34 (%)	40.9	54.3
35–54 (%)	18.2	17.1
55+ (%)	0.0	1.4
Average	22.5	26.1
Number	22	70

Source: PERSFILE; all migrants enumerated in sample of San Marcos.

TABLE 4.17
MEXICAN OCCUPATION OF MIGRANTS TO THE UNITED STATES IN TWO PERIODS:
SAN MARCOS, GUADALAJARA, JALISCO

Occupation	1940–1964		1965–1982	
	Occupation in Period	Occupation in Period	Occupation in 1982	Occupation in 1982
Professional-technical (%)	0.0	0.0	0.0	0.0
Clerical-sales (%)	0.0	42.9	33.3	25.9
Services (%)	0.0	28.6	0.0	31.5
Skilled manual (%)	7.1	21.4	26.7	24.1
Unskilled manual (%)	14.3	0.0	40.0	3.7
Farmworker (%)	78.6	7.1	0.0	14.8
Number	14	14	15	54

Sources: Occupation in period from LIFEFILE; occupation in 1982 from PERSFILE; all migrants enumerated in sample of San Marcos.

before 1940. Paralleling patterns from the rural communities, there was a modest surge in out-migration during the 1940s and 1950s that peaked in 1950–1954 and disappeared in the early 1960s (fig. 4.7). Since 1965, U.S. migration has increased steadily.

Trends in the legal status of migrants are somewhat erratic because of the small numbers involved and also because the migrants belong to

TABLE 4.18
YEARS OF EDUCATION AMONG MIGRANTS TO THE UNITED STATES
IN TWO PERIODS: SAN MARCOS, GUADALAJARA, JALISCO

	Period	
Education	1940–1964	1965–1982
None (%)	26.3	4.3
1–3 (%)	42.1	24.3
4–5 (%)	15.8	11.4
6 (%)	15.8	32.9
7–9 (%)	0.0	12.9
10–11 (%)	0.0	5.7
12 (%)	0.0	5.7
13+ (%)	0.0	2.9
Average	2.6	5.9
Number	19	70

Source: PERSFILE; all migrants enumerated in sample of San Marcos.

a variety of different networks, each with its own tradition of documentation (see fig. 4.8). In the early 1940s most migrants were braceros, but during the late 1940s and early 1950s the number of undocumented migrants increased rapidly. Following Operation Wetback in 1954, the proportion of documented migrants increased as many people took out papers under the liberal immigration laws prevailing at the time. Beginning in the 1960s, however, undocumented migration became the predominant means of entering the United States, except for a brief period during the early 1970s when many entered as tourists. In the most recent period, nearly 70 percent of U.S. migrants possessed no documents.

Through 1964, 96 percent of migrants were male, but since that time more females have migrated. The average age has also risen, with migrants showing a more pronounced concentration within the central labor force years. Since 1965, some 54 percent of migrants have been between the ages of 20 and 35 (table 4.16). Table 4.17 illustrates the rural origins of most U.S. migrants now living in Guadalajara. Of those leaving before 1965, 79 percent worked in agriculture before going to the United States for the first time. Upon returning to Mexico and settling in Guadalajara, however, most of these people obtained clerical and sales jobs or positions as manual laborers. In the most recent period,

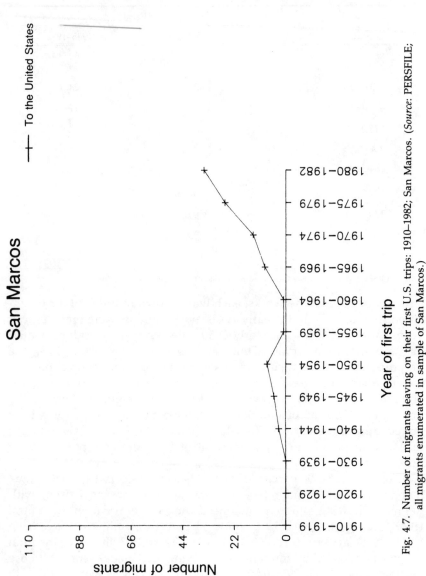

Fig. 4.7. Number of migrants leaving on their first U.S. trips: 1910–1982; San Marcos. (*Source*: PERSFILE; all migrants enumerated in sample of San Marcos.)

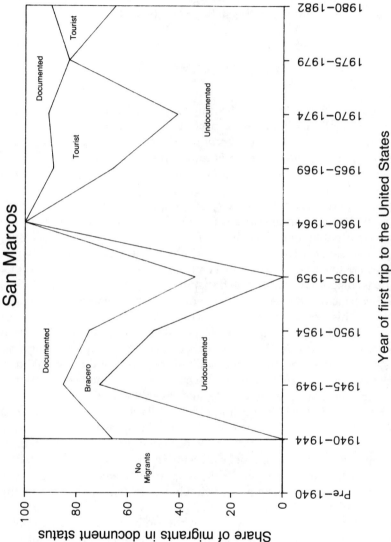

Fig. 4.8. Legal composition of migrant cohorts leaving on their first U.S. trips: 1910–1982; San Marcos. (*Source:* PERSFILE; all migrants enumerated in sample of San Marcos.)

however, no migrants worked in agriculture prior to departure, reflecting the movement of second-generation tapatíos into the U.S. migrant force, people who grew up in Guadalajara and held urban jobs before migrating. Most of these recent migrants are well educated, with a majority having completed the sixth grade (table 4.18).

SUMMARY: INTERNATIONAL MIGRATION IN COMPARATIVE PERSPECTIVE

This historical survey of four Mexican communities suggests that international migration originates in profound socioeconomic transformations that affect sending and receiving areas and that, once begun, it develops a strong internal momentum and expands in similar fashion across widely different socioeconomic settings, suggesting the operation of a common social process.

In the two rural communities, out-migration originated in the era before the Reparto Agrario and was rooted in the economic transformation of Mexico that took place during Porfirian modernization. Enclosure and mechanization concentrated land and production in a few hands and turned the vast majority of rural dwellers into landless laborers. Railroads displaced traditional transport workers, flooded the towns with cheap factory goods that rendered many crafts workers redundant, and made this uprooted population very mobile.

Across the border, the sparsely populated states of the American southwest were also in the throes of socioeconomic transformation resulting from development of the railroad industry. Suddenly linked to the burgeoning industrial states of the northeast, commercial agriculture and mining became quite profitable, and given the local scarcity of labor and the impossibility of importing it from Asia, U.S. employers turned to the mobile masses of Mexico. Mexican workers, including those from Altamira and Chamitlán, were heavily recruited for work in U.S. mines, in agriculture, and on railroads, especially in the years during and after World War I. Throughout the 1920s, migration between the two towns and the United States expanded, slowing only with the onset of the Great Depression in 1929.

During the 1930s, the Mexican Revolution bore fruit in the Reparto Agrario, which redistributed land to many households but did not provide the capital necessary to undertake production. Rather than farming their land, the new ejidatarios found themselves leasing it to the wealthy or going into debt to local moneylenders, a situation that was aggravated by a series of droughts and crop failures. World War II created another labor shortage in the United States, however, and in 1942 the Bracero program was created as a means of importing temporary workers from Mexico. This program provided access to capital that the ejidatarios needed to farm their lands, and they went north eagerly.

Although originally enacted as a temporary wartime measure, this program lasted until 1964 and revived traditions of migration that had largely lapsed during the depression years. As time passed, migrant streams from Altamira and Chamitlán developed an intricate series of supporting social networks, and wage labor in the United States became a common feature of households' economic strategies. Migrants began to establish roots in the United States and formed daughter communities in U.S. cities. By the time the Bracero program ended, U.S. migration had become independent of the official mechanisms of recruitment and hiring.

The institutionalization of U.S. migration came to fruition just as a wave of agricultural modernization surged in Mexico. With government encouragement, large farmers and private companies increasingly came to dominate farming in rural towns such as Altamira and Chamitlán. Through rentals and purchases, they consolidated land and production and shifted to a more mechanized, capital-intensive style of farming. The mix of crops changed from traditional staples such as corn and beans to cash crops such as sorghum, alfalfa, and strawberries. This transformation of agriculture in the mid-1960s displaced many people from traditional vocations, and they turned to wage labor. Because of the well-established social infrastructure linking their communities with United States, people from Altamira and Chamitlán were readily able to find work in an expanding U.S. economy.

The history of migration from the two urban-industrial communities is quite different from that in Altamira and Chamitlán. The pioneer migrants who left Santiago before 1940 were mainly agrarian workers who had been excluded from factory employment. Widespread out-migration from the core industrial workforce did not begin until modernization was forced on the textile mill following World War II. The substitution of machines for human labor displaced about 70 percent of the factory's workers, and many took advantage of migrant networks emanating from nearby agrarian towns to obtain work in the United States.

Given their industrial background, migrants from Santiago quickly switched to nonagricultural jobs and began to establish roots in U.S. cities, a process that was hastened by the end of the Bracero Accord in 1964. By the mid-1960s, daughter communities connected to particular factories and employers had formed in Los Angeles, providing a solid

U.S. anchor upon which the social infrastructure for widespread migration could be built.

Out-migration from Santiago never developed on the scale as in the two rural communities, however. Because of the town's strategic location near the confluence of major lines of transportation and communication near Guadalajara, during the early 1970s Santiago was incorporated into that city's industrial expansion. In spite of the town's recent rapid growth in industrial employment, however, U.S. migration has continued to increase at a steady rate and today represents a well-known and widely used resource within the array of choices available to the town's families.

Guadalajara, in contrast to the other three communities, has no indigenous tradition of U.S. migration. Its link to the United States is through networks based in the small towns from which its inhabitants originally came. The history of out-migration from Guadalajara is thus the history of migration from a myriad of rural communities throughout western Mexico. Nonetheless, Guadalajara has come to occupy an important position in the migrant networks of many towns, and U.S. migration fulfills an important role in the city's dynamic economy.

Guadalajara houses a large sector of small businesses run by independent entrepreneurs, and U.S. migration is quite important to its smooth functioning, providing the capital with which many businesses are initially formed. The profitability of many small firms also depends on a social understanding that permits owners to employ and release labor as the demand for products fluctuates; this tacit understanding depends, in turn, on the knowledge that employment in the United States is always a viable option to local employment. Given the extensive personal and familial links to U.S. migrant communities in Los Angeles and elsewhere, these workers can easily be recalled when business improves.

There are several important lessons to be learned from this brief history of migration from four Mexican communities. The first lesson is that contemporary out-migration from Mexico is rooted in the same causes as the great European migrations of the past century. Both reflect the inevitable dislocations brought by industrialization and development. As industrialization spread throughout the world, it stimulated successive waves of emigration from different countries (Thomas 1954; Hicks 1969; Reynolds 1980; Baletic 1982). As land is consolidated, as machines are substituted for human labor, and as scientific methods are applied to increase agricultural productivity, people are displaced from traditional livelihoods. Historically, displaced Europeans migrated to the United States, just as do Mexicans now. International migration from Mexico does not reflect a stagnant society but a dynamic, developing one.

There are important differences between modern Mexico and historical Europe that exacerbate the former's development pains, however. First, progress in science and technology since the nineteenth century has produced a very high level of agricultural productivity with the potential to displace more workers than in Europe. Second, dramatic reductions in mortality and high levels of fertility have given Mexico a high rate of population growth, so the magnitude of the displacement from rural areas is much larger than in nineteenth century Europe. Third, as the history of Santiago demonstrates, manufacturing is now more capital intensive than before, so Mexican factories do not absorb as many workers as did the early industrial factories of Europe. Finally, the situation of the United States has changed considerably since the years of mass European migration, when it was a frontier society in the process of rapid industrial development. It is now a settled country beset with its own problems of economic dislocation and scarcity and has become a grudging, rather than an open, country of immigration.

The second lesson from this historical review is that the causes of migration from Mexico are exclusively neither "push" nor "pull" factors but an interaction between the two. The creation of a large mass of displaced rural workers during the Porfirian era coincided with the economic development of the American Southwest, and movement between the two areas was stimulated by recruitment. Labor recruitment also played a key role later on, when the later Reparto Agrario created a large class of capital-poor ejidatarios in Mexico and the U.S. war effort generated a labor shortage in the United States. International migration occurred because of complementary transformations in the United States and Mexico, incited by recruitment initiated in the United States.

The third lesson is that, once begun, international migration tends to acquire its own momentum and become progressively more widespread. In each of the three towns, U.S. migration began in some relatively narrow, distinct segment of the population that could be characterized in terms of age, sex, and socioeconomic position. Wherever it started, however, migration eventually broadened to encompass all segments of the occupational hierarchy, all ages, and both sexes. This expansion occurred because migration is inherently a social process, and in each community, networks of interpersonal ties eventually developed to put a job within easy reach of all community members. Various facets of this social process of international migration are explored in greater detail in the remainder of the book.

5
Current Migration Patterns

Chapter 4 gave a historical description of the development of international migration; the present chapter focuses on contemporary patterns. Using quantitative data gathered in the four Mexican communities, it presents a snapshot of the migration process in the years immediately prior to fieldwork. It depicts the prevalence of international migration in each community and the socioeconomic background of U.S. migrants as of 1980–1982. This analysis provides a set of standard statistics against which other studies of Mexican migration can be compared. Although the chapter is important in documenting the current context of migration and providing a benchmark for other researchers, the lengthy presentation of data is somewhat tedious. Readers not interested in knowing all the details about current migration patterns may read the chapter summary and skip to the next chapter without serious loss of continuity.

EXTENT OF MIGRATION

The historical analysis in chapter 4 suggested that, by 1982, migration had become a common feature of life in each of the four communities. Table 5.1 examines this contention by measuring the prevalence of migrants among working-age men and women in each place. One's migrant status is determined by the destination and recency of one's most recent trip outside the community. "Active migrants" left on their last trip in 1980 or later or were away at the time of the survey, while "inactive migrants" left before 1980.[1] These two categories plus "never migrants" are mutually exclusive and total 100 percent. Active and inactive migrants are composed of "U.S. migrants" and "Mexican mi-

---

[1] A three-year reference period (1980–1982) was chosen to define active migration because labor migration is often sporadic. Many recurrent migrants do not leave every year, only once every two or three years. A three-year period is long enough to capture any person who might conceivably be an active migrant but short enough to exclude those who do not migrate regularly.

TABLE 5.1

MALES AND FEMALES AGED 15–64 CLASSIFIED BY MIGRANT STATUS: FOUR MEXICAN COMMUNITIES, 1982

	Community and sex							
	Altamira		Chamitlán		Santiago		San Marcos	
Migrant status	Males	Females	Males	Females	Males	Females	Males	Females
Active migrants (%)	38.6	13.2	30.2	7.0	10.5	3.4	5.5	0.8
To United States (%)	20.4	3.2	25.2	5.2	4.0	0.7	5.5	0.8
Within Mexico (%)	19.5	10.0	6.9	2.0	7.6	2.6	0.0	0.0
Inactive migrants (%)	22.8	8.7	24.2	4.1	28.3	5.6	9.8	1.6
To United States (%)	18.0	1.9	21.1	3.8	16.3	2.6	9.8	1.6
Within Mexico (%)	15.9	8.4	12.9	0.6	19.6	3.4	0.0	0.0
Not active migrant (%)	61.4	87.3	69.8	93.0	89.5	94.5	94.5	99.2
Never migrant (%)	38.6	78.6	45.6	88.9	61.2	91.1	84.7	97.6
Total 15–64	334	310	318	345	276	269	346	369

Source: PERSFILE; household members enumerated in Mexican community samples.

grants," however, depending on the destination of the latest trip, and these categories are not mutually exclusive, since it is possible for someone to have migrated both within Mexico and to the United States in the reference period.

Table 5.1 shows that migration is indeed common in the four communities, especially among men in the rural towns, where 30 percent to 39 percent of working-age males are active migrants. In Altamira, U.S. and Mexican migrants are roughly equal in number (about 20 percent of males are active in each case), but U.S. migrants clearly outnumber their Mexican counterparts in Chamitlán (where 25 percent are active U.S. migrants but only 7 percent are active Mexican migrants). Considering inactive migrants, the prevalence of out-migration assumes even larger proportions. Of working-age men in Altamira, 18 percent are inactive U.S. migrants and 16 percent are inactive Mexican migrants, while in Chamitlán the respective figures are 21 percent and 13 percent. A *majority* of working-age men have migrated at some point in their lives (61 percent in Altamira and 54 percent in Chamitlán), therefore, and a sizable number have been to the United States (38 percent and 46 percent, respectively).

Female migration from the two rural communities occurs on a much smaller scale than male migration. Nonetheless, female participation in the migrant stream is not trivial, although there are relatively few active U.S. migrants in either place. Of working-age women, 13 percent are active migrants in Altamira, compared to 7 percent in Chamitlán. In the former community, most women are internal migrants to nearby Guadalajara (10 percent). Another 9 percent of women from Altamira and 4 percent of those from Chamitlán are inactive migrants, so the percentage of working-age women who have *never* migrated is 78 percent in the former community and 89 percent in the latter. Thus, neither of these towns has reached a stage in the migration process where large numbers of women are involved (cf. Reichert and Massey 1979; Mines 1981), although historical trends do indicate rising female participation.

In both rural communities, active migrants generally outnumber inactive migrants, but when we turn to Santiago this pattern is reversed: only 11 percent of working-age men are active migrants, compared to 28 percent inactive. This contrast reflects a basic difference in the rhythms of rural and urban economic growth over the past forty years. In rural areas, the transformation of agriculture brought widespread displacement during the late 1960s and 1970s, contributing to a progressive upswing in later years and a very recent culmination of the migration process. In Santiago, however, mechanization peaked in the 1950s, and was followed by a rapid expansion of local industrial employment in the late 1960s and 1970s. As the prospects for employment in Santiago improved, the growth in out-migration slackened and many former migrants returned to take jobs opening up in one of the new factories. The relatively large number of inactive migrants attests to the importance of labor migration as a basic strategy for economic adjustment. Almost 40 percent of Santiago's working-age men have become migrants at some point in their lives, and 20 percent have gone to the United States.

As in Altamira, internal migration from Santiago tends to overshadow migration to the United States, again reflecting its closeness to Guadalajara. Twice as many active male migrants remain in Mexico as go to the United States (8 percent vs. 4 percent), and inactive Mexican migrants also outnumber inactive U.S. migrants (20 percent vs. 16 percent). Moreover, there are very few female migrants in Santiago, either active or inactive. Only 3 percent of women have *ever* been to the United States, and only 6 percent have ever migrated within Mexico. Temporary migration for wage labor thus seems to be primarily a male preserve in Santiago.

Since San Marcos is composed largely of in-migrants from elsewhere in Mexico, table 5.1 does not consider the extent of internal migration. Rather, it focuses exclusively on migration to the United States. Even in this large metropolis, with its diversified industrial economy, U.S. migration plays a significant, albeit more modest, role. Of working-age males, 5 percent are active and 10 percent are inactive U.S. migrants. The fact that 15 percent of working-age males have experience in the United States again suggests the importance of U.S. migration as an economic option for workers in Guadalajara. Although very few women are migrants (98 percent have never been to the United States), this reflects the small number of migrants in general rather than a dearth of women migrants in particular.

The importance of migration as an economic strategy is better understood by focusing on the household, since this is the basic institution within which labor is allocated and resources distributed (Wood 1981; Pressar 1982; Griffith 1986). Table 5.2 classifies households by the migrant status of their members. Analogous to our previous definitions, active migrant households have members who left during or after 1980 or were outside the community at the survey date, and inactive migrant households have members who migrated before 1980. As before, the categories "active migrant," "inactive migrant," and "never migrant" are mutually exclusive, while the categories "U.S. migrant" and "Mexican migrant" are not.

Obviously, migrants are more widely distributed among households

TABLE 5.2
HOUSEHOLDS CLASSIFIED BY MIGRANT STATUS OF MEMBERS:
FOUR MEXICAN COMMUNITIES, 1982

	Community			
Migrant status	Altamira	Chamitlán	Santiago	San Marcos
Active migrant (%)	46.0	45.5	21.0	10.5
To United States (%)	22.5	36.0	8.5	10.5
Within Mexico (%)	30.5	13.0	13.5	0.0
Inactive migrant (%)	29.0	38.0	39.0	20.0
To United States (%)	29.0	38.5	23.0	20.0
Within Mexico (%)	23.0	21.0	30.5	0.0
No active migrants (%)	64.0	54.5	79.0	89.5
Never migrant (%)	25.0	16.5	40.0	69.5
Total households	200	200	200	200

Source: HOUSEFILE; households enumerated in Mexican community samples.

than among working-age people in general. Nearly 50 percent of all households in the two rural towns contain active migrants. As before, however, Mexican migrants predominate among households in Altamira, while U.S. migrants predominate in Chamitlán. In the former community, 23 percent of households contain active U.S. migrants, while 31 percent contain active Mexican migrants; but in Chamitlán 36 percent have U.S. migrants, compared to 13 percent with Mexican migrants.

When inactive migrant households are added in, the conclusion that out-migration has become a mass phenomenon is difficult to avoid. An additional 29 percent of households in Altamira contain inactive migrants, as do 38 percent of households in Chamitlán. A cross-sectional look at migration in two rural communities in 1982 thus reveals that at least 75 percent of all households contain members with migrant experience (75 percent in Altamira and 83 percent in Chamitlán). Breaking these figures down separately for U.S. and Mexican migrants, 52 percent of households in Altamira have U.S. migrant members and 54 percent contain Mexican migrants; in Chamitlán, 75 percent contain U.S. migrants and 34 percent contain Mexican migrants. In other words, very few households contain neither a Mexican nor a U.S. migrant, and a majority (in Chamitlán, a vast majority) contain someone who has been to the United States. Seasonal migration for wage labor is obviously a very important component of socioeconomic organization in these communities.

One reaches a similar conclusion by studying the data from Santiago and San Marcos. Roughly a third of all households in San Marcos have members with U.S. migrant experience: 11 percent contain active migrants and 20 percent have inactive migrants. In Santiago, 21 percent of households have active migrants and 39 percent contain inactive migrants, leaving a distinct minority of households (40 percent) with no migrants at all. Although the relative number of Santiago's households with active U.S. migrants is quite modest (9 percent), the total number with any U.S. migrant experience is much larger: about a third of Santiago's households contain someone who has been to the United States. Similarly, while only 14 percent of households contain active Mexican migrants, 44 percent have members who have migrated within Mexico at some point in their lives. In this industrial town, then, migrant labor has been quite important to households in times past, and it continues to play an important, although less extensive, role today.

The foregoing ethnosurvey results permit a ranking of the four communities by the relative prevalence of U.S. out-migration during 1980 to 1982. Migration to the United States is most extensive in Chamitlán, where 25 percent of working-age men are active U.S. migrants and 36 percent of households contain active U.S. migrant members. Next is Altamira, where 20 percent of working-age males actively migrate abroad and 23 percent of households contain a current international migrant. Third is the barrio of San Marcos, in which the relative prevalence of active U.S. migration is 6 percent among working-age males and 11 percent among households. Finally, U.S. migration is least prevalent in Santiago, with an incidence of active migration of 4 percent among working-age males and 9 percent among households.

A comparison of these figures with recent data from community studies elsewhere in Mexico suggests that these four communities are by no means extreme examples of migrant sending areas. For example, using the same definitions, Reichert and Massey (1979) found that in 1978, 75 percent of the households in the rural town of Guadalupe, Michoacán, contained an active U.S. migrant; and using 1979 data, Mines and Massey (1985) found that 74 percent of working-age males in the agrarian community of Las Animas, Zacatecas, went to the United States. In another sample from the rural community of el Bajío, in Guanajuato, 15 percent of households contained someone who had been to the United States during 1973 (Roberts 1982), and in his study of Villa Guerrero in Jalisco, Shadow (1979) found that 33 percent of the adult population in 1976 had prior U.S. migrant experience. Similarly, Cornelius (1978) estimated that 50 percent of 1,001 adult males in six communities in Los Altos, Jalisco, had been to el Norte. Belshaw (1967) found that 33 percent of adult males from Huecorio, Michoacán, had worked in the United States as braceros during the 1960s, and Foster (1967) found that among household heads in Tzintzuntzan the figure was 53 percent for adult males during this period. Finally, Seligson and Williams (1981) found that 15 percent of factory workers in eight border cities had experience working in the United States, and in a representative sample of households from five Mexican urban areas, Selby and Murphy (1984) found the percentage of migrant-sending households to range from 2 percent in Querétaro to 17 percent in San Luis Potosí.

The accumulated evidence thus suggests that migration to the United States is a widespread phenomenon in western Mexico and that our four sample communities are by no means unusual in the extent to which they have integrated U.S. migration into the fabric of their socioeconomic organization. In the three towns, particularly, a majority of households have relied on U.S. migrant earnings at some point in time, and a large plurality of men have worked in the United States.

CHARACTERISTICS OF THE TRIP

Probably the most important aspect of a trip to the United States, at least from the migrant's point of view, is whether it is made with legal documents. Undocumented migrants face a constant risk of apprehension and deportation, and this fact affects all aspects of their lives in the United States: how much they earn, the work they do, where they live, how they travel, how long they stay, and with whom they go (Samora 1971; Reichert and Massey 1979; Browning and Rodriguez 1985). On the other hand, the most important aspect of a trip in Mexico is the size of the place of destination, since opportunities for employment and advancement are generally greater in large metropolitan areas (Balán et al. 1973).

Table 5.3 presents the legal status of U.S. migrants and the size of Mexican migrants' place of destination, each on the most recent trip. Obviously, the vast majority of U.S. migrants in each community is undocumented. This fact is not terribly surprising since recent changes in U.S. policy have made it increasingly difficult for Mexicans to obtain a green card, or U.S. residence permit. Most legal migrants obtained their papers through a relative (usually a father or husband) who began to migrate some time ago (often during the Bracero program) and managed to obtain a green card under the more liberal immigration rules that prevailed before the 1965 Amendments to the U.S. Immigration and Nationality Act (Keely 1979). The upswing in migration in recent years

TABLE 5.3
LEGAL STATUS OF U.S. MIGRANTS AND SIZE OF DESTINATION FOR MEXICAN
MIGRANTS ON MOST RECENT TRIP: FOUR MEXICAN COMMUNITIES, 1982

Legal status and size of place	Community			
	Altamira	Chamitlán	Santiago	San Marcos
U.S. migrants				
Documented (%)	6.4	16.4	20.5	20.6
Undocumented (%)	73.2	67.8	61.6	51.5
Bracero (%)	13.4	9.8	12.3	13.2
Tourist (%)	7.0	6.0	5.5	14.7
Number	157	214	73	68
Mexican migrants				
1,000,000+ (%)	46.2	45.5	71.6	—
100,000–999,999 (%)	17.9	6.5	10.5	—
20,000–99,999 (%)	11.4	39.0	6.3	—
5,000–19,999 (%)	9.2	2.6	7.4	—
Under 5,000 (%)	15.2	6.5	4.3	—
Number	184	77	95	0

Source: PERSFILE; household members enumerated in Mexican community samples.

has thus been composed almost entirely of undocumented migrants, and three-quarters of all U.S. migrants from Altamira and two-thirds of those from Chamitlán are undocumented. In Santiago and San Marcos, the respective figures are 62 percent and 52 percent.

There are relatively more legal migrants in Santiago and San Marcos because migrants from these areas moved out of U.S. farmwork earlier and to a greater extent than did migrants from the two rural towns. Legal documentation greatly facilitates the shift from mobile agricultural labor to settled urban work and is an important step in establishing a settled existence in the United States. Although many legal migrants may have settled abroad, this does not imply a severing of connections with the home community. Even after long years of U.S. experience, legal migrants return periodically, often every year, and we thus find a relatively large number of such legal "shuttle" migrants based in the communities.

Compared to Altamira, Chamitlán also has a relatively large number of documented migrants, reflecting its earlier and more extensive involvement in the Bracero program. When the program began to wind down in the early 1960s, many braceros from Chamitlán began to take out U.S. residence papers for themselves and their families. Often the applications were filled out and supported by growers themselves, who sought a stable and reliable work force to harvest their crops (Reichert and Massey 1979; Mines and Anzaldua 1982). As in Santiago and San

Marcos, however, obtaining legal documents does not imply a rupture with the home community. Rather, in communities with a tradition of U.S. agricultural employment, it facilitates short-term rather than long-term migration. Among migrant farmworkers, green cards are often used not so much as residence documents as work permits, providing unrestricted access to the U.S. labor market (Reichert and Massey 1979; Reichert 1982; Mines 1981).

The data in table 5.3 also show that internal migration from the communities is directed principally to large metropolitan areas within Mexico. Nearly 50 percent of all Mexican migrants from Altamira and Chamitlán and 72 percent of those from Santiago migrate to cities of one million or more—namely, Guadalajara—and with the exception of Altamira, around 90 percent migrate to cities or towns with populations exceeding 20,000. Very few migrants migrate to towns of under 5,000 population. Internal migration from the three towns under study is thus primarily to large urban areas.

Another relevant characteristic of the trip is when it was made. Table 5.4 shows the year of the most recent visit to the United States or a destination in Mexico. Most U.S. migrants made their latest trips quite recently. Roughly 50 percent of all U.S. migrants from Altamira and Chamitlán have been to the United States since 1978, and in San Marcos 50 percent have gone since 1977 (see the median years shown in table 5.4). Only in Santiago was the median date relatively early—1971. In all four communities, between 70 percent and 80 percent of all U.S. migrants made their most recent trip after 1965, one year after the expiration of the Bracero program.

The recency of most trips to the United States is explained by two factors: (1) the upswing in migration that has taken place since 1965, so that most migrants alive today are relative beginners; and (2) the strong tendency for repeat migration. Relatively few migrants make one or two trips and then stop. Many of the migrants represented in table 5.4 began at some point in the past and then made several subsequent journeys to bring them up to the present. People who made their most recent trips before 1965 are basically "retired" migrants who are unlikely to migrate further. The relatively small number of retired migrants and the larger number of recent migrants produce a distribution with a long "tail" extending into the past, so that in all cases the mean date of the last trip is several years before the median date.

The temporal pattern of internal migration roughly follows the international pattern in Altamira and Santiago. As the historical analysis showed, in both these communities the ebb and flow of Mexican migration has roughly followed the ups and downs of migration to the United

TABLE 5.4
YEAR OF LAST U.S. TRIP AND LAST MEXICAN TRIP BY MIGRANTS FROM
FOUR MEXICAN COMMUNITIES, 1982

| | Community and destination | | | | | | |
| | Altamira | | Chamitlán | | Santiago | | San Marcos |
Year of last trip	U.S. migrants	Mexican migrants	U.S. migrants	Mexican migrants	U.S. migrants	Mexican migrants	U.S. migrants
1900–1939 (%)	1.9	3.2	1.8	3.9	6.8	2.1	0.0
1910–1919 (%)	0.0	0.5	0.9	0.0	1.4	0.0	0.0
1920–1929 (%)	1.9	0.5	0.0	0.0	2.7	0.0	0.0
1930–1939 (%)	0.0	2.2	0.9	3.9	2.7	2.1	0.0
1940–1964 (%)	19.7	18.8	18.6	30.2	21.9	22.2	24.2
1940–1944 (%)	1.3	0.5	2.7	2.6	4.1	3.2	0.0
1945–1949 (%)	1.3	3.2	2.3	2.6	2.7	3.2	5.7
1950–1954 (%)	1.9	4.9	3.2	7.9	4.1	2.1	7.1
1955–1959 (%)	9.5	4.3	5.9	2.6	4.1	8.4	4.3
1960–1964 (%)	5.7	5.9	4.5	14.5	6.9	5.3	7.1
1965–1982 (%)	78.3	77.8	79.5	65.8	71.2	75.8	75.7
1965–1969 (%)	2.5	7.6	3.6	9.2	15.1	12.6	2.9
1970–1974 (%)	10.2	10.8	9.0	15.8	16.4	24.2	11.4
1975–1979 (%)	26.1	27.6	28.0	17.1	20.5	22.1	31.4
1980–1982 (%)	39.5	31.9	38.9	23.7	19.2	16.8	30.0
Mean year	1973	1971	1973	1968	1967	1969	1972
Median year	1978	1977	1978	1970	1971	1972	1977
Number of migrants	157	185	221	76	73	95	70

Source: PERSFILE; household members enumerated in Mexican community samples.

States, both being rooted in the same socioeconomic transformations. In Chamitlán, however, the median date of the last Mexican trip is eight years before the median date of the last U.S. trip, reflecting the different historical development of migration in that community. As shown in chapter 4, levels of domestic and international migration were roughly parallel through the mid-1960s, but after 1965 migration focused almost exclusively on the United States. In Chamitlán, the migration decision is now a choice between U.S. migration or no migration at all.

The temporary nature of migration from the four communities is suggested by table 5.5, which shows the duration of the latest U.S. and Mexican trips. In the two rural communities, two-thirds of trips to the United States lasted a year or less, and among migrants from Santiago and San Marcos the figure was three-quarters; however, in each case there was a small but significant number of migrants with very long stays in the United States. In Altamira, Chamitlán, and Santiago, 7 percent to 8 percent of all migrants spent more than five years abroad on their most recent U.S. visit. This long tail produces a large mean trip length (eighteen months to two years), but a short median length (eight to nine months). Whereas the vast majority of U.S. migrants stay abroad for less than a year, then, inevitably there are some who extend their stays for two, three, four, five or more years.

Table 5.5 also indicates that trips within Mexico are longer than those to the United States. Only about 50 percent of internal migrants from Altamira and Chamitlán stayed away for a year or less, and only 37 percent of migrants from Santiago did so. On average, Mexican trips are 1.5 to 2.7 times longer than U.S. trips. This pattern reflects the greater ease of settlement and communication within Mexico. Compared to a protracted residence in the United States, fewer hardships are imposed on migrants or their families by staying for a long time in a Mexican urban area. Naturally, the migrant does not experience the sense of isolation and cultural estrangement that accompanies a long visit to the United States. Moreover, it is easier to maintain contact with loved ones, especially if one's hometown is near the urban destination. For example, even if a man from Altamira holds a full-time job in Guadalajara, he can come home regularly—on weekends, for example—to visit his wife and children. Thus the disincentives to long-term settlement are much weaker in Mexico than in the United States.

The last two tables in this section pertain to U.S. migrants only, since the information required to construct them was not collected from internal migrants. Table 5.6 classifies migrants by the total number of U.S. trips made, and table 5.7 shows migrants classified by cumulative months of U.S. experience. The vast majority of migrants from the four

TABLE 5.5
DURATION OF LAST U.S. AND LAST MEXICAN TRIP BY MIGRANTS
FROM FOUR MEXICAN COMMUNITIES, 1982

Community and destination

Duration of last trip	Altamira		Chamitlán		Santiago		San Marcos
	U.S. migrants	Mexican migrants	U.S. migrants	Mexican migrants	U.S. migrants	Mexican migrants	U.S. migrants
<1 year (%)	65.0	47.0	66.7	53.2	74.3	37.0	76.0
1–3 months (%)	21.7	15.1	25.7	21.5	21.6	17.0	38.0
4–6 months (%)	21.0	13.0	18.0	19.0	18.9	10.0	15.5
7–9 months (%)	12.7	7.0	13.1	3.8	20.3	2.0	7.0
10–12 months (%)	9.6	11.9	9.9	8.9	13.5	8.0	19.7
≤2 years (%)	15.9	13.0	15.3	13.9	8.1	18.0	7.0
≤3 years (%)	3.8	9.2	2.7	3.8	4.1	10.0	8.5
≤4 years (%)	4.5	4.3	5.9	7.6	2.7	8.0	4.2
≤5 years (%)	3.2	4.3	2.3	2.5	2.7	5.0	1.4
5+ years (%)	7.6	22.2	7.2	19.0	8.1	22.0	2.8
Mean duration (months)	23.3	43.9	24.5	37.9	18.1	49.7	19.0
Median duration (months)	8.8	17.0	8.7	10.9	8.5	23.2	8.3
Number of migrants	157	185	222	79	74	100	71

Source: PERSFILE; household members enumerated in Mexican community samples.

TABLE 5.6
NUMBER OF TRIPS MADE BY MIGRANTS TO THE UNITED STATES:
FOUR MEXICAN COMMUNITIES, 1982

Number of U.S. trips	Community			
	Altamira	Chamitlán	Santiago	San Marcos
1–4 trips (%)	89.2	81.6	85.2	84.6
1 trip (%)	46.5	44.1	69.5	62.0
2 trips (%)	22.3	21.2	16.2	11.3
3 trips (%)	16.6	9.5	6.8	8.5
4 trips (%)	3.8	6.8	2.7	2.8
5–9 trips (%)	9.0	9.6	11.0	9.8
5 trips (%)	4.5	2.7	4.1	1.4
6 trips (%)	2.6	2.3	4.1	2.8
7 trips (%)	1.3	1.4	1.4	2.8
8 trips (%)	0.0	2.3	1.4	1.4
9 trips (%)	0.6	0.9	0.0	1.4
10–14 trips (%)	1.3	5.9	4.1	2.8
15–19 trips (%)	0.0	1.4	0.0	1.4
20+ trips (%)	0.6	1.8	0.0	1.4
Mean number of U.S. trips	2.4	3.3	2.3	2.7
Median number of U.S. trips	1.2	1.3	1.0	1.0
Number of U.S. migrants	157	222	74	70

Source: PERSFILE; household members enumerated in Mexican community samples.

communities have made very few trips to the United States and have
accumulated relatively small amounts of time abroad. In each place,
between 80 percent and 90 percent of migrants have made fewer than
five U.S. trips. Significant rural-urban differences become apparent on
more detailed study of these first few trips. For instance, more than 60
percent of migrants from Santiago and San Marcos have made only one
trip to el Norte, while the figure is closer to 45 percent in Altamira and
Chamitlán.

The very small number of trips made, on average, by U.S. migrants
does not necessarily contradict our earlier statement that migrants display a strong tendency to make repeated trips. Because of the recent
upswing in U.S. migration, a large number of migrants began to migrate
only within the last five years, and they literally have not had enough
time to make another trip. Moreover, despite the low average number,

TABLE 5.7
TOTAL MONTHS OF U.S. MIGRANT EXPERIENCE ACCUMULATED BY MIGRANTS
TO THE UNITED STATES: FOUR MEXICAN COMMUNITIES, 1982

Total months of U.S. experience	Community			
	Altamira	Chamitlán	Santiago	San Marcos
0–5 years (%)	82.8	70.6	75.5	75.6
0–12 months (%)	37.2	30.3	48.0	50.0
13–24 months (%)	18.6	17.2	11.0	7.1
25–36 months (%)	10.3	7.2	1.4	5.7
37–48 months (%)	9.0	6.8	4.1	5.7
49–60 months (%)	7.7	9.1	11.0	7.1
5–10 years (%)	11.0	14.9	20.6	11.4
61–72 months (%)	3.9	5.9	6.9	5.7
73–84 months (%)	2.7	4.5	5.5	2.9
85–96 months (%)	0.6	2.7	1.4	1.4
97–108 months (%)	1.9	0.9	2.7	1.4
109–120 months (%)	1.9	0.9	4.1	0.0
11–14 years (%)	3.2	5.4	2.7	5.7
15+ years (%)	3.2	9.1	1.4	7.1
Mean months of U.S. experience	40.9	59.8	38.8	51.4
Median months of U.S. experience	22.5	28.9	12.5	12.0
Number of U.S. migrants	156	221	73	70

Source: PERSFILE; household members enumerated in Mexican community samples.

in each community a significant minority have made enough trips to be classified as recurrent migrants. For example, in Chamitlán, where U.S. out-migration has developed most fully, nearly 20 percent of all migrants have made five or more trips, and in the other towns this figure ranges from 10 percent to 15 percent.

Table 5.7 shows roughly the same pattern in terms of cumulative U.S. migrant experience. The vast majority of migrants—70 percent to 80 percent—have accumulated five or fewer years of U.S. migrant experience, leaving 20 percent to 30 percent with relatively large amounts of time spent abroad. Because of the long tail of the distribution, the mean amount of U.S. experience is much greater than the median.

The tables in this section permit a general characterization of a trip from one of the four communities to the United States. The typical visit was made after 1977 by an undocumented migrant who stayed abroad for a year or less. He was probably making his first or second trip and had accumulated a total of less than two years of migrant experience. On the other hand, the typical migrant within Mexico went to a large urban area in the middle to late 1970s and stayed longer, up to two years.

DEMOGRAPHIC BACKGROUND OF MIGRANTS

Demographic characteristics of migrants are also important in the definition of current migration patterns. Table 5.8 presents the sex distribution and table 5.9, the age composition of U.S. and Mexican migrants, classified by migrant status. As before, active migrants left on their most recent trip in 1980 or later or were in the United States at the time of the survey, and inactive migrants left before 1980.

Consistent with the earlier historical analysis, table 5.8 shows that U.S. migrants are primarily males. The percentage male among active U.S. migrants ranges from 80 percent to 85 percent and among inactive U.S. migrants, from 80 percent to 90 percent. The predominance of men among U.S. migrants is explained partly by the fact that most are undocumented. Male migrants are quite wary of the risks involved in undocumented migration. Tales of molestation by unscrupulous coyotes and immigration officers abound, and most men do not want to subject their wives, mothers, sisters, or daughters to the risks involved in surreptitious entry. When women migrate to the United States, therefore, they usually do so in the company of male relatives, and typically with documents.

This impediment to female migration does not exist within Mexico; therefore, the relative number of women among internal migrants is much greater. In Altamira and Chamitlán, the percentage of women among active Mexican migrants is about 30 percent, and among inactive migrants the respective percentages are 48 percent and 14 percent. The share of women among active Mexican migrants in Santiago is somewhat lower (8 percent), although women do make up 25 percent of inactive migrants.

The age data in table 5.9 show that people actively migrating to the United States are heavily concentrated in the central labor force ages between twenty and thirty-four years, while inactive migrants are somewhat older, centered more in the thirty-five- to fifty-four-year age range. The age distribution of active migrants from Altamira stands out from the others in having a relatively large number of teenagers. Over 25 percent of Altamira's active U.S. migrants are aged fifteen to nineteen, making it the second largest age category. In contrast, the second-largest age group in the other towns is thirty-five to fifty-four. Active U.S.

TABLE 5.8
SEX DISTRIBUTION OF MIGRANTS AND NONMIGRANTS FROM FOUR MEXICAN
COMMUNITIES, 1982

	Migrant status					
	Active migrants		Inactive migrants		Never	Total
Community and sex	U.S.	Mexico	U.S.	Mexico	migrant	population
Altamira						
Male (%)	85.5	71.1	90.5	51.8	42.9	50.7
Female (%)	14.5	28.9	9.5	48.2	57.1	49.3
Number	62	52	95	85	907	1,201
Chamitlán						
Male (%)	81.2	70.0	81.3	86.4	41.5	50.3
Female (%)	18.8	30.0	18.7	13.6	58.5	49.7
Number	85	10	134	22	891	1,142
Santiago						
Male (%)	84.6	91.7	87.7	75.4	46.2	51.3
Female (%)	15.4	8.3	12.3	24.6	53.8	48.7
Number	13	12	57	57	864	1,003
San Marcos						
Male (%)	80.0	—	85.7	—	46.4	48.1
Female (%)	20.0	—	14.3	—	53.6	51.9
Number	20	0	49	0	1,160	1,229

Source: PERSFILE; household members enumerated in Mexican community samples.

migrants from Chamitlán, Santiago, and San Marcos have average ages in the middle thirties, whereas the mean age in Altamira is only twenty-nine.

Very few children migrate to the United States. Only Chamitlán, with the most developed migration tradition, has a significant number of U.S. migrants under the age of fifteen; 4 percent of active U.S. migrants and 8 percent of inactive U.S. migrants there are children. Altamira is the only other town where there are children with U.S. migrant experience; 2 percent of inactive U.S. migrants in that town are less than fifteen years old. None of the communities has yet developed a widespread pattern of family migration, therefore, as has been observed elsewhere (Reichert 1979; Mines 1981; Mines and Anzaldua 1982), although the beginnings of such a pattern can be discerned in Chamitlán.

Turning to age patterns of migration within Mexico, we find a basic contrast between Chamitlán on one hand and Altamira and Santiago on the other hand. In the two towns where Mexican migration continues to play an important role, Altamira and Santiago, the age data reveal a

TABLE 5.9
AGE DISTRIBUTION OF MIGRANTS AND NONMIGRANTS
IN FOUR MEXICAN COMMUNITIES, 1982

| | Migrant status | | | | | |
| | Active migrants | | Inactive migrants | | Never | Total |
Community and age	U.S.	Mexico	U.S.	Mexico	migrant	population
Altamira						
Under 15 (%)	0.0	3.8	2.1	0.0	53.4	40.7
15–19 (%)	25.8	42.3	4.2	7.1	13.1	13.9
20–34 (%)	46.8	36.5	23.2	44.7	12.1	18.2
35–54 (%)	22.6	13.5	36.8	30.6	11.6	15.6
55+ (%)	4.8	3.9	33.7	17.6	9.6	11.6
Mean	28.9	25.2	45.2	37.4	20.8	24.5
Number	62	52	95	85	906	1,200
Chamitlán						
Under 15 (%)	3.6	0.0	8.2	0.0	45.2	36.6
15–19 (%)	7.2	0.0	3.0	4.5	19.7	16.4
20–34 (%)	48.2	50.0	30.1	27.3	14.5	19.4
35–54 (%)	27.7	40.0	28.6	63.6	12.6	16.8
55+ (%)	13.3	10.0	30.1	4.6	7.9	10.8
Mean	34.7	35.6	42.5	38.1	21.2	25.2
Number	83	10	133	22	887	1,135
Santiago						
Under 15 (%)	0.0	0.0	0.0	0.0	48.9	42.0
15–19 (%)	15.4	16.7	1.8	0.0	12.5	11.2
20–34 (%)	38.5	58.3	29.8	55.4	19.7	23.1
35–54 (%)	23.1	25.0	42.1	28.6	12.8	15.7
55+ (%)	23.1	0.0	26.3	16.1	6.1	8.0
Mean	36.9	27.5	44.8	35.9	20.3	22.9
Number	13	12	57	56	851	989
San Marcos						
Under 15 (%)	0.0	—	0.0	—	43.4	41.0
15–19 (%)	10.0	—	2.1	—	15.8	15.1
20–34 (%)	55.0	—	31.3	—	21.1	22.1
35–54 (%)	30.0	—	41.7	—	14.9	16.2
55+ (%)	5.0	—	25.0	—	4.7	5.6
Mean	31.8	—	44.1	—	21.2	22.2
Number	20	0	48	0	1,159	1,227

Source: PERSFILE; household members enumerated in Mexican community samples.

typical concentration of people between the ages of twenty and thirty-four, with average ages in the late twenties. Internal migrants from Chamitlán are much older, with no active migrants below the age of twenty and half above the age of thirty-five. With the disappearance of internal migration as a viable part of households' economic strategies in the late 1960s, few new migrants left for work in Mexican cities, leaving only aging Mexican migrants from previous times.

Altamira again stands out in exporting a large number of teenagers for wage labor in Mexican urban areas, with 42 percent of active internal migrants in the age interval fifteen to nineteen years. When combined with the 26 percent of active U.S. migrants in this age range, the number of active migrants—internal and international—constitutes roughly a 25 percent of all teenagers and a much higher percentage of teenage men, graphically illustrating the extent to which out-migration has come to represent the path to opportunity for young people in Altamira.

The last two tables in this section describe the family situation of migrants in the four communities. Table 5.10 gives the marital status and table 5.11, the household position of U.S. and Mexican migrants. Altamira again stands out in comparison to the other communities.

TABLE 5.10
MARITAL STATUS OF MIGRANTS AND NONMIGRANTS IN
FOUR MEXICAN COMMUNITIES, 1982

Community and marital status	Migrant status				Never migrant	Total population
	Active migrants		Inactive migrants			
	U.S.	Mexico	U.S.	Mexico		
Altamira						
Never married (%)	61.3	71.1	24.2	48.2	72.9	66.6
Currently married (%)	37.1	28.9	72.6	47.1	24.7	30.9
Divorced or separated (%)	0.0	0.0	1.1	0.0	0.0	0.0
Widowed (%)	1.6	0.0	2.1	4.7	2.4	2.4
Number	62	52	95	85	907	1,201
Chamitlán						
Never married (%)	40.0	20.0	25.2	31.8	74.7	65.0
Currently married (%)	60.0	80.0	72.4	68.2	23.0	32.9
Divorced or separated (%)	0.0	0.0	0.0	0.0	0.5	0.4
Widowed (%)	0.0	0.0	2.2	0.0	1.8	1.7
Number	85	10	134	22	890	1,141
Santiago						
Never married (%)	15.4	16.7	21.0	15.8	66.6	59.8
Currently married (%)	84.6	83.3	77.2	84.2	32.6	39.4
Divorced or separated (%)	0.0	0.0	1.8	0.0	0.2	0.3
Widowed (%)	0.0	0.0	0.0	0.0	0.6	0.5
Number	13	12	57	57	862	1,001
San Marcos						
Never married (%)	45.0	—	12.5	—	67.3	64.3
Currently married (%)	50.0	—	83.3	—	31.4	33.7
Divorced or separated (%)	0.0	—	2.1	—	0.0	0.1
Widowed (%)	5.0	—	2.1	—	1.7	1.9
Number	20	0	48	0	1,156	1,224

Source: PERSFILE; household members enumerated in Mexican community samples.

TABLE 5.11
HOUSEHOLD POSITION OF MIGRANTS AND NONMIGRANTS IN
FOUR MEXICAN COMMUNITIES, 1982

| | Migrant status | | | | | |
| Community and household position | Active migrants | | Inactive migrants | | Never migrant | Total population |
	U.S.	Mexico	U.S.	Mexico		
Altamira						
Head (%)	29.0	21.1	72.6	40.0	7.5	16.6
Spouse (%)	3.2	3.9	3.2	9.4	16.9	14.0
Child (%)	66.1	67.3	20.0	48.2	67.4	62.2
Other (%)	1.6	7.7	4.2	2.4	8.3	7.2
Number	62	52	95	85	907	1,201
Chamitlán						
Head (%)	49.4	70.0	64.2	59.1	5.5	17.2
Spouse (%)	9.4	10.0	9.7	9.1	16.6	15.1
Child (%)	38.8	20.0	23.9	22.7	73.9	63.9
Other (%)	2.4	0.0	2.2	9.1	4.0	3.8
Number	85	10	134	22	891	1,142
Santiago						
Head (%)	61.5	66.7	82.5	75.4	10.3	19.5
Spouse (%)	15.4	0.0	5.3	8.8	20.4	18.5
Child (%)	23.1	33.3	12.3	15.8	68.4	61.2
Other (%)	0.0	0.0	0.0	0.0	0.9	0.8
Number	13	12	57	57	864	1,003
San Marcos						
Head (%)	45.0	—	75.5	—	12.4	15.4
Spouse (%)	15.0	—	6.1	—	14.6	14.2
Child (%)	35.0	—	16.3	—	67.2	64.6
Other (%)	5.0	—	2.0	—	5.8	5.6
Number	20	0	49	0	1,160	1,229

Source: PERSFILE; household members enumerated in Mexican community samples.

Consistent with the prevalence of teenagers among migrants from Al-tamira, 61 percent of active U.S. migrants and 71 percent of active Mexican migrants are not married. About 67 percent of both groups are children of the household head, principally teenage sons.

This pattern is completely opposite that in Chamitlán, San Marcos, and especially Santiago, where the large majority of active migrants are married household heads. In Chamitlán, 60 percent of active U.S migrants and 80 percent of active Mexican migrants are married. The respective figures in Santiago are 85 percent and 83 percent, while married people make up 50 percent of active U.S. migrants in San Marcos. Similarly, a majority or near majority of active migrants in each place are household heads: 49 percent of U.S. migrants and 70 percent of Mexican migrants in Chamitlán, 62 percent and 67 percent in Santiago, and 45 percent of U.S. migrants in San Marcos. In general, when inactive migrants are considered, the predominance of married household heads, not surprisingly, increases.

The ethnosurvey data thus permit a demographic characterization of current migrants to the United States. In most cases, active migrants are married, male household heads of prime labor force age. A large secondary group consists of unmarried teenage sons, and in Altamira this category is unusually prominent. In general, few women and children migrate because of the difficulties of undocumented migration, but in Chamitlán there is evidence of some family migration. Inactive U.S. migrants tend to be male household heads who are somewhat older.

SOCIOECONOMIC BACKGROUND OF MIGRANTS

Another important characteristic of migrants is their occupational background, since this factor strongly affects how they enter and are incorporated into U.S. socioeconomic structures (North and Houstoun 1976; Chiswick 1978, 1979, 1984; Mullan 1986). Table 5.12 shows the occupational composition of migrants classified by migrant status and destination.

In the two rural towns, the three lowest groups in the occupational hierarchy account for the vast majority of active U.S. migrants: jornaleros, campesinos, and unskilled workers, with the two agricultural occupations containing most migrants in both cases (63 percent in Altamira and 82 percent in Chamitlán), although in Altamira, a relatively large share (20 percent) of active U.S. migrants are unskilled workers. Although the stereotype of undocumented Mexican migrants as farmworkers is generally upheld, some migrants, even those from rural areas, do come from nonagricultural occupations.

Chapter 4 showed that migrants have been drawn from different occupational groups at different times over the past eighty years. In the rural areas, for instance, we found that out-migration gradually shifted from a concentration among agricultores and a few campesinos in the earliest period to campesinos during and after the Reparto Agrario to landless jornaleros most recently. Consistent with this progression, jornaleros generally dominate among active U.S. migrants (44 percent in Altamira and 57 percent in Chamitlán), followed by campesinos and then agricultores. Among inactive migrants, however, there are relatively more campesinos and agricultores and fewer jornaleros.

In Santiago, migrants first left in large numbers from the ranks of skilled workers during the factory modernization of the mid-1950s, and

TABLE 5.12
OCCUPATION OF MIGRANTS AND NONMIGRANTS IN
FOUR MEXICAN COMMUNITIES, 1982

Community and occupation	Migrant status				Never migrant	Total population
	Active migrants		Inactive migrants			
	U.S.	Mexico	U.S.	Mexico		
Altamira						
Agricultor (%)	1.8	0.0	20.5	1.6	3.5	6.3
Nonmanual (%)	13.0	28.9	12.1	41.7	13.9	19.3
Skilled manual (%)	1.9	2.6	3.6	8.3	6.9	5.2
Campesino (%)	18.5	23.7	34.9	11.7	50.0	33.5
Unskilled manual (%)	20.4	18.4	12.1	20.0	6.2	12.9
Jornalero (%)	44.4	26.3	16.9	16.7	19.4	22.7
Number	54	38	83	60	144	379
Chamitlán						
Agricultor (%)	1.6	0.0	1.1	5.3	0.0	2.7
Nonmanual (%)	13.1	11.1	14.7	47.4	31.8	23.8
Skilled manual (%)	1.6	0.0	6.3	15.8	2.6	4.2
Campesino (%)	24.6	11.1	32.6	0.0	17.2	21.8
Unskilled manual (%)	1.6	0.0	3.2	10.5	8.6	5.7
Jornalero (%)	57.4	77.8	42.1	21.1	35.8	41.8
Number	61	9	95	19	151	335
Santiago						
Professional (%)	10.0	18.1	0.0	16.9	8.5	9.2
Clerical-sales (%)	10.0	9.1	15.2	9.4	13.7	12.8
Skilled manual (%)	30.0	45.5	52.2	37.7	42.5	42.9
Services (%)	20.0	9.1	8.7	9.4	3.9	6.6
Unskilled manual (%)	10.0	18.2	13.0	26.4	28.8	24.5
Farmworker (%)	20.0	0.0	10.9	0.0	2.6	4.0
Number	10	11	46	53	153	273
San Marcos						
Professional (%)	0.0	—	0.0	—	7.0	6.0
Clerical-sales (%)	46.1	—	28.2	—	30.7	31.0
Skilled manual (%)	30.8	—	28.2	—	34.8	34.0
Services (%)	7.7	—	15.4	—	8.6	9.3
Unskilled manual (%)	15.4	—	23.1	—	17.6	18.1
Farmworker (%)	0.0	—	5.1	—	1.3	1.6
Number	13	0	39	0	313	365

Source: PERSFILE; household members enumerated in Mexican community samples.

later migration spread to a wider array of occupations. The largest occupational group among both active and inactive U.S. migrants from Santiago is thus skilled manual workers: 30 percent in the former case and 52 percent in the latter. The next largest categories are quite different, depending on which activity category one considers. Among inactive U.S. migrants, unskilled manual and clerical-sales workers are the next largest categories; among active migrants, farmworkers and services are the next largest categories. The recent expansion of industry in Santiago has induced many skilled and unskilled factory workers to stop migrating, ceding their places to service personnel and farmworkers. In San Marcos, active U.S. migrants are drawn mainly from the clerical-sales and skilled manual categories (constituting 46 percent and 31 percent, respectively), while inactive migrants are more evenly distributed among occupational groups. Migrants from the two urban areas are thus mainly from nonfarm occupations that reflect the occupational composition of each place: in Santiago, factory work; and in San Marcos, diversified manufacturing and services.

Considering the occupational distribution of internal migrants, the contrast between active and inactive migrants is somewhat different from that for international migrants. In the two rural towns, for example, nonmanual workers play a much larger role among both active and inactive migrants. In Altamira, they are the largest occupational group for all Mexican migrants, whether active or inactive, but especially in the latter case. Nonmanual workers do predominate among inactive Mexican migrants in Chamitlán, while jornaleros represent nearly 80 percent of active ones. In Santiago, active and inactive Mexican migrants have basically the same occupational structure, with skilled manual workers predominating, followed by unskilled manual and professional-technical workers. In general, then, in the towns where internal migration has remained a viable economic strategy (Altamira and Santiago), farmworkers make up a smaller share of Mexican than U.S. migrants.

Finally, the educational background of migrants is considered in table 5.13. In general, active U.S. migrants have higher average educations than do either inactive U.S. migrants or nonmigrants, partially reflecting improvements in Mexican public education that have occurred over the years. Since active migrants tend to be younger, they have been better able to take advantage of the recent expansion in public education. The vast majority of active U.S. migrants thus have at least some primary schooling, and many have graduated from grade school. Relatively small percentages (less than 16 percent) are completely illiterate. With the exception of migrants from Chamitlán, however, U.S. migrants generally do not fare well in comparison to Mexican migrants. In Altamira and Santiago, those with the highest average educations become Mexican rather than U.S. migrants.

Active U.S. migrants from rural areas are thus generally drawn from the ranks of jornaleros, with lesser roles played by campesinos, although not all rural-origin migrants are farmworkers: in Altamira 35 percent and in Chamitlán 16 percent come from a nonagricultural background. Rural-origin U.S. migrants generally have some primary education, and a

TABLE 5.13
EDUCATION OF MIGRANTS AND NONMIGRANTS IN
FOUR MEXICAN COMMUNITIES, 1982

Community and education	Migrant status				Never migrant	Total population
	Active migrants		Inactive migrants			
	U.S.	Mexico	U.S.	Mexico		
Altamira						
0 (%)	4.8	5.8	11.5	16.6	25.5	21.9
1–5 (%)	38.7	28.8	64.2	31.8	45.1	44.6
6 (%)	30.5	23.1	13.7	17.7	15.9	17.1
7–11 (%)	14.5	32.7	9.5	15.3	11.5	12.7
12 + (%)	6.5	9.6	1.1	18.8	2.0	3.7
Mean	5.5	6.7	3.8	5.9	3.5	3.9
Number	62	52	95	85	907	1,201
Chamitlán						
0 (%)	15.5	40.0	38.1	22.7	25.4	26.2
1–5 (%)	47.6	50.0	40.3	45.5	44.5	44.3
6 (%)	23.8	0.0	11.9	13.6	18.7	18.0
7–11 (%)	7.1	10.0	7.5	4.6	9.7	9.1
12 + (%)	6.0	0.0	2.2	13.6	1.7	2.3
Mean	4.3	2.2	2.9	4.1	3.5	3.5
Number	84	10	134	22	887	1,137
Santiago						
0 (%)	15.4	0.0	19.3	8.8	24.0	22.5
1–5 (%)	15.4	8.3	31.6	26.3	33.6	32.5
6 (%)	38.5	58.4	31.6	33.4	22.6	24.4
7–11 (%)	23.1	8.3	12.3	14.0	16.7	16.3
12 + (%)	7.7	25.0	5.3	17.5	3.0	4.3
Mean	5.9	7.9	4.8	6.3	4.2	4.4
Number	13	12	57	57	857	996
San Marcos						
0 (%)	5.0	—	16.7	—	17.3	17.1
1–5 (%)	30.0	—	41.6	—	38.1	38.1
6 (%)	30.0	—	27.1	—	20.2	20.6
7–11 (%)	20.0	—	10.4	—	21.0	20.6
12 + (%)	15.0	—	4.2	—	3.4	3.6
Mean	6.3	—	4.4	—	4.6	4.6
Number	20	0	48	0	1,158	1,126

Source: PERSFILE; household members enumerated in Mexican community samples.

large share are grade-school graduates. On average they are better educated than nonmigrants. In Santiago, active U.S. migrants come from a
variety of occupational backgrounds; the largest groups are skilled manual workers, service workers, and farmworkers. The two main occupational groups for U.S. migrants from San Marcos are clerical-sales workers and skilled laborers. Although a majority of active U.S. migrants
from both urban places have completed primary school—a higher level

than in the population as a whole—they are not generally as well educated as Mexican migrants, who have been able to make better use of
their educations in the expanding economy of Guadalajara and its
environs.

SOCIOECONOMIC SELECTION OF MIGRANTS

In the first part of this chapter we concluded that U.S. wage labor was
a pervasive feature of life in each of the four communities. Migrants
may be widely distributed among households in each place, but they
are not evenly distributed. Different social groups are characterized by
varying degrees of wealth and differential access to socioeconomic resources. Migration thus plays a different role in each group's economic
strategy, and its prevalence varies from occupation to occupation. Tables
5.14 and 5.15 examine the extent of out-migration from different occupational groups in rural and urban communities.

In spite of variation across occupations, the extent to which migration has been integrated into the economic strategies of all social groups
in Altamira is impressive and again demonstrates the extent to which
migrant labor has become embedded in the economic organization of
the community. Every occupational category has sent migrants both
to the United States and within Mexico, and every group continues
actively to do so. The percentage of people who have migrated at some
point in their lives varies from a low of 43 percent among campesinos
to a high of 82 percent among unskilled manual workers, with the other
groups clustered mainly at the upper limit of the spectrum (79 percent
among agricultores, 73 percent for nonmanual workers, 67 percent
among jornaleros, and 50 percent among skilled laborers). Active migration is generally greatest among the landless and unskilled—jornaleros
and nonmanual laborers—and lowest among the landed—the agricultores. It is extraordinarily high among unskilled manual workers: 63
percent left the community at some point after 1980, with 29 percent
going to the United States and 37 percent to a Mexican city.

Comparison of U.S. and Mexican migration reveals the relative ranking of occupational groups in terms of lifetime migration percentages to
be very different. The highest levels of U.S. migration are found among
farmworkers; 75 percent of agricultores have been to the United States,
although most are inactive migrants who left in the earliest period. They
are followed in descending order by jornaleros (44 percent), unskilled
workers (43 percent), campesinos (31 percent), nonmanual workers (24
percent), and skilled manual workers (20 percent). In contrast, the extent

TABLE 5.14
MIGRANT STATUS BY OCCUPATIONAL GROUP IN TWO RURAL MEXICAN COMMUNITIES, 1982

Migrant status	Occupation					
	Agricultor	Nonmanual	Skilled manual	Campesino	Unskilled manual	Jornalero
Altamira						
Active migrant (%)	8.3	50.7	25.0	16.5	63.3	48.8
To United States (%)	4.2	13.7	10.0	8.7	28.6	34.8
Within Mexico (%)	4.2	38.4	15.0	8.6	36.7	13.9
Inactive migrant (%)	70.8	21.9	25.0	26.8	18.4	18.6
To United States (%)	70.8	9.6	10.0	22.1	14.3	9.3
Within Mexico (%)	16.7	20.6	20.0	17.3	18.4	17.4
Not active migrant (%)	91.7	49.3	75.0	83.5	36.7	51.2
Never migrant (%)	20.8	27.4	50.0	56.7	18.4	32.6
Number	24	73	20	127	49	86
Chamitlán						
Active migrant (%)	11.1	23.8	21.4	21.6	15.0	39.0
To United States (%)	11.1	16.3	7.1	20.3	10.0	33.3
Within Mexico (%)	11.1	8.6	14.3	2.7	5.0	7.1
Inactive migrant (%)	22.2	16.3	50.0	41.9	20.0	15.9
To United States (%)	11.1	11.3	42.9	41.9	15.0	20.6
Within Mexico (%)	22.2	13.8	35.7	10.8	10.0	10.6
Not active migrant (%)	88.9	76.2	78.6	78.4	85.0	61.0
Never migrant (%)	66.7	60.0	28.6	36.5	65.0	38.3
Number	9	80	14	74	20	141

Source: PERSFILE; household members enumerated in Altamira and Chamitlán.

Migrant status	Occupation					
	Professional-technical	Clerical-sales	Skilled manual	Services	Unskilled manual	Farmworker
Santiago						
Active migrant (%)	32.0	11.4	11.7	15.8	7.3	18.2
To United States (%)	4.0	2.9	3.4	10.5	1.5	18.2
Within Mexico (%)	32.0	8.6	8.4	10.5	5.8	0.0
Inactive migrant (%)	16.0	25.6	32.7	52.6	27.5	45.5
To United States (%)	0.0	20.0	20.2	26.3	10.1	45.5
Within Mexico (%)	16.0	14.3	23.5	36.8	17.4	45.5
Not active migrant (%)	68.0	88.6	88.3	84.2	82.7	81.8
Never migrant (%)	52.0	60.0	55.5	31.6	65.2	36.4
Number	25	35	119	19	69	11
San Marcos						
Active migrant (%)	0.0	5.2	5.5	2.9	2.9	16.7
To United States (%)	0.0	5.2	5.5	2.9	2.9	16.7
Within Mexico (%)	0.0	0.0	0.0	0.0	0.0	0.0
Inactive migrant (%)	0.0	9.5	7.0	17.7	13.2	16.7
To United States (%)	0.0	9.5	7.0	17.7	13.2	16.7
Within Mexico (%)	0.0	0.0	0.0	0.0	0.0	0.0
Not active migrant (%)	100	94.8	94.5	97.1	97.1	83.3
Never migrant (%)	100	72.3	69.5	64.7	70.6	66.7
Number	24	115	128	34	68	6

Source: PERSFILE; household members enumerated in Santiago and San Marcos.

of internal migration is greatest among nonagricultural workers; 59 percent of nonmanual workers and 55 percent of unskilled laborers have migrated internally, followed by 35 percent of skilled laborers, 31 percent of jornaleros, 26 percent of campesinos, and 21 percent of agricultores.

This pattern reflects the state of economic opportunity in Altamira today. Mechanization has reduced the amount of agricultural work available to jornaleros and campesinos, while development patterns have concentrated most skilled and unskilled nonagrarian employment in urban areas. The probability of U.S. migration thus varies inversely with opportunities for both local and urban employment, whereas the extent of internal migration varies directly with opportunities for urban employment. Jornaleros and campesinos migrate to the United States, while nonmanual, skilled, and unskilled workers migrate to Guadalajara or some other Mexican city. Those with access to land, the agricultores, do not migrate.

At a general level, patterns of migration among occupations are much the same in Chamitlán. The highest levels of active migration are found in occupational groups that face the least opportunity for local or urban employment. Jornaleros contain the highest percentage of active migrants, 39 percent, almost all going to the United States, followed by nonmanual workers and campesinos. Most active migrants in the nonmanual category go to the United States, reflecting Chamitlán's specialization in international migration. The main difference from Altamira is that very few unskilled manual workers are active migrants, but this is a smaller and less important occupational group in Chamitlán.

When inactive migrants are considered in tandem with active migrants, we find that migration has become embedded within all occupational groups in Chamitlán, just as it has in Altamira. The level of lifetime out-migration is lowest among agricultores, where only 33 percent have ever become migrants, followed in ascending order by unskilled manual workers (35 percent), nonmanual workers (40 percent), jornaleros (62 percent), campesinos (63 percent), and skilled manual workers (71 percent). As in Altamira, the ordering is quite different for U.S. and Mexican migrants. The highest levels of U.S. migration are found among campesinos and jornaleros, while these groups contain the lowest percentages of internal migrants. Nonagricultural groups are relatively more likely to send migrants to a Mexican urban area than to the United States. As in Altamira, workers with occupations that are salable in the urban sector are drawn to Mexican cities, and those without such skills go to the United States.

Levels of out-migration from Santiago are generally lower than in the rural communities (table 5.15); nonetheless, *all* occupational groups send migrants for work outside the town. Internal migration is relatively much more important than migration to the United States, however. In terms of overall levels of active migration (U.S. and Mexican), professional workers contain the most active migrants (32 percent) and unskilled workers, the least (7 percent), but patterns are completely different for U.S. and Mexican migrants. Farmworkers have the largest percentage of active migrants to the United States (18 percent), yet none migrates within Mexico. After farmworkers come service workers, where 11 percent are U.S. migrants. In each of the remaining occupational groups, active U.S. migrants make up fewer than 5 percent of all workers. In contrast, 32 percent of professional-technical workers are active Mexican migrants, but only 4 percent are U.S. migrants. Of service workers, 11 percent are internal migrants, followed by clerical-sales workers (9 percent), skilled manual laborers (8 percent), and unskilled workers (6 percent).

The important role that migration has played over the years in Santiago is better indicated by combining active and inactive migrants. All groups have sent migrants for work outside the community in significant numbers at some point. The percentage of workers with migrant experience varies from 35 percent to nearly 70 percent. The extent of migration from the different groups is again somewhat different for Mexican and U.S. migrants; 64 percent of farmworkers have been to the United States, while only 4 percent of professionals have gone there. After farmworkers, the next highest group is service workers, where 37 percent have U.S. migrant experience, followed by skilled manual workers (24 percent), clerical-sales workers (23 percent), and unskilled workers (12 percent). Professionals have sent out the most internal migrants (48 percent), followed by service workers (47 percent), farmworkers (46 percent), skilled workers (32 percent), and unskilled and clerical-sales workers (both at 23 percent). Again, those with salable talents migrate within Mexico, and those with fewer marketable skills go to the United States.

Finally, the data for San Marcos show relatively little variation in the extent of U.S. migration across occupations. The smallest occupational group is farmworkers, which also has the highest level of out-migration. Of the six farmworkers enumerated in the ethnosurvey, two were U.S. migrants, one active and the other inactive. In the other groups, the percentage of U.S. migrants (active plus inactive) ranged from about 12 percent to 21 percent, with the exception of professionals, who sent no migrants to the United States.

In summary, data from the four communities suggest that out-migration for wage labor is a viable economic option for workers in all occupational groups. The profound economic impact of migration and its importance as an economic resource are indicated by the relatively large proportions of many groups that have left to work outside the community since 1980. More than a third of all jornaleros, unskilled laborers, and nonmanual workers in Altamira left the community for work in the three years prior to the survey, as did jornaleros in Chamitlán and professionals in Santiago. In general, nonagrarian workers with marketable skills migrate to Mexican urban areas, while farmworkers migrate to the United States. Such a drain of local manpower inevitably affects the economic and social life of the community, a topic that is explored in subsequent chapters.

SUMMARY

The contemporary patterns of migration discussed in this chapter combine with the historical trends noted earlier to show how deeply embedded migration has become within each community. A majority of households in all communities contain a member with migrant experience in either the United States or Mexico, and all social groups contain some migrants. Groups with the fewest opportunities for advancement in Mexico (jornaleros and campesinos in rural areas, farmworkers and service workers in urban areas) are more likely to send workers to the United States, while those with skills appropriate to urban employment (professionals and skilled manual workers) gravitate toward Mexican cities. In both rural and urban areas, U.S. migrants tend to be better educated than nonmigrants but usually less educated than internal migrants.

The typical trip to the United States was made after 1978 and lasted one year or less. The migrant was most likely a married male household head between the ages of twenty and thirty-five, although there were also a relatively large number of unmarried male teenagers, especially in Altamira. The migrant was probably making his first or second trip and had accumulated less than two years of total time in the United States. Because of the rapid increase in U.S. migration from rural areas during the late 1970s, many migrants have not yet had time to make repeated trips and accumulate large amounts of time abroad.

6

The Social Organization of Migration

Migration is not simply a movement of individuals responding to economic opportunities in their place of origin and at their destination, but an organized movement based on social and economic arrangements at both local and national levels.

Bryan Roberts (1974)

Our historical review of U.S. migration showed four very different communities gradually developing a common tradition of international out-migration. Over the years, a growing number of families from a continuously widening variety of social backgrounds was drawn into the migrant stream, until U.S. migration touched virtually all sectors of society. The emergence of mass migration during the 1970s was made possible only by the prior development of a complex social structure that supported and encouraged it. This chapter undertakes a detailed analysis of that social structure, focusing on the organization and operation of migrant networks in the four communities. Using comparative historical, ethnographic, and survey data, we illustrate how social networks develop and expand over time to make U.S. migration accessible to all classes of society, transforming it from an isolated social phenomenon to a mass movement fundamental to community life.

THE SOCIAL BASES OF NETWORK MIGRATION

Migrant networks consist of social ties that link sending communities to specific points of destination in receiving societies. These ties bind migrants and nonmigrants within a complex web of complementary social roles and interpersonal relationships that are maintained by an informal set of mutual expectations and prescribed behaviors. The social relationships that constitute migrant networks are not unique to migrants but develop as a result of universal human bonds that are molded to the special circumstances of international migration. These social ties are not created by the migratory process but are adapted to it and over time are reinforced by the common experience of migration itself.

The most important network relationships are based on kinship, friendship, and *paisanaje*,[1] which are reinforced through regular interaction in voluntary associations. In moving to a strange and often hostile land, migrants naturally draw upon these familiar bonds to share the hazards and hardships of life in exile, and those left behind rely on the same ties to mitigate the loneliness and anxiety of having a loved one far away. As migration continues, however, these well-known social connections acquire new meanings and functions. They are transformed into a set of social relationships whose content and meaning are defined within the migrant context. Over time, shared understandings develop about what it means to be a friend, relative, or paisano within a community of migrants. Eventually these understandings crystallize into a set of interrelationships that define the migrant network.

Kinship

Kinship forms one of the most important bases of migrant social organization, and family connections are the most secure bonds within the networks. The strongest relationships are between male migrants interacting as fathers and sons. Faced with a hostile and alien environment, they have evolved well-established conventions of mutual aid and cooperation in the United States, practices that transcend the stem household itself. Long after sons have grown up to form their own families, fathers travel with them to el Norte, sharing the hardships and risks of undocumented life. From this common experience, the paternal bond is strengthened, and a new relationship between *migrant* fathers and sons develops, one that carries over into the home community. Throughout their lives, migrant fathers and sons are more likely to offer assistance, information, and services to one another.

Migrant brothers also establish a mutual collaboration that builds on and strengthens the fraternal tie. Facing many demands for assistance from various friends and relatives while abroad, migrants naturally display a preference for the tie of brotherhood. Between brothers there is a continual exchange of favors and help, one that cannot be measured in money alone. To a brother arriving in the United States without money, job, or documents, a series of obligations is owed. A place to

---

[1] "Paisanaje" means common origin, or being from the same place, and a "paisano" is someone from the same community of origin. The meaning and importance of these terms with respect to migration are discussed in greater detail later in this section.

stay, help in getting a job, the loan of money, or payment for the trip are just a few examples of how the ties of brotherhood are extended and tested in the migrant context.

The next most important family tie within migrant networks is that between a man and his brothers' sons. The strong relationships that brothers expect and maintain with respect to each other also extends to their sons. Nephews are thus given preference over other relations in the offering of assistance. Arriving in the United States for the first time, a young man can generally count on the aid of his uncle; or an uncle may take it upon himself to accompany a young man on his first trip to el Norte. These ties also carry over to relationships between cousins. Among cousins linked through a common male relative there is a strong family identification, one reinforced by traditional practices of coresidence and mutual assistance between brothers. When parties of young men strike out for the United States together, they are often parallel cousins related through fathers who are brothers.

These kinship connections are reinforced through frequent interaction on important ceremonial occasions. Rituals associated with life milestones are especially important in linking settled migrants in the United States with their relatives back home. A wedding, a baptism, or the *quince* (fifteenth birthday) of a daughter provide opportunities for reuniting family members separated by migration. Relatives from Mexico are invited to share in the festivities, and friends and acquaintances from the home community who happen to be in the United States are also asked to join in, expanding the possibilities for communication and interchange. In this way, settled U.S. migrants lend greater permanence and coherence to the networks.

Kin assistance is generally extended freely and openly up through parallel cousins. Among relatives more distant than these, the strength of ties falls off rapidly, however, and their roles in the migratory process are correspondingly smaller. The most important kin relationships in migrant networks are those between fathers and sons, uncles and nephews, brothers, and male cousins. Beyond these relationships, expectations more appropriate to friendship are relevant in governing behavior between two migrants.

Friendship

Because of its explosive growth, migration has outgrown a social organization based solely on the limited confines of kinship, and networks have increasingly incorporated other close social relationships. The closest bonds outside the family are those formed between people as they grow up together. These are typically friendships between people of roughly the same age who lived near one another and joined together in play and shared formative experiences in church, school, or organized sports.

These formative relationships foster a closeness that becomes relevant when young men later become U.S. migrants, and the migratory experience itself strengthens the basic tie of friendship. A lifetime of shared experiences creates a disposition to exchange favors and provide mutual assistance that benefits both parties in the long run. Friends who find themselves sharing yet another formative experience—international migration—assist one another in a variety of ways: finding an apartment in the United States, sharing information about jobs, pooling resources, and borrowing or loaning money. Although initially concentrated among persons of the same age, friendships gradually extend to other generations, as migrants of all ages are drawn together by the common experience of life in a strange environment.

If migration becomes frequent among a group of friends from the same community, their relationships will eventually overlap with other circles of friends with whom they are brought into frequent contact. Important friendships are formed with migrants from other communities through shared experiences at work, at living (e.g., in grower-provided farm barracks), or at play (in cantinas, bars, dance halls, or other places of entertainment in the United States). In this way, interpersonal relationships within the migrant network are extended and amplified beyond those possible through kinship or local friendship alone. The bonds of kith and kin do not lose their meaning or importance; they are simply augmented by new and different relationships that expand the range of a migrant's social resources in the United States.

Among expatriates, regional allegiances within Mexico also favor the formation of friendships. Common origin from a particular region, such as southern Jalisco or the Zamora Valley, usually implies a series of common experiences, customs, and traditions that permit easy communication and friendship formation. Migrants from the same part of Mexico may even share common relatives or acquaintances or have attended the same fiestas and fairs. As one moves down the geographic hierarchy to more specific regional identities, however, one eventually arrives at another base of social organization that is very important in the migratory process: paisanaje.

Paisanaje

The feeling of belonging to a common community of origin, or paisanaje, is different from the other social relationships we have discussed in that it is a latent dimension of association in the home community. Origin from the same place is not a meaningful basis of social organization for people while they are at home. In general, within the community itself, the concept of paisanaje does not imply any *additional* rights and responsibilities to other paisanos that are not already included in the relationships of friend, family member, or neighbor. It is not a meaningful concept until two paisanos encounter each other outside their home community. Then the strength of the paisanaje tie depends on the strangeness of the environment and the nature of their prior relationships in the community.

Given the cultural distance between Mexico and the United States and the large number of Mexican migrants living and working abroad, it is not surprising that paisanaje has become an important social relationship in recent years. Common origin from Altamira, Chamitlán, or Santiago creates a strong communal identity among migrants in the United States. In an unknown, alien, and often threatening milieu, migrants share a variety of life experiences that draw them together in the pursuit of common goals. Although this sense of paisanaje naturally depends on the nature of migrants' past interactions (whether they were acquaintances, friends, or neighbors), relationships formed abroad have repercussions for social relations at home. They often produce new forms of association that not only promote the cohesion of migrants in the United States but also facilitate their reintegration into the community.

The best example of how paisanaje operates as an integrative force is the annual fiesta held in honor of each town's patron saint. The patron saint, of course, is the personification of paisanaje, the symbolic representation of the town for all its citizens. The celebration held each year to commemorate the patron saint is thus more than a religious holiday. It is a reaffirmation of the community and its people. As such, fiestas have always represented an important integrative mechanism in rural Mexican society (Redfield 1930; Beals 1946; Brand 1951; Lewis 1960; Cancian 1965; Foster 1967; Nutini 1968). With the advent of U.S. migration, however, the symbolic value of the patron saint has been shaped to the new reality of a migrant community, and the traditional importance of the fiesta has been greatly enhanced.

Throughout the months of work and loneliness in the United States, the fiesta of the patron saint looms large in the thoughts and conversations of migrants. It is one day of the year when all who are able to return home do so. Most work long and hard to earn enough money to return for the fiesta with presents for friends and family; in no small way, the fiesta sustains and encourages migrants through their long diaspora. Among the expatriates, it provides a symbolic focal point in their lives. Looking forward to it helps to maintain identity in an alien land. It reaffirms membership in a community where they are loved and respected, where others share their culture and language.

From the townspeople's view, the Saint's Day has become more important as a celebration of the return of *los ausentes* (the absent ones) than as a religious ceremony. They look forward to the fiesta with great anticipation, as a time when wives, children, and mothers are at last reunited with their husbands, fathers, and sons. Without the migrants' return there would not be much to celebrate, and some communities have even changed their fiesta dates to coincide with a period of return migration. A few towns have gone so far as to switch to a patron saint with a more conveniently located holiday.

The patron saint's fiesta provides a very practical framework within which to reunite families and friends. By sponsoring the periodic reunion of migrant and nonmigrant paisanos, it facilitates the reintegration of the former into the larger community and reaffirms their continuing place in its social life. It provides a very public demonstration of commitment to the migrants as true paisanos. In Altamira and Chamitlán, for example, migrants are actively incorporated into the fiesta regardless of whether they are physically present. In both communities, there is a special day assigned to los ausentes. On this date, migrants join together to pay the costs of music, church decorations, fireworks, and other diversions. Those who have been able to return participate in the processions and liturgical acts, and in his sermon the priest reaffirms the collective sentiment of unity, speaking of a single community and of a "great family" with a patron saint who looks over all.

Because of the presence of so many migrants who returned especially for the celebration, a party atmosphere prevails on the day of los ausentes. With so many reunions taking place and so much money being spent on music, floats, and other pageantries, the day seems more festive than others in the fiesta. It seems as if los ausentes were seeking to erase all doubts to themselves and others about their loyalty to the town and their strong identification with it. In el Norte, more than others, these ausentes experienced the meaning of the word "paisano" in its most profound sense.

A traditional cultural manifestation of paisanaje, the patron saint's fiesta, has thus become a very important social institution supporting migration. A more modern manifestation of paisanaje is the "ausente hour," broadcast each weekday at four o'clock in the afternoon on a Zamora radio station. It is run as a public service for the benefit of U.S. migrants and their families in the Zamora Valley. During the program, letters and messages sent from migrants in the United States are read on the air, and special song requests and dedications from migrants abroad are played for wives and sweethearts back home. Some migrants even telephone from Los Angeles with particular requests and messages. The ausente hour supplements the Saint's Day in providing an important symbol of the migrants' continuing membership in the community of paisanos.

Voluntary Organizations

Thus far we have considered various social relationships that make up the migrant networks, but no less important are certain institutional mechanisms that facilitate the formation and maintenance of social ties. A variety of voluntary associations established by migrants in the United States promote regular interpersonal contact, greatly facilitating the process of adaptation and mutual assistance. Although migrants belong to many organizations, probably the most important is the soccer club. It has risen to support international migration in many communities of western Mexico, including Altamira and Chamitlán, but nowhere is it more important than in Santiago.

Most migrants from Santiago go to Los Angeles. In such a large and sprawling city, it is not easy to maintain regular contact with other paisanos. Migrants from Santiago have resolved this problem through their soccer club. People from Santiago originally learned how to play soccer from British technicians at the turn of the century, and this early exposure to the sport soon became a passion. During the early days of U.S. migration, townspeople in Los Angeles began to meet informally and sporadically to play soccer. As interest and attendance grew, the game became a regular weekly event and a club was formed with an affiliation in a local soccer league. Practice is now held once each week, when many paisanos drop by to watch, and a weekly game is played each Sunday before a large and enthusiastic crowd.

A viable soccer club must be able to count on the regular participation of at least twenty-five persons: a dozen players plus a few substitutes, trainers, and coaches. A really good soccer club requires the support of many more fans and supporters, however. Above all, these people provide the financial resources to pay the fees, reserve the playing fields, and purchase the uniforms and the soccer balls. Although the club always had the support of a good number of townspeople, its success on the field caused its popularity to grow so that nearly all out-migrant paisanos became involved. For five consecutive years, the team from Santiago won its league championship in California.

Santiago's club is a social institution to which all out-migrant

paisanos belong as a right, and others may also join if they want to
share in the fun, especially if they happen to be good players. The club
is for all; it does not belong to a particular manager or owner. Decisions
are typically made in assemblies with most members present. The club
represents the home community, and all recognize this as its fundamental end.

The social functions of the club were greatly boosted when it secured
the use of a practice field on which to train, part of a public park in the
Los Angeles area. There, people from Santiago began to meet every
Sunday, bringing their families for free diversion and entertainment.
The field, nicknamed "Los Patos" ("The Ducks") by the townspeople,[2]
became an obligatory place of reunion for all paisanos. It became the
focal point of the out-migrant community, the place where one made
dates, obtained work, located friends, welcomed new arrivals, and ex-
changed news of the town itself. Little by little the field, which had
previously been used by Anglos, became a Latino world. Eventually,
migrants from Santiago began to buy houses close to the field of Los
Patos, and the adjacent barrio became more and more a Hispanic
enclave.

The club has served for many years as a focal point of life for
townspeople in Los Angeles and as a tie to the home community.
Frequently, teams from Santiago have journeyed to the United States
to play those from Los Angeles. The club has also initiated many migrant
careers, especially those of the best soccer players. Coaches in Los
Angeles keep track of promising players at home through the migrant
network and, when the time is right, invite them to come and play in
el Norte. The team pays for transportation, supplies a coyote and ar-
ranges for housing and work. If the player is good enough, his only
obligation is to play for the team.

The case of Santiago is not unique. In some years migrants from
Altamira and Chamitlán have also formed soccer teams to participate in
one of the many leagues in Los Angeles. Sunday after Sunday, the
players meet in the company of other townspeople to play or watch
soccer and to socialize. This reunion breaks up the routine of work and
isolation and provides a forum for communication and interchange.
Migrants share experiences of the past week, discuss events of general
interest in the town or in other places where paisanos go in the United
States, and exchange information about job opportunities. Everyone

---

[2] The park has a small pond on which live a number of ducks. Townspeople soon
began calling the park "El Parque de los Patos" ("Park of the Ducks"), which eventually
was shortened to "Los Patos."

enjoys the conviviality, and they all share expenses for refreshments and foods.

These encounters offer the opportunity to form friendships with people from other places in Mexico who also frequent the athletic fields. On some occasions, when there is a scarcity of players from Santiago, these people join the team and share in the party mood that prevails after each game. Like migrants from Santiago itself, they are also able to take advantage of the information and offers of assistance that spring from these reunions. The parts of the migrant networks that are based on kinship, friendship, or paisanaje thus are broadened and expanded by the soccer clubs. Through the weekly games, migrants from Santiago come into contact with migrants from other social circles and, hence, with new sources of information and exchange.

Through a variety of devices, soccer is also important in promoting the reintegration of migrants into the community. For example, in Santiago a great sporting event is held each year in which the soccer teams from Los Angeles are invited to participate. Young men who return to town after a period of absence typically reenter social life by joining a local soccer team. First they participate in practice, and later they compete in the official matches with teams from other towns. On occasion, men with U.S. migrant experience—some of whom are active members of the clubs in Los Angeles—are actively sought out as team members for a match with a neighboring town. These contacts bring migrants into close contact with numerous nonmigrants, greatly expanding the radius of the migrant network.

In short, the soccer club is an important part of the network linking the town and its daughter communities. It facilitates the movement of migrants back and forth, supports their integration in a foreign land, and later promotes their reincorporation into the home community. Different voluntary organizations may serve the functions of migrant cohesion and integration in other communities. Whatever their purpose, voluntary associations add an important dimension to migrant networks above and beyond the interpersonal ties mentioned before.

DEVELOPMENT OF THE NETWORKS

We have shown how basic human relationships have been adapted to play new roles in the migration process. The familiar relationships of kinship, friendship, and paisanaje are woven into a social fabric that provides migrants with a valuable adaptive resource in a strange environment. Through networks of interpersonal relationships, people, goods, and information circulate to create a social continuum between communities in Mexico and the United States. The networks provide jobs, food, housing, transport, and social life to migrants abroad, and they have made international migration a basic fact of social and economic life in western Mexico.

Such extensive social networks are not created overnight. They emerge gradually as migration moves beyond a few adventurous individuals to involve a wider cross section of the community. The first few migrants return and on subsequent trips initiate others into the migrant process. Every new migrant creates a new set of people with potential connections to the United States. As more people migrate more often, the number of connections expands rapidly and the quality of the ties also improves as people adjust to life abroad. Eventually a few families or individuals settle in the United States, and very strong, direct links are established to particular locales. As the quantity and quality of network connections grow, the cost of migration is progressively reduced, encouraging others to try their luck. As more people take up migration, the number of people with network connections increases. Ultimately, the network expands until nearly everyone has a direct connection to someone with U.S. migrant experience.

The progressive development and elaboration of networks emanating from each of the four communities is clearly revealed in the ethnosurvey data. Table 6.1 examines the number of family members and paisanos that migrants reported knowing in the United States on their most recent trip. In order to show the development of the network over time, the data are broken into three periods based on the date of the trip: pre-1940, 1940 to 1964, and 1965 to the present. As the networks mature over time, we expect migrants to report a growing number of family and kinship ties in the United States.

Such a pattern is, indeed, found in each community. The earliest migrants had few social ties to draw upon in traveling to the United States, whereas recent migrants have at their disposal a large number of kin and friendship connections. The trends are best exemplified in Santiago, where the average number of family members in the United States increases from sixteen people among those whose most recent trip was before 1940 to twenty-six people among those whose last trip was after 1965. The number of paisanos that townspeople reported knowing similarly increases from about six before 1940 to eighteen in the most recent period. Similar trends are found in Altamira. In Chamitlán, however, migrants reported knowing an unusually large number of paisanos in the United States before 1940. This number indicates the early importance of its Chicago networks, which were eliminated by the

TABLE 6.1
AVERAGE NUMBER OF RELATIVES AND PAISANOS IN THE UNITED STATES ON THE
MOST RECENT U.S. TRIP BY PERIOD: MIGRANTS FROM FOUR MEXICAN COMMUNITIES

Community and number	Period			
	Pre–1940	1940–1964	1965–1982	Total
Altamira				
Mean number of relatives	5.0	7.1	7.7	7.4
Mean number of paisanos	4.7	12.2	12.0	11.8
Number	3	37	88	128
Chamitlán				
Mean number of relatives	14.7	13.5	21.9	19.7
Mean number of paisanos	55.0	27.3	35.6	33.8
Number	3	38	120	161
Santiago				
Mean number of relatives	15.7	33.1	26.0	26.9
Mean number of paisanos	6.3	10.1	18.0	15.2
Number	8	24	80	112
San Marcos				
Mean number of relatives	—	5.3	4.5	4.8
Mean number of paisanos	—	3.6	22.6	15.4
Number	0	13	26	39

Source: MIGFILE; migrant household members enumerated in Mexico or California, including those in twenty-five extra households in Santiago.

Great Depression. As new networks were rebuilt after 1940, the number of paisanos falls and then increases. The data for San Marcos are difficult to interpret because the networks are not based there and because no migrants reported making their last trip before 1940. Nonetheless, the average number of paisanos increases considerably between the two most recent periods.

A more sensitive indicator of family connections within the networks is the percentage of migrants who report having a U.S. migrant parent or grandparent, which is classified by period in table 6.2. The earliest migrants, of course, were the pioneers who had no prior family ties in el Norte. Among those migrating before 1940, none reported having migrant parents or grandparents, except in Santiago, where 14 percent had a migrant parent. Over time, migrant experience accumulates in the population, so that subsequent migrants are able to draw upon parents' and grandparents' knowledge and connections in migrating to the United States. In the most recent period, the percentage having parents with U.S. migrant experience rises to 37 percent in Altamira, 62 percent in Chamitlán (where the migrant networks are most developed), 26

TABLE 6.2
PERCENTAGE HAVING PARENTS AND GRANDPARENTS WITH U.S. MIGRANT
EXPERIENCE BY PERIOD: MIGRANTS FROM FOUR MEXICAN COMMUNITIES

Community and relative	Period			
	Pre–1940	1940–1964	1965–1982	Total
Altamira				
With migrant parent (%)	0.0	20.0	37.1	30.0
With migrant grandparent (%)	0.0	0.0	4.8	3.0
Number	3	35	62	100
Chamitlán				
With migrant parent (%)	0.0	31.4	62.0	53.4˙
With migrant grandparent (%)	0.0	8.6	14.8	13.0
Number	3	35	108	146
Santiago				
With migrant parent (%)	14.3	8.7	25.8	20.8
With migrant grandparent (%)	0.0	4.4	6.1	5.2
Number	7	23	66	96
San Marcos				
With migrant parent (%)	—	23.1	33.3	29.4
With migrant grandparent (%)	—	0.0	10.0	6.1
Number	0	13	21	34

Source: MIGFILE; migrant household members enumerated in Mexico or California, including those in twenty-five extra households in Santiago.

percent in Santiago, and 33 percent in San Marcos. Similarly, the percentage having grandparents with migrant experience rises from 0 percent before 1940 to between 5 percent and 15 percent after 1965.

Family and friendship connections build up among migrants with time, therefore, providing new aspirants with a kind of "social capital" they can draw upon to begin a migrant career. The importance of kinship, friendship, and paisanaje in the migratory process is indicated in table 6.3, which shows how migrants obtained their most recent jobs in the United States. In Santiago and San Marcos, 46 percent of migrants said they got their last job through a friend, relative, or paisano. The respective figures for Altamira and Chamitlán were 39 percent and 29 percent. In the two rural towns, labor contractors play a more important role, holding 21 percent and 17 percent of jobs, respectively. Only in Chamitlán did a majority of migrants report obtaining their last job through their own efforts. Interpersonal ties are thus very important to migrants entering the U.S. labor market.

The importance of social connections is further highlighted by table 6.4, which shows where migrants turned for financial assistance when

TABLE 6.3
How U.S. Jobs Were Obtained by Migrants from Four Mexican Communities

How job was obtained	Community			
	Altamira	Chamitlán	Santiago	San Marcos
Migrant looked for it (%)	36.8	53.7	42.8	40.0
Through a friend, relative, or paisano (%)	39.1	29.4	45.6	46.8
Through a labor contractor (%)	20.7	16.9	9.4	12.9
Through a coyote (%)[a]	2.1	0.0	1.1	0.0
Other (%)	1.3	0.0	1.1	1.3
Number of U.S. jobs	386	354	276	77

Source: LIFEFILE; migrant household members enumerated in Mexico or California, including those in twenty-five extra households in Santiago.

[a] A coyote guides undocumented migrants across the border between Mexico and the United States.

TABLE 6.4
Where Migrants Sought Financial Assistance on Most
Recent U.S. Trip: Migrants from Four Mexican Communities

Where migrant sought money	Community			
	Altamira	Chamitlán	Santiago	San Marcos
Friend (%)	50.0	75.8	32.1	20.0
Relative (%)	25.0	6.1	17.9	40.0
Other paisano (%)	3.1	3.0	0.0	30.0
Employer (%)	3.1	12.1	3.6	0.0
Bank (%)	12.5	3.0	25.0	0.0
Other (%)	6.3	0.0	21.4	10.0
Number needing money	32	33	28	10

Source: MIGFILE; migrant household members enumerated in Mexico or California, including those in twenty-five extra households in Santiago.

last in the United States. The vast majority reported asking a friend or a relative for financial assistance. In Altamira, 50 percent said they turned to a friend and 25 percent to a relative. The respective figures in Chamitlán were 76 percent and 6 percent; in Santiago, 32 percent and

18 percent; and in San Marcos, 20 percent and 40 percent. In short, family and friends are an invaluable socioeconomic resource for U.S. migrants.

Finally, as migrant networks grow and mature, we expect a gradual increase in the number of townspeople who belong to various U.S.-based organizations. As table 6.5 shows, membership in voluntary associations does increase over time in each community except San Marcos. Moreover, the pattern is sharpest for the organization that is most important in facilitating network migration: the soccer club. In Santiago, the percentage of migrants reporting membership in an athletic club grows from 0 percent among those making their last trips before 1940 to 53 percent among those leaving after 1965. The increase is from 0 percent to 21 percent in Altamira and from 0 percent to 13 percent in Chamitlán.

These data demonstrate quantitatively what we previously argued from an ethnographic view: that recent migrants have at their disposal

TABLE 6.5

PERCENTAGE OF MIGRANTS BELONGING TO SELECTED VOLUNTARY ORGANIZATIONS ON MOST RECENT TRIP, BY PERIOD: MIGRANTS FROM FOUR MEXICAN COMMUNITIES

Community and organization	Period			
	Pre–1940	1940–1964	1965–1982	Total
Altamira				
In social club (%)	0.0	5.4	3.6	4.1
In religious club (%)	0.0	2.7	1.2	1.6
In sports club (%)	0.0	5.4	20.5	15.5
Number	3	37	88	128
Chamitlán				
In social club (%)	0.0	2.9	7.8	6.5
In religious club (%)	0.0	8.6	7.8	7.8
In sports club (%)	0.0	2.9	12.9	10.5
Number	3	38	120	161
Santiago				
In social club (%)	0.0	4.2	5.0	4.5
In religious club (%)	0.0	8.3	7.5	7.1
In sports club (%)	0.0	8.3	52.5	39.3
Number	8	24	80	112
San Marcos				
In social club (%)	—	0.0	0.0	0.0
In religious club (%)	—	0.0	0.0	0.0
In sports club (%)	—	0.0	4.0	2.7
Number	0	13	26	39

Source: MIGFILE; migrant household members enumerated in Mexico or California, including those in twenty-five extra households in Santiago.

a wider array of social connections in the United States than do those who left earlier. Compared to the earliest pioneers, recent migrants have many more relatives, friends, and paisanos to whom they can turn for information and assistance while abroad. Moreover, these ties function with greater effectiveness than before, as soccer clubs have evolved to provide a dependable weekly forum for communication and interchange between people in the network.

FORMATION OF DAUGHTER COMMUNITIES

In each of the three towns we have studied, the emergence of established communities in the United States was a crucial step in the maturation of the migrant networks. The settlement of a few families transformed the migration process by directing the streams to work sites in particular U.S. towns and cities. Around these families a socioeconomic organization grew, drawing subsequent migrants in ever increasing numbers to specific points of destination, a process Jones (1982b) has labeled "channelization."

The channeling of migrants occurs as social networks focus increasingly on specific communities. As daughter settlements of Mexican outmigrants develop, the social infrastructure linking them to the parent communities becomes more directed and reified and the network becomes self-perpetuating. More migrants move to a particular place because that is where the networks lead, and because that is where the social structure affords them the greatest opportunities for success. As more migrants arrive, the range of social connections is further extended, making subsequent migration to that place even more likely.

This channeling of migrants is clearly evident in the ethnosurvey data that we collected. Figures 6.1 through 6.3 depict the state of destination among U.S. migrants leaving Altamira, Chamitlán, and Santiago on their first U.S. trip from 1900 through 1982. In each case, the earlier periods display far more diversity in destinations than in later periods, by which time 90 percent to 100 percent of all migrants are traveling to California. Before 1940 the percentages of migrants going to this state were only 60 percent in Altamira, 40 percent in Chamitlán, and 38 percent in Santiago. Other prominent states in early periods of migration were Texas, Illinois, and Arizona. During the 1940s and 1950s, however, migration rapidly shifted away from these states and became directed almost exclusively to California. At present, driving through western Mexico during the months of December and January, one notices the large number of cars having California license plates.

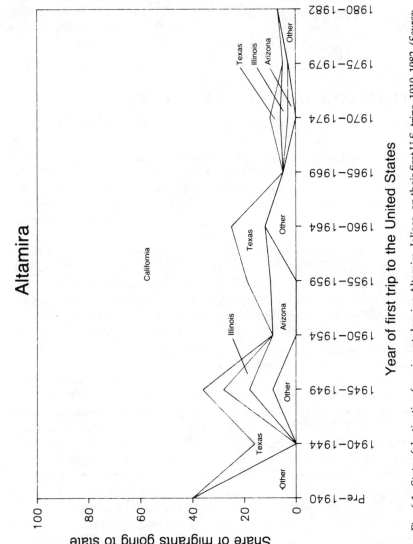

Fig. 6.1. State of destination for migrants leaving Altamira, Jalisco, on their first U.S. trips, 1910–1982. (*Source:* PERSFILE; all migrants from Altamira enumerated in Mexico or California.)

Chamitlán

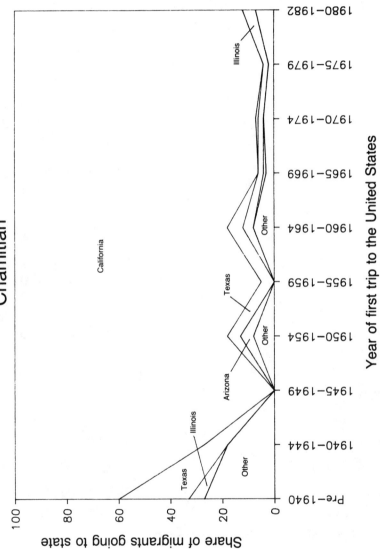

Fig. 6.2. State of destination for migrants leaving Chamitlán, Michoacán on their first U.S. trips, 1910–1982. (*Source:* PERSFILE; all migrants from Chamitlán enumerated in Mexico or California.)

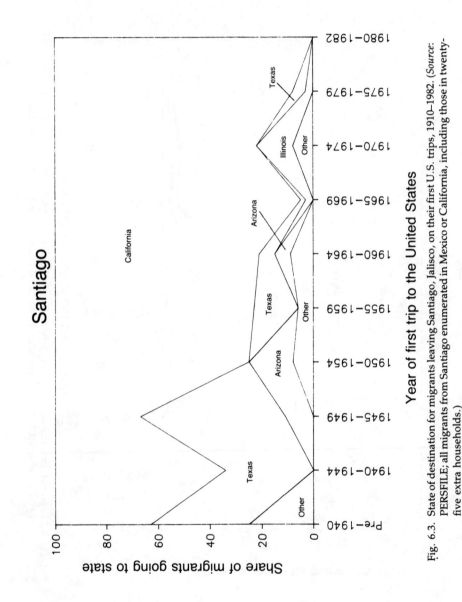

Fig. 6.3. State of destination for migrants leaving Santiago, Jalisco, on their first U.S. trips, 1910–1982. (*Source:* PERSFILE; all migrants from Santiago enumerated in Mexico or California, including those in twenty-five extra households.)

These state statistics show the increasing specificity of the migrant networks over time, but only at a gross level. A better indication of the channeling process can be obtained by examining trends over time in more specific points of destination. Figures 6.4 through 6.6 examine the share of migrants going to different areas in California on their first U.S. trips from 1900 through 1982. Specific place names could have been used to illustrate the increasing specificity of out-migration. To protect the anonymity of respondents, we classified particular towns and cities into broader geographic areas; however, underlying these broad groupings are specific communities within California.

Points of destination for migrants from Altamira fluctuated considerably up through the 1950s. The very earliest migrants to California went largely to the San Francisco Bay area, but this early network was effaced during the Great Depression. With the advent of the Bracero program in the early 1940s, the Imperial Valley became the predominant destination. The connection with this agricultural area can be traced to the large bracero recruitment center at the border-crossing of Calexico-Mexicali, just south of the Imperial Valley, which was one of the first bracero centers established. The importance of the Imperial Valley declined steadily over the years, finally dying out when the Bracero Accord expired in 1964. During the late 1940s and early 1950s, two new locations began to emerge as important poles of attraction for migrants from Altamira: a city in the middle San Joaquin Valley and the Los Angeles urban area. These areas declined in importance during 1955–1959 and the diversity of destinations increased somewhat, as indicated by the rise in the "Other" category.

After 1960, however, the range of U.S. destinations steadily dwindled as Los Angeles and the middle San Joaquin Valley emerged as the two predominant destination areas. Los Angeles predominated during the late 1960s and early 1970s, peaking during 1965–1969, when 68 percent of new migrants left for that urban area. In the late 1970s and early 1980s, the middle San Joaquin Valley increasingly came to the fore, capturing 58 percent of all new migrants after 1980. In each period since 1960, therefore, 50 percent to 80 percent of all migrants from Altamira have gone to one of these two U.S. destination areas.

Specific points of destination emerged earlier and in greater number among migrants from Chamitlán. Since the 1940s, four destination areas have consistently received a significant share of the town's migrants: the middle San Joaquin Valley (but a different community than that of Altamira), the San Francisco Bay area, the Los Angeles metropolitan area, and the Salinas Valley. The array of receiving areas remained quite

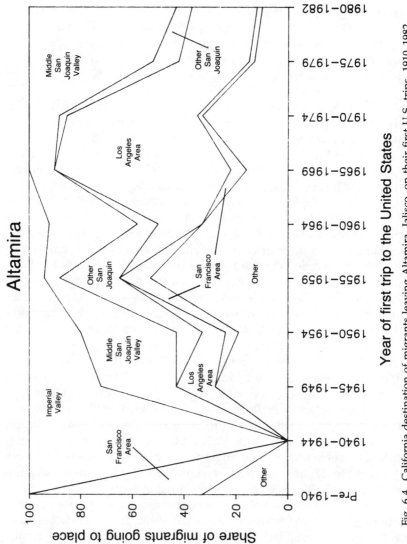

Fig. 6.4. California destination of migrants leaving Altamira, Jalisco, on their first U.S. trips, 1910–1982. (*Source:* PERSFILE; all migrants from Altamira interviewed in Mexico or California.)

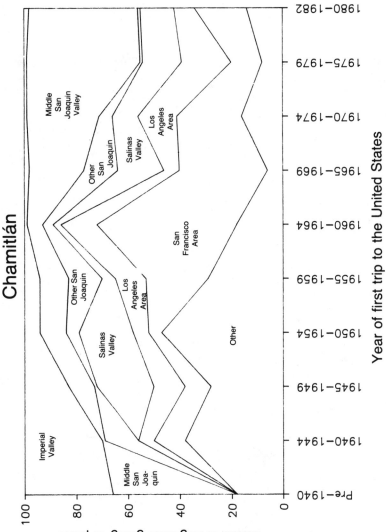

Chamitlán

Share of migrants going to place

(y-axis: 0, 20, 40, 60, 80, 100)

Year of first trip to the United States

(x-axis: Pre-1940, 1940–1944, 1945–1949, 1950–1954, 1955–1959, 1960–1964, 1965–1969, 1970–1974, 1975–1979, 1980–1982)

Labels: Imperial Valley, Middle San Joaquin, Other San Joaquin, Salinas Valley, Los Angeles Area, San Francisco Area, Other, Middle San Joaquin Valley, Other San Joaquin, Salinas Valley, Los Angeles Area

Fig. 6.5. California destination of migrants leaving Chamitlán, Michoacán, on their first U.S. trips, 1910–1982. (*Source:* PERSFILE; all migrants from Chamitlán interviewed in Mexico or California.)

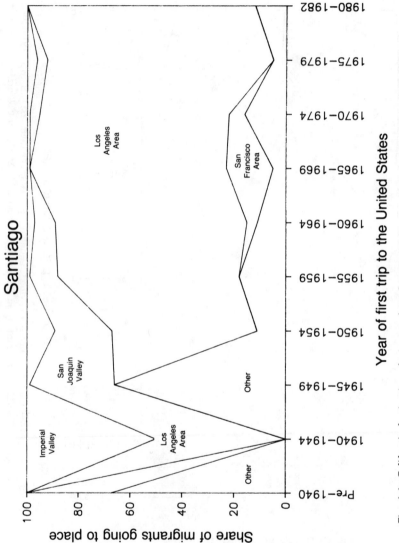

Fig. 6.6. California destination of migrants from Santiago, Jalisco, on their first U.S. trips, 1910–1982. (*Source:* PERSFILE; all migrants from Santiago interviewed in Mexico or California, including those in twenty-five extra households.)

diverse, until 1960, as indicated by the relatively large percentage in the "Other" category.

Los Angeles and the Salinas Valley have remained important poles of attraction for Chamitlán up to the present; however, the two other communities eventually came to dominate the outflow of migrants. Between 1955 and 1975, the San Francisco Bay area was the primary destination area. At its peak during 1960 to 1964, 55 percent of the migrants leaving Chamitlán were going there. Since 1970, a town in the middle San Joaquin Valley has increasingly come to predominate. These two destination points have accounted for at least 55 percent of all out-migrants in each period since 1960.

Santiago displays the simplest trend in out-migration of the three sending communities. During the 1940s, the Bracero program recruited townspeople into agricultural areas such as the Imperial and the San Joaquin Valleys, but since 1950 Los Angeles has become the favorite destination of new U.S. migrants. By the most recent period, roughly 90 percent of all migrants were going to work somewhere in the Los Angeles urban area.

In each case, therefore, specific daughter communities ultimately developed around a core of settled migrant families. Settlement is an intrinsic part of the migration process, occurring as migrants build up significant amounts of time abroad. As people turn away from their former economic pursuits at home and specialize increasingly in U.S. wage labor, a life of seasonal commuting back and forth is difficult to sustain. At the same time, migrants become enmeshed in a web of social and economic ties in the United States that bind them increasingly to specific locations and employers, and settlement eventually occurs. The migrant brings his wife and children to live with him in el Norte, and a permanent residence is established.

These social processes take time to operate, so the daughter communities develop slowly at first, and then more rapidly as a critical mass of out-migrants anchors the networks more firmly to stable settlements, which then serve as magnets for further migration. This fact is illustrated by table 6.6, which classifies household heads in the California sample and all "settlers" from the Mexican sample by the date of their last trip to the United States (on which they presumably "settled"). "Settlers" are those with three continuous years of residence in the United States. In each community, the vast majority of these long-term U.S. residents settled after 1965. Regardless of whether one considers the settlers or the California household heads, 70 percent to 95 percent reported leaving after this date. In contrast, very small percentages (under 5 percent)

TABLE 6.6
DATE OF LAST TRIP FOR SETTLED MIGRANTS AND CALIFORNIA
HOUSEHOLD HEADS: MIGRANTS FROM THREE MEXICAN COMMUNITIES

Date of last U.S. trip	Altamira		Chamitlán		Santiago	
	U.S. settlers	Calif. heads	U.S. settlers	Calif. heads	U.S. settlers	Calif. heads
Pre–1940 (%)	1.4	0.0	1.0	0.0	4.8	0.0
1940–1964 (%)	20.3	25.0	14.3	10.0	25.3	5.0
1965–1982 (%)	78.4	75.0	84.7	90.0	69.9	95.0
Number	74	20	203	20	83	20

Source: PERSFILE; all migrants enumerated in Mexico or California, including those in twenty-five extra households in Santiago.

made the transition to settled U.S. life before 1940. Settlement thus begins at a slow pace and accelerates over time.

The emergence of daughter communities qualitatively changes the nature of the migration process. The permanent social infrastructure that they provide makes a strategy of recurrent migration—the repeated movement of migrants back and forth—viable on a mass basis. It also permits the widespread use of settled migration as a strategy, where young men may work in the United States for long periods—three, four, or five years—before returning home. Given the extensive links between the parent and daughter communities and the dynamic, fluid nature of the networks, recurrent or settled migrants may spend considerable time abroad without rupturing their ties to the home community.

The emergence of daughter communities also produces a qualitative change in the concept of paisanaje. With the emergence of U.S. settlements, men begin to acquire American-born wives and father a generation of sons and daughters born in the United States. The ideal of paisanaje must, therefore, be expanded to incorporate a class of people not born in the home community. Table 6.7 cross-classifies respondents in the California sample by U.S. legal status and position in the household. There are, of course, no native U.S. citizens among household heads. In U.S. agricultural zones, nearly 50 percent are documented and 50 percent undocumented, compared to 63 percent documented and 34 percent undocumented in metropolitan areas. A surprisingly high number of men have wives who are U.S. citizens: 42 percent in the agricultural zones and 10 percent in the metropolitan areas. The percentages of wives with and without documents are equal in each set of areas:

TABLE 6.7
LEGAL STATUS BY POSITION WITHIN HOUSEHOLD AND METROPOLITAN STATUS:
MEMBERS OF CALIFORNIA SAMPLE HOUSEHOLDS

Metropolitan and legal status	Position in household		
	Household head	Spouse	Child
Agricultural areas[a]			
Native U.S. citizen (%)	0.0	42.1	79.7
Legal resident (%)	48.0	26.3	6.8
Undocumented (%)	48.0	26.3	13.6
Unknown (%)	4.0	5.3	0.0
Number	25	19	59
Metropolitan areas[b]			
Native U.S. citizen (%)	0.0	10.0	65.6
Legal resident (%)	62.9	40.0	4.4
Undocumented (%)	34.3	40.0	21.4
Unknown (%)	2.9	10.0	8.9
Number	35	30	90

Source: PERSFILE; all migrants enumerated in Mexico or California, including those in twenty-five extra households in Santiago.

[a] Agricultural = places in agricultural regions of California.

[b] Metropolitan = places in San Francisco or Los Angeles urban area.

about 26 percent in agricultural areas and 40 percent in metropolitan areas. A telling indicator of the degree to which these families have become rooted in their new soil is indicated by the large proportion of children born in the United States; 80 percent of children in agricultural areas and 66 percent of those in metropolitan areas were born in California.

By 1983, therefore, the core of settled out-migrant families had developed connections to the United States not easily erased. They had begun to raise a generation of children with strong attachments on both sides of the border—born in the United States and raised in its schools and neighborhoods, but with strong ties to Mexico and the parent community, constantly reinforced through the circulation of people and information from home. These attachments inevitably extend to the parents, giving them a greater stake in U.S. society, drawing even those without legal documents ever more deeply into U.S. society. For example, roughly two-thirds of undocumented household heads in the California sample have children born in the United States. The deep roots that these daughter communities now have in the United States suggest that the networks they support are also permanent social fixtures and will continue to sustain migration to the United States for years to come.

CASE STUDIES OF NETWORK MIGRATION

The foregoing discussion has established the fundamental elements of the migration process as it has unfolded in three communities over the past five decades: the gradual emergence of a social structure based on the ties of kinship, friendship, and paisanaje; the concomitant development of social institutions supporting migration; the eventual appearance of a core of settled families about which an out-migrant community coheres; the channeling of migrants to these daughter communities; and the deepening of ties within the United States. All of these developments reflect the operation of international migration as an emergent social process.

Thus far, we have sketched the process of migration at a general level and illustrated it with examples and ethnosurvey data. These abstract processes are ultimately based on real-life experiences of actual communities; therefore, we present four case studies drawn from the historic experience of Altamira, Chamitlán, Santiago, and San Marcos. Through these case studies, the manifold processes we have described are exemplified and made real.

Altamira

In the mid-1970s, a small city in the middle San Joaquin Valley extended its zone of fruit cultivation by applying new intensive methods that provided higher profits for local growers. As cultivation increased and output expanded, the need for seasonal labor grew with it, since the work of harvesting and maintaining orchards could be done only by hand. Through prior contacts in the area, several workers from Altamira heard of the new opportunities and began to migrate there to take advantage of the strong seasonal demand for farmworkers. One of these migrants met and fell in love with a U.S. citizen, a daughter of Mexican parents, whom he eventually married. Through this marriage he was able to arrange his papers without difficulty, and he settled down to raise a family in the city.

Because of his knowledge of the agricultural scene in the middle San Joaquin Valley, his growing command of English, and his legal status in the United States, this worker was soon chosen by his employer, a large agricultural company, to be a field foreman. As such, he was the boss of a work crew that he had to recruit and supervise. To secure workers for his crew, he turned to his fellow townspeople and to other Mexicans whom he knew in the United States. Over the years, he recruited many relatives and acquaintances from Altamira, building up an assured pool of migrant workers who always enabled him to put together his crew without problems.

The pay of the foreman depended on the quantity and quality of his team's work. His preference for paisanos stemmed not only from his affective ties with friends and former neighbors but also from the greater control he was able to exercise through the ties of kinship, friendship, and paisanaje. Drawing upon these bonds, he could elicit greater speed and quality from his workers without having to resort to coercive methods such as threatening or firing. In this way, a communality of interests between the foreman and workers was established, one that primarily benefited the company for whom they all worked.

In a short time, this place became the principal point of arrival for people from Altamira seeking work in the United States. When more paisanos arrived than the foreman could use for this team (about thirty-five persons), he placed them with other foremen he knew, and in this way the opportunities for migrants from Altamira expanded. Today there are two foremen from Altamira, and nine families have settled in the city permanently. Together they form a nucleus of people who support the growing social network by maintaining steady contact with seasonal migrants from Altamira.

Chamitlán

In Chamitlán, two networks have come to dominate the migration process. The first leads to a small city in the middle San Joaquin Valley. In the early 1960s, a campesino from Chamitlán who had worked regularly as a bracero went with several other paisanos to work in one of the agricultural fields near this city. After a few years of working as a common laborer, this person was chosen as a foreman on the condition that he gather together a group of workers and take charge of supervising them. The owners arranged legal documentation for him and his family, and they all settled in town.

With time, other families from Chamitlán began to settle in the city and the surrounding area, attracted by the employment that this paisano could offer. Today this city has become the most important center of U.S. employment for people from Chamitlán. In addition to several settled families, there are many temporary migrants, who appear year after year to perform the necessary seasonal agricultural tasks, usually working for the same employer or labor contractor.

Chamitlán's second network leads to the eastern shore of San Francisco Bay, where one finds the cities of Richmond, Berkeley, and Oakland. Within this area, there is a restaurant that employs many migrants from Chamitlán. Employment in this restaurant was not the original reason for the congregation of people from Chamitlán in the San Francisco Bay area; nonetheless, it has been very important in making the region an important magnet for out-migration from that Mexican community.

In the early 1970s, a campesino from Chamitlán who had worked as a bracero for many years took a job in this restaurant as helper to the headwaiter. After a few years, this person himself became headwaiter, and the restaurant owner helped him arrange resident visas for himself and his family, who moved to the San Francisco Bay area to live with him. His position as headwaiter gave him the chance to offer work to friends, relatives, and paisanos from Chamitlán. As word of his position in the United States spread within the home community, townspeople began to appeal to him in large numbers, and he became a man of some importance, a key contact for people seeking to enter the United States.

Over the past decade this restaurant has served as the principal point of entry for a large number of townspeople. Of the 250 workers who now work the restaurant's three shifts, around 100 are from Chamitlán. They are employed as dishwashers, cooks' helpers, cooks, meat cutters, and janitors. Migrants use the restaurant as a launching pad for their new lives in the United States. Few stay at the restaurant permanently. After working for a time in the restaurant, adjusting to life in the United States, and acquiring work experience, most move on to other better-paying jobs available in nearby steel mills, hotels, or other restaurants. This single person, therefore, has been the principal conduit for most migrants from Chamitlán to the San Francisco Bay area.

Santiago

In Santiago, the migratory process really began with the modernization of the textile factory in 1954. Before this time, there were only sporadic cases of international migration, especially among the town's factory workers. The early contacts of these few solitary migrants were sufficient to provide the key links that enabled the later development of migrant networks. Moreover, there was also an extensive web of migrant contacts based in neighboring Ixtlán, which early on had become involved in the migrant process. From these two bases of support, migrants from Santiago constructed an intricate system of social relationships linking the town with specific U.S. destination points.

In spite of its industrial origins, Santiago is notable in having evolved social networks very similar to those in the two rural towns. Townspeople began to migrate in large numbers during the mid-1950s at the height of the Bracero period, and many obtained their first

jobs as farmworkers through this program. Ironically, the development of the networks was greatly spurred by the crackdown on undocumented migration in 1954, when millions were deported during
Operation Wetback. The hostility of the sociopolitical environment in
the United States brought the migrants together for their mutual protection and made network connections even more valuable as socioeconomic resources.

From the start, however, migrants from Santiago preferred industrial over agricultural labor, and although many initially entered the
United States as farmworkers, the migrant outflow was eventually directed to urban work in Los Angeles. Arriving in that city, townspeople
first looked for textile factories but, finding none, took whatever jobs
they could get. Little by little they were able to improve themselves,
and one migrant eventually discovered a factory that made wire nets
and screens, where he went to try his luck.

The result was surprising. In a few days he had learned to use all
the machinery in the factory, which was very similar to that in Santiago's
textile mill, and in a few more days he had learned to control and work
the raw materials. In subsequent years, many townspeople were recruited for work in this factory, finding jobs at first through this person,
and later through many other townspeople who worked there. The
prior factory experience of people from Santiago rendered them immediately qualified to be skilled workers, and the company was very
satisfied with their work. This factory became the point of entry for
many migrants in Los Angeles.

Another factory that served to initiate workers to the Los Angeles
economy, and continues to do so today, is the lamp factory. As in the
screen factory, one migrant worker from Santiago found a hearty wel-
come there because of his prior industrial training. Through the factory
owner, he was able to obtain his residence documents, and since he had
prior union experience, his fellow workers elected him as their union
representative. Through this position, he was able to arrange work in
the factory for many townspeople. Over the years, a true colony grew
up around the lamp factory, and almost all townspeople passed through
it, especially during their first few months in the United States. Because
the work is very difficult and not well paid, employment there serves
as a springboard to better-paid and lighter work elsewhere.

In recent years, later generations of migrants have been employed
in a variety of industries: metalworking, furniture making, automobile
parts manufacturing, and food processing. In each case a similar process
was repeated, with one person finding a job and then inviting other
paisanos to come and work in the same firm. With time, a few became

foremen and gave preference to family members, friends, and towns-people. Currently, a few migrants from Santiago have even founded their own businesses in Los Angeles and have turned to fellow towns-people for employees.

San Marcos

The mechanisms that migrants employ in moving from Guadalajara to the United States are the same as those from rural areas. The difference is that the city in general, and the barrio of San Marcos in particular, do not generate their own social networks. Rather, migrants from the city use the long-established networks of their home communities, which have demonstrated efficacy. People from San Marcos migrate through contacts based in the town of their family's origin. Those not of cam-pesino origin typically do not have access to a set of relationships sufficiently broad to enable them to migrate. Rather, they try to integrate themselves into existing networks, in which one of their neighbors is likely to participate.

The most effective network connections combine the bonds of kin-ship and paisanaje. Urban barrios do not have the same intense kind of community identification as towns, however. In an urban barrio, one generally knows one's neighbors but does not have contact with all the families that live there. In towns it is possible to know most resi-dents, or at least to know of them. Moreover, the relationships of paisanaje are reinforced by kinship. Even if a paisano is not known directly, he can instantly be identified by his kin relationship to someone who is known. Friendly ties between urban neighbors may serve as a basis for the exchange of services and occasionally to support migrants, but they are not strong enough to sustain a whole network. In Los Angeles there are thousands of migrants from Guadalajara, but they do not form a group and are not integrated into any kind of association, as is the case for towns.

Neighbor status in a city implies weaker social solidarity than does paisanaje; however, it can sometimes be used for entry into existing smaller town-based networks. A person from Guadalajara may be able to "tag along" with a neighbor as he plies the network emanating from his, or his father's, community of origin. Over time, urban-origin mi-grants who use such a network becomes completely integrated into the social system. They become enmeshed in the binational social structure based in the rural community, even though they were not born there. At times, social cohesion becomes so strong that these outsiders stay integrated into the system and the community after migration has ceased, even to the point of visiting the home community, just as if they were born there.

Considering the four case studies in comparative perspective, most migrant networks can be traced back to the fortuitous employment of some key individual. All that is necessary for a migrant network to develop is for one person to be in the right place at the right time and obtain a position that allows him to distribute jobs and favors to others from his community. Chance factors play a large role in determining where migrant networks eventually become rooted; after the network has begun to develop, however, a universal logic takes hold as the network is extended and elaborated, binding Mexican communities more tightly to specific destinations in the United States.

SUMMARY: SOCIAL NETWORKS AND MIGRATION

Mexican migration to the United States is based on an underlying social organization that supports and sustains it. International migration is an inherently social process that is organized through networks forged from everyday interpersonal connections that characterize all human groups. These connections include the common bonds of kinship, friendship, and paisanaje, which have been adapted to the new reality of mass migration. Together they compose a web of interconnecting social relationships that supports the movement of people, goods, and information back and forth between Mexican sending communities and the United States.

The interpersonal relationships that make up the network are reinforced by institutional arrangements that bring migrants together on a regular basis in the United States. Voluntary organizations are particularly important in fostering regular face-to-face contact among migrants while they are abroad. The most important of these organizations is the soccer club, which brings migrants together on a weekly basis not only for recreation, but also for the exchange of information on jobs and housing in the United States. Soccer clubs also support reintegration of migrants into the home community through frequent team tours and the regular exchange of players. They also ensure the ongoing involvement of migrants in local affairs by encouraging the regular exchange of gossip and news.

One of the most important social institutions promoting contact and involvement with those at home is the fiesta of the patron saint. With the advent of mass migration, this yearly fiesta has become an important instrument of return migration and a symbolic demonstration of the community's cohesion in the face of diaspora. The new social category assigned to los ausentes in the fiesta's proceedings serves as an important vehicle promoting the ongoing integration of migrants within the community of origin.

Migrant networks are gradually built up and elaborated over the years. In the beginning phases, social ties to people in the United States are few in number. Starting from a small base, they extend slowly at first. As migrant experience steadily accumulates in the population, however, the number of connections between migrants and others in the community expands rapidly. As time passes, a growing number of people have friends and relatives who are, or have been, U.S. migrants. Eventually a critical mass of migrants is achieved, one capable of supporting an extensive network of social ties. As the network expands, it incorporates more potential migrants under its umbrella of social relationships. By the late 1970s, nearly everyone in the communities under study could claim some social tie with a U.S. migrant through either kinship, friendship, or paisanaje.

An important step in the maturation of the migrant networks occurs when migrants begin to settle in the United States and bring their families north to live with them. With the definitive settlement of a few families, the flow of migrants is channeled ever more specifically to the settlement area. This process of settlement often accompanies the promotion of migrants to positions of authority, enabling them to offer jobs to friends, neighbors, and other paisanos.

The existence of a settled core of out-migrant families, in turn, accelerates the development of the network by giving it a solid U.S. anchor. The settled families' roots in the United States rapidly extend and deepen as a second generation is born and raised abroad, and the mere existence of a settled core acts as a magnet to further migration. Points of destination are typically diverse in the early phases of network migration; however, migrants are increasingly channeled to specific points of destination that are linked to the home communities by highly developed social structures.

Migrant networks tend to become self-sustaining over time because of the social capital that they provide to prospective migrants. Personal contacts with friends, relatives, and paisanos give migrants access to jobs, housing, and financial assistance in the United States. As the web of interpersonal connections is extended and elaborated, this social capital is increasingly available to prospective migrants throughout the home community, progressively reducing the financial and "psychic" costs to U.S. migration. Landless jornaleros from a town such as Chamitlán may be poor in financial resources, but they are wealthy in social capital, which they can readily convert into jobs and earnings in the United States. For someone from Chamitlán, which has a particularly well developed migrant network, it is much easier to move and find a job in Los Angeles or San Francisco than in Guadalajara or Mexico City.

The self-feeding character of the migrant networks and the wealth of social capital they provide to people seeking entry into the U.S. labor market explain why U.S. migration has spread to involve all social groups in the communities under study and has become a common feature of life throughout western Mexico. As the costs of migration steadily drop, migration becomes more widely accessible and eventually emerges as a mass phenomenon encompassing all sectors of society. Through the steady growth and elaboration of migrant networks, then, international migration comes to be seen as a reliable resource on which families can regularly rely in adapting to changing economic circumstances.

7

Migration and the Household Economy

Women used to cry when their husbands would go to the United
States. Now they cry when they don't.

Old Man from Chamitlán

Thus far, we have made only passing reference to the role that migration
plays in the household economy. With the development of extensive
migrant networks, however, employment within the United States has
come within reach of virtually all households in the four communities.
In adapting to changing economic circumstances, families always have
the option of sending someone to work in the United States. When
family needs change as a result of childbirth, illness, or misfortune, the
household budget can always be supplemented with U.S. earnings. In
formulating a strategy for family maintenance or improvement, therefore, international migration is an ever-present possibility. It is a constant feature of socioeconomic life in western Mexico.

The potential value of U.S. migration as a socioeconomic resource
is illustrated by table 7.1, which presents average U.S. incomes for
migrants who worked in the United States in 1982. Across the four
communities, average wage rates varied from $4.90 to $5.30 per hour,
and depending on the number of hours worked per week and the
number of months worked per year, U.S. migrants earned between
$5,200 and $8,400 annually. Even after expenses for room and board are
discounted, the average migrant working a season in the United States
brought home somewhere between $4,000 and $5,000.

These sums are relatively modest by U.S. standards; however, when
translated into Mexican pesos, they are quite large and can appear
astronomical to poor jornaleros with limited prospects for work in
Mexico. In 1982 the prevailing wage for Mexican farmwork was 200
pesos per day, yielding a maximum yearly income of 52,000 pesos
(assuming five days per week for fifty-two weeks). In fact, steady agricultural work is nearly impossible to obtain, so most workers earn

TABLE 7.1
ESTIMATED GROSS AND NET ANNUAL INCOMES OF U.S. MIGRANTS FROM
FOUR MEXICAN COMMUNITIES (1982 U.S. DOLLARS)

Components of annual U.S. income	Community			
	Altamira	Chamitlán	Santiago	San Marcos
Average hourly wage	$4.95	$4.89	$5.28	$5.00
Average hours worked per week	43.2	40.3	40.8	53.3
Average months worked per year	6.1	7.1	9.8	6.7
Estimated gross annual income	$5,218	$5,597	$8,445	$7,142
Average expenses in United States	$1,267	$1,300	$3,767	$3,015
Average spent on food	$774	$850	$2,003	$1,675
Average spent on rent	$493	$450	$1,764	$1,340
Estimated net annual income	$3,951	$4,297	$4,678	$4,127
Number of migrants working in United States in 1982	20	42	10	3

Source: MIGFILE; migrant household members enumerated in Mexican community samples, including those in twenty-five extra households in Santiago.

considerably less than this sum—perhaps a few thousand pesos per year. In contrast, the net annual income figures in table 7.1 correspond roughly to a range of 281,000 to 352,000 pesos per year, assuming the average exchange rate for 1982, and 620,000 to 775,000 pesos per year, assuming the exchange rate prevailing at the end of the year.[1]

The relative attraction of U.S. employment is considerable; however, relatively few households send migrants to the United States within a given year. Although the incentives to migrate are strong, international migration is not undertaken lightly; rather, it is employed strategically at particular points in time for specific reasons. It is part of a tightly circumscribed socioeconomic process rooted in the household and its needs. Household members are embedded within a set of family relationships that determine when, why, and where they migrate. To understand why migration occurs, one must understand how it fits within the larger household economy.

---

[1] Unfortunately, it is somewhat risky to convert 1982 dollar earnings into pesos, since that year was one of economic crisis and hyperinflation in Mexico. On January 1, 1982, for example, the Mexican peso traded at 26.3 to the dollar, but by December 31, the figure was around 155. The monthly average exchange rate during 1982 was about 70.3 pesos to the dollar.

STRATEGIES OF MIGRATION

There is a large body of theoretical and empirical literature on the
economy of peasant households. Scholars generally agree that peasants
are small-scale cultivators who maintain certain rights with respect to
land and are somehow connected to a larger society, but beyond this
broad conceptualization they disagree (de la Peña 1981). Some have
attributed a particular psychology, or global view, to peasant households
in order to explain their economic behavior (Foster 1967; Maccoby 1967;
Ingham 1970). Others have attributed peasant economic traits to the
nature of their political and cultural relationships with the larger society
(Redfield 1956; Wolf 1966; Foster 1967; Marriott 1969). Still others have
linked the distinctive character of peasant economies to the fact that
exchange relationships are deeply embedded within larger social structures based on kinship and reciprocal exchange (Kroeber 1948; Foster
1953, 1967; Wolf 1966; Saul and Woods 1971).

Chayanov (1966) provides the most influential and comprehensive
treatment of the peasant economy. He argues that peasant households
are characterized by an economic orientation that emphasizes sustenance and employment instead of output and profit. Rather than maximizing production by substituting new technologies for hand labor,
peasant households seek to achieve subsistence while providing work
to all members. Output is determined not by the market but by the size
and composition of the household. Since peasant households are simultaneously production and consumption units, their lowest limit of production is determined by their minimum consumption requirements
and their highest limit, by the number, age, and sex of available workers.

In spite of this large literature, much of it centered on Mexico, the
concept of a peasant household economy is not very useful for the study
of international migration from western Mexico. As the microhistories
clearly reveal, communities in this region are not backward peasant
villages. Rather, they are dynamic participants in a rapidly changing
society. Through radio and television, households are linked to mass
Mexican culture. Labor migration is widespread, and community members have long been accustomed to the conventions and attitudes of a
capitalist economy. The fact that Santiago and San Marcos are not peasant communities is patently obvious from their occupational structures;
that Altamira and Chamitlán are not peasant communities is equally
clear when one appreciates the large number of landless wage laborers
they contain and the degree to which most campesinos and agricultores
engage in market-oriented production-maximizing behavior. In short,
Chayanov's hypotheses, and other theories of the peasant economy, are

not applicable to Mexico's situation of accelerated change and dynamic development (de la Peña 1981: 7–8).

Rather than focusing on households as units in a peasant economy, it is more useful to consider them as flexible economic entities evolving strategies for survival and improvement (Deere and de Janvry 1979; Wood 1981; Pressar 1982). Structural transformations within Mexico have created an extremely volatile political economy, and household strategies represent the primary mechanism through which individuals adapt to economic flux and change. Each household faces life with a basic set of resources that are fixed in the short run, including land (farmland or urban lots), labor (determined by the number, age, and sex of household members), and capital (money, seeds, tools, livestock, etc.). Each household also has needs of consumption and reproduction that depend primarily on its age-sex composition and on the family's aspirations of socioeconomic advancement. Survival strategies consist of flexible, emergent plans that households develop to match available resources with basic needs and aspirations.

Household resources can be combined productively in an endless variety of ways to meet the requirements of family maintenance and economic improvement. The behavior of household members in meeting these needs can be conceptualized as a series of dynamic, flexible survival strategies that shift in complex ways as needs and economic conditions change. International migration has become a key component of these strategies within the four communities under study. It provides a very attractive way of maximizing the return on a key household resource—its labor power. It is easy, inexpensive, well paid, and reliable.

With the maturation of the migrant networks in the 1970s, U.S. employment became easily accessible to virtually all segments of society. Households in the four communities now assume that international migration is a basic resource constantly at their disposal, and they use it at particular points in time in clear and deliberate ways within larger strategies of survival. Depending on their economic circumstances, available resources, consumption needs, aspirations, and stage in the life cycle, households in the four communities employ one of three clearly discernible strategies of international migration. These strategies are defined by the intersection of three dimensions of movement: duration, frequency, and regularity. Migrants may go abroad once or many times, may stay briefly or for a long time, and may go regularly or intermittently.

The first strategy is *temporary migration*. Migrants who adopt it generally make one to three trips at different points in their lives, with each trip lasting a year or less. These migrants are target earners who seek to make money quickly, often for a specific purpose, before returning home. Although temporary migration is usually undertaken for wage labor, it may also occur for more social reasons, such as to visit family members abroad, help in the care of a sick relative, attend school, study English, or simply have an adventure. Moves initiated for noneconomic reasons often last longer than anticipated, however, and most such migrants eventually take a job. This subset of temporary migration is of great importance in the construction and perpetuation of the migrant networks.

Temporary migration does not imply a disarticulation between the migrant and the community. In all cases, temporary migrants reincorporate themselves into the local economy when they return home and invest their savings in the home community. While abroad they communicate continuously with friends and family at home by means of letters and telephone calls, and through other migrants who constantly move back and forth from the home community. Information travels with a surprising rapidity, and los ausentes are present in the daily conversations of townspeople, while the migrants themselves speak of home constantly, referring to what they have done there or what they will do when they return. They see their stays in the United States as limited and continue to regard themselves as full-fledged members of their communities, and so they are seen by other paisanos.

While in the United States, temporary migrants maintain ongoing relationships with other paisanos. Together they search for housing and organize chores such as food shopping, cooking, house cleaning, and laundry. In agricultural areas, they often live together in barracks provided by growers for housing of dozens, or even hundreds, of migrants during peak work periods. These buildings are generally large, unsanitary sheds in need of repair for which the migrant pays a weekly rent, and the adverse conditions bring the men together. Temporary migrants spend nearly all of their free time with other paisanos, participating, as we have seen, in a variety of associations that generally revolve around sports. As a rule, temporary migrants do not learn English, although in urban areas they may acquire enough familiarity with the language to deal with routine situations.

The incorporation of temporary migrants into the economic, social, and political life of the United States is constrained by the fact that most are "illegal." As a result, they face a constant threat of deportation and are subject to various forms of discrimination. Illegality also means that most are employed in temporary, short-term jobs with little chance for advancement. In a hostile and alien land, temporary migrants thus confine their social relationships to the migrant networks, which serve to reinforce their identification with the home community and its people.

The second strategy is *recurrent migration*. Those who adopt it regularly travel back and forth between Mexico and the United States. Typically, they are married men who leave their families behind and support them with U.S. savings and remittances. Their occupation is literally that of a migrant worker, and most of their income is earned abroad. Although they maintain a residence in Mexico, they endeavor to support a high standard of living through regular work in the United States. Part of the money earned in the United States is devoted to productive investments in the community, which supplement the family income and promote the migrant's later return. Recurrent migrants have chosen a unique strategy, one based on socioeconomic relationships rooted on both sides of the border.

Recurrent migration has two main variants, depending mainly on whether migration is to a rural or an urban area and whether the job held is in agriculture. *Seasonal migration* is a strategy corresponding to the natural cycles of agricultural work (harvest, pruning, gleaning, sowing, etc.), primarily in intensive agricultural areas of California, and to a lesser extent in the Rio Grande valley in Texas. Seasonal migrants in the United States work very hard; however, the demand for farm labor is highly variable. During the harvest, many migrants are employed, but as it ends, work in the fields abates and migrants return home, where living is less costly and they can be with their families. There they may undertake some other economic activity, possibly employing savings compiled abroad.

The classic example of seasonal migration was that promoted by the Bracero program, which recruited Mexicans for farm labor in the United States on six-month contracts. After the end of the program, seasonal migration continued principally among those who had been able "to immigrate," that is, to obtain green cards enabling them to live in Mexico and regularly commute to work in the United States (Reichert 1979; Mines 1981; Mines and Anzaldua 1982). Although undocumented migrants also employ recurrent strategies, repeated migration is greatly facilitated by the acquisition of legal documents, which gives the bearer virtually unrestricted access to the United States.

The second category of recurrent migration is *cyclical migration*, which is directed to certain industries characterized by regular periods of unemployment. Work in these industries is also highly variable, and for a variety of reasons large segments of the work force are regularly furloughed, or hired only under short-term contract. Examples of industries likely to employ cyclical migrants include food processing, fisheries, construction, railroad repair, and highway maintenance, all of which tend to be highly seasonal, with markedly reduced demand during certain months of the year (usually in winter). Many manufacturing industries also experience periodic reductions of demand when workers are laid off (Morales 1983). In order to assure their continued employment season after season, recurrent migrants generally establish a personal relationship with a boss, labor contractor, or foreman in the United States.

During their time abroad, recurrent migrants must save between $150 and $200 to cover the costs of transportation to and from the United States. In addition, undocumented migrants must pay a coyote to guide them across the border, which adds another $350. As a result, there are marked differences in the amount that can be saved in the United States by documented and undocumented migrants. The higher costs of transportation and border-crossing faced by undocumented migrants causes their "overhead" expenses to be much higher. Moreover, legal migrants can move freely, without risk of being deported, so they are better able to look for lucrative work opportunities wherever they may be found (Reichert 1982).

The social world of recurrent migrants in the United States is limited largely to family members, fellow townspeople, and other Mexicans known from work. Patterns of contact with family members and paisanos are similar to those of temporary migrants. In fact, temporary and recurrent migrants often travel jointly to the United States and cooperate in solving the problems of daily living. Together they arrange for food, housing, and transportation to places of employment. Recurrent migrants, through their knowledge and experience in the United States, help temporary migrants adapt to the conditions of life abroad.

Migration becomes a way of life for workers who repeatedly go to the United States, and the life of the family is structured around the regular absence of the household head. He is responsible for obtaining the income necessary for the family to survive and prosper, and to do it, he leaves for much of the year. In exchange, his wife assumes total responsibility for the care and education of the children and, on occasion, for their support (if the husband is laid off or has problems crossing the border).

The last strategy, *settled migration*, occurs when a migrant decides to live permanently in the United States. Migrants who adopt this strategy are characterized by a relatively high degree of integration in the economic, social, and cultural life of the United States, by long years of residence there, and usually by an individual or family decision to settle abroad. They have adopted a strategy of long-term work *and* residence in the United States.

We could have labeled this strategy "permanent migration" or "legal immigration," but these terms are problematic in ways that transcend mere semantics. For example, the "permanence" of migrants in the United States is never assured except in a very few cases, even after many years of settled U.S. life; it is not an indispensable condition of settlement. Some migrants intend to "settle" in the United States for a few years but expect ultimately to return to their home communities. Legal documentation also does not necessarily imply that a person lives in the United States or that that person is fully integrated into the life there. In addition, many settled migrants do not have documents. Settled migration is thus the most ambiguous and hard to identify of the migrant strategies. The most important characteristic of settled migrants is a high degree of integration within the United States, a subjective trait, to be sure, but a valid one nonetheless. In general, those who are not integrated into life in the United States have not settled and do not plan to do so.

Integration implies an ability to cope with U.S. language and customs, even if the migrant lives and works in a Mexican enclave. Settled migrants are generally well versed in the ways of the United States. They know how to get around in a variety of social environments, find work, exercise their rights, undertake purchases, and make investments. They are accustomed to speaking English, or, at the very least, they can understand it. Most men have mastered the technical language of their places of work, while their children are usually bilingual. They participate in a fuller social life than that offered by family members or paisanos alone, although they do not lose their relationships with these people.

Many years of residence in the United States is an important condition of settlement but difficult to make precise. Obviously, the number of years spent abroad is an important variable, and settled migrants generally have three or more years of continuous U.S. residence; however, some have fewer. There are a few cases of migrants on the first trip who decide once and for all to settle and immediately put all their efforts into achieving this goal, even though they may risk deportation and have little hope of acquiring documents. Undocumented migrants may even have to return at times to avoid legal difficulties, but if they are committed to life in the United States, it is an easy matter to return.

Settled migrants naturally have a stable residence in the United States, and the preferred location is an urban center. In general, settled household heads live with their families, and their children are typically legal residents or U.S. citizens. In their financial dealings they give priority to investments in the United States. Earnings and savings are directed to consumption, especially to durable goods such as houses, cars, and furniture, as well as to subsistence and the daily comforts. Settled migrants typically have a stable job in the industrial or service sector. Those who work in agriculture usually hold a specialized job such as foreman, labor contractor, or machinery operator. Some settled migrants operate their own businesses or offer professional-technical services.

Often a personal, or in some cases a family, decision plays a role in the settlement process. At some point, every migrant must decide whether to stay or return. Sometimes it is a conscious decision; at other times it is a product of circumstances that accumulate over the years. In many cases the option of returning simply never materializes, and little by little the migrant makes—although not always accepts—the decision to stay.

Ethnographic work in the four communities thus suggests three principal strategies of migration to the United States. Temporary migration is sporadic, with migrants making a few brief trips and maintaining a high degree of commitment to the home community. Recurrent migration involves repeated movement back and forth across the border, with migrants maintaining social and economic connections in both countries, but with a preference toward Mexico. Finally, settled migration implies integration and long-term residence in the United States and a corresponding weakening of ties to the home community. The relative importance of these strategies in the four communities is difficult to determine from ethnographic information alone, however; for that we turn to the quantitative ethnosurvey.

A TYPOLOGY OF MIGRANTS

Migrants in the four study communities employ all three strategies in going to the United States. It is easy to sketch strategies at a general level, but it is more difficult to associate them with particular migrants in real life. Construction of a typology of migrants based on the patterns we have identified requires some inevitable, arbitrary simplifications. Table 7.2 summarizes a scheme that we developed for classifying migrants by the strategy they employ, using quantitative ethnosurvey data from the four communities. In order to keep procedures clear and simple, we based the scheme on three objective dimensions: the number, length, and relative frequency of trips to the United States.

TABLE 7.2
OPERATIONAL DEFINITION OF MIGRANT STRATEGIES USING ETHNOSURVEY DATA

Migrant strategy	Definition
New	Began migrating 1980 or later
Retired	Last U.S. trip in 1972 or earlier
Settled	Spent at least three continuous years in the United States on most recent trip
Recurrent	Has taken at least three trips, and since first trip has averaged at least one trip every two years or has spent at least half the time abroad
Temporary	Has taken fewer than three trips, has averaged less than one trip every two years, and has spent less than half the time abroad

Assignment of migrants to a strategy type is straightforward. One begins at the top of the table and moves down sequentially. Whenever a migrant fits the criteria for a particular strategy, he is placed in that category, and the next migrant is considered. According to our operational definition, new migrants are those who began to migrate within the last three years. Their entry into the migrant work force is too recent for us to know whether they will be temporary, recurrent, or settled migrants. Retired migrants are those who stopped migrating at least ten years ago and will probably not go again, while settled migrants have spent at least three continuous years in the United States. Recurrent migrants have made three or more trips and have averaged at least one trip every two years or have spent at least half their time in the United States since they began to migrate. Temporary migrants have averaged less than these quantities over the course of their migrant careers and have made fewer than three trips.

Table 7.3 classifies migrant household heads and all migrants by the strategy they were employing as of the survey date. For each group, two sets of figures are presented. The first refers to the representative community samples. These samples underrepresent people who employed a settled migrant strategy, of course, so a second set of figures includes migrants enumerated in the California samples, plus migrants who were enumerated in the community samples but were not household members. (Recall that the ethnosurvey questionnaire solicited information on children of the household head regardless of whether they were members of the household.)

TABLE 7.3
CURRENT STRATEGIES OF MIGRANTS FROM FOUR MEXICAN COMMUNITIES, 1982

	Migrant household heads		All migrants	
Community and strategy	Community sample	With Californians and others	Community sample	With Californians and others
Altamira				
New (%)	4.6	3.7	19.7	16.3
Temporary (%)	36.8	31.8	28.0	23.8
Recurrent (%)	4.6	7.5	10.8	13.3
Settled (%)	6.9	10.3	12.7	15.5
Retired (%)	47.1	46.7	28.7	31.1
Number	87	107	157	264
Chamitlán				
New (%)	5.4	4.7	14.5	12.6
Temporary (%)	36.2	32.0	30.3	20.8
Recurrent (%)	15.4	14.0	17.2	12.3
Settled (%)	4.6	9.3	10.7	22.9
Retired (%)	38.5	40.0	27.2	31.4
Number	130	150	221	481
Santiago				
New (%)	3.7	2.9	8.2	4.4
Temporary (%)	18.3	16.7	23.3	13.8
Recurrent (%)	12.2	11.8	6.9	9.3
Settled (%)	2.4	8.8	6.8	9.9
Retired (%)	63.4	59.8	54.8	62.6
Number	82	102	73	182
San Marcos				
New (%)	8.7	8.7	18.8	22.6
Temporary (%)	30.4	30.4	29.0	23.7
Recurrent (%)	8.7	8.7	7.3	8.6
Settled (%)	4.4	4.4	8.7	11.8
Retired (%)	47.8	47.8	36.2	33.3
Number	46	46	69	93

Source: PERSFILE; all migrants enumerated in Mexico or California, including those in twenty-five extra households in Santiago.

Among household heads, both sets of figures tell the same story. Retired migrants predominate, with their percentage varying from 39 percent to 64 percent depending on the community and sample used, and the percentage of new migrants is quite small, varying from 3 percent to 9 percent of household heads. The most prevalent strategy among those actively going to the United States is temporary migration. In all communities except Santiago, people employing this strategy make up between 30 percent and 40 percent of those with migrant experience. Santiago's percentage is much lower (around 18 percent) because of the unusually large number of retired migrants. In Chamitlán, Santiago, and San Marcos, recurrent migrants make up the next largest group, with percentages ranging from 9 percent to 15 percent. Among household heads from Altamira, however, settled migration is a slightly more prevalent strategy than recurrent migration, both before and after the Californians are added in.

When all migrants—not only household heads—are considered, the relative size of the categories shifts somewhat. In Santiago there are still many retired migrants (55 percent to 63 percent) and few new migrants (4 percent to 8 percent), reflecting that community's history of migration and development in recent decades. In the other communities, however, there are many more new migrants and the relative number of retired migrants is much smaller. As with household heads, temporary migration is the most popular strategy among nonretired migrants, with percentages ranging from 20 percent to 30 percent.

Current data thus suggest that most U.S. migrants adopt a temporary migration strategy, with settled and recurrent migration playing subordinate roles. This conclusion is clouded somewhat by the large number of retired migrants, people who had no definable strategy as of 1982 because they had stopped migrating long before. The relative popularity of the three strategies in a broader historical context is indicated in table 7.4, which considers migrants during their period of active migration. In other words, migrants are classified according to the strategy they employed during the time between their first and last trip to the United States.

This reconsideration of the data reveals even more clearly the predominance of temporary migration. In the representative community samples two-thirds to three-quarters of the household heads, and 55 percent to 65 percent of all migrants, employed a temporary strategy during their years of active migration. Among household heads, recurrent migration generally represents the second most important strategy, followed by settled migration. When all migrants are considered, however, settled migration is more important than recurrent migration. Since migrants who are not household heads are generally young, these results suggest that settlement usually occurs at the early stages of the migrant career. Inclusion of the California respondents in the samples does not change the picture a great deal, except that it naturally boosts the relative number of settlers.

The ethnosurvey data are thus consistent in showing that temporary migration is the predominant strategy employed by most migrants to the United States. Although temporary migration is numerically dominant, our understanding of migrant networks and the way they operate

TABLE 7.4
STRATEGIES EMPLOYED BY MIGRANTS FROM FOUR MEXICAN COMMUNITIES
DURING PERIOD OF ACTIVE U.S. MIGRATION

Community and strategy	Migrant household heads		All migrants	
	Community sample	With Californians and others	Community sample	With Californians and others
Altamira				
New (%)	4.6	3.7	19.8	16.3
Temporary (%)	75.9	64.5	57.3	48.9
Recurrent (%)	10.3	11.2	7.0	6.8
Settled (%)	9.2	20.6	15.9	28.0
Number	87	107	157	264
Chamitlán				
New (%)	5.4	4.7	14.5	12.7
Temporary (%)	66.2	58.6	53.4	33.9
Recurrent (%)	16.9	14.7	14.5	11.2
Settled (%)	11.5	22.0	17.6	42.2
Number	130	150	221	481
Santiago				
New (%)	3.7	2.9	8.2	4.4
Temporary (%)	64.6	55.9	64.4	42.3
Recurrent (%)	17.1	13.7	9.6	7.7
Settled (%)	14.6	27.4	17.8	45.6
Number	82	102	73	182
San Marcos				
New (%)	8.7	8.7	18.8	22.6
Temporary (%)	65.2	65.2	56.5	41.2
Recurrent (%)	17.4	17.4	11.6	10.7
Settled (%)	8.7	8.7	13.0	21.5
Number	46	46	69	93

Source: PERSFILE; all migrants enumerated in Mexico or California, including those in twenty-five extra households in Santiago.

suggests that recurrent and settled migrations are crucial to supporting temporary migration and making it widespread. Indeed, the different strategies are interdependent and reinforce one another.

CHARACTERISTICS OF MIGRANT STRATEGIES

Having broadly sketched the three migrant strategies from an ethnographic perspective, we now establish their character more precisely. The first facet of the strategies we consider is the kind of trip that each involves. Table 7.5 presents information on the journey to the United States for the various strategy types we have defined. In this table,

TABLE 7.5
AVERAGE CHARACTERISTICS OF LAST U.S. TRIP BY STRATEGY EMPLOYED DURING
PERIOD OF ACTIVE MIGRATION: MIGRANTS FROM FOUR MEXICAN COMMUNITIES

Community and characteristic	Migrant strategy			
	New	Temporary	Recurrent	Settled
Altamira				
Length of trip (months)	13.2	9.2	6.8	147.3
Percent documented (%)	11.6	13.3	16.7	32.4
Percent farmworkers (%)	53.7	65.9	66.7	25.7
Total number of trips	1.1	2.2	7.7	1.7
U.S. experience (months)	16.0	27.9	76.0	157.4
Number	43	129	18	74
Chamitlán				
Length of trip (months)	11.3	9.1	9.1	127.8
Percent documented (%)	15.0	21.0	44.4	52.0
Percent farmworkers (%)	56.1	68.0	57.4	28.4
Total number of trips	1.1	2.6	8.0	1.9
U.S. experience (months)	12.8	33.9	123.0	137.2
Number	61	163	54	203
Santiago				
Length of trip (months)	9.5	8.1	6.5	165.4
Percent documented (%)	25.0	26.0	35.7	50.0
Percent farmworkers (%)	25.0	27.8	30.8	3.8
Total number of trips	1.2	1.8	7.5	1.5
U.S. experience (months)	12.5	27.8	105.9	163.6
Number	8	77	14	83
San Marcos				
Length of trip (months)	10.9	7.8	16.3	99.6
Percent documented (%)	35.0	31.7	40.0	27.8
Percent farmworkers (%)	5.6	21.9	60.0	5.3
Total number of trips	1.0	2.1	8.9	1.4
U.S. experience (months)	11.1	27.5	174.2	112.1
Number	21	42	10	21

Source: PERSFILE; all migrants enumerated in Mexico or California, including those in twenty-five extra households in Santiago.

migrants are classified by the strategy employed when they were active migrants, since data pertain to the most recent trip to the United States and not the current period.

The information in table 7.5 generally conforms to the ethnographic sketch of the migrant strategies presented earlier. Temporary migrants are mostly undocumented and have made a small number of short trips to the United States. The percentage documented ranges from 13 percent to 32 percent, the mean trip length is about eight or nine months, and the average temporary migrant has made around two trips to the United

States. Total lifetime experience in the United States averages only two to three years (twenty-seven to thirty-four months). In the two rural towns, temporary migrants are mainly seasonal farmworkers, but those from the urban-industrial settings work predominantly outside of agriculture.

Recurrent migrants similarly conform to ethnographic expectations. Like temporary migrants, only a minority have U.S. residence documents, although the percentage with papers is somewhat higher among them. With the exception of San Marcos, the trip length of recurrent migrants is extremely short—nine months or less, but recurrent migrants have made a large number of trips: an average of eight or nine trips to two for temporary migrants. Over the course of these many trips, recurrent migrants accumulate significant amounts of time in the United States. The shortest average accumulation was just over six years for recurrent migrants from Altamira (76 months), extending up to fourteen years among those from San Marcos (174 months). With the exception of those from Santiago, most recurrent migrants were employed as seasonal farmworkers. In Santiago, nearly 70 percent worked outside of agriculture, employing a strategy of cyclical migration to urban jobs.

Turning to settled migrants, in each community they were very unlikely to work in agriculture, with the percentage of farmworkers ranging from 2 percent in Santiago to 28 percent in Chamitlán, and a relatively large share were documented. Roughly 50 percent of the settlers from Chamitlán and Santiago possessed legal residence papers, compared to 32 percent of those from Altamira and 28 percent of those from San Marcos. Settled migrants have made relatively few trips to the United States, confirming our earlier suggestion of a tendency to settle early in the migrant career. On average, settled migrants only made one or two trips to the United States before settling abroad. They have accumulated considerable amounts of time in the U.S., however, with total experience ranging from twelve to fourteen years.

We stated earlier that a high degree of integration in the United States is the most important characteristic of migrants adopting a settled strategy. Table 7.6 corroborates this statement by examining selected indicators of U.S. integration by migrant strategy. As in table 7.5, these data pertain to the most recent trip to the United States, so the strategy given was that employed during the subject's active migration phase. Because of the small number of cases in San Marcos, data for the two urban-industrial communities are combined.

As one moves from left to right in table 7.6, from new migrants to settled migrants, one generally progresses from low integration in the United States and high degree of attachment in Mexico to precisely the

TABLE 7.6
INDICATORS OF INTEGRATION IN THE UNITED STATES BY STRATEGY EMPLOYED
DURING PERIOD OF ACTIVE MIGRATION: MIGRANTS FROM FOUR MEXICAN COMMUNITIES

Community and indicator	Migrant strategy			
	New	Temporary	Recurrent	Settled
Altamira				
With Anglo friends (%)	33.3	19.7	41.7	66.7
With Chicano friends (%)	66.7	27.9	50.0	80.9
Children in U.S. schools (no.)	0.3	0.5	0.0	1.6
Belong to sports club (%)	25.0	6.3	23.1	39.1
Know "some" English (%)	0.0	3.2	16.7	70.0
Number	9	82	13	24
Chamitlán				
With Anglo friends (%)	20.0	18.5	33.3	26.7
With Chicano friends (%)	0.0	23.5	38.1	40.0
Children in U.S. schools (no.)	4.5	1.6	2.3	2.9
Belong to sports club (%)	0.0	8.9	9.1	17.1
Know "some" English (%)	0.0	2.4	23.1	40.6
Number	8	94	23	36
Santiago and San Marcos				
With Anglo friends (%)	50.0	25.5	40.0	38.7
With Chicano friends (%)	50.0	42.2	73.6	77.3
Children in U.S. schools (no.)	0.0	0.2	0.2	4.5
Belong to sports club (%)	50.0	47.8	20.0	22.7
Know "some" English (%)	50.0	25.0	26.4	67.3
Number	4	90	20	37

Source: MIGFILE; migrant household members enumerated in Mexico or California, including those in twenty-five extra households in Santiago.

opposite. Of the fifteen indicators shown in the table (five indicators in three places), settled migrants show the greatest integration on eleven, and if we ignore new migrants, the increase in integration from temporary to settled migrants is monotonic. In general, settled migrants are most likely to have friends in the United States, to have children in U.S. schools, and to speak and understand English. The last measure is particularly telling, rising in Altamira from 3 percent to 70 percent as one moves from temporary through settled migrants, with similar increases in the other communities.

The pattern of results is clouded somewhat by new migrants, who appear to be quite integrated on some indicators. Part of the anomaly may be attributed to the small number of people in this category; however, new migrants are problematic in other ways. They are younger and, hence, more likely to be involved in athletics and, being unattached, are more open to forming new friendships. Moreover, although we cannot identify the strategy these people employ, they may have selected one for themselves. Some may, indeed, be nascent settlers seeking rapid integration in the United States.

Our earlier ethnographic profiles also mentioned the demographic and family characteristics of the different migrant types, which is the subject of table 7.7. Because the variables in this table were defined as of the survey date, migrants are classified according to their current migrant strategy, and retired migrants are not shown in the table. In all strategy groups, the vast majority of migrants are men (61 percent to

TABLE 7.7
DEMOGRAPHIC AND FAMILY CHARACTERISTICS OF MIGRANTS BY CURRENT STRATEGY:
MIGRANTS FROM FOUR MEXICAN COMMUNITIES

Community and characteristics	Migrant strategy			
	New	Temporary	Recurrent	Settled
Altamira				
Mean age	22.9	37.0	29.5	30.2
Male (%)	76.7	87.3	77.1	82.9
Married (%)	27.9	80.9	65.7	61.5
Household head (%)	9.3	54.0	22.9	26.8
Son or daughter (%)	67.4	42.9	57.1	58.5
Number	43	63	35	41
Chamitlán				
Mean age	28.2	38.0	36.1	28.1
Male (%)	68.9	85.0	79.7	60.9
Married (%)	47.5	85.0	76.3	70.9
Household head (%)	11.5	48.0	35.6	12.7
Son or daughter (%)	67.2	44.0	52.5	75.5
Number	61	100	59	110
Santiago				
Mean age	31.9	38.9	34.5	33.8
Male (%)	75.0	76.0	76.5	66.7
Married (%)	75.0	88.0	88.2	83.3
Household head (%)	37.5	68.0	70.6	50.0
Son or daughter (%)	37.5	16.0	17.6	33.3
Number	8	25	17	18
San Marcos				
Mean age	28.9	33.9	37.9	30.5
Male (%)	85.7	81.8	100.0	81.8
Married (%)	52.4	86.4	87.5	72.3
Household head (%)	19.1	63.6	50.0	25.0
Son or daughter (%)	71.4	22.7	37.5	75.0
Number	21	22	8	11

Source: PERSFILE; all migrants enumerated in Mexico or California, including those in twenty-five extra households in Santiago.

100 percent). New migrants just beginning their careers tend to be young unmarried men who are still members of the families in which they were raised, with average ages in the late twenties or early thirties. Temporary migrants are older married household heads, with average ages in the late thirties. Recurrent migrants are also relatively old, with average ages in the low to middle thirties. In the rural towns, recurrent migrants tend to be unmarried members of their parents' household; in the two urban communities, most are married household heads. Finally, settled migrants are young married children who have not yet formed independent households. Moreover, the relative number of males is lowest among settled migrants, suggesting the importance of wives in the settlement process.

Finally, table 7.8 shows the occupation of migrants using each strategy type. There are few strong patterns in these data. The only clear trend is that migrants with higher skills tend to form the strongest attachments to the United States. The percentage of skilled workers among migrants from Santiago rises from 17 percent among new migrants to 75 percent among settled migrants; the respective percentages for San Marcos are 25 percent to 38 percent. In the two rural towns, the percentage of farmworkers is markedly lower in the settled category than in the other migrant types. These data thus suggest that those most likely people to settle in the United States—those migrants most likely to put down roots in a U.S. city—are people from an occupational background that is most readily transferable to an urban setting.

The ethnosurvey data thus offer clear portraits of people employing the various migrant strategies. New migrants leave for the United States in the young adult years before marriage and make short trips for farmwork (if from rural areas) or urban labor (if from urban areas). In subsequent trips, migrants adopt one of three basic strategies. Temporary migrants make one to three short trips without documents, display a low degree of integration into the United States, and are older married male household heads from unskilled or farm backgrounds. Recurrent migrants make many trips back and forth between the two countries and are younger married household heads from unskilled or farm backgrounds. They tend to be undocumented, although more have papers than do temporary migrants, and more have acquired attachments to the United States. Finally, settled migrants are highly integrated, long-term residents of the United States who are predominantly young male household heads from nonagricultural occupational backgrounds. In many cases, settled migrants possess legal documents, and many are women.

These generalizations are, of course, abstractions that apply to no

TABLE 7.8
OCCUPATION IN MEXICO BY CURRENT STRATEGY:
MIGRANTS FROM FOUR MEXICAN COMMUNITIES

Community and occupation	Migrant strategy			
	New	Temporary	Recurrent	Settled
Altamira				
Agricultor (%)	0.0	8.8	6.7	0.0
Nonmanual (%)	12.1	15.8	3.3	25.0
Skilled manual (%)	9.1	5.3	0.0	6.2
Campesino (%)	12.1	21.0	16.7	9.4
Unskilled manual (%)	21.2	12.3	36.7	25.0
Jornalero (%)	45.5	36.8	36.6	34.4
Number	33	57	30	32
Chamitlán				
Agricultor (%)	0.0	0.0	2.2	0.0
Nonmanual (%)	20.0	14.8	20.0	19.7
Skilled manual (%)	0.0	8.6	4.4	18.2
Campesino (%)	5.0	25.9	20.0	1.5
Unskilled manual (%)	10.0	6.2	2.2	18.2
Jornalero (%)	65.0	44.4	51.1	42.4
Number	40	81	45	66
Santiago				
Professional (%)	0.0	10.0	8.3	0.0
Clerical-sales (%)	16.7	15.0	8.3	8.3
Skilled manual (%)	16.7	45.0	58.3	75.0
Services (%)	50.0	5.0	8.3	8.3
Unskilled manual (%)	0.0	20.0	16.7	8.3
Farmworker (%)	16.7	5.0	0.0	0.0
Number	6	20	12	12
San Marcos				
Professional (%)	0.0	0.0	0.0	0.0
Clerical-sales (%)	37.5	27.8	0.0	12.5
Skilled manual (%)	25.0	27.8	33.3	37.5
Services (%)	12.5	11.1	33.3	25.0
Unskilled manual (%)	25.0	27.8	33.3	12.5
Farmworker (%)	0.0	5.6	0.0	12.5
Number	16	18	6	8

Source: PERSFILE; all migrants enumerated in Mexico or California, including those in twenty-five extra
households in Santiago.

single migrant. Behind the ethnographic and quantitative abstractions, however, are real people whose lives ultimately give meaning to the typologies we have constructed. In order to flesh out the generalities and give them a more tangible meaning, the following section presents these life histories as case studies that exemplify the strategies hitherto discussed hypothetically.

CASE STUDIES OF MIGRANT STRATEGIES

A Temporary Migrant from Altamira

Don Felipe Guevara is a temporary migrant from Altamira who has made three trips to the United States in his lifetime. The motivations for each trip were different, as were the socioeconomic and family contexts within which the trips took place. He was born in 1936, the oldest in a family of four children. At an early age, Don Felipe began working at the principal family business—sheepherding—because of his father's untimely death. The drought of 1940–1941 dried up pasture land and forced the family to sell a substantial part of its livestock. In 1942 the weather improved, although in the succeeding years the rains continued to be scarce. In 1949, because of the family's desperate straits, 13-year-old Don Felipe left with a group of villagers to work in the United States. His mother had to sell some of the few animals that remained in order to pay for his passage.

Don Felipe had trouble finding a job in the United States. He was under age, and little work was available. He says that he went hungry much of the time, and on various occasions he did odd jobs just to get something to eat. He wandered with other paisanos from place to place in southern California until the cotton harvest arrived and he found steady work. He sent practically his entire first week's salary to his family in Mexico and thereafter continued sending home most of his earnings. When the cotton harvest ended, he worked for various truck farmers in the Imperial Valley. During this time, the U.S. Border Patrol deported him and his friends several times, "but at least they only took us to Mexicali, and from there we could return."

After two years in the United States, he returned home to Altamira. On arrival, he found that a new dirt highway to Guadalajara had opened and that opportunities for agricultural work had significantly improved. New wells had expanded the amount of land under irrigation, creating new possibilities for employment.

The money that he had regularly sent home from the United States had gone mainly to support his mother and three younger siblings, and the $200 in cash he brought with him was spent mostly to repair their house and buy new beds. The little money that remained was saved to help feed the family while Don Felipe got started in sharecropping. In February 1951 he solicited land to work as a mediero and began working it along with one of his younger brothers. Both of them had experience in this work. The remaining money from Don Felipe's U.S. earnings enabled the family to survive without having to borrow or sell their crops cheaply before the harvest.

After the first harvest, Don Felipe decided to marry and brought his bride to live with him in his mother's house. With his brother he farmed as a sharecropper for two more seasons. After this time, he did so with the help of his wife and a few hired hands, for his brother had gone to work in the United States. The mother divided up the family plot and gave part to Don Felipe so that he could construct, little by little, his house. After five years of living with his mother, he moved with his wife and two children into a large room that he and a mason friend had attached to the house. At about this time, his younger sister married and his two bachelor brothers began to support his mother.

Don Felipe went to the United States for the second time at the beginning of the 1960s. By then he had five young children and, because of changes in farm technology and crops, found it increasingly difficult to find work during the dry season. At the same time, his house was becoming increasingly crowded, and he wished to enlarge it. For these reasons, he borrowed money and with other villagers went to California once again without documents. After two months of work, however, the U.S. Border Patrol caught him and deported him to Tijuana. During his two months in the United States, he had been able to earn enough only to pay off the coyote and to send a little money home. He had very little cash on him when he was deported, and he suffered many hardships on his way back to Altamira.

The situation he faced on his return was distressing. He had outstanding debts, the time for planting had passed, and he could get by only on day labor, which was scarce. He went further into debt to support his family, and he was able to pay off his debts only after four growing seasons. His oldest child, a daughter, and later on his next oldest, a son, helped him with the agricultural tasks because he did not have enough money to hire his own jornaleros. His wife stayed at home with the two youngest children, where they shelled walnuts to earn a little extra money.

In 1968 Don Felipe decided once again to strike out for el Norte. Working as a sharecropper, he had not been able to save any money, and he wanted his children to attend school. Remembering his bad luck on the prior trip, this time he left his plot seeded and under the care of his spouse, so that, with the help of one of his brothers, she could harvest it to feed the family. With proceeds from the sale of a few animals and a little borrowed money, he left, this time for Florida. The villager with whom he was traveling assured him that they would find work there and that the coyote would be willing to defer payment until after they had jobs, and so it was. With the money he sent home, his wife hired some jornaleros and harvested his plot. For his part, Don Felipe worked "like a slave" in the orange harvest, with payment by piece rate.

After he had finished a season of work in the orange groves, he decided to remain and wait for the next one. He worked sporadically through that winter and spent part of the savings he had compiled. In the next season he was able to save around $1,200 in cash, even while sending back money periodically to his wife, and when the work ended he returned home to his family. This time he showed off his money. He constructed his house with better materials, using brick, cement, and mosaic tile. He bought clothes for the whole family. He paid for the enrollment of his oldest son in secondary school and expanded his herds of domestic animals. He continued working as a mediero and jornalero, but without having to sell his crops before the harvest.

The visits to the United States, although not always free of failure and hardship, permitted this campesino to overcome the difficulties that life put before him: economic stress brought about by drought and technological change and, on two occasions, pressing needs originating in the family life cycle. Migration briefly interrupted his career as a farmer, without really changing his position in the community social structure. He continued to be a mediero who sharecropped a small plot and supplemented his existence through local wage labor.

Don Felipe's one migratory failure put him and his family in a difficult economic situation for several years because of the high cost of going to the United States. Moreover, on each occasion his migration disrupted the family's economic life by depriving the household of its most productive member, forcing it to sell some of its property or go into debt in order to make ends meet. Migration thus involved a certain risk that the household was willing to take because of the economic difficulties it confronted and because of its inability to satisfy its basic requirements. Earnings obtained in the United States went primarily for the maintenance of the family and the improvement of its standard of living, through the construction of a better and more spacious dwelling, and through the acquisition of domestic consumer goods.

A Recurrent Migrant from Chamitlán

Antonio is forty-four years old, and his story exemplifies the logic of recurrent migration. He is married to Jovita, with whom he has two children: Antonio, thirteen years old, and Elena, eleven years old. They all live together in a one-room adobe and tile house in Chamitlán lent to them by some relatives who live permanently in the United States. Antonio is the oldest son of a large family in which nearly all have been U.S. migrants. His father and brothers all worked in the United States, and two of his sisters presently live in California, where they are married to men from Chamitlán. Jovita comes from a very poor family of jornaleros, also with ample migratory experience. At present, three of her brothers live in the San Francisco Bay area.

Antonio, who is illiterate, began working at the age of seven, when he helped his father farm as a medium. When he was eighteen years old, he went with some cousins to work for three weeks picking cotton in Apatzingán, Michoacán. On his return, he continued to help his father while working occasionally as a jornalero, mainly in the potato harvest. During harvest times, he would take the morning bus to nearby Zamora and return home each night to Chamitlán. He followed this pattern of work for seven years. Then in 1965, when he was twenty-five, he went with some other villagers to Mexico City, where he worked for six months as a mason's assistant and another six months as a gardener. At the end of a year, he again returned to Chamitlán, where he began to combine his work as a mason's assistant with that of a jornalero.

In 1967 he went to the United States for the first time, taking advantage of contacts that his parents had made when they had previously worked there. His first destination was Oxnard, California, where he worked for a while in the peach harvest. Later he worked for a few months picking grapes in the middle San Joaquin Valley, where an important colony of people from Chamitlán had emerged in one city. After about two years abroad, he returned home and continued to occupy himself as a jornalero and a mason's assistant.

Antonio married Jovita in 1970, and children soon followed. Nevertheless, he continued working at the same activities until 1979, when he decided once again to try his luck in el Norte. With the help of one of his brothers-in-law, he was able to obtain work in a fruit dehydration plant in the Sacramento Valley, where he was offered the minimum wage and the chance to work extra hours. In the three years since then, Antonio has returned every year to work in this same plant, taking advantage of the good relationships he was able to establish with the owner and the foreman from the beginning.

In the month of May each year, Antonio says good-bye to his family and friends and, usually in the company of other villagers, sets out for the city of Tijuana to look for a way of crossing the border surreptitiously. When Antonio arrives at the city in Sacramento Valley, where the factory is located, he immediately reconfirms his employment and then looks for a room to rent. While he is working at the factory, until November, he periodically sends money to Jovita. During this time, Antonio interacts with the family of his brother-in-law and other towns-people who live nearby.

When November arrives, Antonio loads himself down with a sack of plums and after buying clothes and some gifts for his family, he returns to Chamitlán. He spends the Christmas holidays in town and, while waiting for the reactivation of work in California, works as a jornalero or a mason's assistant. And so, year after year, the cyclical existence of Antonio and his family is repeated. Even after having worked for a considerable length of time in the United States, Antonio has never been able to acquire many consumer goods aside from those that are strictly necessary. A good part of the money he has earned has been spent on Jovita, who has been sick.

Recurrent migration thus began at a stage in the life cycle when there were small children, a time when important economic needs were pressing upon the family. The initial trip was followed by others because needs persisted and migration offered a well-paid and dependable means of satisfying them. The family will probably continue to rely on recurrent migration until the children grow older and their needs subside. Recurrent migration helps the United States by saving the cost of maintaining its labor force, since during periods of unemployment migrants like Don Felipe return home, and shift the cost of unemployment to their families.

A Settled Migrant from Santiago

Señor Fernández was born and raised in the town of Santiago and, like his father, went to work in the textile factory at the age of fourteen, where he spent the next thirty years of his life. He married young and immediately began to raise a family. It was a great hardship to maintain his numerous brood of nine children on his meager factory wages. The first two children were boys, the next five were girls, and the last two were boys. The oldest sons continued in their father's footsteps and began to work in the factory at an early age. Until they were married, they helped their father with household expenses.

Señor Fernández had always assumed that he would continue work-ing in the factory until his retirement. He had a long history of work experience and had also taken on various political, union, and municipal posts. Precisely because of his political connections, however, he was compelled to stop working and leave town. In the mid-1960s, an opposition faction gained control of the union; and as often happens in Mexico, the political losers were forced to resign or retire. He opted for resignation and asked for severance pay from the company.

His situation was different because he was already over fifty years old and the other factories around Santiago were not hiring men that old. He thus decided to take advantage of family connections in the United States and left to try his luck in el Norte. He arrived in Los Angeles in 1966 without documents and began to work in a factory that manufactured ceramic bases for lamps. The work was difficult because handling the molds and working the clay involved much physical wear and tear. The first years were especially difficult. He worked constantly just to survive and to send money home to his family. His situation was aggravated because he was arrested and deported three times.

Whereas politics and union experience had given him trouble in Mexico, in the United States they would be a principal source of his success. Since the factory employed many other paisanos and other Latinos, he was elected to represent them before the company and the union. As a union leader, he became an intermediary between labor and management. He knew how to exercise his rights and those of his fellow workers, but he also knew how to manage people. Above all, through his post he was able to admit to the factory many other paisanos. People from Santiago knew that they could arrive in Los Angeles and find immediate work in the lamp factory. As the work was very difficult, people typically worked for only a few months, found better jobs, and then vacated their posts to others. In this way, many migrants were initiated into the industrial work force of Los Angeles.

In a short time, Señor Fernández became indispensable to the lamp company. All labor conflicts and disagreements were routed through him, and he knew how to manage them. One occurrence in particular established him in his post and led to his definitive settlement in the United States. The spouse of the owner was ill, and Señor Fernández, together with a group of workers, had the sensitivity to visit her in the hospital and give her a bouquet of flowers. This detail did not pass unnoticed, and the boss, pressured by his wife, began to arrange documentation for the legal entry of Señor Fernández. There were some problems concerning his age, but because the owner considered him to be a valued and specialized worker, he pressed on. Señor Fernández returned to Mexico, and in a few months, in December 1969, he received his papers and crossed the border with his documents in order.

Months later his wife arrived with his five daughters and the two youngest sons. The oldest sons were already employed and had families, so they remained in Mexico. His daughters soon began to work in the factory, and when they married, with other migrants, his sons-in-law also got jobs there. From the lamp factory, all went on to other more agreeable and better-paid work.

Given his legal status and his position as a union leader, Señor Fernández was able to obtain a mortgage to buy a house. He purchased a piece of property that contained two separate houses. The Fernández family lived in one of them, and the other was rented to one of his sons-in-law. Over time, the rental from the second house served to pay off the whole mortgage.

When he reached the required age, Señor Fernández retired and, with his pension, busied himself with travel and relaxation. He went frequently to Mexico and stayed for long intervals in Santiago, later returning to Los Angeles to visit his family and oversee his business interests. On one of these trips, he was killed in a car accident; however, his family—spouse, various sons and daughters, in-laws, and grandchildren—remained in Los Angeles. One of his sons learned to speak English well and decided to return to Mexico, where he is now employed as an English teacher. The other son works in a factory in Los Angeles, as do the daughters, with the exception of one who has stopped working to become a housewife.

For a migrant to settle in the United States, various conditions of integration must exist, although which are necessary may vary from person to person. In Señor Fernandez's case, a good job, documentation, immigration of the family, and the purchase of property were the determining factors. In others it could be language ability, the opening of a business, or simply the desire to live in the United States. In many cases, children force the parents to remain by studying in schools and learning the language and the culture of the United States. A multitude of factors intervene in the settlement process such that, compared to other migrant types, the number of people who actually come to settle is relatively small. Moreover, settlement is now much more difficult to accomplish than it was ten or fifteen years ago, primarily because of the many legal and bureaucratic restrictions that impede the process of obtaining documents.

MIGRATION AND THE LIFE CYCLE

The preceding sections frequently mentioned links between the life cycle and the propensity to migrate. The ethnographic sketches, the case studies, the typologies, and the quantitative characterizations of migrant types all underscored the role played by life cycle changes in promoting, or discouraging, migration to the United States. Additions to the family through marriage or birth increase dependence within the household and create pressing needs for support. Given the relatively large amount of money that can be earned during a season of work in the United States and the comparative ease of migration through social networks, an increase in the propensity to migrate during the early stages of family formation is expected. Similarly, when household needs decrease as children grow up, begin to work, and finally leave to form their own families, the economic pressure for migration lessens. In short, the role of migration within household survival strategies should closely parallel stages in the family life cycle, which reflect shifting levels of dependence and economic need within the household.

In Mexico, as elsewhere, the family is the basic social institution, and most people live within its confines throughout their lives, playing active roles in the various transitions of the life cycle. First they are part of their parents' household and later gradually become integrated into society. As they grow older, they venture more widely into the socio-economic world and begin to establish work and friendship relationships with people outside the household. Eventually they marry and begin their own households and start to raise new families that in time will give rise to other families.

Table 7.9 presents a scheme for classifying individuals and households by stage in the life cycle by means of the ethnosurvey data. For individuals, we have identified six phases in the life cycle. We begin considering a person at age eighteen, when most people are still unmarried and living with their parents. Marriage puts a person into the second, "newly married," stage, and the arrival of the firstborn child advances them to the third stage, "young children." When the oldest child reaches age thirteen, the fourth phase, "some teens," is entered; when the youngest child achieves this age, one enters the fifth stage, "all teens." The sixth and final stage, "children gone," occurs when all children have grown up and left home.

The five life cycle stages for households are based on an analogous series of changes within the household. The first, "unmarried," stage is omitted, since unmarried people generally remain in their parents' households. "Newly married" households consist of a married couple without children, while those in the "young children" phase have at least one child under thirteen years of age. Households progress to the "some teens" category when the oldest child in the family reaches age thirteen and to "all teens" when the youngest reaches this age. Finally, the "children gone" stage pertains to households in which all children have grown up and left home.

TABLE 7.9
Definition of Life Cycle Stage for Individuals and Households
in Four Mexican Communities

Stage in life cycle	Persons aged 18+	Households
Unmarried	Never married	—
Newly married	Married with no children ever born	No children in household and none ever born
Young children	Married with all children under 13	All children in household under age 13
Some teens	Married with eldest child 13 or older	Eldest child in household 13 or older
All teens	Married with youngest child 13 or older	Youngest child in household 13 or older
Children gone	Married, all children have left home	All children have left home

The most salient fact about migration within the household has already been noted earlier: most U.S. migrants are men. Other studies in Mexican communities also report that migration to the United States is a "male-led" phenomenon (Wiest 1973; Reichert 1979; Mines 1981). Although women eventually become involved as the social process of migration develops, the initial migrants from a community and from a family are almost always men.

The dominance of men in the migration process reflects two conditions. First, it stems from a basic division of labor within the family, one reflecting the role that each sex plays in socioeconomic organization. Traditionally, the role of women as mothers is assigned great importance in the Mexican family, and much of their time is taken up with biological and social reproduction. During stages of the life cycle devoted to pregnancy and child care, it is difficult for women to migrate, especially to a distant place such as the United States. When women do go, they are typically young and single, recently married and without children, or long married with older children. They generally move as part of larger family groups, when the whole family changes residence.

Migration of women to the United States is also less frequent because most would have to enter the country without documents. In recent years it has been increasingly difficult for anyone, male or female, to acquire U.S. residence papers. A lack of documents exposes both sexes to a variety of exploitations in the United States, but women are especially vulnerable. They are exposed to personal risks and abuses not faced by men (molestation by unscrupulous coyotes, employers, or border patrol officials). For these reasons, most men are reluctant to allow their wives and daughters to undertake the hazardous crossing of the border without documents, and women are usually afraid to try. When women do go to the United States, it is usually only after a male relative has gone before her to arrange legal documentation or, at least, safe passage across the border.

Given this dominance of males, our consideration of migration and the life cycle focuses on men. Table 7.10 presents males eighteen and older classified by migrant status and life cycle stage, with migrant status defined as in chapter 5. The general pattern revealed in this table is quite clear. Active migration begins at a high level among young unmarried men, falls after marriage, rises with the arrival of children, and then falls again as the children mature and leave home. In short, over the course of a man's life cycle, active migration rises and falls depending on family needs, while the number with migrant experience steadily grows. By the end of the life cycle, most men have been to the United States but are no longer active migrants.

This overall pattern seems clear; however, there are some interesting exceptions in each of the four communities. For example, in Altamira the incidence of active migration among young unmarried males is extraordinarily high, even compared to Chamitlán, which has a more extensive tradition of migration and more highly developed networks. Over 60 percent of young men from Altamira are active migrants, compared to only 32 percent in Chamitlán. In both towns, the migration of single men is directed more to the United States than within Mexico, but this is especially true in Chamitlán.

The high percentage of migrants among young unmarried men in Altamira reflects the limited economic alternatives facing them. From age fifteen onward, ambitious young men look to the United States, or at least to Guadalajara, for opportunity and advancement. The fathers, principally inactive migrants, stay in town to participate in local economic activities, while these young men head off to try their fortunes elsewhere. Chamitlán, with its more dynamic farm economy, provides young unmarried men with more opportunities for agricultural employment, rooting them more strongly to the community. Once they are married, however, young men from Chamitlán migrate to the United States in greater numbers, using the more extensive range of network connections at their disposal.

In the two urban-industrial settings, overall levels of out-migration are much lower and fluctuations over the life cycle less pronounced as

TABLE 7.10
MEN AGED 18 AND OLDER CLASSIFIED BY MIGRANT STATUS AND
STAGE IN THE LIFE CYCLE: FOUR MEXICAN COMMUNITIES

Community and migrant status	Person's stage in life cycle					
	Never married	Newly married	Young children	Some teens	All teens	Children grown
Altamira						
Active migrant (%)	60.5	20.0	36.5	31.0	10.8	0.0
To United States (%)	35.1	5.0	21.2	14.1	2.7	0.0
Within Mexico (%)	26.3	15.0	21.2	16.9	8.1	0.0
Inactive migrant (%)	4.4	30.0	32.7	47.9	54.1	38.5
To United States (%)	3.5	25.0	25.0	32.4	43.2	23.1
Within Mexico (%)	0.9	15.0	17.3	28.2	18.9	30.8
Number	114	20	52	71	37	13
Chamitlán						
Active migrant (%)	31.7	26.1	50.0	35.5	22.7	26.7
To United States (%)	28.7	21.7	37.0	29.0	15.9	26.7
Within Mexico (%)	3.0	8.7	19.6	8.1	9.1	0.0
Inactive migrant (%)	8.9	34.8	34.8	51.6	50.0	60.0
To United States (%)	5.0	30.4	30.4	41.9	50.0	53.3
Within Mexico (%)	4.0	4.3	15.2	21.0	9.1	13.3
Number	101	23	46	62	44	15
Santiago						
Active migrant (%)	4.8	9.1	16.3	11.5	15.6	0.0
To United States (%)	3.2	4.5	4.6	5.8	6.3	0.0
Within Mexico (%)	4.8	4.5	12.8	5.8	9.4	0.0
Inactive migrant (%)	7.9	22.7	40.8	44.2	46.9	37.5
To United States (%)	6.3	13.6	19.8	34.6	31.3	25.0
Within Mexico (%)	1.6	18.2	32.6	23.1	25.0	12.5
Number	63	22	86	52	32	8
San Marcos						
Active U.S. migrant (%)	10.0	6.9	3.3	7.5	0.0	0.0
Inactive U.S. migrant (%)	3.3	3.4	13.1	15.0	16.6	0.0
Number	90	29	61	80	36	3

Source: PERSFILE; household members enumerated in Mexican community samples.

a result of their recent histories of economic growth and development. In Santiago, especially, the recent expansion of local industries has given young men a wide array of opportunities for skilled work, so that single males generally do not migrate. Older married men, however, had to face the displacements that followed the modernization of the factory in the 1950s. In adapting to this profound change, they resorted to migration, both to the United States and within Mexico, so there are many with migrant experience in the later stages of the life cycle. The expansion of factory employment in the 1970s helped many find new jobs in Mexico, however; thus most of those with U.S. migrant experience are now inactive. Nonetheless, older men with few skills had more difficulty reincorporating into the industrial work force and have continued to migrate, accounting for the small peak at the "all teens" stage of the life cycle.

Results thus far have considered migration and the life cycle from the viewpoint of the individual. In doing so, we have linked migration to changes in the level of family dependence by inference only. We have not actually considered patterns of migration and labor utilization within the household itself. Table 7.11, therefore, examines levels of employment and active migration for various household members at different stages of the family life cycle. It demonstrates quite clearly how households strategically allocate family labor to migrant and nonmigrant activities in response to changes in the level of dependence and worker availability within the household.

At the point of household formation, just after marriage, fathers are primarily responsible for the economic maintenance of the couple (88 percent to 100 percent are employed), and relatively few wives work (never more than 25 percent). With no young dependents yet in the household, however, the economic pressure on family heads is low, so relatively few fathers migrate to the United States. There are no U.S. migrants among newly married husbands in Santiago and no more than 14 percent in the other communities.

With the arrival of children the situation changes, however. The already low employment of mothers falls sharply or ceases altogether. At the same time, successive births increase the number of mouths to feed and bodies to clothe but provide no additional workers for the family's support. Because of the resultant strain on household resources during the "young children" phase of the life cycle, the percentage of migrant fathers rises sharply. Indeed, during this stage of family growth and development fathers are most intensely involved in labor migration. In Altamira, the percentage with U.S. migrant fathers rises to 14 percent, while the percentages for Chamitlán, Santiago, and San Marcos are 36 percent, 7 percent, and 7 percent, respectively. The share of fathers migrating within Mexico similarly increases: to 24 percent in Altamira, 19 percent in Chamitlán, and 13 percent in Santiago.

As the children grow older, they gradually begin to contribute to the support of the household, progressively reducing the stress on

TABLE 7.11

EMPLOYMENT AND MIGRANT STATUS OF HOUSEHOLD MEMBERS BY STAGE
IN THE LIFE CYCLE: HOUSEHOLDS IN FOUR MEXICAN COMMUNITIES

Migrant status, employment status, and community	Household's stage in life cycle				
	Newly married	Young children	Some teens	All teens	Children grown
Altamira					
Father					
Employed (%)	100.0	100.0	98.6	89.2	81.8
U.S. migrants (%)	6.3	14.3	11.4	2.7	18.2
Mexican migrants (%)	12.5	23.8	17.1	8.1	0.0
Number	16	42	70	37	11
Mother					
Employed (%)	20.0	13.6	1.4	11.4	25.0
U.S. migrants (%)	6.7	0.0	1.4	4.5	6.3
Mexican migrants (%)	0.0	2.3	2.7	0.0	0.0
Number	15	44	73	44	16
Sons					
Employed (%)	0.0	1.4	36.2	86.8	0.0
U.S. migrants (%)	0.0	0.0	7.8	23.5	0.0
Mexican migrants (%)	0.0	0.0	9.7	17.6	0.0
Number	0	71	257	68	0
Daughters					
Employed (%)	0.0	0.0	7.1	29.6	0.0
U.S. migrants (%)	0.0	0.0	0.0	7.4	0.0
Mexican migrants (%)	0.0	0.0	7.5	18.6	0.0
Number	0	70	227	54	0
Chamitlán					
Father					
Employed (%)	92.9	97.9	98.4	84.4	71.4
U.S. migrants (%)	14.3	36.2	30.7	13.3	14.2
Mexican migrants (%)	14.3	19.1	8.1	8.9	0.0
Number	14	47	62	45	14
Mothers					
Employed (%)	0.0	0.0	3.2	5.8	5.6
U.S. migrants (%)	16.7	0.0	3.2	7.7	5.6
Mexican migrants (%)	8.3	2.1	0.0	3.9	0.0
Number	12	47	62	52	18
Sons					
Employed (%)	0.0	0.0	2.6	67.9	0.0
U.S. migrants (%)	0.0	1.5	3.9	21.0	0.0
Mexican migrants (%)	0.0	0.0	0.0	2.5	0.0
Number	0	68	231	81	0
Daughters					
Employed (%)	0.0	2.7	9.2	22.9	0.0
U.S. migrants (%)	0.0	2.7	0.0	4.8	0.0
Mexican migrants (%)	0.0	0.0	0.0	2.4	0.0
Number	0	73	195	83	0

TABLE 7.11 Continued

Migrant status, employment status, and community	Household's stage in life cycle				
	Newly married	Young children	Some teens	All teens	Children grown
Santiago					
Father					
Employed (%)	100.0	97.7	88.7	67.7	66.6
U.S. migrants (%)	0.0	6.8	5.7	11.8	0.0
Mexican migrants (%)	0.0	12.5	5.7	8.8	0.0
Number	6	88	53	34	9
Mother					
Employed (%)	25.0	13.3	15.1	2.7	0.0
U.S. migrants (%)	0.0	2.2	0.0	0.0	0.0
Mexican migrants (%)	0.0	1.1	1.9	0.0	0.0
Number	4	90	53	37	11
Sons					
Employed (%)	0.0	2.4	19.2	59.6	0.0
U.S. migrants (%)	0.0	0.0	2.0	0.0	0.0
Mexican migrants (%)	0.0	0.0	2.6	3.8	0.0
Number	0	123	151	52	0
Daughters					
Employed (%)	0.0	0.0	15.2	40.0	0.0
U.S. migrants (%)	0.0	0.0	0.0	0.0	0.0
Mexican migrants (%)	0.0	0.0	2.3	5.4	0.0
Number	0	119	132	37	0
San Marcos					
Father					
Employed (%)	87.5	93.2	92.4	83.3	66.7
U.S. migrants (%)	12.5	7.4	7.6	0.0	0.0
Number	8	54	79	36	3
Mother					
Employed (%)	14.3	12.3	8.3	15.9	0.0
U.S. migrants (%)	0.0	0.0	4.8	2.3	0.0
Number	7	57	84	44	3
Sons					
Employed (%)	0.0	1.3	30.5	66.7	0.0
U.S. migrants (%)	0.0	0.0	1.5	7.4	0.0
Number	0	76	259	54	0
Daughters					
Employed (%)	0.0	0.0	10.8	42.2	0.0
U.S. migrants (%)	0.0	0.0	0.0	0.0	0.0
Number	0	83	259	64	0

Source: PERSFILE: household members enumerated in Mexican community samples.

family resources. In Altamira the percentage of working sons rises from 1 percent in the "young children" stage, to 36 percent in the "some teens" stage, and to 87 percent in the "all teens" stage, and similar increases typify the other communities. The percentage of working daughters likewise increases over the three child-rearing phases of the life cycle, although to a lesser extent. By the time all children in the household have become teenagers, therefore, the vast majority of sons and many daughters are contributing to the household economy. At the same time, many of these working sons and daughters begin to migrate to the United States, and migration and employment by mothers also increase as children enter the teenage years.

In the next to last life cycle stage, just before the few remaining teenage children marry and leave home, the relative number of workers is greatest and the strain on household resources the smallest. Most sons have begun to work, and many have begun to migrate, and a large minority of daughters a few mothers have also entered the work force. At the same time, no young children are left in the household to raise and care for. Given the relative abundance of workers and few dependents, at this stage the employment of fathers drops sharply, as does the incidence of U.S. migration. At this stage, fathers also tend to return from the United States to supervise the behavior of teenage daughters and to introduce sons into the world of work.

In the final stage of the life cycle, all children have left home and fathers retire from the active labor force in larger numbers. In the two rural communities the international migration of fathers increases somewhat at this stage, possibly to compensate for the loss of migrant sons to whose income the household has grown accustomed. Also at this stage, some women begin to be widowed and enter the labor force to support themselves.

These results strongly suggest that household economic strategies are dynamic and constantly adjusting over the course of the life cycle. Available workers within the household are shifted back and forth between migrant and nonmigrant pursuits depending on the family's economic burden. This conclusion is further supported by table 7.12, which shows household size, number of workers, and number of migrants by stage in the life cycle. As one progresses through the various life cycle stages, the number of household members increases at first, peaks in the "some teens" stage, and then declines back close to its starting point. Numbers of workers and migrants similarly increase, peak, and fall.

The most interesting data in table 7.12 are the ratios of workers per household member and migrants per household worker, which are

TABLE 7.12

AVERAGE NUMBER OF HOUSEHOLD MEMBERS, WORKERS, AND MIGRANTS BY STAGE IN THE LIFE CYCLE: HOUSEHOLDS IN FOUR MEXICAN COMMUNITIES

Community and variable	Household's stage in life cycle				
	Newly married	Young children	Some teens	All teens	Children grown
Altamira					
Number of members	2.30	5.23	8.77	5.43	2.06
Number of workers	1.10	1.11	2.47	2.50	0.90
Number of migrants	0.30	0.39	1.18	1.13	0.18
To United States	0.15	0.14	0.41	0.50	0.18
Within Mexico	0.15	0.25	0.77	0.63	0.00
Workers/member[a]	0.48	0.21	0.28	0.46	0.44
Migrants/worker[b]	0.27	0.35	0.48	0.45	0.20
Number of households	20	44	73	46	17
Chamitlán					
Number of members	2.35	5.09	8.97	4.80	2.33
Number of workers	0.82	1.09	2.27	2.09	0.89
Number of migrants	0.53	0.64	0.58	0.75	0.17
To United States	0.35	0.43	0.48	0.55	0.17
Within Mexico	0.18	0.21	0.10	0.20	0.00
Workers/member[a]	0.35	0.21	0.25	0.44	0.38
Migrants/worker[b]	0.64	0.59	0.26	0.35	0.19
Number of households	17	47	62	56	18
Santiago					
Number of members	1.43	4.72	7.24	4.38	1.75
Number of workers	1.00	1.12	1.93	1.89	0.50
Number of migrants	0.00	0.22	0.31	0.27	0.00
To United States	0.00	0.09	0.11	0.11	0.00
Within Mexico	0.00	0.13	0.20	0.16	0.00
Workers/member[a]	0.70	0.24	0.27	0.43	0.29
Migrants/worker[b]	0.00	0.20	0.16	0.14	0.00
Number of households	7	90	54	37	12
San Marcos					
Number of members	2.78	5.04	8.19	5.02	1.50
Number of workers	1.44	1.16	2.27	2.38	0.50
Number of U.S. migrants	0.11	0.09	0.16	0.11	0.00
Workers/member[a]	0.52	0.23	0.28	0.47	0.44
Migrants/worker[b]	0.08	0.08	0.07	0.05	0.00
Number of households	9	57	85	45	4

Source: HOUSEFILE; households enumerated in Mexican community samples.

[a] Ratio of number of workers per household member.

[b] Ratio of number of migrants per household worker.

plotted in figure 7.1 for Altamira, Chamitlán, and Santiago. In general, the two ratios are inversely related. As the relative number of workers falls over the early stages of family development, the relative number of migrants rises. Then as the relative number of workers begins to grow once again in the later stages, the relative number of migrants falls.

This pattern is best demonstrated by Altamira and Santiago. Chamitlán displays the same pattern of peaks and valleys in the relative number of workers, but the pattern of migrants per worker is distorted by an exceptionally high ratio in newly married households. This high ratio reflects both an unusually small number of workers and a large number of migrants. The relatively large number of migrants originates from Chamitlán's extensive tradition of migration and its well-developed networks.

There is thus a generally inverse relationship between the number of workers and the number of migrants across stages in the life cycle. The *incidence* of migration is not the only facet of the household economy that varies over the life cycle stage; the *way* in which migration is employed also relates to the particular needs of the family at different points in time. Depending on the nature of demands faced and the reasons for exporting workers, household strategies of migration will differ. Temporary migration should be most prevalent during phases of the life cycle devoted to child rearing, when men migrate to support young children but cannot leave frequently or stay away for long periods because of the many responsibilities of fatherhood. Settled migration should be more common among single or recently married men without family responsibilities and, hence, weaker attachments to the community. Recurrent migration should similarly occur most frequently just after marriage and then late in the life cycle, when men have family ties binding them to Mexico but fewer responsibilities that demand their presence.

These hypotheses are generally confirmed in table 7.13, which classifies male migrants eighteen and over by their life cycle stage and current migrant strategy. This table considers only nonretired migrants, since the increase in retired migrants over the life cycle complicates the picture needlessly and does not reveal any trends that we have not already considered. Because of the relatively small number of migrants, a three-way cross-classification by strategy, life cycle stage, and community produces very small cell sizes, so the table is broken down only by rural and urban status. Moreover, because settled migrants are underrepresented in the representative community samples, we have also added the Californian samples to this table. Their addition or deletion, however, does not affect the general pattern of results.

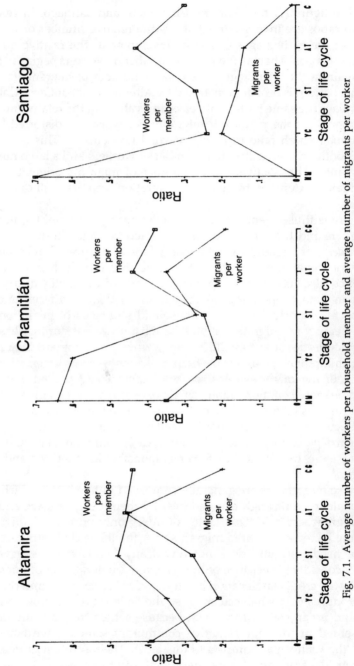

Fig. 7.1. Average number of workers per household member and average number of migrants per worker by stage in the life cycle: three Mexican communities (NM = newly married, YC = young children, ST = some teens, AT = all teens, CG = children gone. *Source*: HOUSEFILE; households enumerated in Mexican community samples.)

TABLE 7.13
NONRETIRED MALE MIGRANTS 18 AND OLDER CLASSIFIED BY CURRENT STRATEGY,
LIFE CYCLE STAGE, AND RURAL VERSUS URBAN STATUS: FOUR MEXICAN COMMUNITIES

Rural-urban status and migrant strategy	Person's stage in life cycle					
	Never married	Newly married	Young children	Some teens	All teens	Children grown
Rural areas						
New (%)	40.7	14.3	9.5	5.1	13.3	0.0
Temporary (%)	17.3	21.4	44.4	59.3	60.0	100.0
Recurrent (%)	19.8	28.6	27.0	10.2	26.7	0.0
Settled (%)	22.2	35.7	19.0	15.3	0.0	0.0
Number	81	14	63	59	15	4
Urban areas						
New (%)	52.9	28.6	7.7	9.5	10.0	0.0
Temporary (%)	23.5	14.3	50.0	47.6	50.0	50.0
Recurrent (%)	5.9	28.6	30.7	19.0	10.0	50.0
Settled (%)	17.6	28.6	11.5	23.8	30.0	0.0
Number	17	7	26	21	10	2

Source: PERSFILE; all migrants enumerated in Mexico or California, including those in twenty-five households in Santiago.

Table 7.13 shows very clearly that migrants shift from one strategy to another as they progress through life. Most unmarried men are new migrants who have just entered the migrant work force and cannot yet be assigned to a particular strategy type. Among those unmarried men whose strategy can be identified, there is a clear rank ordering, although it is slightly different in rural and urban areas. In rural areas, settled migration is most popular, followed by recurrent migration and temporary migration. In urban areas, temporary migration is most popular, followed by settled and recurrent migration.

Among married men without children, settled and recurrent migrants clearly predominate in both urban and rural areas. In rural areas, especially, settled migration is by far the most popular strategy at this stage. With the arrival of children and the beginning of family building, new migration begins to disappear and the percentage of migrants pursuing settled and recurrent strategies falls off. Over the remaining stages of the life cycle, temporary migration comes increasingly to dominate the strategies of migrants, constituting at all times no less than 44 percent of those migrating. Recurrent migration is generally the second most frequent strategy during these phases of life.

In summary, during stages of the life cycle devoted to family growth and development, men are enmeshed in a series of very strong social and economic connections that bind them firmly to the home community. Because of their pressing obligations and strong affective ties to wives and children, most men are willing to absent themselves only sporadically and for brief periods. If they must spend extended periods working abroad, they pursue a strategy of recurrent migration rather than settlement. By the time all their children have left the household, few men are still migrating, but those who continue to go to el Norte make exclusive use of a temporary or recurrent strategy.

Migration to the United States thus represents a fundamental resource that is employed by the household in a strategic way to meet shifting needs at different stages of family development. The sporadic or even the regular absence of family members through migration does not destroy family life. On the contrary, it permits the family to survive and prosper through difficult times brought about internally by the addition of young dependents and externally through the dislocations that have accompanied recent economic developments in Mexico.

MIGRATION AND THE HOUSEHOLD BUDGET

The relative importance of migration within the household economy can be ascertained by considering the cash contributions of migrants and nonmigrants to the household budget. The ethnosurvey questionnaire asked a detailed series of questions about each wage earner's contribution to household income, and table 7.14 was constructed from responses to these inquiries. The table presents average monthly income for households by source and migrant status in 1982. It is important to recognize that these data consider only *earned* cash income, and not noncash support, such as that realized through subsistence farming. Local earnings thus do not represent the only source of family support for nonmigrant households, and it would be misleading to consider monthly earned income to be an accurate index of their true economic status.

In spite of these caveats, the data in table 7.14 do indicate that U.S. migration has a large impact on the monthly budget of Mexican households. Among rural households, U.S. migration raises monthly earnings to a level comparable with advantaged households in Mexican urban areas. For example, nonmigrant households in the two urban communities earned about $207 per month. By comparison, U.S. migrant households in the rural town of Altamira earned a monthly average of $243, while those in Chamitlán earned $158. In each case, money earned in the United States comprised more than 80 percent of monthly cash

TABLE 7.14
MONTHLY EARNED INCOME OF HOUSEHOLDS BY SOURCE OF INCOME AND
MIGRANT STATUS OF HOUSEHOLD IN 1982: FOUR MEXICAN COMMUNITIES (1982 DOLLARS)

| Community and source of income | Migrant status of household in 1982 | | | | | |
| | Has U.S. migrants | | Has Mexican migrants | | Has no migrants | |
	Income	Percent	Income	Percent	Income	Percent
Altamira						
U.S. migrant labor	201	82.7	0	0.0	0	0.0
Mexican migrant labor	7	2.9	117	75.0	0	0.0
Local labor	35	14.4	40	25.0	70	100.0
Total household income	$243	100.0	$157	100.0	$70	100.0
Number	44	44	39	39	117	117
Chamitlán						
U.S. migrant labor	137	86.7	0	0.0	0	0.0
Mexican migrant labor	3	1.9	84	65.1	0	0.0
Local labor	18	11.4	45	34.9	90	100.0
Total household income	$158	100.0	$129	100.0	$90	100.0
Number	57	57	16	16	127	127
Santiago and San Marcos						
U.S. migrant labor	42	65.6	0	0.0	0	0.0
Mexican migrant labor	0	0.0	194	74.3	0	0.0
Local labor	22	34.4	67	25.7	207	100.0
Total household income	$64	100.0	$261	100.0	$207	100.0
Number	17	17	25	25	383	383

Source: HOUSEFILE; households enumerated in Mexican community samples, including twenty-five extra households in Santiago.

income, and households with U.S. migrants had significantly higher incomes than did those containing Mexican migrants or no migrants.

In the two urban communities, however, the monthly income of U.S. migrant households is markedly lower than that of households in the other two migrant status groups. There are two sources of this deficit. First, these households reported practically no locally earned income in 1982. The fact that few of their members were able to secure paid employment in the dynamic economy of Guadalajara and its environs suggests that they are unusually poor households with unskilled members especially unsuited to urban employment. Second, remittances sent by migrants from Santiago and San Marcos tend to be lower because most of them hold urban jobs in the United States. Since the cost of living is higher in U.S. cities, the amount of money available to send home is less.

As important as the amount of U.S. income is, equally important is how it is spent. We stated earlier that migration plays a central role in family support at critical junctures in its life cycle. We have implied, but not demonstrated, that money earned in the United States goes mostly to support current consumption. Unfortunately, the ethnosurvey questionnaire did not ask about how U.S. income was spent, but it did ask migrants whether they saved any money while working abroad, and then asked how these savings were spent. This information is presented by life cycle stage and rural versus urban origin in table 7.15.

The percentage of migrants that spend savings on consumer goods tends to begin high and then fall throughout the life cycle. Young unmarried migrants are the most likely to spend money on consumer goods, usually durables such as stereos, cassette recorders, televisions, records, and automobiles. In this category of migrant, 47 percent of those from rural areas and 67 percent of those from urban areas reported spending their U.S. savings on such consumer items. This kind of consumer spending remains quite prevalent among newly married migrants but drops markedly with the arrival of children.

In contrast, the percentage spent on family support is initially low among never-married and newly-married migrants, then peaks among those with teenage children, and finally falls again for migrants whose

TABLE 7.15
HOW U.S. SAVINGS WERE SPENT CLASSIFIED BY STAGE IN LIFE CYCLE AND
RURAL VERSUS URBAN STATUS: MIGRANTS FROM FOUR MEXICAN COMMUNITIES

Rural-urban status and how savings spent	Person's stage in life cycle					
	Never married	Newly married	Young children	Some teens	All teens	Children grown
Rural areas						
Family support (%)	6.7	11.8	8.7	13.5	20.0	12.5
Housing (%)	13.3	41.2	37.0	34.6	40.0	50.0
Consumer goods (%)	46.7	41.2	32.6	25.0	23.3	25.0
Productive investment (%)	13.3	0.0	13.0	19.2	13.3	12.5
Other (%)	20.0	5.9	8.7	7.7	3.3	0.0
Number	15	17	46	52	30	8
Urban areas						
Family support (%)	0.0	0.0	0.0	18.8	21.4	0.0
Housing (%)	33.3	0.0	28.6	37.5	35.7	100.0
Consumer goods (%)	66.7	25.0	42.9	37.5	21.4	0.0
Productive investment (%)	0.0	25.0	14.3	6.3	21.4	0.0
Other (%)	0.0	50.0	14.3	0.0	0.0	0.0
Number	3	4	14	16	14	1

Source: MIGFILE; migrant household members enumerated in Mexico or California, including those in twenty-five extra households in Santiago.

children have grown and left home. Spending on housing, however, is initially low and continues to grow throughout the life cycle, presumably reflecting the growing need for space as family size increases. In rural areas, a sharp increase in spending for housing is registered immediately after marriage, while in urban areas it does not increase until children arrive.

There are no strong trends in productive investment over the life cycle, although there is some evidence that investment is most likely during phases of the life cycle when family needs are least pressing. Migrants from rural areas tend to invest productively when some of their children have reached the teenage years, whereas those from urban areas generally do so when all children are teenagers.

In general, these figures provide further evidence that migration is employed by households in a very deliberate, self-conscious way. Migrant households use U.S. earnings to increase their monthly income when family needs warrant it and spend the money in characteristic ways depending on the stage of family development.

SUMMARY

Migration to the United States represents a substantial socioeconomic resource for households in western Mexico. A typical migrant working a season in the United States earns between $4,000 and $5,000, even after expenses for food and lodging are deducted, and when converted into pesos, these sums appear very large. In spite of the obvious incentives to international migration, only a small percentage of potential migrants go to the United States in any given year. Migration is a valuable resource that is used judiciously by households, which employ it in a strategic fashion at particular stages of the life cycle. Within larger household survival strategies, international migration is used in one of three ways.

Migrants employing a temporary strategy make a small number of short trips to the United States. This strategy is most prevalent at stages in the life cycle devoted to the raising of young children and is by far the most common strategy in the communities under study. Temporary migrants are generally married fathers in their middle to late thirties who travel to the United States without documents. While abroad, they generally hold unstable urban jobs or perform seasonal agricultural work. They display a low degree of integration within the United States and retain strong ties to their community of origin.

Recurrent migrants make repeated short trips to the United States over prolonged periods. They seek to maintain a high standard of living in Mexico by working regularly in the United States. Over the years, those employing a recurrent strategy make many trips and accumulate much time abroad. They tend to be in their late twenties or early thirties and are single or recently married. They are predominantly undocumented, although a large minority have acquired documents. Like temporary migrants, they are employed as seasonal workers in agriculture or in industries with a cyclical character. They are more integrated into the United States than are temporary migrants, but they still display a preference for life in Mexico.

Settled migration is the last strategy. Migrants who adopt it generally make a small number of trips to the United States before deciding to stay. A settled strategy is usually employed early in the life cycle by single or recently married men in their late twenties or early thirties. They typically settle in U.S. cities and work at steady urban jobs. When a settled migrant works in agriculture, it is generally as a foreman or a labor contractor. As settlers, migrants accumulate many years of experience in the United States and are highly integrated within its socioeconomic and cultural environment. A majority or large minority obtain legal residence documents, and most have children born and raised in the United States. Although ties to the home community are never broken, they are weaker than those for other strategies.

The prevalence of U.S. migration among households and the use of the different strategies are highly related to stage of the life cycle. In the early stages of the life cycle, just before and just after marriage, many migrants employ settled and recurrent strategies, but as life progresses and responsibilities accumulate, temporary migration comes increasingly to dominate the migration process. Migration is high among young unmarried males, who go to the United States to learn the ropes of migration, to earn some extra spending money, or to have an adventure. After marriage, the level of migration falls, but it rises again with the advent of childbearing and peaks during the stage of the life cycle when there are many young children and few workers. Migration falls again as children grow up and leave the household.

Changes in the level of migration over the life cycle are associated with fluctuations in the level of household dependence. The number of migrants per worker varies inversely with the number of workers per household member. As children are born into the family, fathers maximize the return to their labor—and their support for the family—by going to the United States. As their children mature and begin to join the work force, fathers migrate less frequently and migration by their children begins to rise. Consistent with these patterns, spending for consumer goods is most prevalent early in the life cycle, while spending for housing and family maintenance predominates later on.

Together these results indicate that U.S. migration is employed in a deliberate, strategic fashion by households in the four communities. It is manipulated according to definite strategies at different points in a family's growth and development. The migration of Mexicans to the United States is not a haphazard movement of poor people seeking high wages. Rather, it is a calculated movement by household members seeking to remedy specific pressures brought about by family growth or economic dislocation. Because migration has been institutionalized through extensive social networks, it constitutes a basic element in the socioeconomic organization of households and is an omnipresent socioeconomic resource open to all.

When a household member is working in the United States, the money that person sends home can have a profound impact on household income. In rural areas, remittances from the United States can easily raise monthly incomes to levels usually available only to Mexican urban dwellers with stable industrial or service jobs, and often higher positions. Such a large amount of money flowing into the communities from the United States has inevitably had a strong impact on patterns of socioeconomic organization, especially in the rural towns. We examine these impacts in chapter 8.

8

The Socioeconomic Impact of Migration in Mexico

The widespread movement of migrants to the United States naturally affects the internal life of Mexican communities. The large volume of remittance dollars flowing into towns and neighborhoods and the periodic absence of productive family members inevitably affect patterns of socioeconomic organization. The profundity of change depends, of course, on how long international migration has been occurring and on the number of migrants involved. Among the four communities under study, Chamitlán provides the best opportunity to observe migration's effects since it has a longer and more extensive history of migration than the others.

The subject of the impact of international migration on sending areas has received widespread attention by researchers in many regions, including Turkey, Yugoslavia, Spain, Portugal, the Middle East, and the Caribbean.[1] Many studies have focused specifically on Mexico, beginning with the early work of Taylor (1933) and continuing through recent studies by Wiest (1979, 1984), Cornelius (1976, 1978), Reichert (1981, 1982), Shadow (1979), Mines (1981, 1984), Roberts (1982, 1984), and Dinerman (1978, 1982). The international research literature covers a variety of social, cultural, and economic settings and differs on certain points; however, it shows remarkable consistency in several key findings.

Studies agree that migrant income allows households to improve their material standards of living dramatically but that earnings are spent in relatively unproductive ways. Remittances and savings generally go to current consumption rather than investment. Studies specifically cite the purchase and repair of homes and the acquisition of consumer goods as priority spending goals. The little investment that occurs

---

[1] The specific studies for each country include Paine (1974) and Pennix (1982) for Turkey; Baucic (1972), Bennett (1979), and Baletic (1982) for Yugoslavia; Brandes (1975), Rhoades (1978, 1979), and Bretell (1979) for Spain and Portugal; Trebous (1970), Fergany (1982), and Swanson (1979) for the Middle East; and Rubenstein (1979), Pressar (1982), Grasmuck (1982), and Griffith (1986) for the Caribbean.

goes to small commercial activities that generate little employment. To the extent that they are able, migrants do buy farmland; however, when land is acquired by migrants, it is often held fallow while they continue migrating or is retained as a source of security and prestige in the community. As a result of these developments, studies report a decline in agricultural production and a constriction of local economic activity linked to international migration.

In this chapter we analyze these issues through a detailed examination of the impact of migration on the four communities. Following issues addressed in prior research, we consider the effect of migration on spending patterns, housing, living standards, business activities, employment, land distribution, and agricultural production. Although the data pertain to 1982, the impact of migration cannot be fully understood apart from the historical-structural context within which it occurs. Where appropriate, we thus interpret our cross-sectional findings relative to broader historical trends and draw special attention to structural factors in the conclusion.

SPENDING PATTERNS

In chapter 7 we suggested that family sustenance is the most common goal of U.S. migrants. Although spending patterns differ between households depending on their life cycle stage, size, and economic resources, migrant earnings generally go first to cover the costs of basic necessities such as food, clothing, and shelter. Only after these needs are met do families spend on goods and services to improve their standard of living or to increase production. Studies have revealed that migrant earnings go primarily to consumption rather than investment.

It is very difficult to establish precisely the amount of U.S. income sent home and how it is spent. Money comes in irregular quantities and at sporadic intervals and arrives in a variety of forms: money orders, cashier's checks, personal checks, traveler's checks, electronic drafts, cash sent through relatives and friends, and savings brought back by migrants themselves. Given the irregular and sporadic nature of migrant remittances, the ethnosurvey did not ask how they were spent; rather, in order to assess how U.S. earnings were used, it focused on migrant savings.

Table 8.1 reports how migrants in the four communities spent money saved on their most recent trip to the United States. This information confirms the finding that migrants spend primarily on current consumption, a category that includes family sustenance, housing, the

TABLE 8.1
HOW MONEY SAVED ON LAST U.S. TRIP WAS SPENT: MIGRANTS FROM
FOUR MEXICAN COMMUNITIES, 1982

How savings were spent	Community			
	Altamira	Chamitlán	Santiago	San Marcos
Productive investments (%)	15.4	8.9	11.5	21.1
Buy land (%)	10.6	2.5	5.7	15.8
Buy livestock (%)	3.8	1.3	0.0	0.0
Buy tools (%)	0.0	1.3	2.9	0.0
Buy or start business (%)	1.0	3.8	2.9	5.3
Current consumption (%)	71.1	86.1	71.4	68.4
Support family (%)	19.2	3.8	5.7	21.1
Build or repair house (%)	18.3	25.3	0.0	36.8
Buy house or lot (%)	11.5	22.8	22.9	10.5
Buy consumer goods (%)	13.5	32.9	31.4	0.0
Recreation (%)	8.6	1.3	11.4	0.0
Other (%)	13.4	5.1	17.2	10.6
Buy vehicle (%)	3.8	0.0	8.6	5.3
Pay off debt (%)	1.9	1.3	2.9	5.3
Savings not spent (%)	7.7	3.8	5.7	0.0
Total with savings	104	79	35	19

Source: MIGFILE; migrant household members enumerated in Mexico or California, including those in twenty-five extra households in Santiago.

purchase of consumer goods, and recreation. In Altamira, Santiago, and San Marcos, about 70 percent of savings were spent in these categories, compared to 86 percent in Chamitlán. In each community, housing was the most popular spending target. The percentage of households that used their savings to build, repair, or buy a home varied from 23 percent in Santiago (where a large share of homes are provided free of cost by the factory) to 48 percent in Chamitlán; however, focusing on savings probably overstates the importance of housing relative to family support. Money spent on family support usually arrives in the form of remittances, while money saved during a trip is more often spent on large durable goods, such as housing.

Relatively few savings go to productive investment. Among the four communities, the percentage of migrants spending in a potentially productive way varied from only 9 percent in Chamitlán to 21 percent in San Marcos. As prior studies have revealed, land was the most popular of such investments, even among urban migrants, who typically purchase land in their rural communities of origin. A few respondents reported spending on motor vehicles, which may or may not be a productive investment, depending on the use of these vehicles. In rural communities, pickup trucks, larger trucks, and tractors are purchased for use in agricultural production. Even if we assume that spending on vehicles always represents a productive investment, our general conclusion is not altered. Migrant savings are spent primarily on consumption.

HOUSING

Spending patterns thus suggest that home ownership is a universal aspiration among families in the four communities and that migration is employed as a means to achieve this end. In this section, we consider the extent to which people have been able to become home owners or to improve their existing homes through U.S. migration; we then examine the effects that migration has had on the distribution of housing among migrants and nonmigrants in each community.

Table 8.2 shows how home owners in the four communities acquired money to buy their houses. The first (top) subdivision in the table considers all owned homes and the second subdivision, all purchased homes. A modest but significant percentage of all homes owned by residents in each place was purchased with money earned in the United States. As one would expect, the largest percentage is found in Chamitlán, where 26 percent of all homes owned were bought with U.S. earnings, followed by 11 percent in Altamira, 9 percent in San Marcos, and 8 percent in Santiago. If we consider only those homes that were purchased, the percentages are even larger: 33 percent in Chamitlán, 26 percent in Altamira, 10 percent in San Marcos, and 9 percent in Santiago.

One-quarter of all homes bought in Altamira and one-third of those in Chamitlán were thus purchased with money earned in the United States. The percentages in Santiago and San Marcos are lower because in urban areas there are other ways of acquiring a home besides migration. Urban dwellers have greater access to credit, to means of accumulating cash, and to subsidized housing provided by companies or the government. In Santiago, for example, many families take advantage of free housing provided by the textile company, and in San Marcos, a significant part of the survey area contains houses constructed with "social interest loans" given by banks at government-subsidized rates. Even in the latter case, U.S. migration often plays a crucial role. Informants report that many people use U.S. savings for down payments on a social interest loan and then rely on remittances to help meet the monthly payments.

The bottom two subdivisions in table 8.2 indicate the extent to which migrants, as opposed to all home owners, have used U.S. earnings to

TABLE 8.2
HOW MONEY TO BUY HOME WAS OBTAINED: HOUSEHOLDS IN
FOUR MEXICAN COMMUNITIES, 1982

Source of money	Community			
	Altamira	Chamitlán	Santiago	San Marcos
Owned homes				
Local labor (%)	48.6	48.3	62.8	70.4
Mexican labor (%)	6.3	6.2	2.0	14.4
U.S. labor (%)	10.6	26.2	7.8	8.8
Inherited (%)	25.4	17.2	12.8	2.4
Other (%)	9.2	2.0	14.7	4.0
Number	142	145	102	125
Purchased homes				
Local labor (%)	65.1	58.3	71.9	72.1
Mexican labor (%)	8.5	7.5	2.3	14.8
U.S. labor (%)	26.4	32.5	9.0	9.8
Other (%)	0.0	1.7	16.9	3.3
Number	106	120	89	122
Homes owned by migrants				
Local labor (%)	43.2	42.1	44.9	50.0
Mexican labor (%)	2.3	6.5	0.0	18.2
U.S. labor (%)	17.1	33.6	16.3	22.7
Inherited (%)	22.7	15.9	16.3	2.3
Other (%)	14.7	1.9	22.5	6.8
Number	88	107	49	44
Homes purchased by migrants				
Local labor (%)	55.9	50.0	53.7	51.2
Mexican labor (%)	2.9	7.8	0.0	18.6
U.S. labor (%)	41.2	41.1	19.5	25.6
Other (%)	0.0	1.1	26.8	4.6
Number	68	90	41	43

Source: HOUSEFILE; households enumerated in Mexican community samples.

acquire homes. In Chamitlán, 33 percent of all homes owned by migrants and 41 percent of those purchased by them were bought with money earned in the United States. The respective figures for Altamira were 17 percent and 41 percent; and for San Marcos, 23 percent and 26 percent, with 16 percent and 20 percent in Santiago. In other words, among those eligible to have bought homes with U.S. money (migrants who did not inherit their homes), between 20 percent and 41 percent did so.

Migrants display a preference for investing their savings in housing, therefore, and a significant share of their homes were bought with U.S. money. Table 8.3 suggests the effect that this has had on the distribution of home ownership in the four communities. In general, migrants have been more successful in becoming home owners than nonmigrants. The

TABLE 8.3
OWNERSHIP AND SOURCE OF PURCHASE MONEY FOR HOMES IN FOUR MEXICAN COMMUNITIES
BY YEARS OF U.S. MIGRANT EXPERIENCE, 1982

Community, ownership, and source	Nonmigrant	U.S. migrants × years of experience				
		<1 year	1–4 years	5–9 years	10+ years	Total
Altamira						
Homes owned (%)	56.0	83.0	89.0	78.0	93.0	86.4
Bought with U.S. earnings (%)	0.0	10.0	26.0	29.0	85.0	27.2
Number	97	24	47	18	14	103
Chamitlán						
Homes owned (%)	76.0	76.0	74.0	79.0	73.0	75.2
Bought with U.S. earnings (%)	0.0	4.0	29.0	50.0	59.0	24.8
Number	51	34	57	28	30	149
Santiago						
Homes owned (%)	40.0	77.0	74.0	75.0	86.0	76.6
Bought with U.S. earnings (%)	0.0	0.0	18.0	11.0	67.0	12.5
Number	136	22	23	12	7	64
San Marcos						
Homes owned (%)	60.0	70.0	70.0	78.0	80.0	72.6
Bought with U.S. earnings (%)	0.0	13.0	7.0	71.0	38.0	17.7
Number	138	23	20	9	10	62

Source: HOUSEFILE; households enumerated in Mexican community samples.

percentage of home owners is greatest among households containing U.S. migrants, with the sole exception of Chamitlán, which is discussed below. The contrast is especially marked in Altamira, where 86 percent of U.S. migrant households, but only 56 percent of nonmigrants, own their homes. In Santiago the respective percentages are 77 percent and 40 percent and in San Marcos, 73 percent and 60 percent.

When migrant households are grouped according to total U.S. experience (the sum total of individual members' migrant experiences), the contrast in home ownership is heightened. Among those with ten or more years of cumulative U.S. experience, 93 percent own homes in Altamira, 86 percent in Santiago, and 80 percent in San Marcos, and the percentage of homes purchased with U.S. money rises steadily as the amount of experience in the United States increases. This pattern is consistent with the idea that migrants turn to home buying only after pressing family needs have been met. The first few trips are made in response to immediate demands of family growth. Only after these demands subside or are satisfied will buying a home become a realistic goal.

The prevalence of home ownership among both migrants and non-migrants in Chamitlán stems from the advanced state of its migratory stream. Its social networks are now so well developed that U.S. migration is open even to the very poor, and most migrants are now landless jornaleros. Since migrant families in Chamitlán are quite likely to buy and own homes, and since 75 percent of households in Chamitlán contain migrants, home ownership has become very widespread, and more families own a home there than in any other community. Even the poorest groups have a chance for home ownership. Those few households without migrants are relatively well off and do not need to migrate to earn money to acquire homes.

An important phenomenon in the two rural towns that cannot be appreciated from the tables is the high percentage of houses on loan. Of all families in Chamitlán, about 33 percent live in a borrowed house and 20 percent do so in Altamira. The respective figures for Santiago and San Marcos are only 9 percent and 5 percent. The high rural percentages reflect the extent to which the social process of migration has progressed in the two towns. Although migration begins with men, wives and children eventually become involved, and at advanced stages of the process entire families migrate. When all members of a home-owning family migrate, the house is typically loaned to relatives or friends so that it will not be left vacant. With so many families gone, many houses are available for loan in this way. This situation does not arise in Santiago or San Marcos, where migration is less pervasive and there is a stronger rental market for unused homes.

The strong demand for houses from U.S. migrants in Altamira and Chamitlán has brought inflation to their housing markets. In Chamitlán, particularly, townspeople report that prices are near those found in Zamora or Guadalajara. Since migrants want to own homes in the community even if they spend most of their time abroad, home buyers face a paradoxical situation of many vacant homes with few for sale, and in recent years it has become increasingly difficult to purchase a house.

Migration-induced demand and inflation have made home construction very profitable and a dynamic factor of growth in local economies. In Altamira, construction is the second largest source of employment after agriculture; the situation is similar in Chamitlán, where a building boom has increased the employment of masons and carpenters and has supported the formation of several new construction supply businesses. The boom has been encouraged by the recent period of high inflation, since the devaluation of the peso greatly enhanced migrants' ability to buy houses. In Santiago and San Marcos, particularly, many formerly settled migrants returned to buy or construct houses. Having purchased houses in southern California during the late 1960s and early 1970s, these immigrants found that their homes had appreciated markedly by 1982. During the economic crisis, they took advantage of favorable exchange rates to sell their houses in California and build or buy new ones in Mexico.

Often homes constructed with migrant earnings are second dwellings. Rural migrants frequently buy houses in Zamora or Guadalajara as investments and rent them out to relatives or lease them on the open market. Migrant families from San Marcos very often purchase second homes in the neighborhood, partly for investment, but also to keep friends and relatives nearby. In this way, the loaning and leasing of second homes reinforces the network of ties that link Guadalajara to the rural communities of origin.

There are also differences between migrants and nonmigrants with respect to housing quality. The data in table 8.4 indicate that where differences in housing quality exist, U.S. migrants generally live in better homes. This is especially true in Altamira, where variability in housing quality is greatest. Here, 52 percent of U.S. migrant families live in brick homes, compared to only 34 percent of nonmigrants, who typically live in adobe. Similarly, 47 percent of migrant homes have cement or tile floors (as opposed to dirt), while the percentage is only

TABLE 8.4

QUALITY OF HOUSING IN FOUR MEXICAN COMMUNITIES BY YEARS OF U.S. MIGRANT EXPERIENCE, 1982

Community and kind of house	Nonmigrant	U.S. migrants × experience				
		<1 year	1–4 years	5–9 years	10+ years	Total
Altamira						
Made of brick (%)	34.0	50.0	53.0	39.0	71.0	52.4
Cement or tile floor (%)	34.0	46.0	45.0	33.0	71.0	46.6
With running water (%)	77.0	83.0	87.0	72.0	79.0	82.5
With electricity (%)	63.0	79.0	96.0	72.0	86.0	86.4
Number	97	24	47	18	14	103
Chamitlán						
Made of brick (%)	29.0	9.0	21.0	29.0	10.0	17.4
Cement or tile floor (%)	80.0	71.0	88.0	82.0	83.0	81.9
With running water (%)	86.0	97.0	95.0	89.0	100.0	95.3
With electricity (%)	92.0	97.0	98.0	100.0	100.0	98.7
Number	51	34	57	28	30	149
Santiago						
Made of brick (%)	61.0	77.0	65.0	100.0	86.0	78.1
Cement or tile floor (%)	93.0	95.0	91.0	92.0	86.0	92.2
With running water (%)	97.0	100.0	96.0	100.0	100.0	98.4
With electricity (%)	98.0	100.0	100.0	100.0	100.0	100.0
Number	136	22	23	12	7	64
San Marcos						
Made of brick (%)	93.0	91.0	95.0	100.0	100.0	95.2
Cement or tile floor (%)	92.0	96.0	100.0	100.0	90.0	96.8
With running water (%)	100.0	100.0	100.0	100.0	100.0	100.0
With electricity (%)	98.0	96.0	100.0	100.0	100.0	98.4
Number	138	23	20	9	10	62

Source: HOUSEFILE; households enumerated in Mexican community samples.

34 percent for nonmigrant homes. Migrant homes are also more likely to have running water and electricity. In the other communities, housing quality is generally much higher, so the contrasts between migrants and nonmigrants are not as great. Nonetheless, migrants are more likely to live in higher-quality homes in nine of the twelve comparisons, and in most cases the percentage with higher-quality homes increases as migrant experience grows.

STANDARD OF LIVING

Returning migrants not only want to acquire homes; they also want to stock them with consumer durables that make life easier and more comfortable. Modern appliances such as stoves, refrigerators, washing machines, and sewing machines greatly reduce the drudgery of daily life, especially for women. Electronic products such as radios, television, stereos, and telephones make life much more enjoyable and give residents in rural communities direct access to national cultural life. Possession of these highly desired goods also enhances the social status and prestige of a family within the community.

Table 8.5 examines the presence of selected appliances in homes of migrants and nonmigrants. In the two urban communities, the vast majority of households contain appliances, so differences between migrants and nonmigrants are not great. In Altamira, however, U.S. migrants clearly have greater access to work-saving amenities, and access to these conveniences generally increases with U.S. migrant experience. Only 56 percent of nonmigrant households had a stove, while 85 percent of U.S. migrant households did so, and among those with ten years of migrant experience, the figure was 93 percent. Even smaller percentages of nonmigrant households contained refrigerators (21 percent), but the percentage of migrant households with this appliance was 35 percent, and 71 percent among those with ten or more years of experience. Similarly, the percentage owning washing machines was 11 percent for nonmigrants, 33 percent for all migrants, and 71 percent for the most experienced migrants. Possession of sewing machines similarly rose from 37 percent among nonmigrant households to 93 percent among the most experienced migrant households, with 61 percent of all migrant households possessing this convenience.

Chamitlán is a wealthier community, and ownership of appliances is more widespread, so the overall contrast between migrants and nonmigrants is not as great. Moreover, households with under five years of migrant experience do not fare much better than those with none.

TABLE 8.5

PRESENCE OF SELECTED APPLIANCES IN HOUSEHOLDS OF FOUR MEXICAN COMMUNITIES
CLASSIFIED BY YEARS OF U.S. MIGRANT EXPERIENCE, 1982

Community and appliance	Nonmigrant	U.S. migrants × experience				Total
		<1 year	1–4 years	5–9 years	10+ years	
Altamira						
Stove (%)	56.0	83.0	87.0	72.0	93.0	84.5
Refrigerator (%)	21.0	17.0	34.0	33.0	71.0	35.0
Washing machine (%)	11.0	13.0	34.0	28.0	71.0	33.0
Sewing machine (%)	37.0	33.3	68.0	56.0	93.0	61.2
Number	97	24	47	18	14	103
Chamitlán						
Stove (%)	78.0	71.0	89.0	89.0	90.0	85.2
Refrigerator (%)	33.0	21.0	19.0	21.0	57.0	27.5
Washing machine (%)	18.0	6.0	11.0	21.0	37.0	16.8
Sewing machine (%)	41.0	41.0	33.0	46.0	60.0	43.0
Number	51	34	57	28	30	149
Santiago						
Stove (%)	98.0	100.0	100.0	100.0	86.0	98.4
Refrigerator (%)	79.0	95.0	74.0	83.0	86.0	84.4
Washing machine (%)	69.0	59.0	74.0	75.0	86.0	70.3
Sewing machine (%)	57.0	50.0	61.0	42.0	71.0	54.7
Number	136	22	23	12	7	64
San Marcos						
Stove (%)	99.0	100.0	100.0	100.0	100.0	100.0
Refrigerator (%)	76.0	83.0	90.0	67.0	70.0	80.6
Washing machine (%)	63.0	87.0	75.0	44.0	40.0	69.4
Sewing machine (%)	60.0	70.0	70.0	67.0	70.0	69.4
Number	138	23	20	9	10	62

Source: HOUSEFILE; households enumerated in Mexican community samples.

Nonetheless, the contrast between those with more than ten years of experience and nonmigrants is quite marked. The percentage owning a stove is 78 percent for nonmigrant households but 90 percent for the most experienced migrant households. For refrigerators, washing machines, and sewing machines, the respective percentages are 33 percent versus 57 percent, 18 percent versus 37 percent, and 41 percent versus 60 percent.

Table 8.6 considers ownership of selected electronic components by migrant and nonmigrant households. Goods such as televisions, stereos, and radios are often purchased in the United States and brought home. For some of the goods listed in table 8.6, there is little difference in the prevalence of ownership between migrant and nonmigrant households. For example, radios are virtually universal among sample households, and telephones are so rare that it is difficult to interpret patterns, except in San Marcos, where migrants seem to have slightly greater access. Televisions and stereos are also quite common in the two urban communities, and there are no really clear patterns of ownership by migrant status.

The greatest contrasts between migrant and nonmigrant households occur in the two rural communities with respect to the ownership of televisions and stereos, two highly prized items. In Altamira, 69 percent of households with migrants have televisions, compared to only 37 percent of nonmigrant households. In households with more than ten years of migrant experience, 86 percent have a television set. Similarly, in Chamitlán 60 percent of migrant households and 80 percent of those with ten or more years of migrant experience have televisions, compared to only 53 percent of households without migrants. The percentage owning stereos in Altamira rises from 13 percent among nonmigrants to 43 percent among the most experienced migrants and from 29 percent to 57 percent in Chamitlán.

One final item that is highly desired but very expensive is a motor vehicle, and information on ownership of this good is presented in table 8.7. In the two rural towns, a majority of vehicles are owned by U.S. migrants, and a sizable proportion were purchased directly with U.S. money. Of the thirty-five vehicles enumerated in Altamira, 51 percent were migrant-owned and 26 percent were bought directly with U.S. earnings; of the sixteen vehicles in Chamitlán, 63 percent were owned by migrants and 31 percent were purchased with money from the United States. The impact of U.S. migration is particularly evident in the ownership of automobiles. Of the five cars listed for Altamira in table 8.7, four were owned by U.S. migrants, three were purchased with U.S.

TABLE 8.6
PRESENCE OF SELECTED ELECTRONIC GOODS IN HOUSEHOLDS OF FOUR MEXICAN COMMUNITIES
CLASSIFIED BY YEARS OF U.S. EXPERIENCE, 1982

Community and electronic good	Nonmigrant	U.S. migrants × experience				Total
		<1 year	1-4 years	5-9 years	10+ years	
Altamira						
Radio (%)	91.0	96.0	98.0	94.0	93.0	96.1
TV (%)	37.0	71.0	66.0	61.0	86.0	68.9
Stereo (%)	13.0	13.0	26.0	28.0	43.0	25.2
Phone (%)	1.0	0.0	9.0	0.0	7.0	4.9
Number	97	24	47	18	14	103
Chamitlán						
Radio (%)	90.0	91.0	91.0	86.0	83.0	88.9
TV (%)	53.0	56.0	54.0	54.0	80.0	59.7
Stereo (%)	29.0	24.0	21.0	39.0	57.0	32.2
Phone (%)	10.0	0.0	0.0	0.0	10.0	2.0
Number	51	34	57	28	30	149
Santiago						
Radio (%)	86.0	73.0	87.0	92.0	86.0	82.8
TV (%)	89.0	95.0	100.0	100.0	71.0	95.3
Stereo (%)	68.0	55.0	43.0	58.0	86.0	54.7
Phone (%)	10.0	5.0	9.0	0.0	29.0	7.8
Number	136	22	23	12	7	64
San Marcos						
Radio (%)	87.0	91.0	95.0	89.0	90.0	91.9
TV (%)	91.0	91.0	90.0	89.0	90.0	90.3
Stereo (%)	55.0	74.0	50.0	33.0	60.0	58.1
Phone (%)	25.0	30.0	50.0	22.0	50.0	38.7
Number	138	23	20	9	10	62

Source: HOUSEFILE; households enumerated in Mexican community samples.

TABLE 8.7
PERCENT OF VEHICLES OWNED BY U.S. MIGRANTS, PERCENT OF VEHICLES
BOUGHT WITH U.S. EARNINGS, AND PERCENT OF VEHICLES REGISTERED IN THE
UNITED STATES BY TYPE OF VEHICLE: FOUR MEXICAN COMMUNITIES, 1982

| | Type of vehicle | | | | |
Community and variable	Pickup truck	Large truck	Tractor	Car	Total vehicles
Altamira					
U.S.-migrant-owned (%)	60.0	45.5	33.3	80.0	51.4
Bought with U.S. earnings (%)	30.0	9.1	22.2	60.0	25.7
Registered in United States (%)	10.0	0.0	0.0	20.0	8.6
Number of vehicles	10	11	9	5	35
Chamitlán					
U.S.-migrant-owned (%)	37.5	66.7	0.0	75.0	62.5
Bought with U.S. earnings (%)	25.0	33.3	0.0	25.0	31.3
Registered in United States (%)	25.0	16.7	0.0	25.0	25.0
Number of vehicles	8	6	2	4	20
Santiago					
U.S.-migrant-owned (%)	6.0	—	—	41.7	20.7
Bought with U.S. earnings (%)	0.0	—	—	8.3	3.4
Registered in United States (%)	0.0	—	—	8.3	3.4
Number of vehicles	17	0	0	12	29
San Marcos					
U.S.-migrant-owned (%)	44.4	—	—	25.0	40.9
Bought with U.S. earnings (%)	5.6	—	—	25.0	9.1
Registered in United States (%)	16.7	—	—	0.0	13.6
Number of vehicles	18	0	0	4	22

Source: HOUSEFILE; households enumerated in Mexican community samples.

earnings, and one was actually registered in the United States. Similarly, in Chamitlán three of the four cars were migrant-owned, and one was bought and registered in the United States.

In rural farm communities such as Altamira and Chamitlán, pickup trucks, larger trucks, and tractors are obviously productive investments, and migrant earnings have played an important role in their acquisition. In Altamira, six of the ten pickup trucks were owned by migrants, three were purchased directly with U.S. money, and one was registered in the United States. Five of the eleven trucks and three of the nine tractors were migrant-owned, and one truck and two tractors were bought with migrant money. In Chamitlán, 25 percent of the pickup trucks and about 33 percent of the larger trucks were purchased with funds from the United States, and 67 percent of all larger trucks and 38 percent of all pickup trucks were owned by migrants.

In short, U.S. migration has played an important role in building the stock of vehicles in the two rural communities, with a quarter to a third purchased directly with U.S. money and a majority owned by U.S. migrants. In Santiago and San Marcos, the effect of migration has been less pronounced, because of greater opportunities for earning and borrowing money and because of less extensive migration. Only 21 percent of vehicles in Santiago were migrant-owned, and in San Marcos the figure was 41 percent. Fewer than 10 percent were purchased with U.S. earnings in each case.

In the rural communities, the widespread investment of migrant earnings in homes, consumer goods, and vehicles creates ancillary demands for other services, particularly urban amenities such as running water, electricity, sewers, and roads. New appliances require a reliable source of electric power, modern plumbing facilities require sewer systems, and cars and trucks must be driven on paved roads. Migration to the United States often results in additional demand for "urban modernization" programs designed to bring basic services and utilities to rural towns. Reichert (1981, 1982) has described one case where public buildings and municipal improvements were undertaken with the crucial support of U.S. migrants and their earnings, supplemented by funds from the Mexican government.

Altamira and Chamitlán have also undertaken initiatives to expand urban services; however, the role played by international migrants in the two towns was very different. In Altamira, there was no unusual monetary participation of migrants. Rather, most funding for these works came from the government, which established a special commission between 1970 and 1975 that funded several projects in Altamira and other municipios in southern Jalisco. Roads were constructed, potable water supplies were introduced, towns were electrified and publicly lighted, and sewers and schools were built. In Chamitlán, however, most public works were paid for by the residents themselves and migrant earnings played a much larger role. Streets were paved, and piped potable water was extended to most of the town, along with electricity and sewage. The main plaza was remodeled and dirt roads connecting the town to its rancherías improved. Informants report that migrant earnings represented a significant portion of private contributions to these projects.

One example of the leading role taken by migrants in local development is a project now under way on the outskirts of Chamitlán. The developers are a group of young men, all of whom have worked in the United States. They are trying to build a new country club organized around a new social and athletic facility. They are financing this project partly through a bank, but they also plan to sell memberships to patrons, who by contributing money for the construction of playing fields, courts, and an auditorium, will have the right to own land in the development and to build there. Contributors would be considered founding members of the club, and the developers expect them to come largely from the ranks of successful U.S. migrants.

BUSINESS AND EMPLOYMENT

Prior studies have concluded that international migration does little for economic growth and development in sending communities, a conclusion that follows from the small share of migrant money invested in production and from the fact that businesses formed by migrants tend to be small and unproductive. These studies disregard the context of Third World development, however. They implicitly assume that migrant earnings *could* have activated local economies if the right investments had been made. This position disregards the structural character of economic development in countries such as Mexico: the concentration of productive and commercial activities in a few large metropolitan centers. Given the advantages that such cities have with respect to infrastructure, services, credit availability, labor supply, and market access, the ability of migrants to promote local development in small towns is really quite limited. As we have seen, in competition with urban manufacturing centers, once-thriving artisan and commercial sectors in Altamira and Chamitlán have dwindled to a few small enterprises.

This fact is reflected in table 8.8, which examines characteristics of businesses operated by households in the four communities under study. In the two rural towns, most household business activity consists of small operations employing one or two family members and few outside workers. The average business in Altamira consisted of 1.6 family workers and 0.3 employees, and in Chamitlán the figures were 2.3 and 0.2, respectively. The most common business activities were street vending (typically food products), retail sales (usually small grocery stores), wholesaling (primarily local farm products), and small workshops (for shoemaking, carpentry, sewing, etc.).

Chamitlán's businesses, which are so close to booming Zamora, have been particularly hard hit by the Mexican pattern of regional concentration. Today, the few remaining merchandisers simply redistribute to neighboring rancherías products bought from Zamora. Most local merchants specialize in the sale of food, the one consumable for which

TABLE 8.8
SELECTED CHARACTERISTICS OF BUSINESSES OPERATED BY HOUSEHOLDS IN
FOUR MEXICAN COMMUNITIES

Community and characteristic	Kind of business					
	Street vendor	Retail	Wholesale	Taller	Other	Total
Altamira						
Migrant-owned (%)	0.0	50.0	44.4	62.5	30.8	36.2
Bought with U.S. earnings (%)	0.0	0.0	22.2	12.6	7.7	8.5
Mean number of employees	0.3	0.4	0.0	0.8	0.0	0.3
Mean number of farmworkers	1.4	2.0	1.4	2.3	1.3	1.6
Number	9	8	9	8	13	47
Chamitlán						
Migrant-owned (%)	37.5	71.4	28.6	80.0	40.0	50.0
Bought with U.S. earnings (%)	12.5	14.3	14.3	20.0	20.0	15.6
Mean number of employees	0.1	0.0	0.4	0.3	0.4	0.2
Mean number of family members	2.8	2.4	2.6	1.4	1.8	2.3
Number	8	7	7	5	5	32
Santiago						
Migrant-owned (%)	50.0	52.9	16.7	16.7	85.7	47.4
Bought with U.S. earnings (%)	50.0	11.8	0.0	0.0	16.7	10.5
Mean number of employees	0.0	0.8	0.2	0.5	0.6	0.6
Mean number of family members	2.0	2.3	1.7	2.0	1.3	2.0
Number	2	17	6	6	7	38
San Marcos						
Migrant-owned (%)	83.3	17.6	14.3	25.0	14.3	26.7
Bought with U.S. earnings (%)	33.3	5.9	14.3	25.0	14.3	15.6
Mean number of employees	0.0	0.5	0.6	1.8	1.4	0.8
Mean number of family members	4.0	2.6	3.7	2.3	2.3	2.9
Number	6	17	7	8	7	45

Source: HOUSEFILE; households enumerated in Mexican community samples.

frequent trips into the city are impractical. According to our data, about half of Chamitlán's businesses deal with food: eight street vendors plus another seven retail outlets, out of thirty-two sampled. This data accords with information obtained from the municipal government, which indicates that 46 percent of businesses are grocery stores and another 18 percent are made up of bakeries, tortilla factories, milk stores, and butchers. The absence of productive activities in the town is notable. A canvass of the town revealed only six manufacturing enterprises: a small furniture assembly shop, a metalworking shop, a small factory for children's clothes, and three woodworking shops.

In spite of the limited opportunities for business in the two rural communities, migrants do invest their earnings in productive enterprises. Of Altamira's businesses, 36 percent are migrant-owned and 9 percent were established directly with U.S. money. In Chamitlán, the figures are even higher: 50 percent of businesses are owned by migrants and 16 percent were founded with money earned in the United States. Migrants in Altamira were especially likely to own and invest in wholesale businesses or in small talleres, whereas those in Chamitlán tended to be involved in talleres and retail stores.

The overall patterns of business ownership and investment are not markedly different in Santiago and San Marcos. Their business sectors are likewise dominated by small commercial ventures dedicated to the sale of food. Street vendors and retail stores together make up roughly half of all businesses in both places, and over 40 percent of these food outlets are owned by migrants and 14 percent were capitalized with U.S. earnings. Considering all business ventures together, 47 percent of those in Santiago and 27 percent of those in San Marcos are managed by returned migrants, and 11 percent of the former and 16 percent of the latter were founded with capital earned in the United States.

The importance of U.S. earnings to the creation and maintenance of businesses was repeatedly stressed by informants in the urban areas. We have already noted the dynamic, small-scale manufacturing sector of Guadalajara and its environs. There is some evidence of the importance of this sector in table 8.8. Businesses in San Marcos generally employ more workers than in the other communities: an average of 3.7 workers per firm (2.9 family members and 0.8 employees); the next closest community is the industrial suburb of Santiago, with 2.6 workers per firm.

The backbone of Guadalajara's informal economy is the myriad of small talleres, which produce everything from clothing to candy, and talleres in San Marcos employ more nonfamily workers than any other business category represented in table 8.8: some 1.8 employees per firm, which, in addition to 2.3 family members, gives an average firm size of 4.1 people. The talleres, in turn, support a thriving wholesale trade network, and this is the largest single business category represented in table 8.8, with 4.3 workers overall (2.6 family members and 0.6 employees). In both of these categories, U.S. migration has played a significant role, as it is directly responsible for the capitalization of 14 percent of wholesale businesses and 25 percent of the talleres.

Given the structural constraints, the extent of investment in economic activities is impressive, even in rural areas, where economic opportunity is quite limited. The importance of U.S. migration is further suggested by table 8.9, which examines the impact of U.S. earnings on employment. Taking all four places together, 32 percent of hired workers

TABLE 8.9
Number of Workers Employed by Businesses in Four Mexican Communities by Kind of Worker, Migrant Status of Owning Household, and Source of Capital, 1982

Community, migrant status, and source of capital	Kind of worker					
	Hired workers		Family workers		Total workers	
	Number	Percent	Number	Percent	Number	Percent
Altamira						
Migrant-owned	3	25.0	30	39.0	33	37.1
Bought with U.S. earnings	0	0.0	6	7.8	6	6.7
Not migrant-owned	9	75.0	47	61.0	56	62.9
All businesses	12	100.0	77	100.0	89	100.0
Chamitlán						
Migrant-owned	4	50.0	44	60.3	48	59.3
Bought with U.S. earnings	2	25.0	20	27.4	22	27.2
Not migrant-owned	4	50.0	29	39.7	33	40.7
All businesses	8	100.0	73	100.0	81	100.0
Santiago						
Migrant-owned	15	68.2	32	43.2	47	49.0
Bought with U.S. earnings	3	13.4	9	12.2	12	12.5
Not migrant-owned	7	31.8	42	56.8	49	51.0
All businesses	22	100.0	74	100.0	96	100.0
San Marcos						
Migrant-owned	3	8.3	36	27.9	39	23.6
Bought with U.S. earnings	8	22.2	17	13.2	25	15.2
Not migrant-owned	33	91.7	93	72.1	126	76.4
All businesses	36	100.0	129	100.0	165	100.0
All Communities						
Migrant-owned	25	32.1	142	40.2	167	38.7
Bought with U.S. earnings	13	16.7	52	14.7	65	15.1
Not migrant-owned	53	67.9	211	59.8	264	61.3
All businesses	78	100.0	353	100.0	431	100.0

Source: HOUSEFILE; households enumerated in Mexican community samples.

were employed in businesses owned by U.S. migrants, and 17 percent were employed in enterprises directly established with money from the United States. When family workers are added in, we find that of the 431 people working in sampled firms, 15 percent owed their jobs directly to the investment of U.S. earnings and 39 percent worked in migrant-owned firms. Among the four communities, Chamitlán showed the most extensive impact of migration on employment: 27 percent of all jobs in family-run businesses could be traced directly to U.S. earnings, and 59 percent worked in firms owned by migrants. The number of workers employed in U.S.-owned businesses appears to be quite small; nonetheless, it represents a significant share of the work force in each community. Workers in migrant-owned businesses represent about 12 percent of Santiago's estimated work force, about 9 percent of Chamitlán's, 8 percent of San Marcos's, and 6 percent of Altamira's.

Migrant remittances are not only spent on consumption or invested in businesses; they are also deposited into savings accounts in Mexican banks. Indeed, the flow of migrant dollars into Chamitlán was the determining factor in the establishment in 1978 of the Chamitlán branch of *Bancomer*, a large commercial bank, through which occurs a large share of the municipio's current economic transactions. The branch makes a few loans to townspeople who can provide collateral for repayment, but its most important function has been to provide fixed-term investment accounts for migrants with dollars. Depositing of U.S. earnings into a rural branch of a large Mexican bank drains the community of scarce capital, since the money is rarely invested there but is usually channeled to more profitable undertakings in urban areas.

Recognizing this fact, in 1960 the Catholic Diocese, with the encouragement of a local priest, founded the People's Savings Fund, a cooperative venture completely staffed and run by townspeople. This organization has become the savings bank of a majority of Chamitlán's families. Its 6,622 members participate as associates on condition that they remain town residents. The fund serves an important redistributive function through a low-interest loan program that it offers to its members. According to the 1980 report of the fund's Board of Directors, 1,161 loans were authorized that year for various purposes, including the acquisition of agricultural machinery, the purchase of seeds, the purchase of livestock, the expansion of business, the improvement or purchase of a home, the acquisition of medical care or equipment, a business trip, and even the repair of a school. The People's Savings Fund has thus been a very important institution enabling migrants to invest their earnings productively within the town itself.

In Santiago and San Marcos, the most popular form of savings for migrants remains the fixed-term investment account. From informants in area banks, we know that many branches in working-class neighborhoods of Guadalajara and surrounding small towns serve primarily to capture U.S. dollars; for example, the San Marcos branch in 1982 received a daily average deposit of 5,000 U.S. dollars in cash and between $15,000 and $20,000 in draft form. Most of these deposits represent money sent or brought home by migrants.

Finally, one last economic impact of migration that has been mentioned in the research literature is the detrimental loss of productive workers through migration abroad. In order to assess this possibility, table 8.10 shows the extent of migration in 1982 among labor force members and households in the four communities. Even though migration may be a very common experience and over the course of a three-year period many families and the work force as a whole will lose productive members, the potentially deleterious effects of labor migration are muted by the fact that migration is sporadic. Within any single year, a relatively small percentage of the work force is absent, and relatively few families are left without their most productive worker. Even in Chamitlán, where migration is most extensive, only 13 percent of the work force was absent in 1982 and only 14 percent of families experienced the temporary absence of the father. In most cases, these absences did not occupy the entire year.

OWNERSHIP AND DISTRIBUTION OF FARMLAND

In prior research, farmland has consistently emerged as one of the most popular productive investments, and many studies have noted the tendency for migrants to purchase land in their home communities. In most developing areas the supply of land is limited, however, and given the superior buying power of migrants, studies also report that land prices have been bid up significantly. In some communities, this price inflation has, in turn, placed the ability to buy land beyond the means of all but a few successful migrants, creating a basic cleavage between landowning migrants and landless nonmigrants, and perpetuating an unequal property distribution.

A basic issue is the extent to which migrants have channeled their earnings into landholdings. In both Altamira and Chamitlán—especially Chamitlán—the amount of land for sale at any given time is quite limited; however, the ethnosurvey data do indicate that migrants have

TABLE 8.10
MIGRANT STATUS OF WORKERS AND FATHERS IN 1982: FOUR MEXICAN COMMUNITIES

Migrant status	Community			
	Altamira	Chamitlán	Santiago	San Marcos
Workers				
U.S. migrant (%)	6.6	12.8	1.0	2.5
Mexican migrant (%)	5.0	1.8	1.0	0.6
Nonmigrant (%)	88.4	85.3	98.0	96.9
Number	518	545	408	484
Fathers				
U.S. migrant (%)	5.7	13.5	2.7	2.4
Mexican migrant (%)	3.4	2.8	2.2	0.6
Nonmigrant (%)	90.9	83.7	95.1	97.1
Number	175	178	184	170

Source: PERSFILE; household members enumerated in Mexican community samples.

made significant use of their U.S. earnings to buy land. Among all parcels owned by migrants in Altamira, 25 percent were purchased with money earned in the United States, representing 37 percent of all land bought by migrants (i.e., excluding inherited land). Given the greater scarcity of land in Chamitlán, fewer migrants have been able to acquire it. Only 16 percent of all parcels owned by migrants were bought with U.S. earnings, or 19 percent of all land purchased by migrants.

Table 8.11 examines the percentage of households owning different kinds of farmland by years of migrant experience. As can be seen, migrants generally have greater access to farmland than do nonmigrants, and this access increases with years of U.S. migrant experience. In Altamira, 39 percent of nonmigrant households own some kind of agricultural land, but 51 percent of migrants do so, and among those with greater than ten years of experience, the percentage is 57 percent. A similar pattern holds in Chamitlán, where only 8 percent of nonmigrant families own land, compared to 15 percent of migrants. The highest percentage owning land is among those with more than ten years of experience (33 percent).

The contrast in ownership patterns between migrants and nonmigrants is clearest in the case of irrigated land, the most highly prized and valuable of agricultural resources. In Altamira, the percentage of migrant households owning irrigated land is four times that of nonmigrant households, and this percentage increases steadily from 4 percent among households with the least U.S. experience to 14 percent among those with the most. No nonmigrant household in Chamitlán owns

TABLE 8.11
PERCENTAGE OF HOUSEHOLDS OWNING FARMLAND BY KIND OF LAND AND YEARS OF
U.S. MIGRANT EXPERIENCE, 1982

Community and kind of land	Nonmigrant	U.S. migrants × experience				
		<1 year	1–4 years	5–9 years	10+ years	Total
Altamira						
Irrigated (%)	3.1	4.2	17.0	11.1	14.3	12.6
Dryland (%)	27.8	8.3	40.4	55.6	35.7	35.0
Pasture (%)	8.2	4.2	8.5	16.7	14.3	9.7
Orchards (%)	18.6	16.7	23.4	33.3	28.6	24.3
Any land (%)	39.2	25.0	57.4	66.7	57.1	51.4
Number	97	24	47	18	14	103
Chamitlán						
Irrigated (%)	0.0	5.9	5.3	3.6	23.3	8.7
Dryland (%)	7.8	17.6	12.3	17.9	13.3	14.8
Pasture (%)	0.0	2.9	1.8	0.0	0.0	1.3
Any land (%)	7.8	26.5	14.0	21.4	33.3	22.1
Number	51	34	57	28	30	149

Source: HOUSEFILE; households enumerated in Mexican community samples.

irrigated land, while the percentage of such owners among migrant households rises from 6 percent among those with less than a year of migrant experience to 23 percent among those with more than ten.

We also considered migrants' access to land through leasing or sharecropping arrangements, but this did not change the basic conclusions indicated in table 8.11. Migrants have greater access than do nonmigrants to the limited land available in each community, and this advantage increases as migrant experience grows. Moreover, migrants' advantage is greatest with respect to irrigated land and dryland, the most productive classes of farmland. These facts imply a basic inequality in the distribution of farmland among migrant and nonmigrant families. Table 8.12 examines the total number of hectares owned by households in the two towns and calculates the percentage owned by migrant and nonmigrant households.

A quick glance at this table reveals that most of the farmland in each community is owned by migrant households. In Altamira, 52 percent of all households contain someone with U.S. migrant experience, while such households own 68 percent of all dryland and 79 percent of all irrigated land in the community. In addition, migrant households rent 75 percent of the dryland that is currently under lease. Similarly, while 75 percent of Chamitlán's households contain a U.S. migrant, they own all the community's irrigated land and 81 percent of its dryland. They also rent 100 percent of the irrigated land that is leased out and 66 percent of the dryland.

These figures understate the real concentration of land. Migrant households do own most of Altamira's dry and irrigated land and such households do represent a sizable share of the population; however, not all migrant households own land. In fact, only thirty-six migrant families own dryland, and a mere thirteen own irrigated land. In other words, 68 percent of the community's dryland is owned by 18 percent of its households, and a mere 7 percent of all households own 79 percent of the irrigated land. The distribution is even more skewed in Chamitlán, where 7 percent of the community's households, all migrants, own 100 percent of the irrigated land and 22 percent own 81 percent of its dryland.

The unequal distribution of farmland was not completely a result of migration to the United States, of course. Many migrants were landowners or ejidatarios before going to the United States. To the extent that migration helped households to consolidate a privileged position in the communities, however, it has perpetuated the inequities. Moreover, most of the migrants who acquired land did so before 1970, when

TABLE 8.12
PERCENTAGE DISTRIBUTION OF OWNED AND LEASED FARMLAND AMONG
MIGRANT AND NONMIGRANT HOUSEHOLDS IN TWO COMMUNITIES, 1982

Community and migrant status	Kind of land				
	Irrigated	Dryland	Pasture	Orchards	Total
Altamira					
Owned land					
Nonmigrant (%)	21.3	32.5	30.0	47.7	31.8
U.S. migrant (%)	78.7	67.5	70.0	52.3	68.2
<5 years (%)	48.6	42.7	37.4	39.2	42.0
5+ years (%)	30.1	24.4	32.6	13.0	26.2
Hectares (no.)	65.8	548.6	213.5	46.5	874.4
Leased land					
Nonmigrant (%)	91.0	25.5	—	43.3	32.0
U.S. migrant (%)	9.0	74.5	—	56.7	68.0
<5 years (%)	7.2	37.9	—	35.7	35.0
5+ years (%)	1.8	36.7	—	21.0	33.0
Hectares (no.)	27.8	276.8	0	14.6	319.2
Chamitlán					
Owned land					
Nonmigrant (%)	0.0	19.2	0.0	—	13.2
U.S. migrant (%)	100.0	80.8	100.0	—	86.8
<5 years (%)	39.7	54.1	0.0	—	51.9
5+ years (%)	60.3	26.7	0.0	—	34.9
Hectares (no.)	58.0	146.0	8.0	0	212.0
Leased land					
Nonmigrant (%)	0.0	33.8	32.8	—	30.6
U.S. migrant (%)	100.0	66.2	67.2	—	69.4
<5 years (%)	36.4	25.1	54.5	—	37.4
5+ years (%)	63.6	41.2	12.7	—	31.7
Hectares (no.)	11.0	68.0	52.4	0	131.4

Source: HOUSEFILE; households enumerated in Mexican community samples.

commercial agricultural development and increased migration brought inflation of land prices. At present, only successful U.S. migrants, agricultores, and large agribusinesses can afford to acquire land within the communities, and most of the land owned by townspeople is held by a small number of migrant families.

Prior research has also revealed that while migrant households are keenly interested in owning land, they are not always as interested in farming it. Rather, they lease out land to nonmigrant families while continuing to migrate for better-paid work abroad. This practice does not seem to be very widespread in either Altamira or Chamitlán, although there are some indications that it does occur. We calculated the percentage of farmland leased out by migrant and nonmigrant households. The letting of farmland is not widespread; it is restricted primarily to migrant households. In Altamira, no irrigated land is leased out by nonmigrant households, but 10 percent of that owned by migrant households is. Similarly, while 8 percent of nonmigrants' dryland holdings are leased out, the percentage for migrant households is 35 percent. In Chamitlán, only migrant households lease farmland to others.

AGRICULTURAL PRODUCTION

An issue related to land distribution is agricultural production. Previous research has suggested that migration inhibits production in two ways. First, as households become more involved in the migratory process, they begin to specialize in recurrent migration to the exclusion of agricultural production. If they own land, they lease it out, use it for grazing, or let it lie fallow. If they are landless, they give up sharecropping at home in favor of wage labor abroad. Second, even when migrant households continue to farm the land, they do so less intensively. The end result is a reduction in total farm production within the sending community and a decline in agricultural productivity.

In order to examine the extent to which migration leads to withdrawal from production, we considered migrant households in which the head reported an agricultural occupation and examined the percentage that produced some crop during 1982. In general, increasing involvement in migration does seem to lead to a decline in cultivation. In Altamira, 60 percent of nonmigrant households farmed a crop in 1982, compared to only 49 percent among migrant households. The percentage cultivating fell from 56 percent among households with less than a year of U.S. migrant experience to only 25 percent among those with ten or more years of experience. Similar findings were obtained for Chamitlán, where the percentage cultivating fell from 68 percent among the least experienced migrant households to 42 percent among the most experienced. Overall, 49 percent of migrant households engaged in cultivation, compared to 54 percent of nonmigrants.

In addition to affecting the prevalence of cultivation among households, migration influences *how* it is practiced: the methods that are used and the intensiveness of the effort. Migration lessens the amount of labor available within the household but also provides a source of capital for investment in productive inputs such as machinery and fertilizers. The issue is how these two opposite effects balance out.

Prior research suggests that as the cumulative total of U.S. experience in a household grows, the commitment of its members to the various tasks of farming falls. The migrant himself is absent and cannot contribute his labor to the household, and other members may not be able to work (as when the wife is caring for very young children) or may be less motivated to work because they expect the migrant's earnings to provide for the family. The data shown in table 8.13 somewhat support the view that migration leads to a decline in family labor inputs.

Migrant households are generally less likely to use family workers for agricultural tasks, especially in Altamira, and in both rural towns the commitment of family members to farming drops as U.S. migrant experience increases. The smallest percentage using family workers is always found among households with the most U.S. migrant experience. The strongest trends are found for clearing and plowing, which occur in May and June, when U.S. migrants are most likely to be away. In Altamira, the percentage of households using family members for clearing falls from 77 percent among those with less than one year of U.S. migrant experience, to 50 percent among those with more than ten; in Chamitlán, the drop is from 58 percent to 30 percent.

Members of households with U.S. migrant experience may be less willing or able to devote their labor to agricultural production; however, they are in a better position to invest capital in other inputs to offset the loss of family workers. One possibility is to substitute hired labor for family workers, and table 8.14 examines the use of jornaleros by households in the two communities. As can be seen, migrant households generally increase the use of nonfamily workers as they accumulate U.S. migrant experience, although the trends are somewhat erratic. The pattern is best exemplified in Altamira, where households with ten or more years of migrant experience are always the most likely to employ hired laborers. There, 70 percent of such households used a jornalero for some task, compared to 48 percent among nonmigrants. The trends were especially strong for the tasks of clearing and plowing.

A similar pattern is observed when we consider households' use of machinery in table 8.15. In both communities there is a very clear relationship between the percentage using farm machinery and the amount of U.S. migrant experience. In Altamira, for example, only 27 percent of nonmigrant households used machinery for any agricultural task but 47 percent of migrant households did so, with the percentage rising from 29 percent among those with the least experience to 60 percent among those with the most; exactly the same pattern is seen in Chamitlán, where only 24 percent of nonmigrant households employed any kind of machinery, compared to 32 percent among the least experienced migrant households and 77 percent among the most.

Table 8.16 considers the use of modern agricultural inputs such as

TABLE 8.13.
PERCENTAGE OF FARMING HOUSEHOLDS USING FAMILY WORKERS FOR AGRICULTURAL TASKS
BY YEARS OF U.S. MIGRANT EXPERIENCE, 1982

Community and task	Nonmigrant	U.S. migrants × experience				
		<1 year	1–4 years	5–9 years	10+ years	Total
Altamira						
Clearing (%)	76.3	76.5	57.1	87.5	50.0	66.7
Plowing (%)	72.9	41.2	51.4	75.0	50.0	53.8
Sowing (%)	81.4	76.5	62.9	93.8	50.0	70.5
Harvesting (%)	83.1	76.5	60.0	93.8	60.0	70.5
Any task (%)	83.1	76.5	62.9	93.8	60.0	71.8
Farm households (no.)[a]	59	17	35	16	10	78
Chamitlán						
Clearing (%)	81.0	57.9	80.8	50.0	30.8	60.0
Plowing (%)	76.2	73.7	84.6	66.7	69.2	75.7
Sowing (%)	95.2	94.7	96.2	100.0	84.6	94.3
Harvesting (%)	95.2	94.7	100.0	91.7	92.3	95.7
Any task (%)	95.2	94.7	100.0	100.0	92.3	97.1
Farm households (no.)[a]	21	19	26	12	13	70

Source: HOUSEFILE; households enumerated in Mexican community samples.

[a] Only households engaged in agricultural production.

TABLE 8.14
PERCENTAGE OF FARMING HOUSEHOLDS USING HIRED LABORERS FOR AGRICULTURAL TASKS
BY YEARS OF U.S. MIGRANT EXPERIENCE, 1982

Community and task	Nonmigrant	U.S. migrants × experience					Total
		<1 year	1–4 years	5–9 years	10+ years		
Altamira							
Clearing (%)	6.8	17.6	22.9	12.5	50.0		23.1
Plowing (%)	6.8	11.8	8.6	12.5	40.0		14.1
Sowing (%)	35.6	23.5	28.6	18.8	40.0		26.9
Harvesting (%)	39.0	35.3	40.0	25.0	70.0		39.7
Any task (%)	47.5	52.9	48.6	25.0	70.0		47.4
Farm households (no.)[a]	59	17	35	16	10		78
Chamitlán							
Clearing (%)	19.0	0.0	3.8	0.0	7.7		2.9
Plowing (%)	19.0	5.3	11.5	0.0	23.1		10.0
Sowing (%)	28.6	5.3	23.1	25.0	38.5		21.4
Harvesting (%)	38.1	31.6	65.4	33.3	53.8		48.6
Any task (%)	47.6	36.8	65.3	33.3	54.8		50.0
Farm households (no.)[a]	21	19	26	12	13		70

Source: HOUSEFILE; households enumerated in Mexican community samples.

[a] Only households engaged in agricultural production.

TABLE 8.15
PERCENTAGE OF HOUSEHOLDS USING FARM MACHINERY FOR SELECTED TASKS
BY YEARS OF U.S. MIGRANT EXPERIENCE, 1982

Community and task	Nonmigrant	U.S. migrants × experience				Total
		<1 year	1–4 years	5–9 years	10+ years	
Altamira						
Clearing (%)	15.3	17.6	25.7	18.8	30.0	23.0
Plowing (%)	10.2	11.8	11.4	18.8	20.0	14.1
Sowing (%)	6.8	5.9	11.4	18.8	20.0	12.8
Harvesting (%)	22.0	17.7	48.6	37.5	60.0	41.0
Any task (%)	27.1	29.4	51.4	43.8	60.0	46.2
Farm households (no.)[a]	59	17	35	16	10	78
Chamitlán						
Clearing (%)	23.8	31.6	34.6	41.7	69.2	41.4
Plowing (%)	19.0	10.5	23.1	25.0	46.2	24.3
Sowing (%)	19.0	5.3	11.5	25.0	46.2	18.6
Harvesting (%)	23.8	10.5	19.2	33.3	53.9	25.7
Any task (%)	23.8	31.6	34.6	41.7	76.9	42.9
Farm households (no.)[a]	21	19	26	12	13	70

Source: HOUSEFILE; households enumerated in Mexican community samples.

[a] Only households engaged in agricultural production.

TABLE 8.16
PERCENTAGE OF HOUSEHOLDS USING SELECTED AGRICULTURAL INPUTS
BY YEARS OF U.S. MIGRANT EXPERIENCE, 1982

Community and input	Nonmigrant	U.S. migrants × experience				
		<1 year	1–4 years	5–9 years	10+ years	Total
Altamira						
Improved seeds (%)	32.2	23.5	54.3	62.5	60.0	50.0
Chemical fertilizer (%)	79.7	70.5	68.6	87.5	60.0	71.8
Insecticide (%)	71.2	82.4	60.0	93.8	60.0	71.8
Any input (%)	83.1	88.2	82.9	100.0	80.0	87.2
Farm households (no.)[a]	59	17	35	16	10	78
Chamitlán						
Improved seeds (%)	38.1	68.4	46.2	66.7	76.9	61.4
Chemical fertilizer (%)	85.7	94.7	96.2	100.0	100.0	97.1
Insecticide (%)	61.9	78.9	76.9	83.3	100.0	82.9
Any input (%)	85.7	100.0	96.2	100.0	100.0	98.6
Farm households (no.)[a]	21	19	26	12	13	70

Source: HOUSEFILE; households enumerated in Mexican community samples.

[a] Only households engaged in agricultural production.

scientifically improved seeds, chemical fertilizers, and insecticides. The clearest trends are observed for the use of improved seeds. Nonmigrant households are relatively unlikely to use this input; only 32 percent of those in Altamira and 38 percent of those in Chamitlán did so. In Altamira, the percentage reporting the use of improved seeds rose from 23 percent for migrant households with under one year of experience to 60 percent for those with more than ten years; in Chamitlán, the increase was from 68 percent to 77 percent. Altamira's households display no strong trends for the other two inputs, and overall, migrants and nonmigrants are equally likely to employ them in production. In Chamitlán, however, household use of fertilizers and insecticides increases steadily to 100 percent in the highest experience category, although their use is also quite common among nonmigrant households.

Migration thus bears a complex relationship to factors that influence agricultural productivity. Increasing migration is associated with less commitment by family workers to the tasks of farmwork, but also with increasing use of other inputs such as hired labor, machinery, and scientifically improved seeds. Table 8.17 suggests how these effects balance out with respect to agricultural productivity by examining the relationship between productivity and years of U.S. migrant experience. In order to correct for erratic patterns resulting from small numbers, we have collapsed the four experience classes into two.

In general, increasing migration has a positive effect, or no effect, on agricultural productivity. Only for sorghum cultivation in Altamira is there evidence of a negative impact. There, nonmigrant households produce an average of 1.85 metric tons of sorghum per hectare, compared to 1.65 tons per hectare among those with less than five years of U.S. migrant experience and 1.47 among those with more. In Chamitlán, migrant experience is always positively related to productivity. Corn productivity increases from 0.69 to 0.94 tons per hectare for households below and above five years of U.S. migrant experience, respectively, compared to 0.66 tons per hectare among nonmigrant households. The gains in sorghum productivity are even more dramatic. Nonmigrant households produce only 0.33 tons per hectare, while the least experienced migrant households produce 1.29 and most experienced households, 2.37.

Finally, table 8.18 considers productivity per household. Migrant households possess more land and make greater use of hired labor and capital inputs, so the amount produced per household is greater for them. Indeed, in all cases household productivity increases with U.S. migrant experience, and migrant households tend to sell larger shares

TABLE 8.17
AGRICULTURAL PRODUCTIVITY (METRIC TONS PER HECTARE) FOR CORN AND
SORGHUM BY YEARS OF U.S. MIGRANT EXPERIENCE, 1982

		U.S. migrants × experience		
Community and crop	Nonmigrant	<5 years	5+ years	Total
Altamira				
Corn	1.08	0.95	1.05	0.98
Sorghum	1.85	1.65	1.47	1.49
Farm households (no.)[a]	59	52	26	78
Chamitlán				
Corn	0.66	0.69	0.94	0.88
Sorghum	0.33	1.29	2.37	1.87
Farm households (no.)[a]	21	45	25	70

Source: HOUSEFILE; households enumerated in Mexican community samples.

[a] Only households engaged in agricultural production.

TABLE 8.18
HOUSEHOLD PRODUCTION OF CORN AND SORGHUM AND PERCENT OF CROP
SOLD BY YEARS OF MIGRANT EXPERIENCE, 1982

		U.S. migrants × experience		
Community and crop	Nonmigrant	<5 years	5+ years	Total
Altamira				
Corn				
Tons grown	122.7	108.0	61.1	169.1
Tons per household	2.1	2.1	2.4	2.2
Percent sold (%)	8.9	14.4	48.4	26.7
Sorghum				
Tons grown	137.5	168.0	145.5	313.5
Tons per household	2.3	3.2	5.6	4.0
Percent sold (%)	43.4	45.0	35.9	40.8
Farm households (no.)[a]	59	52	26	78
Chamitlán				
Corn				
Tons grown	25.1	55.5	65.5	121.0
Tons per household	1.2	1.2	2.6	1.7
Percent sold (%)	28.8	33.6	63.0	49.5
Sorghum				
Tons grown	10.2	82.0	143.6	225.5
Tons per household	0.5	1.8	5.7	3.2
Percent sold (%)	60.6	35.4	79.1	63.2
Farm households (no.)[a]	21	45	25	70

Source: HOUSEFILE; households enumerated in Mexican community samples.

[a] Only households engaged in agricultural production.

of this expanded production on the market rather than retaining it for household consumption. The percentage destined for market also tends to increase with years of migrant experience. Of the corn grown by nonmigrant households in Altamira, 9 percent was destined for market; this figure increased from 14 percent among households with under five years of U.S. migrant experience to 48 percent among those with over five years of experience. The percentage of corn sold in Chamitlán similarly increased from 29 percent among nonmigrant households to 34 percent among the least experienced migrant households to 63 percent among the most experienced households. These figures suggest that as involvement in migration increases, households become more oriented toward commercial agriculture.

Migration thus appears to affect the level of agricultural production in two different directions simultaneously. On the one hand, increasing migration brings about a decline in the number of households engaged in cultivation; on the other hand, through the application of capital it increases productivity and production among those migrant households still engaged in farming. Which effect influences a community's total agricultural output more strongly—the decline in cultivation or the increase in productivity—cannot be determined from the ethnosurvey data alone.

CONCLUSIONS

The foregoing analyses are based primarily on ethnosurvey data pertaining to 1982. Current socioeconomic patterns inevitably reflect larger historical processes of economic development and social change, however, and migration did not always play the role it does today. During the first three decades of the century, international migration was practiced by a small number of young men who could afford the trip, and migration had little impact on the communities. During the period of the Bracero Accord and the Reparto Agrario, migration began to play a more dynamic role in economic development, as bracero migration provided a way for newly landed ejidatarios to acquire the funds necessary for cultivation.

During the 1960s the current context of international migration was established with the beginnings of agricultural modernization. Machinery and new crops displaced agrarian workers and changed the organization of farmwork, substituting wage labor for sharecropping. The centralization of trade and manufacturing in large urban areas displaced workers in traditional industries and dried up local commercial opportunities, while factory mechanization reduced employment opportunities in urban areas. Within this context, international migration assumed greater importance as a survival strategy, allowing households to adjust to the ongoing structural transformations in Mexican society. Within this context our cross-sectional analysis unfolded.

Like previous investigations in Mexico and elsewhere, our data confirm that migrant earnings are dedicated primarily to current consumption. At least 70 percent of migrants from each of the four communities reported spending their savings on ends such as family support, shelter, consumer goods, or recreation. Fewer than 21 percent of respondents reported making potentially productive investments. These estimates are probably conservative, since savings are more likely to be invested productively than are remittances, which typically go directly to family support.

The most popular destination for migrant savings was housing, and international migration had a strong impact on the ownership and quality of homes, especially in the rural communities. A large share of homes was purchased with money earned in the United States, and migrants were more likely to be homeowners and to live in higher-quality homes than were nonmigrants. Both ownership and housing quality tended to increase as households accumulated migrant experience in the United States.

International migration also permits rural households to enjoy modern consumer goods usually associated with urban life. Migrant families are more likely than nonmigrants to own modern conveniences such as stoves, refrigerators, washing machines, and sewing machines, which greatly enhance the ease of daily life, and access to these goods increases as migrant experience grows. International migration also provides rural dwellers greater exposure to entertainment and diversion in the form of television and stereo. Vehicle ownership remains quite rare in rural areas; most cars and trucks are owned by migrants, and many were bought directly with U.S. earnings. Ownership of these urban-industrial products also improves rural infrastructure by generating a demand for amenities such as power, water, sewers, and paved roads, and migrants have at times been active in organizing and financing these municipal improvements. In the urban communities, the impact of migration on standards of living is not as pronounced, because most urban households enjoy access to household and municipal amenities.

Our conclusions regarding the effect of migration on business activity differ somewhat from those of earlier studies. In contrast to the prevailing wisdom on the economic effects of migration, we find that U.S. earnings do play a positive role in local nonagrarian economies.

Most money earned in the United States is spent on current consumption; however, migration does play a role in the formation and operation of small businesses. Between 9 percent and 16 percent of businesses in the two communities were capitalized with U.S. money, and between 27 percent and 50 percent were migrant-owned. Businesses founded by migrants provided jobs to a modest number of family workers and a few paid employees, who together constituted between 6 percent and 12 percent of the active work force, just about balancing out the annual absence of workers lost through U.S. migration. Migrants' demand for new housing also generated employment in the construction sector, and one town founded a community savings fund to accumulate and invest migrant earnings in the community.

The distribution of agricultural land in the two rural communities has also been affected by migration. Most farmland is owned by a small number of migrant families. Some of these families were landowners before becoming migrants; others were ejidatarios who became migrants after the Reparto Agrario in order to finance cultivation, or they were recurrent migrants who purchased land with the savings they accumulated over many trips. In general, migrants have greater access to farmland than do nonmigrants, and this access increases with the amount of U.S. migrant experience. The higher the quality of the land, the more likely migrants are to own it.

Migration has two contrary effects on agricultural production. The more that a household migrates, the less likely it is to engage in cultivation but the higher the degree of productivity among those continuing to farm. Increasing migration decreases the number of family workers engaged in farming but increases the use of hired labor, machinery, and modern inputs. As a result, migrant households that engage in cultivation produce more than do nonmigrant households; however, they produce a larger output of cash crops and sell a higher percentage of their output on the open market.

Migration originates in profound transformations of agrarian society, involving processes of mechanization, capitalization, and commercialization, but over time it produces socioeconomic changes that encourage these trends and make subsequent migration more likely. When the transformation of agriculture began in the 1960s, workers were displaced. Given ready access to the United States through networks established during the Bracero era, many displaced workers took up international migration as a strategic adjustment. Given the way that networks operate and the attraction of high wages, inevitably some households employed recurrent or settled strategies. As migration became more widespread, more households were able to invest in capital-intensive production methods, and as recurrent migration spread, more families withdrew from cultivation. In this way, migration exacerbated the falling demand for agricultural labor and accelerated the shift to commercial agriculture. Meanwhile, the example of successful migrants living in well-built houses stocked with modern amenities encouraged others to begin to migrate. In short, although the root causes of migration lie in structural economic transformations, over time international migration operates in such a way as to promote the very changes that brought it about, encouraging still more migration. In this sense, migration comes to fuel itself.

9

Integration in the United States

We have already described the formation of U.S. daughter communities as an important step in the maturation of migrant networks. As these communities develop over time, they anchor the networks more firmly to particular sources of U.S. employment and channel migration to increasingly specific points of destination in the United States. The development of these daughter communities, in turn, reflects larger processes of integration that engage migrants as they experience life abroad.

The integration and settlement of Mexican migrants in the United States are not recent phenomena. The first migrants from Altamira and Chamitlán settled in the United States during the 1920s, primarily around Chicago. During the 1960s a second wave of settlement occurred when former braceros took out permanent residence papers and began to establish themselves in California, forming enclaves in cities such as Los Angeles and San Francisco, as well as in agricultural areas. At this time, the first migrants from Santiago also began to settle in Los Angeles. Throughout the 1970s the California communities grew as migrants became increasingly integrated into life abroad and opted in growing numbers for settlement in the United States.

This chapter examines the social processes that generate settled communities of Mexican migrants in the United States. After considering the process of integration in general theoretical terms, we employ ethno-survey data to document the ongoing personal, social, and economic integration of migrants in our sample. A special section examines the role that legal status plays in the process of integration, and another section explores the shift in orientation to Mexico as opposed to the United States that occurs among migrants as they spend more time abroad. This chapter concludes with two case studies that personify the inherent ambiguities and complexities of a process that bridges two cultures, two societies, two economies, and two overlapping sets of social relationships.

THE INTEGRATION PROCESS

We have argued that migrants adopt strategies of migration on the basis of their stage in the life cycle and economic needs. At the outset, most migrants adopt a temporary strategy, staying for a short time to meet some particular income goal. A few, mostly young, migrants adopt a settled strategy, lingering for several years to accumulate money, visit relatives, or gain experience. In no case are new entrants well integrated into the socioeconomic life of the receiving society, however, and rarely do they intend to stay permanently. Integration is an emergent process that occurs gradually as migrants accumulate time in the host country (Bohning 1972; Piore 1979).

Since migration is accomplished through personal ties based in communities of origin, during the initial trip social and economic relationships are confined primarily to other paisanos; these relationships constitute core connections in the migrant networks. Temporary migrants display a strong tendency for return migration, however, and settled migrants often find their visits extending longer than originally anticipated. As they build up time in the United States, migrants gradually become enmeshed in an array of personal, social, and economic ties rooted north of the border, connections that make long-term settlement progressively more likely. Over time migrants are drawn into permanent residence abroad.

Although the pattern of growing integration with increasing migrant experience is a general one, the process of integration is strongly conditioned by several variables. A crucial factor is rural versus urban origin. Urban migrants are much more likely to opt for city residence than are rural migrants, and the prospects for integration are generally much greater in urban areas. Work is steadier, residences tend to be more stable, and there are more opportunities for advancement. Diverse urban labor markets give spouses more opportunities for work, supporting stronger household economies. Urban areas also offer a wider range of leisure activities than rural areas and more chances for social contact. The probability of interaction between migrants and natives is much higher, and urban life demands a greater knowledge of U.S. culture and the English language.

A related conditioning variable is occupational background. Migrants from an agrarian background display a strong tendency to seek agricultural work in the United States, while nonfarmworkers gravitate to urban jobs, even if they come from rural areas. This fact is important because farmwork provides few opportunities for integration. The work itself is unstable and highly seasonal, lasting between six and eight months each year. Opportunities for economic advancement are also restricted, with the only avenue for mobility a promotion to foreman or row boss. Moreover, farmwork provides few chances for contact with natives, since fields are generally isolated, and workers often live in barracks and travel in special vehicles. Few farmworkers learn English, since most other workers are Mexican, and relationships with growers are funneled through Spanish-speaking foremen.

Finally, legal status obviously plays an important role in the integration process. Undocumented migrants are less likely than legals to acquire social and economic ties to the United States, even after many years of residence. They experience a constant insecurity while working abroad, and their integration is ultimately constrained by the fact that they may be deported at any time. Given the hazards and risks of undocumented life, they must be circumspect regarding the social and economic connections they make, and they are reluctant to expose their families to a clandestine, insecure existence. Some undocumented migrants do have stable, well-paid jobs and live in cities with their families; however, legal migrants generally enjoy a much more secure existence in the United States, encouraging the process of integration.

Unlike urban origin and occupational background, which are determined largely by accidents of birth and family background, legal status is an artifact of shifting political and economic conditions in the United States, which exert fluctuating pressures for and against integration in different periods. From 1942 to 1964, for example, the Bracero Accord channeled migrants into agricultural work on six-month work visas, discouraging integration and settlement. The end of the Bracero program in 1964 combined with an urban employment boom in California to encourage the entry of migrants into low-wage urban occupations, thereby promoting integration. Until 1968, it was relatively easy for Mexican migrants to obtain legal residence documents, but successive amendments to U.S. immigration law have made it increasingly difficult for Mexicans to acquire legal papers, and the economic dislocations of the 1970s have created a public environment hostile to immigrant assimilation.

Our general hypothesis is, therefore, that integration increases as migrants spend more time in the United States but that this process of progressive integration is facilitated by an urban background and a nonfarm occupational status. Integration is also encouraged by the possession of legal documents, with the avenues for legalization determined primarily by immigration policies prevailing in different periods. In considering the social process of integration among migrants from the four communities, therefore, we apply controls, as appropriate, for rural versus urban origin, occupational background, and legal status.

PERSONAL INTEGRATION

Although initial trips to the United States are social in the sense that they are accomplished through networks, people generally do not migrate for social reasons. Rather, they are in the United States to work, and most of their time is devoted to this end. The emphasis on work is especially strong among temporary migrants, who usually have a wife and children to support at home. On their first few trips, they generally have a Spartan existence, often sharing living quarters in order to save money. If they are agricultural workers, they sleep in communal barracks provided by growers; if they are urban workers, they rent a room or apartment together or sleep on a spare sofa in the home of friends or relatives. They work long hours and have little time for social life. Most of their free time is spent in the company of other migrant workers, usually paisanos.

If a migrant makes one or two temporary trips or stays as a settler for a short time, there is no problem with this way of life. The migrant knows that it will end and does not define himself with respect to the foreign setting. The labor may be menial and life unpleasant, but he will return home with a good deal of money. As migrants accumulate time in the United States, however, an anomic social life becomes increasingly prevalent. People are intrinsically social beings, and inevitably migrants begin to spend more time on social activities in the United States. At first, social relationships are concentrated within the network of out-migrant townspeople, but eventually they encompass migrants from other communities, U.S.-born *Chicanos*, and finally native Anglo-Americans. Ultimately, the migrant becomes enmeshed in a web of social ties based in the United States.

The progressive acquisition of personal ties abroad is suggested by table 9.1, which shows the relative frequency of U.S. ties by migrant experience and rural versus urban origin. A common view is that Mexican migrants are young males traveling without family dependents; however, this view is valid only in the aggregate, not when migrants are categorized according to experience. As the migrant experience lengthens and begins to appear more open-ended, enforced separation from wives becomes difficult to sustain, and the percentage of migrants

TABLE 9.1
Interpersonal Ties Within the United States by Years of Migrant Experience and Rural versus Urban Origin: Migrants from Four Mexican Communities, 1982

Origin and tie	Years of U.S. migrant experience					Total
	Under 1	1-4	5-9	10-14	15+	
Rural origin						
Family and home ties						
With spouse in United States (%)	1.8	7.4	30.2	56.0	64.0	21.0
With son in United States (%)	1.7	6.3	11.6	40.0	54.2	14.3
With daughter in United States (%)	1.7	5.3	7.0	36.0	45.8	11.8
With child born in United States (%)	3.4	11.1	29.5	45.8	46.4	20.2
Relatives in United States (no.)	9.6	9.6	17.3	25.4	30.5	14.7
Paisanos in United States (no.)	29.1	23.6	23.3	22.5	22.5	24.6
Ties with U.S. groups						
With Chicano friend (%)	14.8	28.9	45.2	58.3	58.3	34.6
With black friend (%)	7.4	11.1	23.8	8.3	25.0	13.7
With Anglo friend (%)	11.1	20.0	38.1	33.3	62.5	26.9
With Latino friend (%)	7.4	27.8	31.0	20.8	54.2	25.6
Number of migrants	66	121	49	27	26	289
Urban origin						
Family and home ties						
With spouse in United States (%)	12.2	21.1	25.0	44.4	42.9	23.1
With son in United States (%)	7.5	21.1	14.3	33.3	35.7	17.8
With daughter in United States (%)	5.0	7.9	17.9	33.3	35.7	14.0
With child born in United States (%)	9.8	18.6	16.1	30.0	42.9	18.1
Relatives in United States (no.)	9.3	9.0	15.1	14.8	25.1	12.6
Paisanos in United States (no.)	25.4	11.0	30.4	27.8	39.3	23.9
Ties with U.S. groups						
With Chicano friends (%)	39.0	52.6	64.3	75.0	85.7	55.8
With black friends (%)	4.9	18.4	10.7	12.5	35.7	13.9
With Anglo friends (%)	17.1	31.6	35.7	25.0	71.4	31.8
With Latino friends (%)	29.3	36.8	39.3	25.0	78.6	38.8
Number of migrants	45	47	32	12	15	151

Source: MIGFILE; migrant household members enumerated in Mexico or California, including those in twenty-five extra households in Santiago.

with spouses rises smoothly with increasing time abroad. Among rural-origin migrants, the percentage accompanied by spouses rises from 2 percent for new migrants to 64 percent among those with the most experience, while the respective figures are 12 percent and 43 percent for urban-origin migrants. Although over 75 percent of all migrants do not have wives in the United States (see "Total" column), this figure reflects the fact that most have accumulated little experience (see rows giving numbers of migrants) and thus does not give a true picture of migrant integration.

The percentage of migrants with sons or daughters in the United States similarly rises with U.S. migrant experience. Among those of rural origin, the proportion accompanied by migrant sons increases from 2 percent in the lowest experience interval to 54 percent in the highest and from 8 percent to 36 percent among those of urban origin. A similar increase is observed for daughters. Fieldwork suggests that integration is greatly encouraged by having children raised abroad, since their social relationships are concentrated in the United States rather than among migrants from the home community. Through their children, migrant parents generally become more integrated into U.S. life.

A particularly telling indicator of integration is the percentage of migrants with children born in the United States. Having children who are native American citizens greatly increases the strength of ties to U.S. society. These children grow up speaking English and learning Anglo-American culture and thus draw the rest of the family into the social world of the United States. Among rural-origin migrants the percentage with native children rises steadily from 3 percent in the lowest experience interval to 46 percent in the highest, and a similar increase is observed among migrants from urban areas.

Table 9.1 also clearly documents the gradual development of social relationships between Mexican migrants and members of various U.S. ethnic groups. It is not surprising that, in general, the most prevalent social relationships are with Chicanos and other Latinos (who may also be Spanish-speaking immigrants). As the amount of time spent in the United States increases, the percentage knowing Anglos (non-Hispanic white Americans) increases quite dramatically, from 11 percent to 63 percent among rural migrants and from 17 percent to 71 percent among urban migrants. Indeed, by the time rural-origin migrants have accumulated fifteen years of experience in the United States, they are more likely to be friendly with Anglos than *either* Chicanos or Latinos.

The last piece of information we consider in table 9.1 is the average number of paisanos that migrants reported knowing on their last trip to the United States. On this measure, rural and urban migrants display contrasting patterns. Among urban-origin migrants, the number of out-migrant paisanos increases with years of migrant experience, while among those of rural origin it falls slightly but steadily. This contrast stems from the progressive shift of rural-origin migrants into the nonagricultural sector as they accumulate U.S. migrant experience. Migrant networks from rural communities feed primarily into areas of U.S. agricultural employment. Family and friendship connections are widely used to secure jobs with specific growers at specific times. There is, therefore, a disproportionate concentration of paisanos in certain farms and fields. When a migrant from a rural area opts for a settled strategy and takes up nonagricultural employment, he drifts away from a close connection with this network, leading to a decrease in the intensity of his relationships with paisanos. Networks from Mexican urban areas, in contrast, lead directly into U.S. urban areas and associations with non-agricultural employers in particular factories and service establishments.

SOCIAL INTEGRATION

A crucial step in the social process of integration is the movement from transitory seasonal employment to a steadier, more sedentary job in the United States. This transition usually involves moving from agricultural to nonagricultural employment. Table 9.2 documents a very marked shift in the rural migrants sector of employment as years of migrant experience increase. Among rural-origin migrants with less than a year of migrant experience, 91 percent were farmworkers; but after fifteen years of experience, this percentage had fallen to 38 percent. In contrast, urban-origin workers are predominantly nonagricultural regardless of their experience category, although the percentage still tends to increase with U.S. migrant experience.

Another crucial variable in the settlement process is legal status. Although it is not perfectly correlated with integration, legal status is important for migrants seeking to incorporate more fully into life in the United States. Even among those who do not desire closer integration, the green card is a highly prized document, providing security and ready access to most classes of employment; and once obtained, even if integration was not intended, it greatly facilitates the formation of social, economic, and cultural ties within the United States. The possession of legal documents is thus an important indicator of social integration, as well as an important conditioning variable.

Given the importance of legal status in the integration process, it is

TABLE 9.2
INDICATORS OF SOCIAL INTEGRATION WITHIN THE UNITED STATES BY YEARS OF MIGRANT EXPERIENCE AND RURAL VERSUS URBAN ORIGIN: MIGRANTS FROM FOUR MEXICAN COMMUNITIES, 1982

Origin and indicator	Years of U.S. migrant experience					
	Under 1	1–4	5–9	10–14	15 +	Total
Rural origin						
Nonagricultural workers (%)	9.1	30.6	46.9	44.4	61.5	32.5
With legal papers (%)	1.5	5.0	10.2	44.4	69.2	14.6
English language ability[a]	0.1	0.2	1.2	2.0	2.4	0.8
With child in U.S. schools (%)	7.6	9.1	16.4	37.0	69.2	18.0
Member of athletic club (%)	6.6	9.5	20.8	23.1	16.0	12.7
Member of social club (%)	1.6	3.4	8.3	7.7	16.0	5.4
Ever receiving:						
Unemployment (%)	12.7	8.6	24.4	40.0	56.0	20.5
Food stamps (%)	0.0	2.2	0.0	12.0	16.0	3.8
Welfare (%)	0.0	2.2	0.0	4.0	12.0	2.5
Social Security (%)	0.0	3.2	0.0	4.0	28.0	4.6
Medical services (%)	22.2	35.5	69.0	64.0	80.0	46.0
Number of migrants	66	121	49	27	26	289
Urban origin						
Nonagricultural workers (%)	60.0	80.9	65.6	100.0	80.0	72.9
With legal papers (%)	13.6	25.5	25.0	41.7	73.3	28.0
English language ability[a]	0.5	1.2	1.4	1.9	2.6	1.2
With child in U.S. schools (%)	13.3	10.6	21.9	33.3	53.3	19.9
Member of athletic club (%)	15.9	25.5	40.6	33.3	64.3	30.2
Member of social club (%)	2.3	4.3	3.1	0.0	7.1	3.4
Ever receiving:						
Unemployment (%)	4.9	15.8	25.0	50.0	50.0	20.2
Food stamps (%)	7.3	2.4	7.1	0.0	14.3	6.2
Welfare (%)	2.4	0.0	3.6	0.0	28.6	4.7
Social Security (%)	0.0	5.3	7.1	0.0	7.1	3.9
Medical services (%)	24.4	34.2	60.7	66.7	85.7	44.6
Number of migrants	45	47	32	12	15	151

Source: MIGFILE; migrant household members interviewed in Mexico or California, including those in twenty-five extra households in Santiago.
[a] English language ability: (0) doesn't speak or understand English; (1) doesn't speak but understands some; (2) doesn't speak but understands well; (3) speaks and understands some; (4) speaks and understands well.

not surprising to find a steady, sharp increase in the proportion of migrants with legal papers over years of U.S. migrant experience. Only about 2 percent of rural-origin migrants and 14 percent of urban-origin migrants with less than a year of experience in the United States have green cards. Most of these people acquired their documents through a legally resident relative (usually a spouse or a parent) under the family reunification provisions of U.S. immigration law. After fifteen years of migrating to the United States, however, the vast majority of migrants have regularized their status—69 percent of those from rural areas and 73 percent of those from urban areas.

English language ability is another obvious indicator of social integration, implying a basic skill at managing daily life in the United States. Overall, the English ability of the migrants in the sample is quite limited. The average rural-origin migrant barely understands spoken English and cannot speak it at all, while the typical urban migrant understands it only slightly better. There is, nonetheless, an obvious improvement in English skills with increasing years of U.S. migration experience. After fifteen years in the United States, most migrants from both areas report that they understand well and can speak at some level of proficiency.

A natural concomitance of the growth in interpersonal and family ties to the United States is an increase in social ties of a more institutional nature. For example, we saw earlier how the accumulation of U.S. migrant experience was accompanied by the growing presence of migrant children. Most of these children are minors and are enrolled in U.S. schools. Indeed, the percentage of migrants reporting a child in U.S. schools grows steadily over the years of U.S. migrant experience, from 8 percent to 69 percent among rural migrants and from 13 percent to 53 percent among urban migrants.

Another kind of social tie is membership in a voluntary organization, the most important of which is the soccer club. As discussed earlier, these sports clubs play very important roles in the elaboration and maintenance of the migrant networks and contribute greatly to the cohesion of daughter communities in the United States. As migrants spend more time abroad, they are drawn to increasing participation in leisure activities. Membership in U.S. athletic clubs thus increases with migrant experience, particularly among urban-origin migrants, where the percentage of migrants belonging to an athletic club rises from 16 percent in the lowest to 64 percent in the highest experience interval. Among rural-origin migrants membership increases from 7 percent to 17 percent. Similarly, the percentage who report an affiliation with a U.S. social club rises as the amount of migrant experience grows.

The use of social services is also a strong indicator of integration among migrants, demonstrating a detailed knowledge of the benefits accruing from membership in U.S. society and a willingness to take advantage of them. Looking at the overall totals, we find that migrants are quite unlikely to use most U.S. social services. Only 2 percent to 6 percent of migrants have *ever* received food stamps, welfare, or Social Security; however, some 20 percent have used U.S. unemployment compensation, and roughly 45 percent have made use of U.S. medical facilities. These results generally concur with those of other studies (Avante Systems 1978; Bustamante 1977, 1978; Cornelius 1976; North and Houstoun 1976; Van Arsdol et al. 1979; North 1983).

When the overall figures are broken down by years of migrant experience, however, a different pattern emerges. Service utilization generally increases over the years of migrant experience. Although increases in the use of food stamps, welfare, and Social Security are unimpressive, the percentages of migrants who have ever received unemployment compensation and medical care display more regular, crescive increases over the course of the migrant career. After fifteen years of migrant experience, the vast majority have made use of U.S. medical facilities, and around half have received unemployment compensation, findings that are again congruent with other research (Blau 1984; Simon 1984).

ECONOMIC INTEGRATION

Migrants tend to be employed within the secondary labor market, a class of unstable, marginal jobs in labor-intensive industries subject to intense competitive pressures (Piore 1979; Portes and Bach 1985). Employers in these firms try to maintain profits through a variety of tactics: by keeping some or all employees off of official employment books or dealing strictly in cash in order to avoid paying taxes or by not conforming to minimum-wage legislation. Over time migrants should experience a formalization of economic status in the United States, however, moving into more regularly taxed, better-paid, and more legitimate jobs.

Table 9.3 presents selected measures of economic integration within the United States by U.S. migrant experience and sector of employment. These data generally support the notion of a gradual regularization of migrant economic status over time. Those with little U.S. migrant experience are less likely to be paid by check or have taxes withheld from their pay and more likely to earn less than the minimum wage, compared to experienced migrants. Even among those with the least experience,

TABLE 9.3

INDICATORS OF ECONOMIC INTEGRATION WITHIN THE UNITED STATES BY YEARS OF MIGRANT EXPERIENCE SECTOR OF U.S. EMPLOYMENT: MIGRANTS FROM FOUR MEXICAN COMMUNITIES, 1982

Sector and indicator	Years of U.S. migrant experience					
	Under 1	1-4	5-9	10-14	15+	Total
Agricultural workers						
Below minimum wage (%)[a]	30.0	17.0	17.2	0.0	33.3	19.5
Paid by check (%)	77.0	93.2	94.3	93.3	100.0	88.4
With taxes withheld (%)	74.3	91.0	88.9	93.3	84.6	85.0
With checking account (%)	0.0	11.6	0.0	0.0	15.4	5.1
With savings account (%)	0.0	14.3	11.8	20.0	15.4	9.5
Number of migrants	78	93	37	15	13	236
Nonagricultural workers						
Below minimum wage (%)[a]	33.3	18.2	5.9	8.3	14.3	16.0
Paid by check (%)	75.9	88.4	95.3	86.9	100.0	89.5
With taxes withheld (%)	78.6	82.9	90.7	86.4	100.0	86.8
With checking account (%)	10.7	6.8	11.8	22.2	37.5	14.7
With savings account (%)	10.7	8.5	21.2	17.6	29.2	15.5
Number of migrants	33	75	44	24	28	204

Source: MIGFILE; migrant household members enumerated in Mexico or California, including those in twenty-five extra households in Santiago.

[a] Includes jobs held since 1965 only.

however, the vast majority seem to be in reasonably legitimate job situations: roughly 75 percent report being paid by check and having taxes withheld, although about 33 percent did report earning less than the minimum wage. After fifteen years as U.S. migrants, however, all were paid by check and nearly all had taxes withheld from their pay. Moreover, among nonagricultural workers, the percentage earning less than the minimum wage had fallen to 14 percent. Among agricultural workers, the percentage earning under the minimum wage falls for those with up to fifteen years of experience but then increases. This increase stems from the continued labor force attachment of several elderly migrants with many years of U.S. migrant experience. All are above age sixty-five (indeed, one is seventy-seven!), and they continue to do light agricultural work for minimal pay.

The last two indicators of economic integration in table 9.3 measure connections between migrants and U.S. economic institutions—specifically, banks. The more experience migrants build up in the United States, the more likely they are to open U.S. bank accounts. The percentage of farmworkers with savings or checking accounts rises from 0 percent initially to 15 percent after fifteen years. Among nonagricultural workers, the percentage with checking accounts rises from 11 percent to 38 percent and the percentage with savings accounts, from 11 percent to 29 percent.

THE EFFECT OF LEGAL STATUS

The fact that an undocumented migrant's presence in the United States is considered illegal and that deportation can occur at any time has a profound impact on the level and pattern of integration. Undocumented migrants generally have fewer immediate family members in the United States, since they are reluctant to expose wives and children to the dangers of an illicit border-crossing and a clandestine existence. They must also be careful about whom they talk to and whom they associate with. All strangers, especially native Anglos, blacks, or Chicanos, are potential threats. A simple phone call to immigration authorities by anyone could send a hapless migrant back to Mexico in a moment.

The ethnosurvey data in table 9.4 reflect these characteristics of life without documents. Undocumented migrants generally have fewer family and friendship ties in the United States than do legal migrants. Overall, only 16 percent of undocumented migrants have wives in the United States and only 10 percent have sons, compared to corresponding figures of 58 percent and 45 percent among documented migrants.

TABLE 9.4

INTERPERSONAL TIES WITHIN THE UNITED STATES BY YEARS OF MIGRANT EXPERIENCE AND DOCUMENTATION:
MIGRANTS FROM FOUR MEXICAN COMMUNITIES, 1982

Legal status and tie	Years of U.S. migrant experience					
	Under 1	1–4	5–9	10–14	15 +	Total
Documented migrants						
Family and community ties						
With Spouse in United States (%)	66.7	31.3	30.0	87.5	64.3	57.9
With Son in United States (%)	33.3	37.5	20.0	56.3	55.6	45.3
With Daughter in United States (%)	50.0	25.0	30.0	50.0	48.1	41.3
With Child born in United States (%)	15.8	20.4	35.7	61.1	51.6	32.0
Relatives in United States (no.)	21.3	15.2	20.1	28.8	31.6	25.2
Paisanos in United States (no.)	36.7	16.9	9.1	22.9	36.0	25.7
Ties with U.S. groups						
With Chicano friend (%)	66.7	80.0	50.0	87.5	70.4	73.0
With Black friend (%)	0.0	20.0	10.0	12.5	33.3	20.3
With Anglo friend (%)	16.7	33.3	30.0	37.5	63.0	43.2
With Latino friend (%)	66.7	53.3	60.0	31.3	63.0	54.0
Number of migrants	7	18	13	17	29	84
Undocumented migrants						
Family and community ties						
With Spouse in United States (%)	3.1	10.6	30.4	25.0	44.4	15.6
With Son in United States (%)	3.1	9.4	12.5	25.0	33.3	10.3
With Daughter in United States (%)	0.0	4.7	8.9	25.0	33.3	6.9
With Child born in United States (%)	4.0	8.7	21.3	18.8	27.3	11.8
Relatives in United States (no.)	9.0	8.7	16.9	18.8	24.5	12.2
Paisanos in United States (no.)	20.1	23.4	27.9	21.6	12.3	23.0
Ties with U.S. groups						
With Chicano friend (%)	24.2	30.5	52.7	35.7	55.6	35.6
With Black friend (%)	6.5	12.2	20.0	7.1	22.2	12.6
With Anglo friend (%)	17.8	23.2	40.0	28.6	66.7	28.0
With Latino friend (%)	17.8	29.3	30.9	7.1	66.7	26.6
Number of migrants	74	118	63	20	10	285

Source: MIGFILE; migrant household members enumerated in Mexico or California, including those in twenty-five extra households in Santiago.

As shown in table 9.4, 36 percent of undocumented migrants report knowing a Chicano and 28 percent report knowing an Anglo, while the corresponding figures for legal migrants are 73 percent and 43 percent. Documented migrants are also three times more likely to have native American children.

The contrast between those with and without documents is especially marked in the beginning stages of the migrant career. Most legal migrants with under a year of experience have some family or friendship tie in the United States. Two-thirds report having a wife in the country, and the same proportion report friendship with Chicanos and Latinos. About 16 percent have children born in the United States. These connections probably indicate the avenues through which the migrants obtained their legal documents after so little experience in the United States. In contrast, only 3 percent of undocumented migrants in the first experience interval have wives in the United States, while 4 percent have U.S.-born children, 24 percent Chicano friends, and 18 percent Latino friends.

In each case, the data in table 9.4 depict rising integration for undocumented migrants as U.S. migrant experience grows. Over time, undocumented migrants catch up with their documented counterparts, acquiring more family and friendship ties within the United States. After fifteen years of experience as undocumented migrants, 44 percent report having a wife in the United States, 56 percent report having a Chicano friend, and 67 percent report having an Anglo friend. Over 25 percent are parents of native American citizens. In other words, while illegal status inhibits integration in the United States, it does not stop it, nor does it alter the basic nature of the process. Undocumented migrants become more integrated the more time they build up abroad.

Essentially the same pattern of results is found for the indicators of social integration presented in table 9.5. The average level of integration is consistently lower among undocumented migrants, especially among those with the least U.S. migrant experience; nonetheless, social connections to the United States increase steadily with growing migrant experience. English language ability, the percentage holding nonagricultural jobs, the percentage with children in U.S. schools, and membership in social and athletic organizations all increase as undocumented migrants accumulate experience in the United States, although these indicators of integration rarely exceed levels reported by documented migrants with the same experience.

The results shown in table 9.5 suggest that, with the exception of medical services, undocumented migrants are very unlikely to use public services. Fewer than 3 percent have *ever* received food stamps, welfare,

TABLE 9.5
Indicators of Social Integration within the United States by Years of Migrant Experience and Documentation: Migrants from Four Mexican Communities, 1982

Legal status and indicator	Under 1	1–4	5–9	10–14	15+	Total
Documented migrants						
Nonagricultural workers (%)	100.0	72.2	76.9	64.7	72.4	73.8
English language ability[a]	1.3	1.5	2.2	2.9	2.6	2.3
With child in U.S. schools (%)	28.6	38.9	38.5	64.7	72.4	54.8
Member of athletic club (%)	57.1	22.2	30.8	47.1	39.3	37.3
Member of social club (%)	14.3	0.0	7.7	11.8	10.7	8.4
Ever receiving						
Unemployment (%)	50.0	31.3	40.0	75.0	64.3	55.3
Food stamps (%)	16.7	6.3	0.0	18.8	17.9	13.2
Welfare (%)	0.0	6.3	0.0	6.3	21.4	10.5
Social Security (%)	0.0	6.3	10.0	6.3	28.6	14.5
Medical services (%)	66.7	50.0	70.0	93.8	82.1	75.0
Number of migrants	7	18	13	17	29	84
Undocumented migrants						
Nonagricultural workers (%)	28.4	48.3	50.8	60.0	60.0	44.9
English language ability[a]	0.2	0.4	1.2	1.4	2.1	0.7
With child in U.S. schools (%)	12.2	6.8	15.9	15.0	50.0	12.3
Member of athletic club (%)	8.8	14.0	30.6	10.5	22.2	16.5
Member of social club (%)	1.5	4.4	6.5	0.0	22.2	4.4
Ever receiving						
Unemployment (%)	0.0	9.5	24.1	13.3	33.3	11.6
Food stamps (%)	3.2	2.4	3.7	0.0	11.1	3.1
Welfare (%)	1.6	1.2	1.9	0.0	11.1	1.8
Social Security (%)	0.0	3.6	1.9	0.0	0.0	1.8
Medical services (%)	19.4	35.7	65.5	37.5	77.8	40.2
Number of migrants	74	118	63	20	10	285

Source: MIGFILE; migrant household members enumerated in Mexico and California including those in twenty-five extra households in Santiago.

[a] English language ability: (0) doesn't speak or understand English; (1) doesn't speak but understands some English; (2) doesn't speak but understands English well; (3) speaks and understands some English; (4) speaks and understands English well.

or Social Security, and only 12 percent have children in public schools or have ever received unemployment compensation. When these figures are broken down by years of migrant experience, however, some interesting patterns emerge. Basic findings on the use of food stamps, welfare, and Social Security do not really change. No matter how much time undocumented migrants have accumulated in the United States, they are unlikely to use these services. Use of unemployment compensation, however, increases from 0 percent to 33 percent as one moves from less than a year of migrant experience to more than fifteen years. Over the same length of time, the proportion of migrants with children in U.S. schools increases from 12 to 50 percent and the percentage ever receiving medical care, from 19 percent to 78 percent.

Medical services are different from the others in that they may be provided either publicly or privately. The marked increase over time in the percentage who report having received medical care is hardly surprising, since most people eventually need it. Use does not necessarily imply service at public expense, however. The ethnosurvey questionnaire also asked how undocumented migrants paid their U.S. medical bills; 39 percent reported paying the bills themselves, 34 percent said the service was covered by health insurance, 20 percent said their employer paid, 4 percent said a relative paid, and 3 percent reported some other arrangement. Of the 105 undocumented migrants who reported receiving medical attention in the United States, *not one* admitted to receiving treatment at public expense.

Our results, therefore, do not suggest widespread abuse of publicly provided social services by undocumented migrants. The public service that is most likely to be used by them is, understandably, education, which increases as migrants become more integrated into U.S. society and accumulate family members here. Moreover, in many cases, children of undocumented migrants are themselves native American citizens entitled to public education. To a lesser extent, undocumented migrants have made use of unemployment compensation, but very few have ever received other types of governmental transfer.

Undocumented migrants also increasingly pay into U.S. society as they become more integrated economically. The data in table 9.6 indicate a relatively high degree of labor force integration among most undocumented migrants, even though they typically lag behind legal migrants. As indicated in table 9.6, 86 percent of all undocumented migrants are paid by check and 84 percent report having taxes deducted from their pay, compared to respective figures of 97 percent and 92 percent among legal migrants. Among migrants with under one year of experience, however, only 68 percent of those without documents had

TABLE 9.6

INDICATORS OF ECONOMIC INTEGRATION WITHIN THE UNITED STATES BY YEARS OF MIGRANT EXPERIENCE AND DOCUMENTATION: MIGRANTS FROM FOUR MEXICAN COMMUNITIES, 1982

Legal status and indicator	Years of U.S. migrant experience					
	Under 1	1–4	5–9	10–14	15+	Total
Documented migrants						
Below minimum wage (%)[a]	0.0	0.0	0.0	9.1	21.4	8.0
Paid by check (%)	100.0	100.0	92.3	93.8	100.0	97.4
With taxes withheld (%)	83.3	93.3	92.3	88.2	96.4	92.4
With checking account (%)	33.3	21.4	22.2	18.8	34.6	26.8
With savings account (%)	33.3	7.1	22.2	31.3	23.1	22.5
Number of migrants	7	18	13	17	29	84
Undocumented migrants						
Below minimum wages (%)[a]	36.4	20.5	13.5	0.0	16.7	20.8
Paid by check (%)	69.2	88.5	96.7	89.5	100.0	86.1
Paid taxes withheld (%)	68.2	85.0	91.8	94.4	100.0	83.5
With checking account (%)	0.0	1.2	3.7	0.0	22.2	2.2
With savings account (%)	0.0	6.0	17.0	6.7	33.3	8.1
Number of migrants	74	118	63	20	10	285

Source: MIGFILE; migrant household members enumerated in Mexico or California, including those in twenty-five extra households in Santiago.

[a] Includes jobs held since 1965 only.

taxes withheld from their paychecks, compared to 83 percent of those with documents. As in the other tables, economic integration increased with accumulated experience. The percentage of undocumented migrants with taxes withheld rose steadily to 100 percent in the highest experience interval. Similarly, the percentage of undocumented migrants with formal ties to U.S. banks also tended to increase over time.

In short, undocumented status acts as an important damper on the formation of social and economic connections to United States, an effect observed at all levels of migrant experience, but one that is especially pronounced in the early stages of the migrant career. Even with this clear effect in inhibiting the formation of social connections, undocumented status does not change the basic *process* of integration. The prevalence of ties to the United States in each case increases with migrant experience, and after fifteen years, the integration of undocumented migrants usually approaches or equals the level of legals. Documentation is thus clearly an important event in the integration process, greatly facilitating the formation of connections to U.S. society; however, it is not synonymous with integration itself and is not necessarily the most important step in the process.

ORIENTATION TO MEXICO

Progressive integration implies a gradual shift in a migrant's focus of orientation from Mexico to the United States. In the early phases of migration, a migrant's primary frame of reference is the home community. New entrants do not see themselves as part of U.S. society, but as members of their communities of origin. Most of the money they earn is sent home in the form of remittances or savings. There it is used to support the family or to enhance its socioeconomic status in the community through the purchase of land, housing, businesses, or consumer goods. Migrants' social identities are defined with respect to the social context of family, friends, and neighbors in Mexico.

As they spend more time abroad, migrants pay increasing attention to their socioeconomic position in the United States. Their social world increasingly encompasses the community of settled out-migrants and with time even embraces native U.S. citizens. Although an involvement in the social context of the home community is never lost, the social, economic, and cultural environment of the United States gradually assumes greater importance in migrants' daily lives. Eventually, they regard themselves as settlers rather than sojourners, a process strongly encouraged by children born and raised in the United States, whose

aspirations and identities are strongly shaped by Anglo-American culture. A sure sign that a settlement process is under way occurs when
migrants send fewer earnings back home and spend more in the United
States. As integration proceeds, migrants earn more but at the same
time send less to the home community.

Table 9.7 presents information on the components of annual U.S.
income broken down by years of migrant experience and sector of
employment. For both economic sectors (agricultural and nonagricultural workers), there are three major subdivisions of information. The
top subdivision shows the components of gross annual income during
the respondent's most recent trip: hourly wage, hours worked per week,
and months worked per year. The middle subdivision shows average
yearly expenses for food and rent in the United States, and in the bottom
subdivision disposable income is estimated by subtracting annual expenses from annual income. As integration proceeds, the share of income that is disposable, that is, available for remittance home, should
fall.

Considering the components of gross annual income, we see a
rather steep rise in wages over years of U.S. migrant experience. In both
agricultural and nonagricultural jobs, wages roughly triple as one moves
from those with under one year of experience to those with more than
fifteen years; however, wages are consistently higher in the nonagricultural sector. The average hourly wage of farmworkers is $5.40, compared
to $9.65 among nonagricultural workers, and the difference appears to
grow as experience increases. In other words, labor market experience
is much better rewarded in urban jobs than in agriculture.

Among farmworkers, hours worked per week increase up to a point
and then fall abruptly, peaking at about forty-eight hours among those
with five to nine years of experience before falling to a more conventional
forty-hour week thereafter. Months worked per year display exactly the
same pattern, rising from 4.1 to 8.4 months between the intervals of
zero to one years and five to nine years of experience and falling to 7
months thereafter. Among those with up to nine years of experience,
therefore, utilitarian economic motives apparently predominate, as migrants work on maximizing income by working long hours and more
months in their jobs in the United States. After this time the rigor
lessens, with fewer hours and months worked for higher wages. The
higher wages are more than enough to offset the shorter work time, so
that gross income is maintained or rises steadily as years of U.S. migrant
experience accumulate.

In the nonagricultural sector, the pattern of hours worked per week
is somewhat erratic. Starting high at 45.1, the number of hours falls to

TABLE 9.7
COMPONENTS OF ANNUAL U.S. INCOME BY YEARS OF U.S. MIGRANT EXPERIENCE AND SECTOR OF U.S. EMPLOYMENT: MIGRANTS FROM FOUR MEXICAN COMMUNITIES, 1982[a]

Sector and component	Years of U.S. migrant experience					
	Under 1	1–4	5–9	10–14	15+	Total
Agricultural workers						
Annual U.S. income	$2,702	$4,650	$9,564	$9,205	$13,431	$5,263
Hourly wage	$4.02	$4.71	$5.95	$8.58	$12.05	$5.40
Hours worked per week	41.0	43.3	47.8	38.3	39.8	42.7
Months worked per year	4.1	5.7	8.4	7.0	7.0	5.7
Annual U.S. expenses	$610	$1,029	$2,069	$3,451	$4,971	$1,332
Food	$425	$697	$1,497	$2,139	$4,014	$939
Rent	$185	$332	$572	$1,312	$957	$393
Disposable income	$2,092	$3,621	$7,494	$5,754	$8,460	$3,931
As percent of total	77.4	77.9	78.4	62.5	63.0	74.7
Number of migrants	78	93	37	15	13	236
Nonagricultural workers						
Annual U.S. income	$7,009	$9,754	$15,306	$20,983	$32,532	$14,743
Hourly wage	$6.07	$6.47	$9.77	$11.56	$20.09	$9.65
Hours worked per week	45.1	42.8	40.8	46.3	40.9	42.9
Months worked per year	6.4	8.8	9.6	9.8	9.9	8.9
Annual expenses	$1,673	$3,043	$5,679	$10,506	$13,503	$5,303
Food	$1,101	$1,769	$3,413	$7,460	$9,295	$3,428
Rent	$572	$1,274	$2,266	$3,046	$4,208	$1,876
Disposable income	$5,335	$6,710	$9,627	$10,477	$19,029	$9,439
As percent of total	76.1	68.8	62.9	49.9	58.5	64.0
Number of migrants	33	75	44	24	28	204

Source: MIGFILE; migrant household members enumerated in Mexico or California, including those in twenty-five extra households in Santiago.

[a] All amounts in 1982 U.S. dollars.

40.8 in the experience interval from five to nine years, rises to 46.2 hours in the interval from ten to fourteen years, and then falls back again in the over-fifteen-year experience class. Patterns for months worked per year are more regular, however, displaying a steady increase from 6.4 to 9.9 over the range of U.S. migrant experience. The increase in months worked combines with a rising wage rate to almost quintuple the annual gross income of nonagricultural workers from the first to the last experience interval.

At all levels of migrant experience, the gross income of nonagricultural workers is considerably larger than that of farmworkers, and overall, the former exceeds the latter by a factor of 2.8. Expenses of nonfarmworkers are also considerably higher, by a factor of 4 on average. Food and lodging for migrant farmworkers are often provided or subsidized by growers. In cities, however, nonagricultural workers must make their own arrangements; although their expenses are higher, the income differential is not significantly reduced. Instead of exceeding the income of farmworkers by a factor of 2.8, taking account of expenses reduces it to 2.4.

In both groups, expenses rise steadily with years of accumulated migrant experience. As wives and children join the migrants in the United States, household expenses rise. Among farmworkers, these added expenses produce a decline in disposable income between the experience intervals of five to nine years and ten to fourteen years before recovering to a peak of about $8,500 in the highest interval. Among nonagricultural workers, disposable income does not decline, but it clearly stalls at the same point before peaking at $19,000 in the highest interval.

The most important variable in table 9.7, in terms of the settlement process, is disposable income as a proportion of gross income. Obviously, our measure of disposable income is very crude, since it does not include necessary expenses such as utilities and clothing. Nonetheless, among those just beginning migrant careers, over 75 percent of gross income is "disposable" in both agricultural and nonagricultural sectors; that is, the quantity of money that migrants potentially have available to remit back to their home communities amounts to about 77 percent of their gross earnings. Farmworkers maintain this level up through nine years of migrant experience. Beyond this point, it falls to roughly 63 percent of gross pay as more and more of their earnings are spent on maintaining families resident in the United States. The share of nonagricultural workers' income potentially available for remittance home falls immediately and rapidly to 50 percent in the experience interval ten to fourteen years, as the cost of maintaining families is much higher in urban areas and its growth over time exceeds the growth in migrants' wages. In the highest experience interval, the share of nonagricultural income that is disposable recovers somewhat to 59 percent.

A more telling indicator that integration is under way is the use to which disposable income is put. The ethnosurvey questionnaire asked migrants to estimate the average amounts they saved and remitted home each month. The difference between the sum of two quantities and disposable income provides an estimate of the amount spent in the United States on purchases other than food and rent. Percentages of disposable income devoted to each of these three categories—savings, remittances, and other spending—are presented in table 9.8.

Farmworkers begin their careers remitting or saving all the disposable income they earn in the United States. As the years of U.S. experience add up, however, they save and remit less and less and spend more and more in the United States. After fifteen years as migrants, they are spending 65 percent of their U.S. incomes in the United States. Nonagricultural workers begin by spending 59 percent of their disposable incomes. Apparently much more spending is required to establish oneself in a city job, and of course there are many more inducements to spending for recreation and pleasure. After one is established in the city, however, the relative amount spent rather than saved or remitted falls by almost half. In the experience interval one to four years, nonagricultural workers spend only 34 percent of their disposable incomes. As with farmworkers, however, this quantity rises rapidly and steadily thereafter, to 76 percent in the highest experience interval.

In short, the ethnosurvey data provide tangible evidence of an ongoing shift of orientation between Mexico and the United States among migrants from the four communities. As they accumulate experience abroad, migrants acquire more and stronger connections to the United States. As their social worlds consist increasingly of people and institutions north of the border, migrants spend growing amounts of their total U.S. incomes on living expenses in the United States and send smaller shares of their disposable incomes to Mexico. After fifteen years of migrant experience, about 40 percent of money earned is spent on food and lodging (especially lodging), and from what is left, more than 67 percent is spent in the United States.

Even among the most experienced, most integrated U.S. migrants, however, the permanence of settlement is rarely wholly certain. The issue of staying versus returning to Mexico is a constant, problematic issue for migrants in their first generation of U.S. residence. Even after many years in the United States, it is common for migrants to return to their home communities. It is also common for migrants to spend a

TABLE 9.8
Disposition of U.S. Income by Years of Migrant Experience and Sector of U.S. Employment: Migrants from Four Mexican Communities, 1982[a]

Sector and disposition	Years of U.S. migrant experience					
	Under 1	1–4	5–9	10–14	15 +	Total
Agricultural workers						
Percent remitted	59.3	38.8	29.6	18.4	25.8	39.4
Percent saved	40.7	31.4	24.3	10.9	8.9	28.8
Percent spent	0.0	29.8	46.1	70.6	65.3	31.7
Disposable income	$2,092	$3,621	$7,494	$5,754	$8,460	$3,931
Nonagricultural workers						
Percent remitted	21.4	41.6	17.6	17.8	6.0	20.9
Percent saved	19.8	25.0	25.8	13.8	17.8	20.4
Percent spent	58.8	33.5	56.6	68.4	76.3	58.7
Disposable income	$5,335	$6,710	$9,627	$10,477	$19,029	$9,439

Source: MIGFILE; migrant household members enumerated in Mexico or California, including those in twenty-five extra households in Santiago.

[a] All amounts in 1982 U.S. dollars.

lifetime working in the United States and then to retire to Mexico on their pensions or Social Security payments in order to take advantage of the lower cost of living.

The fundamentally ambiguous character of U.S. settlement is suggested by table 9.9, which presents the current residence of migrants who practiced a settled migrant strategy during their active migrant years. That is, each person represented in this table lived at least three consecutive years in the United States at some time. Regardless of whether one includes the California respondents, it is apparent that many migrants who had apparently "settled" at some point in the past eventually returned home to Mexico. The propensity for return following settlement is greatest among urban-origin migrants, among whom nearly 33 percent of those who ever "settled" in the United States had returned home by 1982. Among rural-origin migrants, the figure was 14 percent. These estimates are somewhat crude; however, since it is impossible to gather a representative sample of all migrants who have ever settled, they serve to indicate the ambiguous, problematic meaning of settlement for Mexican migrants. Settlement is never an irreversible, irrevocable step in the social process of migration; rather, it involves a relative shift in the focus of orientation between two very different countries.

CASE STUDIES OF INTEGRATION

A Settler from Altamira

Federico comes from a middle-class family in Altamira, where his father owned a corn flour mill, and was a merchant of grains and fruits produced in the municipio. When Federico's two older brothers finished primary school, there was no secondary school in town, so his father opened up a carpenter shop and employed them in order to initiate them into a trade. When Federico finished sixth grade, however, a secondary school had opened, and he was able to continue his studies. He was not required to contribute much to the work of the household and so was able to finish ninth grade without difficulty.

Given Federico's success in secondary school, his family sent him to preparatory school in Guadalajara and paid all his expenses during the first year. In the second year his father died, and Federico was obliged to find a job in a grocery store owned by a paisano, who several years earlier had settled in Guadalajara. He didn't care for the work, and a year after having set his studies aside, he returned to Altamira.

TABLE 9.9
CURRENT RESIDENCE OF MIGRANTS WHO PRACTICED SETTLED STRATEGIES DURING THEIR
ACTIVE YEARS OF U.S. MIGRATION: MIGRANTS FROM FOUR MEXICAN COMMUNITIES

Current residence	Rural origin		Urban origin	
	Without Californians	With Californians	Without Californians	With Californians
United States (%)	80.7	86.2	41.7	68.6
Mexico (%)	19.3	13.8	58.3	31.3
Number of migrants	109	159	36	67

Source: PERSFILE; all migrants enumerated in Mexico or California, including those in twenty-five extra households in Santiago.

There he worked sporadically helping his older brother as a carpenter's assistant. After several months of irregular work and intermittent pay, he decided to migrate to the United States. In 1975 he left with a group of young men from Altamira, who had found paid work increasingly scarce with the advent of agricultural modernization.

Federico arrived in Los Angeles and stayed with a friend from Altamira who had invited him to come and told him of possible work as a carpenter. Within a few weeks of arriving, he found work as an assistant to a carpenter who was an acquaintance of this friend. The job lasted for only two months, since the carpenter worked very small jobs and didn't need a helper on most of them. After a few weeks of unemployment, Federico obtained seasonal work in a fruit cannery through another paisano living in Los Angeles. He worked there for two months, and his earnings permitted him to pay his debt to his friend and to begin supporting himself. He still did not earn enough to send money to his mother, however. Eventually work in the cannery came to an end, and after a few days of unemployment, he went back to work as a carpenter's assistant, but this job also lasted for only two months.

Given these frequent spells of unemployment, he decided to switch into agricultural work, and he struck out for fields where he knew other paisanos worked. Unfortunately, he lacked experience as a farmworker, and the first few weeks were very difficult for him. Although his competence later improved, he never became one of the better farmworkers, those whom foremen chose when there was little work or when particular expertise was required. For six weeks he worked more or less continuously in the fields, but winter came and he could work for only a few hours per week. Although most of his fellow paisanos had returned home, he resisted the temptation to return because of the little money he had saved. Having paid off the coyote who guided him across the border, worked off his debts to his friend in Los Angeles, and sent his mother a little money, he had accumulated little cash.

He ultimately decided to return to Los Angeles, where another paisano offered him work as a gardener's assistant. This work had many advantages in comparison to his previous jobs. The work was steady, and wages were better than in agriculture. Although the costs of food and lodging were higher in the city, better wages and steadier employment compensated for the disadvantage. The company where he worked employed ten to fifteen people from Altamira, all of whom had obtained their jobs through a woman from town who was married to the owner, a U.S. citizen. Drawing upon the bonds of paisanaje, she chose young men willing to work long, hard hours.

Federico learned the trade during the first few weeks on the job and found that he did not need to know English. He was simply transported from garden to garden according to a route established by the owner, who dealt with the clients and collected the fees. Routes were expanded primarily through the gardeners themselves while they were on the job. When they encountered a homeowner with a garden, and if the homeowner was interested in their services, they simply presented a card containing the telephone number of the company, and the owner arranged for service to begin.

Federico put a great deal of enthusiasm into his new work and learned the trade well, and through his efforts the company's routes grew rapidly. Because he had learned to drive the company's trucks and could navigate easily about the city, the owner promoted him from assistant to gardener and gave him a route of his own. In order to work a route he needed a pickup truck and gardening machinery, and the company advanced him a loan for these expenses. Because the promotion carried a salary increase, Federico was able to pay off the debt in a few months and at the same time send money to his mother to help pay for the education of his younger sister. His remittances, plus contributions from his two older brothers, enabled his mother to send her to study at the normal school in Guadalajara.

For three years, from age twenty-two to age twenty-five, he busied himself with his life as a gardener. During this time he returned to Altamira only once and stayed for only three weeks, since his work in the United States didn't allow him more time off. All the while, Federico managed to avoid crossing paths with immigration officials, so his undocumented status caused him few problems.

At twenty-five years of age, Federico married a woman from Altamira whom he had met in Los Angeles. When they married, she had been working for a year and a half as a seamstress in a small garment factory. In contrast to the usual custom, the wedding was only a civil one, leaving the religious ceremony for a future trip to Altamira. Marriage brought a series of changes for Federico, such as renting an apartment and buying furniture. Since his wife continued working for another year and a half after their marriage, it was not difficult to pay for these new expenses. Federico was impressed, since if he were to establish a new apartment in Mexico, the money required would be difficult to obtain and would necessitate several years of work as an employee in Guadalajara or a carpenter in Altamira.

With the birth of their first child, Federico decided to start his own business. His growing familiarity with English and contacts on the gardening route enabled him to establish direct relationships with prospective clients. Instead of signing them up for the company, he arranged to garden for them himself, and little by little he built up his own route. To handle the additional work, he hired a brother-in-law from Altamira. To avoid problems with the family, Federico clearly explained the terms of employment, and the brother-in-law accepted them.

Eventually the fact that Federico was not reporting new clients aroused suspicion in the company, and after proving that he was gardening on his own account, he was fired. Another worker from Altamira was given his route, but some customers chose to continue with Federico because of the personal relationship he had developed with them. With these customers, together with the new ones whom he had acquired on the side, plus another route that he bought on credit from a different gardener, he was able to make enough money to support his family and to retire from gardening himself. After the break with his former employer, his brother-in-law continued to work for him, and he continued to have cordial relationships with most paisanos who worked for the old company; however, contacts with his old bosses and their close relatives ended.

At thirty years of age, after eight years of residence in the United States, Federico is well adapted to life in Los Angeles and has decided to stay on. Many factors contributed to this decision. Network contacts with other paisanos provided the socioeconomic infrastructure that permitted his incorporation into the permanent and well-paid work that made integration possible. The experience of a high income nurtured consumer tastes that could be satisfied better by working in Los Angeles than in Altamira. His growing facility with English permitted him to conduct a successful business and to meet the needs of daily life. His marriage in the United States to another migrant further cemented his connection to that country, as did the birth of his children, who will grow up as American Chicanos rather than Mexicans. Finally, his growing family spurred him to expand his business operations in Los Angeles, creating stronger economic ties to the United States.

The one problematic aspect of his integration is his lack of legal residence papers. In many employment settings, legal documents are necessary to achieve a stable income, opportunities for advancement, and permanence, especially among farmworkers; in these circumstances documentation plays an important role in the decision to settle. Legal status is of secondary importance in many urban settings, however, where the difficulty of detection and apprehension make immigration enforcement inefficient. Federico doesn't discount the value of arranging legal papers for himself and his wife, because they offer greater security in the United States. Nevertheless, they made the decision to settle without these documents.

Even with his integration into the socioeconomic world of Los Angeles, Federico's "settlement" is not definitive. At times he sounds like an old migrant, speaking with nostalgia about grandiose plans to return to his birthplace in triumph and open a business that will provide work to many people; however, a return to Mexico becomes progressively less likely each day. Given the long time he has been away and his lack of familiarity with economic changes in the region, it will be difficult for him to find opportunities sufficient to maintain his current standard of living. For the foreseeable future, therefore, he has chosen to remain in the United States. As he says, "for now I don't plan to return to town."

A Settled Family from San Marcos

The case of the Domínguez family from San Marcos also helps to illustrate the process of integration and the ambiguity of settlement. The family is originally from Tepatitlán, Jalisco, a small town near Guadalajara, but many years ago, family members left and settled in Guadalajara, where some relatives still live. For the past fifteen years the Domínguez family has lived in a Mexican neighborhood of Los Angeles. The family owns two houses, one of which is home to its eight members, while the other is rented out. The family also owns a small garment workshop that employs twenty workers, located on the same property.

The father went to Los Angeles in the early 1960s when his brother, who was already there, assured him that good work could be found. After three years working in a factory, Señor Domínguez was able to save enough money to bring his spouse and four children from Mexico. Originally all entered without legal documents, but two children were later born in the United States, and the birth of these U.S. citizens enabled Señor Domínguez to arrange the papers of all.[1] Later his wife became a naturalized U.S. citizen in order to facilitate the legalization of other relatives and avoid problems in starting a business.

Following her arrival in the United States, Señora Domínguez worked at home, sewing clothes for a local garment manufacturer. She learned the trade, saved her money, bought a sewing machine, and finally opened her own taller on their property. This arrangement allowed her to work at home and at the same time take care of the house and the children. Meanwhile, the garment shop continued to expand. Since the father had a well-paying factory job, he was able to support the family commodiously on his salary, and what they earned from the taller was reinvested, buying additional machines and hiring more workers.

The shop expanded until there were twenty women working in it, primarily other Mexicans, but all Hispanic. Señora Domínguez ran the workshop and supervised relations with contractors who provided fabrics, accessories, and patterns. Her taller cut, assembled, and sewed patterns from fabrics they were given. Every weekend she would hand over another shipment of finished clothing to the contractor, and she was paid. Eventually, her work in the taller prevented her from attending to housework, so she invited a sister from Mexico. In return for minimal salary and board, the sister helped with household chores. On other occasions the mother came to help out for a few months. Over the years, various siblings and relatives have visited the Domínguez family, and to all she has been able to give work or at least a place to stay.

The taller is fundamentally a family enterprise. The father continues to work in the factory every morning, but he returns in the evening to take charge of repairing and maintaining the sewing machines. He also organizes the older sons in the work of distributing the different garment pieces according to the work schedule. The oldest daughter is in charge of internal accounts, controlling how many pieces each worker makes per day. The other daughters help to put the finishing touches on the clothes and cover them with plastic bags. The whole family helps to unload fabrics and accessories when they arrive at the workshop and to load the finished shirts and garments when they leave for the wholesaler. All participate in the work of the factory in some way, each according to age, capacity, and daily schedule. Only the oldest son,

---

[1] United States immigration law has since been amended, in 1976, to prevent this avenue of entry. Now U.S. citizens can sponsor the immigration of their parents only after reaching the age of twenty-one.

already married, works elsewhere. The children do not have a fixed salary, only the right to ask for what they need from their parents.

The female employees of the taller generally receive the minimum hourly wage, but they have the option of working at piece rate. In this way, many considerably elevate their incomes. One of them, who works very well and very rapidly, earns between $300 and $400 each week. In fact, she works almost all day, and her wages are logged into two separate Social Security accounts registered under different names. The shop is open from seven in the morning to eight at night, and the shifts vary depending on where one is located in the productive chain. Workers who actually sew the garments arrive first, and those who do the finishing and ironing arrive later in the afternoon.

The Domínguez family workshop requires a series of professional and technical services, which are usually provided by other Hispanics. A Puerto Rican bookkeeper pays the business taxes and handles the payroll. Repair work is usually given to friends or relatives who are familiar with the shop or have worked in it. Señor Domínguez has his car serviced in the garage of a paisano, and his wife attends hairdressing courses in a school run by a Mexican woman. In general, most of the activities of daily life are conducted in Spanish with other Hispanics, although all the children speak English, and for the youngest it is the primary language.

The Domínguez family is clearly well integrated into life in the United States, therefore, and would be considered settled migrants under any reasonable definition. The wife is a naturalized American citizen, two of the six children were born in the United States, and the rest have green cards. All have some familiarity with English, and the younger children speak it as their main language. The family has been in the United States for more than fifteen years. All family members of working age are gainfully employed. They own two houses, pay taxes, retain financial advisors, and operate a successful business with twenty employees. Even with this overwhelming evidence of integration in the United States, the family's permanent "settlement" remains ambiguous.

Señor Domínguez is a conspicuous consumer, but when he buys consumer goods, he does so in double portions. One part goes into their house in Los Angeles, and the other is saved to bring back to Mexico. Señor Domínguez makes frequent trips back to Tepatitlán and is constructing a house there. Much of the family's money is spent furnishing this house in sumptuous style. The parents maintain the dream of eventual return to their home community and are investing a great deal of money to make this dream a reality. When and how the family will return and who will go remain unclear, however. The family is divided between a good livelihood and economic security in the United States on one hand and a strong social attachment to their community of origin on the other hand. The case of the Domínguez family reflects the inherent ambiguity of a life that straddles two different economic, social, and cultural worlds.

SUMMARY

This chapter has considered the process of integration in the United States which is one part of a larger social process of international migration. Integration is initially accomplished through social networks that emanate in migrants' home communities. Through them migrants travel north, cross the border, find jobs, and become established in their new environments. Throughout their careers in the United States, migrants never lose contact with these networks or with their home communities. Even if migrants initially have no intention of staying, as they spend more time abroad they tend to acquire social and economic ties that bind them more firmly to American society. Social and economic connections in the United States multiply steadily with increasing migrant experience, although the extent and timing of integration are strongly influenced by urban origin, occupational background, and legal status.

A variety of social and economic connections to the United States were considered, and results uniformly depict a steady process of integration as migrant experience increases. The more time they spend abroad, the more likely migrants are able to establish family and friendship ties in the United States, obtain nonagricultural occupations, possess legal documents, and make use of public services such as education, medicine, Social Security, and unemployment compensation. Facility with the English language also increases with U.S. migrant experience, as does membership in various U.S.-based organizations. Over time, employment is increasingly regularized and various economic connections to the United States are established.

The extent of integration on these dimensions is clearly affected by rural versus urban status, sector of U.S. employment, and legal status, but the basic process of integration is the same. The status of being a farmworker or an undocumented alien decreases the extent of integration relative to nonagricultural and documented workers, but social and economic connections increase with exposure to U.S. society in each case. Undocumented migrants do not appear to make use of public services in the United States, however, with the exception of medical care, education, and—to a lesser extent—unemployment compensation.

Progressive integration into U.S. society brings a gradual shift of orientation away from migrants' communities of origin to the United States. Few of these migrants are ever completely divorced from the social settings of their home communities; however, the more time they spend working abroad, the less inclined they are to remit their earnings back to Mexico and the more money they spend in the United States. Even after many years of international migration, however, the concepts of integration and settlement remain problematic and ambiguous. The issue of settlement versus return is never definitively settled within the migrant generation, and many who at some point "settle" in the United States eventually return to Mexico.

10

Principles of International Migration

The foregoing chapters paint a general picture of international migration as a dynamic social process. Mexican migration to the United States originally occurred as a result of social, economic, and political transformations that altered relations of production in both countries; over time, however, it became institutionalized and acquired a momentum of its own. The emergence of migrant networks put employment in the United States within reach of virtually all segments of society, and international migration became an integral part of household survival strategies, widely seen as a basic socioeconomic resource to be employed during critical phases of the life cycle, during periods of economic stress, or in a sustained effort of socioeconomic improvement. Its widespread use, in turn, induced social and economic changes within sending communities that encouraged more migration.

This brief summary represents a concise distillation of findings from the preceding chapters and describes the concrete case of migration from our sample communities to the United States. At a more abstract level, the social process of international migration can be defined formally in terms of six basic principles:

1. Migration originates historically in structural changes that affect the relations of production in sending and receiving societies.
2. Once international migration begins, social networks develop to make foreign employment increasingly accessible to all classes of the sending society.
3. As international migration becomes more accessible, it is widely incorporated into household survival strategies and is used during stages of the life cycle when dependence is greatest, during periods of economic stress, or in efforts of socioeconomic advancement.
4. The experience of international migration affects individual motivations, household strategies, and community organizations in ways that encourage further migration.

5. The maturation of migrant networks is facilitated by an ongoing process of settlement, whereby migrants build personal, social, and economic ties to the receiving society as they accumulate time abroad.
6. The operation of migrant networks is made possible by an ongoing process of return whereby temporary and recurrent migrants move back and forth between sending and receiving societies and settled migrants reemigrate back to their places of origin.

These six principles provide a general framework for understanding international migration as a developmental social process. They were originally derived in chapter 1, drawing upon studies conducted by other researchers in a variety of settings. The principles are also consistent with the evidence that we have presented to this point; however, they have not yet been subjected to a rigorous quantitative evaluation. Prior analyses have considered only one or two variables at a time, but in reality many factors act simultaneously to determine the course of migration. No effort has been made to sort out the relative impacts of different variables as they jointly influence the social process of migration.

This chapter uses quantitative life histories from the ethnosurvey to undertake such a task. In order to disentangle the complexity of the migration process, we divide the migrant career into four segments corresponding to fundamental decisions that migrants and their families confront at key points in their lives: whether to begin migrating, whether to continue migrating, whether to settle in the United States, and among those who have settled whether to return to Mexico. At each stage, separate analyses are conducted to measure the probability of departure, repetition, settlement, or return and to estimate the impact of selected variables on the likelihood of these events. Together the models capture in succinct form the essence of international migration as a dynamic social process and verify its fundamental principles.

METHODS OF ANALYSIS

Each of the four phases of migration corresponds to a distinct event in the larger social process of migration. The events of departure, repetition, settlement, and return all have measurable probabilities at various points in time, and the magnitudes of these probabilities bear directly on the six principles listed above. For example, principle 1 predicts elevated departure probabilities during particular historical periods, specifically, during periods of identifiable structural change in sending and receiving areas. Likewise, principle 3 predicts an increasing probability of repeat migration with each trip taken, while principle 5 posits an increase in the likelihood of settlement with growing migrant experience, and principle 6 suggests a decreasing probability of return migration among settled migrants as duration of stay lengthens.

The first goal of this chapter is to measure probabilities associated with each event in the social process of migration, using life table methods (Pollard et al. 1974). Originally developed to study the process of mortality, the life table follows people through life, comparing the number of deaths at each age with the number of people who reach that age and computing age-specific probabilities of dying. The life table is not restricted to the study of mortality, however. It is a general method that can be applied to any process involving entries into and exits out of a population. In the case of departure, for example, one enters the population of nonmigrants through birth and exits it through first departure to the United States. If migration is regarded in this way, a life table can be constructed to measure the probability of first departure by age. Analogous operations can be carried out to measure probabilities associated with repeat migration, settlement, and return.

The measurement of these probabilities is important, but it does not directly link variables to outcomes, an operation that is necessary to test our six principles fully. The second goal of this chapter, therefore, is to measure the impact of selected variables on probabilities associated with the fundamental events of international migration, using the method of multivariate logistic regression (Hanushek and Jackson 1977). This statistical technique measures independent effects of explanatory variables on the likelihood of discrete outcomes such as departure, repetition, settlement, or return, while controlling for the effects of other variables. In all except the departure analysis, we make use of quantitative life histories gathered from male migrants to the United States, with person-years of experience as the units of observation. The application of logistic regression procedures to such data yields a discrete-time event history analysis (Allison 1984).

STEPS IN THE MIGRATION PROCESS

Departure

The first principle concerning the structural causes of Mexico–United States migration predicts a specific historical pattern in probabilities of departure from the four communities. In rural areas, we hypothesize that structural shifts in the relations of production increased the likelihood of international migration during two epochs: the 1940s, when agrarian reform provided land but no capital for cultivation, and during the 1960s, when a wave of agricultural modernization brought the displacement of workers from traditional agricultural tasks. In urban areas, we posit an increase in departure probabilities during the postwar recession of 1945–1946 and during the factory modernization of 1954–1955, followed by a decline in the economic boom years of the 1970s.

These basic trends are also affected by political and economic developments in the United States. Mexican immigration was officially encouraged by the Bracero Accord from 1942 to 1954, discouraged by Operation Wetback in 1954–1955, encouraged again by expansion of the Bracero program in 1955–1959, and finally discouraged by phasing out of the Bracero program in the early 1960s. During the late 1960s and 1970s, however, rapid economic growth in the southwestern United States and weak border enforcement again encouraged large-scale Mexican immigration.

In order to examine the correspondence between changes in the structural context of migration and the relative likelihood of leaving the four communities, figure 10.1 presents "lifetime" probabilities of first departure for males from rural and urban areas, estimated for successive five-year periods from 1940 to 1982. The lifetime probability of departure represents the hypothetical probability of making at least one trip to the United States before reaching age sixty. It was estimated by use of a combination of logistic regression and life table methods.[1] For each five-year period, we asked what would happen if men born in that

---

[1] Specifically, we conducted an age-period-cohort analysis (Mason et al. 1973, 1976) of men from the four communities, including those in the Californian samples, employing a discrete-time approach to study person-years of observation. Beginning at birth, each year of a man's life was coded 0 if he had never migrated and 1 if he became a migrant initially in that year. All years subsequent to the one in which a man became a migrant were excluded. Using logistic methods, this 0–1 variable was regressed on dummy variables representing age (in five-year intervals), period (in five-year segments from 1940 to 1982, with the last period truncated), and birth cohort (also in five-year segments). The cohort coefficients proved insignificant and were eliminated. This procedure provided estimates of the yearly probability of becoming a migrant by age and period. For each five-year period between 1940 and 1982, this probability was converted into a life table value known as $_nq_x$, which represents the probability of migrating between ages x and $x + n$, and these values were then used to derive another life table function, l_x, the probability of remaining a nonmigrant up to age x. The quantity $1 - l_x$ represents the probability of becoming a U.S. migrant by age x, and we take $1 - l_{60}$ as our measure of the lifetime migration probability. Estimation of age-period-cohort models raises several technical issues (Fienberg and Mason 1978; Rodgers 1982) that are discussed more thoroughly in Massey (1985).

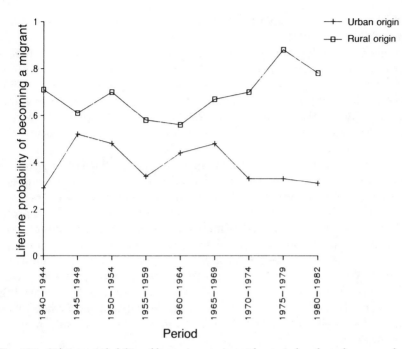

Fig. 10.1. Lifetime probability of becoming a migrant by period and rural versus urban
origin. (*Source*: PERSFILE; male household members enumerated in Mexico and
California, including those in twenty-five extra households in Santiago.)

particular period went through life subject to the rates of departure
prevailing at that time.

Trends in lifetime departure probabilities correspond closely to predicted patterns. In rural areas, the probability of departure begins high,
about .70, during the early Bracero years, then falls to about .60 with
the end of World War II, but revives to its former level during the early
1950s. With the advent of the U.S. government Operation Wetback, the
probability of departure falls steadily to a minimum of about .56 in 1964,
when the Bracero program finally ended. With the advent of agricultural
modernization during the middle 1960s, the pressures for migration
intensified substantially, and by this time migrant networks had rendered the Bracero program irrelevant as a vehicle for entry into the
United States. From 1965 onward, the probability of departure rose
steadily, until by the late 1970s a rural male had a 90 percent chance of
going to the United States over his lifetime.

Urban trends are also consistent with the temporal pattern of structural shifts that we have identified. During World War II the probability

of departure was low, about .30, as factories worked overtime to satisfy foreign demand. When the war ended, a period of recession and a high degree of unemployment ensued and the lifetime probability of departure rose to .52 in 1945 to 1949. With economic recovery, the likelihood of departure fell until the wave of factory modernization began in 1955, ushering in another era of widespread migration culminating in a migration probability of .48 in 1965 to 1969. With the subsequent economic boom of Guadalajara, the likelihood of departure fell rapidly after 1969 to about .30 during the 1970s and early 1980s.

Data from both rural and urban areas suggest that U.S. migration was, indeed, used as a mechanism for adjustment to structural change. Whether the change involved the mechanization of fields or factories, a rise in the probability of international migration ensued. The high probability of departure in all periods indicates the extent to which migration has become a permanent part of survival strategies within the communities, however. Indeed, a *majority* of rural-origin men could always expect to work in the United States (the lowest lifetime probability was .56), as could at least one in three urban-origin migrants. Moreover, the 90 percent chance of departure for men from rural areas in the late 1970s graphically illustrates how U.S. migration has become truly a mass phenomenon.

In order to estimate the effects of particular variables on the departure process, we developed a model to explain the migration behavior of male household heads versus other family members. Unfortunately, we could not undertake a full event history analysis of migration probabilities because the ethnosurvey did not gather life history data from nonmigrants. It is, therefore, impossible to contrast those who did and did not go to the United States in a given year by using retrospective event history data; however, the process of departure can be studied cross-sectionally by comparing migrants and nonmigrants during 1980 to 1982.

Two logistic regression models were estimated to predict the likelihood of different household members migrating to the United States during this period. The first model predicts the probability of U.S. migration for male household heads (fathers), and the second predicts migration probabilities for other household members (primarily wives, sons, and daughters). Models were specified separately for rural and urban areas, and members of the California sample were excluded in each case. The dependent variable was whether the household member in question went to the United States between 1980 and 1982 and was coded 1 if the person migrated and 0 otherwise. Prediction of this outcome is equivalent to predicting the probability of migration over the period.

The models employed three sets of explanatory variables: household characteristics (dependency, land ownership, and business ownership), personal characteristics (age, sex, education, labor force status, and occupation), and characteristics of the migrant experience itself (person's prior migrant experience and father's prior migrant experience). The logistic regression coefficient associated with each variable provides a consistent estimate of its independent impact on the probability of migration. Since it is difficult to visualize the structure of causal models from equations alone, we present the coefficients in the form of a path model, depicted in figure 10.2. Each causal relationship is represented by a path, and the direction of causality is indicated by the arrows. Only relationships that proved to be statistically significant are included in the diagram.

In order to facilitate direct comparison between the variables in the path diagrams, all are measured on a scale of 0 to 1. The relative size of the coefficient thus indicates the relative importance of the effect. Variables were defined to equal 1 if the subject displayed the trait in question and 0 otherwise. Business owners, males, workers, U.S. migrants, primary school graduates, fathers over age thirty-five, and other family members over age fifteen were all coded as 1, and land ownership was set to 1 if households owned at least five hectares, roughly the smallest plot able to support a family (Stavenhagen 1970). Occupation was coded differently in rural and urban areas. In the former it was set to 1 if the subject was a farmworker and 0 otherwise; in the latter, skilled workers were coded 1 and others 0. Dependency equaled the number of dependents per household member.[2]

The rural model provides a clear picture of how various individual and household factors combine to influence the likelihood of a father migrating. The probability of going to the United States is increased by prior migrant experience, by being a day laborer, and by increasing dependency within the household, while the chances of U.S. migration are lowered by owning farmland or a business and by advancing age. The most important factors explaining fathers' migration are prior U.S. migrant experience and access to a means of production.

---

[2] All the models were also estimated by using continuous variables for age, education, and migrant experience to ensure that results were not an artifact of dichotomization. Estimates based on continuous data lead to exactly the same conclusions as the ones given here, which are preferred for heuristic reasons. Estimates corresponding to the continuous specifications of the models are reported in Massey (1987).

Rural Households

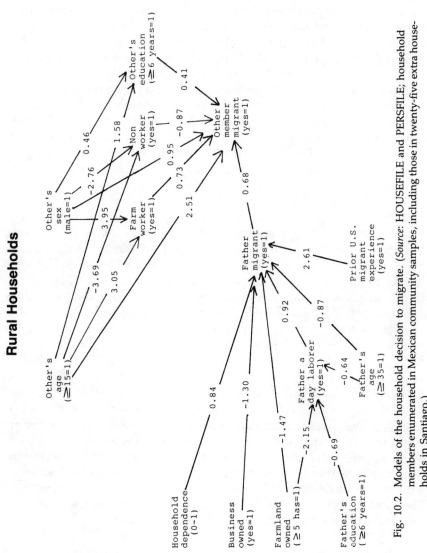

Fig. 10.2. Models of the household decision to migrate. (*Source*: HOUSEFILE and PERSFILE; household members enumerated in Mexican community samples, including those in twenty-five extra households in Santiago.)

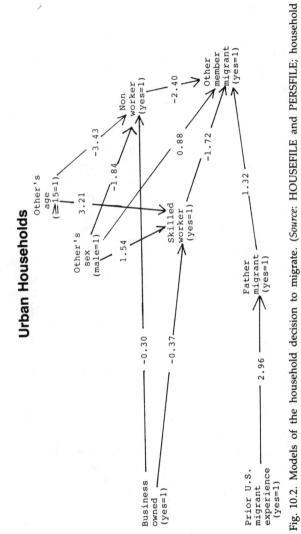

Urban Households

Fig. 10.2. Models of the household decision to migrate. (*Source:* HOUSEFILE and PERSFILE; household members enumerated in Mexican community samples, including those in twenty-five extra households in Santiago.) (continued)

The impact of owning a business on the likelihood of migration is very strong and negative (with a coefficient of –1.30), as is the effect of owning farmland (a coefficient of –1.47), meaning that these factors strongly reduce the probability of a father migrating. Owning land also has a negative *indirect* effect on the likelihood of migration because it sharply reduces the likelihood of a father being a day laborer, which also affects the propensity to migrate. Counterbalancing these inhibiting effects on migration, the strongest single effect in the model is the positive impact of prior migrant experience (coefficient 2.61). Within the context of these more powerful constraints, life cycle factors—dependency and age—determine the likelihood of migration. Fathers are most likely to migrate during phases of the life cycle when they are young (under thirty-five) and have growing families with many dependents.

These results support the structural interpretation of international migration suggested by principle 1 previously. For rural fathers, the strongest determinants of migration reflect patterns of socioeconomic organization rather than individual characteristics such as age, education, and occupation. Access to productive resources such as land and commerce stem from institutional arrangements in society, such as the system of land tenure, access to credit, the extent of urban primacy, and the economic organization of agriculture. The one individual-level variable with a powerful effect on migration is prior migrant experience, which supports the view of international migration as a self-feeding social process. Only within the constraints imposed by these larger forces do life cycle and occupational factors exert their influence, and education plays no direct role in the process.

These conclusions follow from the path diagram shown in figure 10.2; however, it is difficult to visualize what the various effects really mean in terms of concrete migration probabilities. The equations that were estimated to give the path coefficients shown in figure 10.2 can also be employed to predict migration probabilities for fathers with different characteristics, and these are shown in table 10.1.[3] According to this table, a privileged property owner with few dependents—that is, a non–day laborer owning both business and farmland, with a work-

---

[3] For estimation of the migration probabilities, independent variables are given values corresponding to different assumed traits, and these are inserted into the following equation to generate predicted probabilities: $P = 1/(1 + e^{-BX})$, where B is the vector of coefficients corresponding to variables depicted in figure 10.2, and P is the predicted probability. This procedure is an appropriate means of conveying the social significance of results from a logistic regression model (Petersen 1985) and is used to generate predicted probabilities throughout this chapter.

TABLE 10.1
ESTIMATED PROBABILITIES OF MIGRATION FOR RURAL MALE HOUSEHOLD HEADS WITH
DIFFERENT PERSONAL AND FAMILY CHARACTERISTICS, 1980–1982

| Characteristics | Number of dependents per household member | | | | | |
	0.0	0.2	0.4	0.5	0.6	0.8
Day laborer under 35						
without U.S. migrant						
experience						
No land or business	.099	.115	.133	.143	.154	.177
Business and no land	.029	.034	.040	.044	.047	.055
Land and no business	.025	.029	.034	.037	.044	.047
Both land and business	.007	.008	.010	.010	.011	.013
Day laborer under 35 with						
U.S. migrant experience						
No land or business	.599	.638	.676	.694	.712	.745
Business and no land	.289	.325	.363	.382	.402	.443
Land and no business	.255	.289	.324	.343	.362	.402
Both land and business	.085	.100	.116	.125	.134	.155
Non–day laborer under 35						
without U.S. migrant						
experience						
No land or business	.042	.049	.058	.062	.067	.079
Business and no land	.012	.014	.016	.018	.019	.023
Land and no business	.010	.012	.015	.015	.016	.019
Both land and business	.003	.003	.004	.004	.005	.005
Non–day laborer under 35						
with U.S. migrant						
experience						
No land or business	.373	.413	.454	.475	.496	.538
Business and no land	.139	.161	.185	.198	.211	.241
Land and no business	.120	.139	.161	.172	.185	.211
Both land and business	.036	.042	.050	.054	.058	.068

Sources: HOUSEFILE and PERSFILE; household members enumerated in Mexican community samples.

ing wife and no children—had less than a .01 probability of becoming a migrant during 1980 to 1982. In contrast, a young father from the rural proletariat—a day laborer with some prior U.S. experience, a nonworking wife, three small children, and no land or business—had a 75 percent chance of migrating. Indeed, the minimum probability of migration for a day laborer with prior migrant experience and no property was .60; even without the added boost of U.S. experience, day laborers without access to productive resources had relatively high probabilities of migration, ranging from .10 to .18, contingent on the level of household dependency. The fact that two-thirds of the fathers in rural areas own neither land nor a business suggests the great potential for out-migration from these communities.

The model also suggests the momentum inherent in the migration process. Even if there were a radical restructuring of Mexican society, giving everyone access to either land or a business, among those with U.S. experience the probability of U.S. migration would still be in the range of .20 to .40 at high dependency levels. In other words, once U.S. migration is incorporated into a family's survival strategy, it shows remarkable persistence. Even with access to resources sufficient for the general support of a family, once migration has been experienced, there is a strong tendency to use this well-known resource again.

In contrast to the case for fathers, personal rather than household factors are most important in determining the migration of other family members. The member most likely to migrate is a male over the age of fifteen who has entered the work force. The probability of migration for a fifteen-year-old son who has begun to assist his parents in farmwork is about .20. If he has a primary-school education, the probability rises to .28, and if he has a father who is an active U.S. migrant, it increases to .34. With both primary-school education and a migrant father, the probability is .43.

Household variables do not significantly affect the probability of other family members migrating, except indirectly through their influence on the migration of the father. The strong connection between the migration of fathers and sons again illustrates the self-perpetuating nature of international migration. Given prior U.S. experience, it is not only more likely that the father himself will migrate, but that his son will follow his example and also be initiated into the migration process. In essence, the model documents the intergenerational transmission of the migrant tradition.

The bottom half of figure 10.2 shows the migration model for urban households. This diagram provides a much less satisfying explanation of out-migration than that found in the rural model. The only variable significantly related to the likelihood of fathers migrating is prior migrant experience. The lack of significant effects for any of the other individual or household variables probably reflects economic conditions around Guadalajara at the time of the ethnosurvey. Recession and mechanization have led to international migration in the past; however, during 1980–1982 Guadalajara's economy was booming and unemployment among men in our sample was about 1 percent. Prior migrant experience was widespread, but most male household heads were inactive as migrants during the reference period. The only fathers who did migrate were those with prior U.S. migrant experience, consistent with the self-perpetuating nature of the migration process. The probability of migration for a male household head with prior experience was around .24, compared to .02 for one with no experience.

The effects of personal variables on the migration behavior of other household members generally parallel those of the rural model, except that age has no direct effect on migration and education has no effect at all. Those most likely to migrate are males of labor force age who have entered the unskilled labor force. The probability of migration for an unskilled son was roughly .06, while for sons who were not yet in the work force or who were skilled workers, it was practically zero. As in the rural model, there was a strong link between the migration of fathers and sons. The probability of migration for a son who was an unskilled worker with a migrant father was .19.

In summary, the results of this section bear directly on several of the ideas that we have advanced as fundamental principles of international migration. First, fluctuations in departure probabilities have historically followed larger structural developments in Mexican and American society, and path models indicate that the likelihood of migration is strongly determined by access to means of economic production. Second, prior migrant experience and having a migrant parent greatly increase the propensity to migrate, reflecting in part the influence of network connections. Third, the timing of U.S. migration is determined primarily by life cycle factors such as age and dependency. Finally, there is clear evidence of a self-feeding dynamic in the migration process. Having prior U.S. experience greatly increases the probability that a father will migrate again, and there is strong link between the migration propensities of fathers and sons, implying an intergenerational transmission of the migrant tradition.

Repetition

The concept of migration as a social process suggests that while structural factors may initiate migration, they are less important in explaining why it continues. Once someone has gone abroad, the cost of subsequent trips is substantially reduced, since the migrant has become familiar with the social infrastructure of the network. That person has learned how to get around in the foreign setting, made connections with employers and labor contractors, established relationships with settled paisanos, and generally reduced the anxiety of the unknown. Moreover, exposure to an affluent consumer society changes a migrant's outlook, generating aspirations for higher standards of living more easily supported by foreign than domestic labor.

The probability of making a trip generally increases with the number of trips already made. Such "trip progression probabilities" are easily estimated from the ethnosurvey data by applying life table procedures. To calculate these probability values, we selected all men who ever made a trip to the United States,[4] and between each pair of successive trips we counted the number of migrants who moved from trip x to trip $x + 1$. Given some number of prior trips, we could estimate the probability of making another.[5] These trip progression probabilities are plotted in figure 10.3.

Among both rural and urban origin migrants, the probability of making an additional trip to the United States increases with the number of trips already made. The probability rises from .77 for rural-origin migrants who have made one trip, to .94 among those who have made nine trips. Among urban-origin migrants the probability rises from .59 after the first trip to 1.0 after the ninth. Since the probability of making an additional trip steadily rises, the probability that a migrant will make any number of trips falls quite rapidly over the first few trips but then levels off after six or seven trips. The probability that a new rural-origin migrant will eventually go on to make 10 trips to the United States is about .22, therefore, compared to .08 for urban migrants.

The concept of migration as a social process also leads to specific predictions regarding the determinants of making an additional trip. As we have demonstrated, migration originates in the structural organization of society, which determines households' access to productive resources. After the process of migration has begun, however, these structural reasons for migration should matter less. Over the course of the migrant career, aspects of the migrant experience itself should increasingly dominate the decision to make an additional trip.

---

[4] In this and all ensuing analyses, the California samples are pooled with the Mexican community samples.

[5] The estimates are generated by means of a multiple-decrement life table approach. Between each successive trip, the number who go on to make an additional trip and the number who do not are considered. The decrement in the process occurs when a migrant fails to make an additional trip, but this decrement is subject to censoring biases. If a migrant had not yet accumulated five years since the most recent trip or had not returned from this trip, the observation was considered to be censored. Migrants who had not made another trip within five years of the last were considered to have retired. Failure to make another trip, censoring, and retirement define a triple-decrement life table. The associated single decrement table for failure gives $_nq_x$, the probability of not making another trip, so $1 - {_nq_x}$ gives the desired trip progression probability. These procedures are discussed in more detail in Massey (1985).

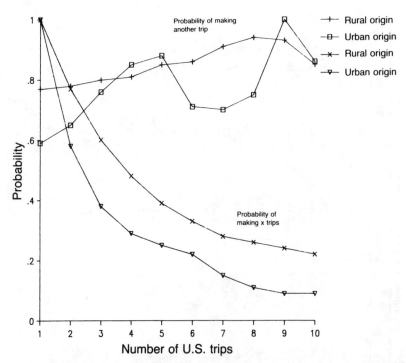

Fig. 10.3. Probability of making an additional trip to the United States and the probability of making *x* trips by rural versus urban origin. (*Source*: PERSFILE; male migrant household members enumerated in Mexico and California, including those in twenty-five extra households in Santiago.)

Table 10.2 tests this conceptualization of the migration process by conducting a logistic regression analysis of trip progression probabilities among male migrants from the four communities. After each trip, a set of independent variables was employed to predict the likelihood of making another trip. For each year of a subject's life, the dependent variable was measured as 1 if a new trip was made and 0 if not; therefore, the units of analysis are person-years of experience subsequent to the most recent trip, making the exercise an event history analysis. As in the departure analysis, three sets of explanatory variables are examined: characteristics of the household (presence of children and property ownership), characteristics of the person (marital status, age, education, occupation, and rural origin), and characteristics of the most recent trip to the United States (time since last trip, accumulated migrant experience, whether the wife or children were migrants, U.S. occupation, and

TABLE 10.2
LOGISTIC MODELS PREDICTING THE PROBABILITY OF MAKING AN ADDITIONAL U.S. TRIP, BY NUMBER OF TRIPS

| | Number of trips already made | | | | | |
| Explanatory variables | 1 trip | | 2 trips | | 3+ trips | |
	B	p	B	p	B	p
Household characteristics						
No children	0.158	0.669	-0.465	0.333	-0.501	0.248
Land owned	-1.113	0.115	0.075	0.894	0.572	0.207
Business owned	0.174	0.671	-0.747	0.247	-0.131	0.776
Home owned	-0.695[a]	0.008	-0.473	0.158	-1.185[a]	0.001
Personal characteristics						
Never married	0.341	0.340	-0.381	0.427	0.577	0.194
Age	-0.096	0.236	0.108	0.558	-0.017	0.814
Age squared	0.001	0.308	-0.001	0.294	0.001	0.699
Years of schooling	0.000	0.994	0.020	0.711	0.013[a]	0.791
Rural origin	0.400	0.168	-0.231	0.489	-0.735[a]	0.020
Characteristics of last U.S. trip						
Years since trip	-0.113[a]	0.001	-0.107[a]	0.004	-0.104[a]	0.001
U.S. migrant experience (months)	0.018[a]	0.001	0.004	0.231	0.008[a]	0.001
Wife a migrant	4.426[a]	0.001	0.995	0.184	0.802[b]	0.090
Children migrants	-0.029	0.965	0.802	0.236	1.337[a]	0.001
Farmworker	0.272	0.323	0.345	0.311	0.619[a]	0.050
Documented	1.787[a]	0.001	0.829[a]	0.044	0.183	0.621
Bracero	0.049	0.728	-0.953[a]	0.008	-0.748[a]	0.023
Period of first trip to United States						
1950–1959	0.103	0.747	-0.024	0.949	0.651[a]	0.030
1960–1969	0.258	0.460	-0.065	0.873	0.796[a]	0.027
1970–1982	0.572	0.131	-0.159	0.708	1.150[a]	0.004
Intercept	-0.526	0.719	-1.507	0.453	-0.240	0.878
Chi square (χ^2)	219.080		143.040		424.800	
Person-years	1,011		819		1,193	

Source: LIFEFILE; male migrant household members enumerated in Mexico and California, including those in twenty-five extra households in Santiago.

[a] $p \leq .05$ [b] $p \leq .10$

legal status). The model also controls for the period when migration began.[6]

The columns in table 10.2 labeled B contain the logistic regression coefficients, which measure the effect of different variables in determining the probability of making another trip; and the p columns give the level of statistical significance associated with these coefficients. The level of significance states the likelihood that the coefficient is due to random sampling error. It provides an indication of the extent to which an effect may be regarded as either "real" or an artifact of the sampling procedure.

A household's access to productive resources and level of dependency strongly influence the probability of departure; however, after the first trip, these variables play a minor role in the migration process. The ownership of a business or farmland and the presence of minor children, key variables in explaining the commencement of migration, are unrelated to the likelihood of making subsequent trips. Only home ownership has a significant impact, strongly reducing the likelihood of making more trips. Once the important earnings target of improved housing is met, migration becomes substantially less likely. Personal variables are also generally unimportant in accounting for repeat migration. Marital status, age, and education are all unrelated to the likelihood of making an additional trip, and being of rural origin influences the process only after the third trip, when the probability of going again reduces.

For the most part, the progression from one trip to the next is determined by variables connected to the migrant experience itself. Accompaniment by a migrant wife strongly increases the probability of

---

[6] In these event history models, time-varying explanatory variables were specified as such. That is, variables that normally change from year to year—whether regularly like age, or irregularly like household dependency—were allowed to vary across years in the event history. Only fixed characteristics like sex or rural origin remained constant over all person-years of observation. However, statistical identification of the models did require making several restrictive assumptions. Right-hand censoring was assumed to be random, making the time between the beginning and end of observation independent of the timing of events. Moreover, while the underlying risk of events was not assumed to be constant over time, it was assumed to change monotonically. Although the models typically included some measure of exposure time on the right-hand side of the equation, so that steadily falling or rising event probabilities could be detected, they did not contain separate dummy variables for each year of observation, so that repeated secular fluctuations in these probabilities could not be measured. These simplifications are warranted by the exploratory nature of the analyses and by the limited size of the data sets, as discussed in Massey (1987).

subsequent trips, and after the third trip, so does having children with U.S. migrant experience. As one might expect, the number of years since the last trip has a negative effect on the probability of going again: the longer a migrant waits after a trip, the less likely he is to make another. In contrast, the effect of prior migrant experience is strongly positive: the more time accumulated abroad, the more likely another trip. Moreover, migrants who work in U.S. agriculture are generally more likely to make another trip than are those who hold nonagrarian jobs. Since it is seasonal, farmwork is more conducive to recurrent migration than is urban employment.

Variables associated with the migrant experience play a predominant role in determining whether a migrant makes another trip, and the influence of these variables increases with each trip. Of the seven characteristics of the last trip shown in table 10.2, four are significant after the first trip and three after the second, but six are significant in predicting trips after the third. Only the impact of legal status declines steadily as the number of trips increases, until it is no longer significant beyond the third trip. Apparently after one gains familiarity with the migrant network on the first few trips, a lack of legal documents no longer acts as a barrier to further U.S. migration.

Finally, beyond the third trip, the period in which a person began to migrate has a strong influence on the probability of going again. The more recently one began to migrate, the higher the probability of making additional trips to the United States. This pattern probably reflects the ongoing development and maturation of the migrant networks. People who began to migrate during the 1970s are more likely to make trips beyond the third because they have better developed and more extensive networks at their disposal, greatly facilitating a strategy of recurrent migration.

Our principles again receive clear support. The evidence suggests that international migration indeed tends to be self-perpetuating. Migration breeds more migration: the probability of going again increases with each subsequent trip and with each month of accumulated migrant experience. Moreover, as the migration experience progresses, the factors that originally stimulated migration become less relevant. Over time, the social process of migration acquires its own momentum and becomes increasing independent of its structural causes. Moreover, the importance of migrant networks in this social process is suggested by the irrelevance of legal status after the first few trips and by the higher probability of repeat migration among those who recently began to migrate.

Settlement

As migrants go back and forth between Mexico and the United States and accumulate experience abroad, they acquire social and economic ties that draw them into settled life abroad. Over time, a growing number of families settle down to form daughter communities in particular U.S. towns and cities. These communities, in turn, greatly facilitate migration by providing a stable anchor in the receiving society for kin and friendship networks based in sending areas. They provide a permanent pool of social and economic contacts for new migrants and form a secure context within which the migrants can arrive, find work, adapt, and live.

An analysis of the settlement process requires a definition of when settlement has occurred. As we have already stated, among Mexican migrants the concept of settlement is highly ambiguous. Even after many years in the United States, families still make annual trips back to their home communities and may invest substantial sums there. "Settled" migrants may even own land and a house in Mexico and may continue to play a significant role in community affairs. Moreover, nearly all settled migrants proclaim an intention to return home eventually, in spite of mounting evidence to the contrary.

In this study we chose to adopt an arbitrary, yet reasonable, criterion for settlement and then to consider return as a possible fourth step in the migration process. Here a settler is defined as a migrant who has been in the United States for three *continuous* years. That is, someone had to report a solid block of thirty-six contiguous months in the United States in order to be defined as a settler. Some such settlers may have returned to Mexico for brief visits; however, unless these visits were reported in their life histories, they would be considered settled. This definition excludes seasonal migrants who reported working several months in the United States during successive years and is a far more stringent criterion than that used by most censuses to determine when someone has moved permanently.

Estimates of settlement probabilities were generated by a life table analysis that followed male migrants as they accumulated experience in the United States, counting the number of settlements that occurred each year. Migrant experience could be accumulated through any combination of trips and trip lengths; thus, four years of experience could be generated by making four trips of one year each or two trips of two years. Figure 10.4 plots the probability of settlement at different intervals of migrant experience (the bottom two lines) as well as the

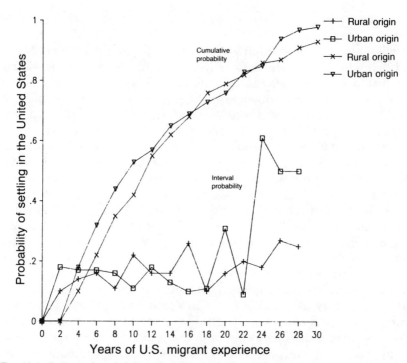

Fig. 10.4. Estimated probability of settlement in the United States by total years of U.S. migrant experience and rural versus urban origin. (*Source*: PERSFILE; male migrant household members enumerated in Mexico and California, including those in twenty-five extra households in Santiago.)

cumulative probability of settling at each point in time (the top two lines).[7]

These graphs suggest that settlement is an incremental process that occurs at a steady, if irregular, pace throughout the migrant career. Up to twenty years of experience, the probability of settlement within any interval does not greatly increase but fluctuates between .10 and .20. Over the long term, however, the cumulative probability of settlement becomes very high. If migrants repeatedly go to the United States, the chances are very great that they will eventually settle there. Seemingly,

---

[7] The estimates were prepared with the use of a double-decrement life table, with settlement representing one decrement and censoring the other. Right-hand censoring of data occurs when migrants do not advance to the next U.S. migrant experience interval because the interview occurs. The quantity $_nq_x$ from the associated single-decrement table for settlement gives the probability of settling in the experience interval from x to $x + n$, while $1 - l_x$ gives the cumulative probability of settling by age x. A fuller elaboration of the underlying life table analysis is presented in Massey (1985).

the only way to preclude settlement is to stop migrating, but as we have seen, the more one migrates, the more likely one is to continue migrating, and the more one continues to migrate, the more likely one is to eventually settle in the United States. According to the data in figure 10.4, if a group of migrants were to begin to migrate and accumulate experience steadily until they settled, after twenty years nearly 80 percent would be settled, and after thirty years the figure would be well over 90 percent.

Determinants of the settlement process were studied by a logistic regression analysis of men's migrant experience, where units of analysis were person-years spent in the United States and the outcome was contingent on whether settlement occurred in a given year (letting migrants receive a score of 1 in the last of three successive years in the United States and 0 otherwise). The U.S. person-years need not have occurred consecutively. Only person-years spent in the United States, and only those after the second year, were considered, however, since only when these criteria are fulfilled are migrants at risk of settling. As before, three sets of explanatory factors were employed to explain this outcome—household, personal, and trip characteristics—and the coefficients associated with each variable are shown in table 10.3.

As with repeat migration, factors related to the household's economic position are not very important in the settlement process. Ownership of farmland or a business is not significantly related to the propensity to settle, nor is home ownership. Lack of access to means of support may lead to migration initially, but it has little relation to the direction the migration process once it has begun, playing no real part in the decision to settle. The household characteristic that is primarily important is the presence or absence of children. The probability of settlement is considerably enhanced by a lack of children.

Among personal characteristics, marital status itself is not strongly related to the propensity to settle: married and single men have roughly the same settlement propensities. As we have seen, it is the presence or absence of children that is important. Age, however, is strongly related to the likelihood of settlement; it is low in the teenage years, rising through the twenties to a peak in the early thirties, and then falling steadily thereafter. In general, then, settlement is most likely to occur at early stages of the life cycle, just before or just after marriage, that is, before one has really formed a family. Rural origin strongly decreases the likelihood of settlement, suggesting that their networks are better adapted to recurrent than settled migration. Education again plays an insignificant role in the process.

Aside from life cycle factors, the propensity to settle is strongly de-

TABLE 10.3
LOGISTIC MODEL PREDICTING THE PROBABILITY
OF U.S. SETTLEMENT FROM SELECTED VARIABLES

Explanatory variables	B	SE[a]	p
Household characteristics			
No children	1.460[b]	0.681	0.032
Land or business owned	−0.574	1.115	0.607
Home owned	0.115	0.418	0.783
Personal characteristics			
Never married	0.708	0.602	0.240
Age	0.516[b]	0.183	0.005
Age squared	−0.008[b]	0.003	0.005
Years of schooling	0.042	0.056	0.447
Rural origin	−1.277[b]	0.412	0.002
Characteristics of U.S. trip			
U.S. migrant experience (months)	0.050[b]	0.008	0.001
Wife a migrant	0.311	0.695	0.655
Children migrants	1.048	0.679	0.123
Farmworker	0.648[c]	0.384	0.091
Documented	0.791[b]	0.357	0.027
Bracero	−2.978[b]	0.054	0.002
Initial U.S. wage	0.101[c]	0.054	0.063
Intercept	−12.268[b]	3.077	0.001
Chi square (χ^2)	96.680		
Person-years	524		

Source: LIFEFILE; male migrant household members enumerated in Mexico and California, including those in twenty-five extra households in Santiago.
[a] Standard error.   [b] $p < .05$.   [c] $p < .10$.

termined by trip characteristics. The likelihood of migration is considerably increased by greater U.S. migrant experience and by the possession of legal residence documents and to a lesser extent by employment in agriculture and by receiving a high initial wage in the United States. (The ethnosurvey did not ask the migrant to state the wage of each job in the United States, only the first and the last.) The prospects for settlement also seem to be enhanced by having children who are migrants. Bracero migrants were very unlikely to settle, which is not surprising since the Bracero program ended before the networks had really come into their own, and it was explicitly designed to discourage settlement.

In order to illustrate the relative importance of variables in the settlement process, table 10.4 presents estimated probabilities of settlement for a typical Mexican migrant: a married, twenty-five-year-old man

TABLE 10.4
PROBABILITY OF U.S. SETTLEMENT FOR A MARRIED MALE MIGRANT AGED 25
WITH NO PROPERTY AND AN INITIAL U.S. WAGE OF $3.40

Characteristics	Years of U.S. migrant experience								
	3	4	5	6	7	8	9	10	15
Rural-origin farmworker									
Documented									
No children	.354	.500	.646	.768	.858	.917	.953	.973	.999
Migrant children	.267	.399	.547	.688	.801	.880	.930	.960	.998
Nonmigrant children	.113	.188	.297	.435	.584	.719	.823	.895	.994
Undocumented									
No children	.199	.312	.453	.601	.733	.833	.901	.943	.997
Migrant children	.141	.230	.352	.498	.643	.766	.857	.916	.995
Nonmigrant children	.055	.095	.161	.259	.389	.537	.679	.794	.987
Urban-origin nonfarmworker									
Documented									
No children	.507	.642	.774	.862	.919	.954	.974	.986	.999
Migrant children	.404	.552	.692	.804	.882	.932	.961	.978	.999
Nonmigrant children	.193	.304	.443	.591	.725	.828	.898	.941	.997
Undocumented									
No children	.319	.460	.608	.739	.838	.904	.945	.969	.998
Migrant children	.235	.359	.505	.650	.772	.861	.918	.953	.998
Nonmigrant children	.098	.165	.265	.397	.545	.686	.799	.879	.993

Source: LIFEFILE; male migrant household members enumerated in Mexico and California, including those in twenty-five extra households in Santiago.

with no property in Mexico who earned the minimum wage on his first trip to the United States. This table estimates the effect of origin, occupation, documentation, and children on such a person's probability of settlement.

The striking finding is that migrant experience ultimately overcomes the effect of other variables to render settlement virtually inevitable in the long run. After accumulating fifteen years of U.S. migrant experience, the typical migrant has a 99 percent chance of settlement, irrespective of legal status, origin, U.S. occupation, or parental status. Differences in the likelihood of settlement with respect to these variables occur primarily within the first ten years of migration. After three years, the probability of settlement within any given year ranges from a low of about .06 for undocumented rural farmworkers with nonmigrant children to a high of .51 for documented urban nonfarm workers without children. After five years, the settlement probability for the former has risen to only .16, while that for the latter's has increased to .77; after ten years of experience, the gap between the two figures has narrowed considerably, to .99 versus .79. At the fifteen-year mark, all the original differences have been erased.

Possession of legal documents but no children and the status of being a nonfarmworker from an urban background all substantially increase the probability of settlement early in the migrant career; as experience progresses, however, these variables matter less and less. As the social process of migration runs its course and migrants acquire increased time abroad, the probability of settlement eventually becomes so great that all other variables become irrelevant. In short, we find dramatic evidence of an ongoing settlement process among Mexican migrants to the United States, supporting the fifth principle.

Return

As we have seen, the probability of U.S. settlement increases considerably when migration is extended indefinitely, but the act of settling abroad rarely implies a break with social life in the home community. Social networks are maintained and reinforced by a constant circulation of people, goods, and capital between sending and receiving communities. Most of this circulation involves the temporary or recurrent migration of people who work seasonally in the United States. Networks are also reinforced by another kind of return migration involving people who once adopted a settled migrant strategy. Even after many years in the United States, migrants may sell their foreign assets and return to live in the community where they were born or in a Mexican urban area; thus return is the last phase in the social process of migration.

Using life history data, we selected all migrants who had ever settled in the United States (i.e., who had ever lived abroad for three consecutive years) and then checked to see whether they returned to Mexico in the years subsequent to their settlement. "Return" occurs when a former settler has spent three consecutive years in Mexico. As before, life table methods were employed to derive the figures graphed in figure 10.5, which shows the probability of return migration at different intervals of time after settlement, together with the cumulative probability of return.[8]

---

[8] As in the analysis of settlement, measurement of probabilities of return migration was accomplished with a double-decrement life table that controlled for censoring biases. For each year after settlement, the number of returned and censored migrants was tabulated to provide data on two decrements, and the associated single decrement for return was used to generate the probabilities plotted in figure 10.5.

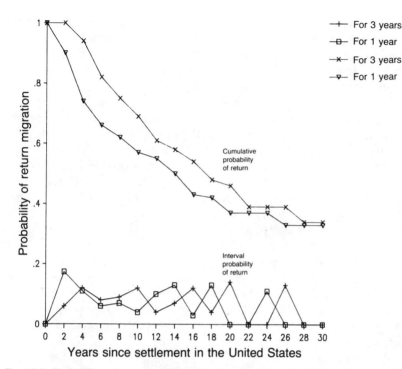

Fig. 10.5. Probability of return to Mexico in the years following U.S. settlement. (*Source:* PERSFILE; male migrant household members enumerated in Mexico and the United States, including those in twenty-five extra households in Santiago.)

The lines in this figure clearly document a process of return migration. The likelihood of return following settlement varies between .04 and .14 up to 20 years but displays no particular trend over time. Return migration seems to be a fairly steady process that occurs throughout the years of settlement. In the long run, this process produces relatively high cumulative probabilities of return. Thirty years after settling in the United States, 67 percent of settled migrants can be expected to have returned to Mexico. In the short run, however, the degree of attachment to the United States remains quite strong: ten years after settlement, 69 percent are still in the United States as settlers, and even after twenty years, 46 percent have not returned.

This pattern is not greatly affected by the definition of "return" that we choose. Even if we require a migrant to be in Mexico for only one complete year in order to be counted as "returned," 57 percent of all migrants still remain abroad after ten years. The main effect of changing the definition is to shorten the process of return by two years, but in the long run the result is the same: about 67 percent return within thirty years of settlement. These probabilities provide a quantitative indication of the ambiguity surrounding the concept of settlement for Mexican migrants, demonstrating at once the long-term lure of Mexico and the short-term attraction of the United States.

Table 10.5 examines the determinants of return migration by conducting a logistic regression analysis in the years following settlement. The outcome variable was coded 1 in the last of three consecutive years spent in Mexico and 0 otherwise. Explanatory factors were essentially the same as in prior analyses: selected household and personal characteristics and variables connected with the migrant's stay abroad.

The key variables in the process of return migration are property ownership, age, and marital status. When a family owns a home in Mexico or operates some productive enterprise there, the likelihood of return migration is substantially increased. In addition, return tends to occur as migrants approach old age. In fieldwork we have encountered many cases of migrants who worked most of their lives in the United States and then retired to Mexico to receive their Social Security payments and pensions. The probability of return is also significantly lowered by being married, although this effect is partially offset if the wife also is a migrant.

All factors relating to aspects of the migrant's stay in the United States are negatively related to the probability of return migration. As the length of the stay and wages both increase, the probability of return steadily diminishes. Having a migrant wife or children also reduces the likelihood of return (although not significantly), as does working in agriculture. Our omission of legal status from the list of characteristics does not imply that the possession of documents is unrelated to the probability of return. On the contrary, it is so highly related that in the years following settlement, *not one* legal migrant returned to Mexico for three consecutive years; that is, the probability of return migration among settled migrants with documents was zero. Since the logistic estimation method requires that at least some documented migrants return, the effect of this variable could not be estimated statistically. Nonetheless, it is clear that the possession of legal documents strongly discourages, if not precludes, return migration to Mexico.

The kind of settled migrant most likely to return to Mexico is thus an older married undocumented migrant with a wife, children, house, and property in Mexico who has been in the United States under five years working at or near the minimum wage in an urban job. It is not very common for settled migrants to have their wives and children in

TABLE 10.5
LOGISTIC MODEL PREDICTING RETURN MIGRATION FROM SELECTED VARIABLES

Explanatory variables	B	SE	p
Household characteristics			
No children	0.454	0.444	0.307
Land or business owned	1.289[a]	0.494	0.009
Home owned	0.684[a]	0.349	0.050
Personal characteristics			
Never married	−0.904[a]	0.462	0.050
Age	0.041[a]	0.018	0.024
Years of schooling	−0.071	0.058	0.220
Rural origin	0.505	0.344	0.142
Characteristics of U.S. stay			
U.S. migrant experience (months)	−0.008[a]	0.003	0.001
Wife a migrant	−0.667	0.591	0.259
Children migrants	−0.442	0.464	0.341
Farmworker	−0.705[a]	0.330	0.033
Most recent wage	−0.220[a]	0.079	0.005
Intercept	−2.658[a]	0.809	0.001
Chi square (χ^2)	61.580		
Person-years	1,557		

Source: LIFEFILE; male migrant household members enumerated in Mexico and California, including those in twenty-five extra households in Santiago.

[a] $p < .05$.

Mexico, however. Settled migrants usually are either single or have their families with them, and they usually work at something more than the minimum wage. Table 10.6 presents probabilities for two typical rural migrants—one single and one married with a migrant family, both earning $5.00 per hour in urban jobs—and then examines the effect of property ownership, age, and time in the United States.

In general, property ownership has the greatest impact on return migration. Among those without any property in Mexico, the *highest* yearly probability of return was only .04, compared to .07 among those with a home, .13 among those with land or a business, and .22 among those with both. In essence, once settlement has occurred, return migration is not very likely unless a migrant owns property in Mexico, and even in this case the prospects for return steadily diminish with time spent in the United States. The highest probability of return, .22, is for an older property owner with a migrant family and five years of residence abroad. His probability of return falls rapidly the longer he re-

TABLE 10.6
PROBABILITY OF RETURN MIGRATION FOR SETTLED RURAL-ORIGIN NONFARM
WORKERS EARNING $5 PER HOUR ON THEIR LATEST U.S. JOBS

Characteristic	Years of U.S. migrant experience				
	5	10	15	20	25
Single, aged 25, with no children					
No property	.017	.011	.077	.004	.003
Home only	.034	.021	.013	.008	.005
Land or business only	.060	.038	.024	.014	.009
Home, land, and business	.112	.072	.046	.029	.018
Married with migrant wife and children					
Aged 25 years					
No property	.014	.009	.005	.003	.002
Home only	.028	.009	.011	.003	.002
Land or business only	.050	.031	.020	.012	.008
Home, land, and business	.094	.060	.038	.023	.015
Aged 50 years					
No property	.038	.024	.015	.009	.006
Home only	.074	.047	.029	.019	.012
Land or business only	.127	.082	.053	.033	.021
Home, land, and business	.224	.152	.100	.064	.041

Source: LIFEFILE; male migrant household members enumerated in Mexico and California, including those in twenty-five extra households in Santiago.

mains in the United States. At ten years it is only .15, falling to .10 after fifteen years, then to .06 after twenty years, and finally to .04 at twenty-five years.

Long periods of U.S. residence considerably reduce the chances of return migration, even among those who are otherwise disposed to go home. We have confirmed our last hypothesis and found clear evidence of a return flow; however, the generally slow pace of return, the steady decline in the likelihood of return over time, and the fact that most settled migrants own no more than a home in Mexico do not suggest a substantial return migration for settled migrants in the short term.

SUMMARY

In this chapter we derived six principles underlying the social process of international migration. Migration begins because of structural changes in sending and receiving societies, which generate unequal access to productive wealth in the former and strong demand for unskilled labor in the latter, stimulating the international movement of workers. Once begun, however, international migration unfolds according to an internal logic that reflects its inherently social nature. Since migrants are human beings enmeshed in a series of interpersonal relationships, persistent migration leads to the development of social networks. These networks, in turn, support and encourage additional migration, which further extends them. Over time, migration acquires momentum and becomes a mass phenomenon widely incorporated into family economic strategies. Subsequent changes in individuals' perceptions and community organization encourage further migration. Over time, international migration becomes more independent of the structural factors that originally caused it.

In order to test this theoretical framework, we conceptualized international migration as a four-step process involving separate decisions on whether to depart, repeat, settle, and return. Each step is characterized by its own set of event probabilities and determinants, and a positive choice at any point moves a person and his family on to the next phase of the migration process. The six principles in our framework received strong support from probabilities computed for the four events and from models estimating their determinants.

There is considerable evidence that departure is determined primarily by variables that reflect structural arrangements in society. Year-to-year fluctuations in the probability of departure closely parallel identifiable changes in the structure of the Mexican political economy, and controlling for the effect of prior experience, the strongest determinants of the decision to migrate are ownership of land and businesses, which reflect the larger distribution of productive resources in Mexico.

The data also indicate a strong social momentum to the migration process. As migrant networks develop and mature, a point is reached where virtually all men can expect to migrate at some point in their lives. By the end of the 1970s, for example, 90 percent of rural men could anticipate at least one trip to the United States. Given such accessibility, migration comes to be regarded as a basic component in family economic strategies, widely employed during stages of the life cycle when dependency is greatest. Moreover, one trip tends to lead to another, as migrants' aspirations are changed by the migrant experience itself. After the first trip, the probability of a second one is quite high, about .60 in urban areas and near .80 in rural areas, and the probability of going again rises with each additional trip, to between .90 and 1.0 after nine trips. Even controlling for the effects of other social and economic variables, prior migrant experience remains the strongest single predictor of migration to the United States. After two or three trips, the original structural causes of migration decline in importance, and the likelihood of making another trip is determined primarily by experience on the last one. The data thus are consistent in showing a self-perpetuating character to the migration process.

There is also strong evidence that settlement is a key phase in the larger process of migration. As migrants make additional trips and stay longer, they accumulate experience in the United States, which increases the likelihood of permanent settlement. As migration continues, daughter communities form, and their growth further stabilizes the networks. After ten years of migrant experience, 42 percent of rural migrants and 53 percent of urban migrants have settled, with the figures rising to 79 percent and 76 percent after twenty years. The likelihood of settlement is determined primarily by rural versus urban origin, life cycle factors, and characteristics of the most recent trip. The people most likely to settle are young childless men from urban areas who possess legal documents and have accumulated extensive experience abroad.

Opposing the settlement process is one of return migration. About 31 percent of migrants can be expected to return to Mexico within ten years of settlement and 54 percent, within twenty years. This return flow ironically reinforces and maintains the migrant networks, thereby increasing the likelihood of departure from the community. The principal determinants of return migration are life cycle factors, property ownership, legal status, and prior U.S. migrant experience. Those most likely to return are older married migrants with property in Mexico, no documents, and little time accumulated in the United States.

In general, structural factors and life cycle variables tend to play important roles during the first and last phases of the migration process. Not having access to productive, lucrative resources and being young with a growing family strongly encourage departure, while owning Mexican property late in life strongly encourages return. Those least likely to leave—people with access to productive wealth—are also those most likely to return. In the intervening stages, the course of migration is most strongly determined by a migrant's origins (rural or urban) and various aspects of experience in the United States.

Multivariate statistical analyses thus support the descriptive tables and ethnographic fieldwork presented in earlier chapters and suggest that international migration is, indeed, a dynamic social process whose operation reflects basic underlying principles. Although these principles may operate in different ways and in different settings, they ultimately lead to the same outcome: a growing prevalence of international migration and the widespread adoption of foreign labor as an adaptive strategy.

11
Conclusions

The four communities considered in this study were chosen to provide a comparative basis for analyzing the social process of Mexican migration to the United States. Two were rural-agrarian towns, and two were urban-industrial communities, ranging in size from a few thousand to several million. Altamira was a town of small property holders and sharecroppers who farmed their own plots, while Chamitlán was one of landless laborers employed by large farmers and agribusinesses. Santiago was an industrial town of skilled and semiskilled factory workers, and San Marcos was a working-class neighborhood of Guadalajara with a diverse urban work force.

In spite of their contrasting socioeconomic structures, the four communities displayed several common elements in the historical development of U.S. migration. The commonalities stem from the similar economic origins of migration in each place and from the operation of a common social process that took hold once migration had begun. In each community, international migration originated in the economic structure of society but was sustained and encouraged by the development and elaboration of social networks.

Historically, U.S. migration can be regarded as a response to changes in the productive organization of Mexican society. International out-migration followed periods of profound socioeconomic transformation that displaced people from productive work. In rural communities, migration rose particularly during three periods: during the late Porfirian era, when enclosure and farm mechanization displaced vast numbers of campesinos from the land; during the Reparto Agrario, when land was redistributed to peasants without an accompanying access to capital and credit; and during Mexico's "green revolution," when the application of new machines, crops, and scientific methods to farming severely constricted the demand for hand labor. Findings are essentially the same for industrial communities: migration increased in two periods of economic dislocation—the post–World War II industrial recession and the wave of factory mechanization in the 1950s—and abated during the urban economic boom of the 1970s.

Mexican-U.S. migration cannot be explained by Mexican "push" factors alone, for each period of extensive out-migration was accompanied by active recruitment from the United States. Porfirian economic policies created a mass of poor, landless campesinos, while the concomitant economic expansion of the American southwest, coupled with the closing of European immigration, led to extensive labor recruitment in Mexico. Similarly, the social transformations wrought by the Reparto Agrario coincided with the establishment of the U.S.-sponsored Bracero Accord, and the era of factory modernization concurred with the program's expansion and peak. Mexico's wave of agricultural modernization in the late 1960s also coincided with an intensification of labor demand on the U.S. side, brought about by the simultaneous boom of the southwestern U.S. economy and the escalation of the war in Viet Nam.

International migration began through a complementarity of supply and demand at the macro level; however, a basic lesson from the four communities is that migration displays a strong intrinsic tendency to become more extensive over time. Although pioneer migrants typically come from a narrow segment of society, migration inevitably diffuses outward to involve an increasingly large and diverse cross section of the population. In each community, migration eventually became a mass phenomenon. Even in the urban-industrial communities, 33 percent of all households contained people with migrant experience in 1982, and in the rural areas 50 percent to 75 percent of all households did so. Migrants can now be found in every socioeconomic class and in all segments of society.

These high levels of international migration are supported and sustained by social networks forged from the relationships of kinship, friendship, and paisanaje, which have been adapted to the migrant enterprise. These interconnecting social links facilitate the movement of people and information between Mexico and the United States. Migrant networks are webs of reciprocal obligations, and by drawing upon these obligations, newly arrived migrants obtain help in getting settled and finding a job in the United States.

Social connections within the networks are reinforced by a variety of institutional mechanisms that promote frequent contact between migrants and nonmigrants and among the migrants themselves. In particular, soccer clubs bring migrants together on a regular basis for the exchange of news and information and promote the periodic reunion of migrants and townspeople through team tours and player exchanges. The annual fiesta for the patron saint also serves as an important vehicle for promoting the reintegration of migrants within the community.

Migrant networks build up gradually over the years. Starting from a small base, they extend slowly at first, and as migration spreads through the community, the number of connections between migrants and others expands rapidly. The formation of networks is greatly boosted by the emergence of daughter communities in the United States, which provide a solid U.S. base from which social connections can multiply. With the settlement of a few families, the flow of migrants is channeled with increasing precision to specific destination points.

Over time, networks become self-sustaining because of the social capital they provide migrants and potential migrants. Personal contacts with friends, relatives, and paisanos give migrants ready access to jobs, housing, and financial assistance in the United States. This social capital dramatically decreases the cost of migrating to the United States. As the cost decreases, more people are induced to become migrants, and as more become migrants, the network expands, leading to still more migration. Over time, the networks become so extensive that almost everyone has a social tie to someone in the United States, putting U.S. employment within reach of all social classes.

With the advent of its widespread accessibility, migration is incorporated into family survival strategies on a permanent basis and foreign wage labor becomes a regular feature of the household economy. It is most often employed to meet pressing demands for support during critical phases of the life cycle and is strongly associated with the level of household dependency, rising and falling as the relative number of children and adults shifts through the different stages of the life cycle. Migration is also employed during periods of unusual economic stress and as a conscious strategy of socioeconomic advancement.

There are three basic strategies of migration, which predominate for different reasons at different stages of the life cycle. Temporary migration involves making a few short trips to the United States, usually when the children are young and the family is growing. It may also be employed sporadically to meet sudden financial emergencies. Recurrent migration entails repeated short trips to the United States over a prolonged period and is usually employed just after marriage, before the arrival of children, or after all the children have grown. Recurrent migration is typically employed as part of a strategy of social mobility within the community. The last strategy, settled migration, involves long-term residence in the United States, and migrants who adopt it are generally single or recently married men seeking opportunities and advancement outside the community.

Migration to the United States can make a critical difference to the household budget, especially in rural areas. In households with members working abroad, U.S. remittances constitute roughly 66 percent of monthly cash income in rural areas and over 80 percent in rural areas. A season of wage labor in the United States can raise a rural family's standard of living to levels associated with only skilled or professional employment in Mexican cities. Migrant households generally contain a greater quantity and variety of consumer goods than do nonmigrant households, and their material standard of living increases steadily as members acquire experience as migrants.

With the advent of mass migration, the flow of dollars into sending communities is considerable and has had a profound impact on community economic and social institutions. Most remittances and savings are spent on current consumption, with housing as the most popular destination for migrant savings. As a result of the additional demand for new and remodeled homes, several communities have experienced booms in construction business and employment. Migration also plays a role in the formation and capitalization of businesses. In a setting where access to credit is restricted, U.S. migration provides an important source of capital; while businesses founded by migrants do not generate extensive employment, they generally create enough work to compensate for the annual loss of labor through international migration.

Migration has also affected the distribution and use of farmland. It has clearly contributed to the unequal distribution of land; however, it is only one factor in a much larger complex of transformations in rural Mexico. In the two agrarian towns, most farmland is owned by a small number of migrant families, and migrant households generally have greater access to higher-quality land. Widespread U.S. migration affects farm production in two contrary ways. Increasing migration makes households less likely to engage in farming, but among those still cultivating it increases productivity by supporting the use of machinery and other inputs to offset declining family labor. Overall, the effect of international migration in discouraging cultivation seems to be stronger than its positive effect in enhancing productivity, so its net effect has been to decrease aggregate production in the community.

In general, the various community-level effects of mass international migration combine to encourage further departures. The positive examples provided by well-known cases of social mobility through migration serve as an inducement to others. At the same time, migration encourages the formation of businesses whose sales depend largely on the steady flow of remittances from abroad (e.g., the construction industry). Finally, international migration contributes to the displacement of labor in rural Mexico by encouraging the trend away from subsistence farming toward capital-intensive production and cash crops and by decreasing local cultivation.

Mexican migration also has important impacts on the United States. A key element in the larger migration process is the process of progressive integration and settlement abroad. As the social process of migration takes its course and people build up increasing experience as migrants, they become progressively enmeshed in series of social and economic connections based in the United States. The timing and extent of integration are affected by variables such as occupation and rural versus urban origin; however, integration on a variety of dimensions always increases with time spent abroad. With greater migrant experience, people are more likely to establish family and friendship ties in the United States, secure nonfarm jobs, possess legal documents, use public services, speak English, and join voluntary associations.

Progressive integration into U.S. society brings a gradual shift away from the home community toward the United States. Migrants seldom are completely divorced from life in their native communities; however, the more time that they spend abroad, the less of their pay they remit back to Mexico and the more money they spend in the United States. Over time, there is a steady shift to long-term residence and permanent settlement, and an inevitable part of the social process of migration is the formation of U.S. daughter communities, which further strengthen and reinforce the networks.

The foregoing results follow from extensive ethnographic fieldwork and exhaustive exploratory analysis of the ethnosurvey data. Together they provide a picture of Mexican migration to the United States as an ongoing social process, one governed by a few key principles. In chapter 10 these principles were put forth as a series of basic propositions and explicitly tested with the use of sophisticated statistical models. In each case, the basic tenets of the models received support.

The social process of migration was conceptualized as a four-step process corresponding to key events faced by migrants and their families over the course of the migrant career: whether to begin migrating, whether to continue migrating, whether to settle in the United States, and whether to return to Mexico. Each event was associated with a measurable probability and a characteristic set of determinants. Estimates of these models supported the core argument of the book: that migration is a social process with a strong internal momentum that reinforces itself over time.

Various conclusions are evident from this study. The first lesson is methodological and is addressed primarily to social scientists: the efficacy of the ethnosurvey method. The ethnosurvey combines the ethnographic approach of anthropology and the survey approach of sociology into a single study. In questionnaire design, interviewing, and analysis, the two approaches inform one another and in the end produce data that are more accurate and valid than those produced by either method alone. The ethnographic and survey data are, in turn, supplemented with microhistorical information gathered through archival research and oral histories. The combination of these three approaches yields unusually rich and accurate information about complex, sensitive topics and is especially well suited to studying dynamic, longitudinal processes that unfold over many years.

A second conclusion concerns the nature of international migration and the way we understand it. Our findings strongly question attempts to conceptualize migration in terms of a single dimension, whether economic, social, historical, or demographic. Unidimensional explanatory models inevitably fail because in reality migration embraces these four dimensions simultaneously. Our findings also question the validity of static models of migration. One cannot understand migration from a synchronic perspective because the process is fundamentally a dynamic one that can be comprehended only from a longitudinal perspective. Since the process of international migration unfolds in a series of developmental stages, it is crucial to know whether a community has just begun to send migrants or has been sending them for many years. In order to understand migration today, one needs to know what happened in the past.

Another conclusion is that arguments regarding whether migration is best understood at the individual, household, community, or regional level are misplaced. Our study has demonstrated the importance of variables and processes at all four levels. National policies produce regional economic imbalances that encourage migration, and national social and economic structures provide the context within which migration occurs. Networks formed at the community level support and sustain its progress over time, while households are the economic units that actually adopt international migration as an economic strategy. Finally, individuals are inevitably influenced and transformed by the migrant experience itself, and their changing aspirations alter the character of the process.

One final issue concerns the generality of our findings. Out of all the migrant communities in Mexico, we chose four and sampled them randomly. To what extent are they representative of Mexican communities in general? To what extent do their inhabitants represent the Mexican population? The answers to these questions depend on the kinds of generalization one wants to make. Specific averages and percentages on various aspects of U.S. migration certainly cannot be generalized to the rest of Mexico. For example, we make no claim about the percentage of households in Mexico that contain present or former U.S. migrants. Such generalizations from small samples of nonrandomly selected communities is inappropriate. Specific facts cannot be generalized; however, we believe that the basic *process* of international migration can be. In a set of diverse communities with contrasting patterns of socioeconomic organization, a strong commonality of process was found. In spite of differences in community structure and socioeconomic organization, the social process of migration unfolded in a remarkably consistent and predictable fashion over time.

If the social process of international migration is, indeed, a general one, then recent thinking on Mexican migration has generally missed the mark. Most scholars and policymakers think primarily in synchronic, short-run terms, considering migration only at the moment, as a phenomenon isolated in time. As we have seen, however, international migration is a developmental process with a strong momentum and an internal logic all its own. The widespread movement of people back and forth between Mexico and the United States cannot be abstracted from the dynamic, historical process that created it.

Governments, in particular, rarely consider the long-run consequences of their policies. The United States government clearly did not seek to instigate mass international migration when it established the Bracero program in the 1940s, nor did the Mexican government when it supported the agricultural revolution in the 1960s. Both countries have now become alarmed about the scale of international migration, however, and the United States, particularly, has sought quick, painless policies to limit it. Viewing international migration as a developmental social process suggests that any change in the status quo will be very difficult to achieve. At this point in the process, the momentum of migration is strongly resistant to change. After forty years, international migration has become so institutionalized, routine, and embedded into the social and economic fabrics of both countries that the human and financial costs of stopping it are probably prohibitive. In spite of all the rhetoric, few people on either side of the border seem willing to pay the costs of stemming the flow.

References

Alba, Carlos. 1985. "La Utilidad de lo Minúsculo." *Relaciones: Estudios de Historia y Sociedad* 6(22): 85–112.

Alba, Francisco. 1978. "Mexico's International Migration as a Manifestation of its Development Pattern." *International Migration Review* 12: 502–113.

Allison, Paul D. 1984. *Event History Analysis: Regression for Longitudinal Event Data.* Sage University Paper Series on Quantitative Applications in the Social Sciences, Series No. 07–046. Beverly Hills and London: Sage.

Arias, Patricia. 1980. "El Processo de Industrialización en Guadalajara: Siglo XX." *Relaciones: Estudios de Historia y Sociedad* 1(3): 9–47.

———. 1983. *Fuentes para el Estudio de la Industrialización en Jalsico: Siglo XX.* Mexico City: Casa Chata.

Arias, Patricia, and Jorge Durand. 1985. "El Impacto Regional de la Crisis." *Relaciones: Estudios de Historia y Sociedad* 6(22): 43–64.

Arizpe, Lourdes. 1978. *Migración, Etnicismo y Cambio Económico: Un Estudio Sobre Migrantes Campesinos a la Ciudad de México.* Mexico, D.F.: El Colegio de México.

———. 1981. "The Rural Exodus in Mexico and Mexican Migration to the United States." *International Migration Review* 15: 626–649.

Arroyo, Jesus. 1985. "Ires y Venires en el Occidente Mexicano." Pages 21–56 in Patricia Arias, ed. *Guadalajara: La Gran Ciudad de la Pequeña Industria.* Zamora, Michoacán: El Colegio de Michoacán.

Avante Systems. 1978. *A Survey of the Undocumented Population in Two Texas Border Areas.* San Antonio, Tex.: U.S. Commission on Civil Rights, Southwestern Regional Office.

Balán, Jorge, Harley L. Browning, and Elizabeth Jelin. 1973. *Men in a Developing Society: Geographic and Social Mobility in Monterrey, Mexico.* Austin: University of Texas Press.

Baletic, Zvonimir. 1982. "International Migration in Modern Economic Development: With Special Reference to Yugoslavia." *International Migration Review* 16: 736–756.

Baucic, Ivo. 1972. *The Effects of Emigration from Yugoslavia and the Problems of Returning Emigrant Workers.* The Hague: Martinus Nijhoff.

Beals, Ralph L. 1946. *Cherán: A Sierra Tarascan Village.* Smithsonian Institution Publications in Social Anthropology No. 2. Washington, D.C.: U.S. Government Printing Office.

Bean, Frank D., Harley L. Browning, and W. Parker Frisbie. 1984. "The Sociodemographic Characteristics of Mexican Immigrant Status Groups: Implications for Studying Undocumented Mexicans." *International Migration Review* 18: 672–691.

Belshaw, Michael. 1967. *A Village Economy: Land and People of Huecorio.* New York: Columbia University Press.

Bennett, Brian C. 1979. "Migration and Rural Community Viability in Central Dalmatia (Croatia) Yugoslavia." *Papers in Anthropology* 20: 75–84.

Blau, Francine D. 1984. "The Use of Transfer Payments by Immigrants." *Industrial and Labor Relations Review* 37: 222–239.

Blejer, Mario I., Harry G. Johnson, and Arturo C. Prozecanski. 1978. "An Analysis of the Economic Determinants of Legal and Illegal Mexican Migration to the United States." *Research in Population Economics* 1: 217–231.

Bohning, Wolf R. 1972. *The Migration of Workers in the United Kingdom and the European Community.* London: Oxford University Press.

Bonfil, Guillermo. 1973. *Cholula: La Ciudad Sagrada en la Era Industrial.* Mexico City: Universidad Nacional Autónoma de México.

Bovenkerk, J. 1974. *The Sociology of Return Migration.* The Hague: Mouton.

Brand, Donald D. 1951. *Quiroga: A Mexican Municipio.* Smithsonian Institution Publications in Social Anthropology No. 11. Washington, D.C.: U.S. Government Printing Office.

———. 1960. *Coalcomán and Motines del Oro: An Ex-Distrito of Michoacán México.* The Hague: Martinus Nijhoff for the Institute of Latin American Studies, the University of Texas at Austin.

Brandes, Stanley. 1975. *Migration, Kinship, and Community: Tradition and Transition in a Spanish Village.* New York: Academic Press.

Brettell, Caroline. 1979. "Emigrar para Voltar: A Portuguese Ideology of Return Migration." *Papers in Anthropology* 20: 1–20.

Browning, Harley L., and Nestor Rodríguez. 1985. "The Migration of Mexican Indocumentados as a Settlement Process: Implications for Work." Pages 277–298 in George J. Borjas and Marta Tienda, eds. *Hispanics in the U.S. Economy.* New York: Academic Press.

Bustamante, Jorge A. 1977. "Undocumented Migration from Mexico: Research Report." *International Migration Review* 11: 149–177.

———. 1978. "Dimensions of the Migration Phenomenon in Mexico and the Caribbean Basin." Pages 22–40 in *Proceedings of the Brookings–El Colegio de México Symposium on Structural Factors in Mexican and Caribbean Basin Migration.* Washington, D.C.: Brookings Institution.

———. 1984. "Changing Patterns of Undocumented Migration from Mexican States in Recent Years." Pages 15–32 in Richard C. Jones, ed. *Patterns of Undocumented Migration: Mexico and the United States.* Totowa, N.J.: Roman and Allanheld.

Cancian, Frank. 1965. *Economics and Prestige in a Maya Community: The Religious Cargo System in Zanacantan.* Stanford, Calif.: Stanford University Press.

Cardoso, Lawrence. 1980. *Mexican Emigration to the United States 1897–1931.* Tucson: University of Arizona Press.

CELADE (Centro Latinoamericano de Demografía). 1982. *México: Estimaciones y Proyecciones de Población. 1950–2000.* Santiago, Chile: CELADE y Las Naciones Unidas.

Chayanov, Alexander V. 1966. *Theory of Peasant Economy.* Homewood, Ill.: Richard D. Irwin.

Chiswick, Barry R. 1978. A Longitudinal Analysis of the Occupational Mobility of Immigrants." Pages 20–27 in B. Dennis, ed. *Proceedings of the 30th Annual Winter Meeting of the Industrial Relations Research Association.* Madison: University of Wisconsin Press.

———. 1979. "The Economic Progress of Immigrants: Some Apparently Universal Patterns." Pages 357–399 in William Feller, ed. *Contemporary Economic Problems, 1979.* Washington, D.C.: American Enterprise Institute.

———. 1984. "Illegal Aliens in the United States Labor Market: Analysis of Occupational Attainment and Earnings." *International Migration Review* 18: 714–732.

Conroy, Michael E., Mario C. Salas, and Felipe V. González. 1980. "Socio-Economic Incentives for Migration from Mexico to the U.S.: Magnitude, Recent Changes, and Policy Implications." *Mexico–U.S. Migration Research Reports.* Austin: Institute of Latin American Studies.

Cornelius, Wayne A. 1976. "Outmigration from Rural Mexican Communities." *Interdisciplinary Communications Program Occasional Monograph Series* 5(2): 1–39. Washington, D.C.: Smithsonian Institution.

———. 1978. *Mexican Migration to the United States: Causes, Consequences, and U.S. Responses.* Migration and Development Monograph C/78–9. Cambridge, Mass.: MIT Center for International Studies.

———. 1982. "Interviewing Undocumented Immigrants: Methodological Reflections Based on Fieldwork in Mexico and the U.S." *International Migration Review* 16: 378–411.

Cossío Silva, Luis. 1965. "La Agricultura." Pages 5–17 in *Historia Moderna de México.* Mexico City: Editorial Hermes.

Craig, Richard B. 1971. *The Bracero Program: Interest Groups and Foreign Policy.* Austin: University of Texas Press.

Dagodag, W. Tim. 1975. "Source Regions and Composition of Illegal Mexican Immigration to California." *International Migration Review* 9: 499–511.

de la Peña, Guillermo. 1977. "Industrias y Empresarios en el Sur de Jalisco: Notas para un Estudio Diacrónico." In Guillermo de la Peña, ed. *Ensayos Sobre el Sur de Jalisco.* Mexico City: Casa Chata.

———. 1981. *A Legacy of Promises: Agriculture, Politics, and Ritual in the Morelos Highlands of Mexico.* Austin: University of Texas Press.

———. 1982. "Regional Change, Kinship Ideology, and Family Strategies in Southern Jalisco." Paper presented at the Conference on Theoretical Aspects of Kinship in Latin America and the Caribbean, New York.

Deere, Carmen Diana, and Alain de Janvry. 1979. "A Conceptual Framework for the Empirical Analysis of Peasants." *American Journal of Agricultural Economics* 61: 601–611.

Díaz, May N. 1966. *Tonalá: Conservatism, Responsibility, and Authority in a Mexican Town.* Berkeley and Los Angeles: University of California Press.

Díez-Canedo, Juan. 1980. *A New View of Mexican Migration to the United States.* Ph.D. dissertation, Department of Economics, Massachusetts Institute of Technology. (Spanish Translation: 1984. *La Migración Indocumentada de México a Los Estados Unidos.* Mexico City: Fondo de Cultura Económica.)

Dinerman, Ina R. 1978. "Patterns of Adaptation among Households of U.S.-Bound Migrants from Michoacán, México. *International Migration Review* 12: 485–501.

———. 1982. *Migrants and Stay-at-Homes: A Comparative Study of Rural Migration from Michoacán, México.* Monographs in U.S.–Mexican Studies No. 5. La Jolla: Program in United States–Mexican Studies, University of California at San Diego.

Durand, Jorge. 1983. *En un Pueblo Obrero.* Tesis de Maestría, Centro de Estudios en Antropología Social, El Colegio de Michoacán, Zamora, Michoacán.

Falasco, Dee, and David M. Heer. 1984. "Economic and Fertility Differences Between Legal and Undocumented Mexican Families: Possible Effects of Immigration Policy Changes." *Social Science Quarterly* 65: 495–504.

Fergany, Nader. 1982. "The Impact of Emigration on National Development in the Arab Region: The Case of the Yemen Arab Republic." *International Migration Review* 16: 757–780.

Fienberg, Stephen F., and William M. Mason. 1978. "Identification and Estimation of Age-Period-Cohort Models in the Analysis of Discrete Archival Data." Pages 1–67 in Karl F. Schuessler, ed. *Sociological Methodology 1979.* San Francisco: Jossey-Bass.

Findley, Sally. 1977. *Planning for Internal Migration: A Review of Issues and Policies in Developing Countries.* Washington, D.C.: U.S. Government Printing Office.

Flores, Roy, and Gilbert Cardenas. 1978. *A Study of the Demographic and Employment Characteristics of Undocumented Aliens in San Antonio, El Paso, and McAllen.* San Antonio,

Tex.: U.S. Commission on Civil Rights, Southwestern Regional Office.

Foglio, Fernando. 1936. *Geografía Económica Agrícola del Estado de Michoacán, México.* Mexico City: Editorial Cultura.

Foster, George M. 1942. *A Primitive Mexican Economy.* Seattle: University of Washington Press for the American Ethnological Society.

———. 1953. "What is Folk Culture?" *American Anthropologist* 55: 159–173.

———. 1967. *Tzintzuntzan: Mexican Peasants in a Changing World.* Boston: Little, Brown.

Frisbie, W. Parker. 1975. "Illegal Migration from Mexico to the United States: A Longitudinal Analysis." *International Migration Review* 9: 3–13.

Fromm, Eric, and Michael Maccoby. 1970. *Social Character in a Mexican Village.* Englewood Cliffs, N.J.: Prentice Hall.

Furtado, Celso. 1970. *Economic Development of Latin America.* New York: Cambridge University Press.

Galarza, Ernest. 1964. *Merchants of Labor: The Mexican Bracero Story.* Santa Barbara, Calif.: McNally and Loftin.

Gamio, Manuel. 1922. *La Población del Valle de Teotihuacán: El Medio que se ha Desarrollado, su Evolución Etnica y Social.* Mexico City: Secretariat of Agriculture and Public Works, Division of Anthropology.

———. 1930. *Mexican Immigration to the United States.* Chicago: University of Chicago Press.

———. 1931. *The Mexican Immigrant: His Life-Story.* Chicago: University of Chicago Press.

García y Griego, Manuel. 1979. *El Volumen de la Migración de Mexicanos No Documentados a los Estados Unidos: Nuevas Hipótesis.* Mexico City: Centro Nacional de Información y Estadísticas del Trabajo.

Gilly, Adolfo. 1971. *La Revolución Interrumpida.* Mexico City: El Caballito.

González, Humberto. 1981. *Terratenientes, Campesinos y Empresarios Capitalistas: Un Estudio Socioeconómico Local: Altamira, Jalisco.* Tésis de Licenciatura, Universidad Iberoamericana, Mexico City.

———. 1984. "Las Migraciones a los Estados Unidos en el Occidente de México." Pages 135–157 in F. Alcantara and F. Enrique Sergio y Sanchez, eds. *Desarrollo Rural en Jalisco: Contradicciones y Perspectivas.* Guadalajara: El Colegio de Jalisco.

González, Luis. 1972. *San José de Gracia: Pueblo en Vilo.* Mexico City: El Colegio de México. (English Translation by John Upton: 1974. *San Jose de Gracia: Mexican Village in Transition.* Austin: University of Texas Press.)

———. 1978. *Monagrafías Municipales: Zamora.* Morelia: Gobierno del Estado de Michoacán.

———. 1982. *La Querencia.* Morelia, Michoacán: Editorial SEP Michoacán.

Goodman, Leo A. 1961. "Snowball Sampling." *Annals of Mathematical Statistics* 32: 117–151.

Grasmuck, Sherri. 1982. "Migration within the Periphery: Haitian Labor in the Dominican Sugar and Coffee Industries." *International Migration Review* 16: 365–377.

Graves, Nancy B., and Theodore D. Graves. 1974. "Adaptive Strategies in Urban Migration." *Annual Review of Anthropology* 3: 117–151.

Griffith, David C. 1986. "Social Organizational Obstacles to Capital Accumulation Among Returning Migrants: The British West Indies Temporary Alien Labor Program." *Human Organization* 45: 34–42.

Hall, Linda B. 1982. *El Refugio: Migración Mexicana a los Estados Unidos, 1910–1920.* Historicas: Boletín de Información del Instituto de Investigaciones Históricas 8. Mexico City: Universidad Nacional Autónima de México.

Hammel, Eugene A. 1969. "The Pink Yo-Yo: Occupational Mobility in Belgrade, ca. 1915–1965." *Research Series No. 13.* Berkeley: Institute of International Studies, University of California at Berkeley.

Hanusheck, Eric A., and John E. Jackson. 1977. *Statistical Methods for Social Scientists*. New York: Academic Press.

Hewitt de Alcantara, Cynthia. 1976. *Modernizing Mexican Agriculture: Socioeconomic Implications of Technical Change, 1940–1970*. Geneva: United Nations Research Institute for Social Development.

Hicks, John R. 1969. *A Theory of Economic History*. Oxford: Oxford University Press.

Hoffman, Abraham. 1974. *Unwanted Mexican Americans in the Great Depression: Repatriation Pressures 1929–39*. Tucson: University of Arizona Press.

Ingham, John M. 1970. "The Asymmetrical Implications of Godparenthood in Tlayacapan." *Man* 6: 615–629.

Jenkins, J. Craig. 1977. "Push/Pull in Recent Mexican Migration to the U.S." *International Migration Review* 11: 178–189.

Jones, Richard C. 1982a. "Undocumented Migration from Mexico: Some Geographical Questions." *Annals, Association of American Geographers* 72: 77–87.

———. 1982b. "Channelization of Undocumented Mexican Migrants to the United States." *Economic Geography* 58: 156–176.

———. 1984. "Macro-Patterns of Undocumented Migration between Mexico and the U.S." Pages 33–57 in Richard C. Jones, ed. *Patterns of Undocumented Migration: Mexico and the United States*. Totowa, N.J.: Rowman and Allanheld.

Jongkind, C. F. 1971. "La Supuesta Funcionalidad de los Clubes Regionales in Lima, Perú." *Boletín de Estudios Latinoamericanos* 11: 1–14.

Keely, Charles B. 1979. *U.S. Immigration: A Policy Analysis*. New York: The Population Council.

Kiser, G., and M. Woody. 1979. *Mexican Workers in the United States: Historical and Political Perspectives*. Albuquerque: University of New Mexico Press.

Kroeber, Alfred. 1948. *Anthropology*. New York: Harcourt.

Lailson, Silvia. 1980. "Expansión Limitada y Proliferación Horizontal: La Industria de la Ropa y el Tejido de Punto." *Relaciones: Estudios de Historia y Sociedad* 1(3): 48–102.

Lewis, W. Arthur. 1954. "Economic Development with Unlimited Supplies of Labour." *The Manchester School of Economic and Social Studies* 22(2): 139–191.

Lewis, Oscar. 1951. *Life in a Mexican Village: Tepoztlán Restudied*. Urbana: University of Indiana Press.

———. 1960. *Tepoztlán: Village in Mexico*. New York: Holt, Rinehart, and Winston.

Lomnitz, Larissa. 1975. *Cómo Sobreviven los Marginados*. Mexico City: Siglo XXI. (English Translation: 1977. *Networks and Marginality*. New York: Academic Press.)

Maccoby, Michael. 1967. "Love and Authority: A Study of Mexican Villagers." Pages 336–346 in Jack Potter, May Díaz, and George Foster, eds. *Peasant Society: A Reader*. Boston: Little, Brown.

MacDonald, John S., and Leatrice D. MacDonald. 1974. "Chain Migration, Ethnic Neighborhood Formation, and Social Networks." Pages 226–236 in Charles Tilly, ed. *An Urban World*. Boston: Little, Brown.

Magnin, William. 1959. "The Role of Regional Associations in the Adaption of Rural Population in Peru." *Sociologus* 9: 23–35.

———. 1970. *Peasants in Cities*. Boston: Houghton Mifflin.

Maram, Sheldon L. 1979. "Hispanic Workers in the Garment and Restaurant Industries in Los Angeles County." *Working Papers in U.S.–Mexican Studies No. 12*. La Jolla, Calif.: Program in United States–Mexican Studies, University of California at San Diego.

Marriott, McKim. 1969. "Little Communities in an Indigenous Civilization." Pages 171–222 in McKim Marriott, ed. *Village India*. Chicago: University of Chicago Press.

Mason, Karen O., William M. Mason, Haliman H. Winsborough, and William K. Poole. 1973. "Some Methodological Issues in Cohort Analysis of Archival Data." *American Sociological Review* 38: 242–258.

Mason, William M., Karen O. Mason, and Haliman H. Winsborough. 1976. "Reply to Glenn." *American Sociological Review* 41: 904–905.

Massey, Douglas S. 1985. "The Settlement Process Among Mexican Migrants to the United States: New Methods and Findings." Pages 255–292 in Daniel B. Levine, Kenneth Hill, and Robert Warren, eds. *Immigration Statistics: A Story of Neglect*. Washington, D.C.: National Academy Press.

———. 1987. "Understanding Mexican Migration to the United States." *American Journal of Sociology* 92: 1372–1403.

Massey, Douglas S., and Brendan P. Mullan. 1984. "A Demonstration of the Effect of Seasonal Migration on Fertility." *Demography* 21: 501–518.

Massey, Douglas S., and Kathleen M. Schnabel. 1983. "Recent Trends in Hispanic Immigration to the U.S." *International Migration Review* 17: 212–244.

Melville, Margarita B. 1978. "Mexican Women Adapt to Migration." *International Migration Review* 12: 225–235.

Meyer, Jean A. 1976. *The Cristero Rebellion: The Mexican People Between Church and State, 1926–1929*. New York: Cambridge University Press.

Mines, Richard. 1981. *Developing a Community Tradition of Migration: A Field Study in Rural Zacatecas Mexico and California Settlement Areas*. Monographs in U.S.–Mexican Studies No. 3. La Jolla, Calif.: Program in United States–Mexican Studies, University of California at San Diego.

———. 1984. "Network Migration and Mexican Rural Development: A Case Study." Pages 136–155 in Richard C. Jones, ed. *Patterns of Undocumented Migration: Mexico and the United States*. Totowa, N.J.: Rowman and Allanheld.

Mines, Richard, and Ricardo Anzaldua. 1982. *New Migrants vs. Old Migrants: Alternative Labor Market Structures in the California Citrus Industry*. Monographs in U.S.–Mexican Studies No. 9. La Jolla, Calif.: Program in United States–Mexican Studies, University of California at San Diego.

Mines, Richard, and Alain de Janvry. 1982. "Migration to the United States and Mexican Rural Development: A Case Study." *American Journal of Agricultural Economics* 64: 444–454.

Mines, Richard, and Douglas S. Massey. 1985. "Patterns of Migration to the United States from Two Mexican Communities." *Latin American Research Review* 20: 104–124.

Morales, Patricia. 1981. *Indocumentados Mexicanos*. Mexico City: Editorial Grijalbo.

Morales, Rebecca. 1983. "Transitional Labor: Undocumented Workers in the Los Angeles Automobile Industry." *International Migration Review* 17: 570–596.

Mullan, Brendan P. 1986. *Mexican Migrants in the United States Labor Market: A Study of Migrants' Occupational Mobility*. Ph.D. dissertation, Graduate Group in Demography, University of Pennsylvania.

North, David S. 1983. "Impact of Legal, Illegal, and Refugee Migrants on U.S. Social Service Programs." Pages 269–286 in Mary M. Kritz, ed. *U.S. Immigration and Refugee Policy: Global and Domestic Issues*. Lexington, Mass.: Heath.

North, David S., and Marion F. Houstoun. 1976. *The Characteristics and Role of Illegal Aliens in the U.S. Labor Market: An Exploratory Study*. Washington, D.C.: Linton.

Nutini, Hugo G. 1968. *San Bernardino Contla: Marriage and Family Structure in a Tlaxcalan Municipio*. Pittsburgh: University of Pittsburgh Press.

Orange County Task Force. 1978. *The Economic Impact of Undocumented Immigrants on Medical Costs, Tax Contributions, and Health Needs of Undocumented Migrants*. Santa Ana,

Calif.: Orange County Board of Supervisors.

Paine, Suzanne. 1974. *Exporting Workers: The Turkish Case*. London: Cambridge University Press.

Parkes, Henry B. 1950. *A History of Mexico*. Boston: Houghton Mifflin.

Passel, Jeffrey S., and Karen A. Woodrow. 1984. "Geographic Distribution of Undocumented Immigrants: Estimates of Undocumented Aliens Counted in the 1980 Census by State." *International Migration Review* 18: 642–671.

Pennix, Rinus. 1982. "A Critical Review of Theory and Practice: The Case of Turkey." *International Migration Review* 16: 781–818.

Petersen, Trond. 1985. "A Comment on Presenting Results from Logit and Probit Models." *American Sociological Review* 50: 130–131.

Philpott, Stuart B. 1973. *West Indian Migration*. London: London School of Economics Monographs in Anthropology.

Piore, Michael J. 1979. *Birds of Passage: Migrant Labor and Industrial Societies*. New York: Cambridge University Press.

Pollard, A. H., Farhat Yusuf, and Geoffrey N. Pollard. 1974. *Demographic Techniques*. New York: Pergamon Press.

Portes, Alejandro, and Robert L. Bach. 1985. *Latin Journey: Cuban and Mexican Immigrants in the United States*. Berkeley and Los Angeles: University of California Press.

Pressar, Patricia R. 1982. "The Role of Households in International Migration and the Case of U.S.-Bound Migration from the Dominican Republic." *International Migration Review* 16: 342–364.

Preston, Samuel H. 1975. "The Changing Relation Between Mortality and Level of Economic Development." *Population Studies* 29: 231–248.

Ramírez Flores, José. 1970. *El Consulado de Guadalajara*. Guadalajara: Edición del Banco Refaccionario de Jalisco.

Randall, Laura. 1962. "Labor Migration and Mexican Economic Development." *Social and Economic Studies* 11: 73–81.

Ranis, Gustav, and J. C. H. Fei. 1961. "A Theory of Economic Development." *American Economic Review* 51: 533–565.

Ranney, Susan, and Sherrie Kossoudji. 1983. "Profiles of Temporary Mexican Labor Migrants to the United States." *Population and Development Review* 9: 475–493.

———. 1984. "The Labor Market Experience of Female Migrants: The Case of Temporary Mexican Migration to the U.S." *International Migration Review* 18: 1120–1143.

Ravenstein, E. G. 1885. "The Laws of Migration." *Journal of the Royal Statistical Society* 48: 167–277.

———. 1889. "The Laws of Migration." *Journal of the Royal Statistical Society* 52: 241–302.

Redfield, Robert. 1930. *Tepoztlán, A Mexican Village: A Study of Folk Life*. Chicago: University of Chicago Press.

———. 1956. *Peasant Society and Culture*. Chicago: University of Chicago Press.

Reichert, Joshua S. 1979. *The Migrant Syndrome: An Analysis of U.S. Migration and Its Impact on a Rural Mexican Town*. Ph.D. dissertation, Department of Anthropology, Princeton University, Princeton, N.J.

———. 1981. "The Migrant Syndrome: Seasonal U.S. Wage Labor and Rural Development in Central Mexico." *Human Organization* 40: 56–66.

———. 1982. "Social Stratification in a Mexican Sending Community: The Effect of Migration to the United States." *Social Problems* 29: 422–433.

Reichert, Joshua S., and Douglas S. Massey. 1979. "Patterns of Migration from a Mexican Sending Community: A Comparison of Legal and Illegal Migrants." *International Migration Review* 13: 599–623.

———. 1980. "History and Trends in U.S.-Bound Migration from a Mexican Town."

International Migration Review 475–491.

———. 1982. "Guestworker Programs: Evidence from Europe and the United States and Some Implications for U.S. Policy." *Population Research and Policy Review* 1: 1–17.

Reisler, Mark. 1976. *By the Sweat of their Brow: Mexican Immigrant Labor in the United States: 1900–1940.* Westport, Conn.: Greenwood Press.

Reynolds, Lloyd G. 1980. "Economic Development in Historical Perspective." *American Economic Review* 70(2): 91–95.

Rhoades, Robert E. 1978. "Intra-European Return Migration and Rural Development: Lessons from the Spanish Case." *Human Organization* 37: 136–147.

———. 1979. "From Caves to Main Street: Return Migration and the Transformation of a Spanish Village." *Papers in Anthropology* 20: 57–74.

Roberts, Bryan R. 1973. *Organizing Strangers: Poor Families in Guatemala City.* Austin: University of Texas Press.

———. 1974. "The Interrelation of City and Provinces in Peru and Guatemala." *Latin American Urban Research* 4: 207–235.

———. 1978. *Cities of Peasants: The Political Economy of Urbanization in the Third World.* London: Edward Arnold.

Roberts, Kenneth D. 1982. "Agrarian Structure and Labor Mobility in Rural Mexico." *Population and Development Review* 8: 299–322.

———. 1984. "Agricultural Development and Labor Mobility: A Study of Four Mexican Subregions." Pages 74–92 in Richard C. Jones, ed. *Patterns of Undocumented Migration: Mexico and the United States.* Totowa, N.J.: Rowman and Allanheld.

Rodgers, William L. 1982. "Estimable Functions of Age, Period, and Cohort Effects." *American Sociological Review* 47: 774–786.

Rosenthal-Urey, Ina. 1984. "Church Records as a Source of Data on Mexican Migrant Networks: A Methodological Note." *International Migration Review* 18: 767–781.

Rossi, Peter H. 1955. *Why Families Move.* Glencoe, Ill.: The Free Press.

Rowe, Patricia M. 1979. *Country Demographic Profiles: Mexico.* U.S. Bureau of the Census Series ISP-DP-14. Washington, D.C.: U.S. Government Printing Office.

Rubenstein, Hymie. 1979. "The Return Ideology in West Indian Migration." *Papers in Anthropology* 20: 21–38.

Rulfo, Juan. 1953. *El Llano en Llamas.* Mexico City: Fondo de Cultura Económica. (English Translation by George D. Schade: 1967. *The Burning Plane and Other Stories.* Austin: University of Texas Press.)

———. 1955. *Pedro Páramo.* Mexico City: Fondo de Cultura Económica. (English Translation by Lysander Kemp: 1959. *Pedro Páramo: A Novel of Mexico.* New York: Grove Press.)

Russell, Philip. 1977. *Mexico in Transition.* Austin, Tex.: Colorado River Press.

Samora, Julian. 1971. *Los Mojados: The Wetback Story.* Notre Dame, Ind.: University of Notre Dame Press.

Saul, John S., and Roger Woods. 1971. "African Peasantries." Pages 103–114 in Teodor Shanin, ed. *Peasants and Peasant Societies.* Baltimore: Penguin Books.

Scudder, Thayer, and Elizabeth Colson. 1980. *Secondary Education and the Formation of An Elite: The Impact of Education on Gwembe District, Zambia.* New York: Academic Press.

Selby, Henry A., and Arthur D. Murphy. 1984. "The Mexican Urban Household and the Decision to Migrate to the United States." *Occasional Papers in Social Change No. 4.* Philadelphia: Institute for the Study of Human Issues.

Seligson, Mitchell A., and Edward J. Williams. 1981. *Maquiladoras and Mexican Workers in the Mexico–United States Border Industrialization Program.* Austin: University of Texas Press.

Shadow, Robert D. 1979. "Differential Out-Migration: A Comparison of Internal and International Migration from Villa Guerrero, Jalisco (Mexico)." Pages 67–84 in Fernando Camara and Rovert Van Kemper, eds. *Migration Across Frontiers: Mexico and the United States.* Contributions of the Latin American Anthropology Group, Volume 3. Albany, N.Y.: Institute of Mesoamerican Studies, State University of New York.

Simmons, James W. 1968. "Changing Residence in the City: A Review of Intra-urban Mobility." *Geographical Review* 58: 622–651.

Simon, Julian L. 1984. "Immigrants, Taxes, and Welfare in the United States." *Population and Development Review* 10: 55–70.

Simon, Rita J., and Margo DeLey. 1984. "The Work Experience of Undocumented Mexican Women Migrants in Los Angeles." *International Migration Review* 18: 1212–1229.

Sotelo Inclán, Jesús. 1970. *Raíz y Razón de Zapata.* Mexico City: Editorial CFE.

Soto, Jesús. 1982. *El Desarrollo Desigual en los Municipios de Jalisco (1950–1978).* Guadalajara: Departamento de Programación y Desarrollo del Estado de Jalisco.

Speare, Alden Jr. 1974. "Residential Satisfaction as an Intervening Variable in Residential Mobility." *Demography* 11: 173–188.

Stark, Oded. 1983. "Migration Decision Making: A Review Essay." *Migration and Development Program Discussion Paper No. 3.* Cambridge: Migration and Development Program, Harvard University.

Stark, Oded, and D. Levhari. 1982. "On Migration and Risk in LDCs." *Economic Development and Cultural Change* 31: 191–196.

State of Jalisco. 1982. *La Situación Industrial en Jalisco.* Guadalajara: Departamento de Programación y Desarrollo del Estado de Jalisco.

Stavenhagen, Rodolfo. 1970. "Social Aspects of Agrarian Structure in Mexico." Pages 225–270 in Rodolfo Stavenhagen, ed. *Agrarian Problems and Peasant Movements in Latin America.* Garden City, N.Y.: Anchor.

Stuart, James, and Michael Kearney. 1981. "Causes and Effects of Agricultural Labor Migration from the Mixteca of Oaxaca to California." *Working Papers in U.S.–Mexican Studies No. 28.* La Jolla, Calif.: Program in United States–Mexican Studies, University of California at San Diego.

Swanson, Jan. 1979. "Some Consequences of Emigration for Rural Economic Development in the Yemen Arab Republic." *Middle East Journal* 33: 34–44.

Taylor, J. Edward. 1984. "Differential Migration, Networks, Information, and Risk." *Migration and Development Program Discussion Paper No. 11.* Cambridge, Mass.: Migration and Development Program, Harvard University.

Taylor, Paul S. 1932. "Mexican Labor in the United States: Chicago and the Calument Region." Pages 25–284 in Carl C. Plehn, Ira B. Cross, and Melvin M. Knight, eds. *University of California Publications in Economics,* vol. 7, no. 2. Berkeley: University of California Press.

———. 1933. "A Spanish-Mexican Peasant Community: Arandas in Jalisco, Mexico." *Ibero-Americana,* vol. 4. Berkeley: University of California Press.

Thomas, Brinley. 1954. *Migration and Economic Growth.* London: Cambridge University Press.

Tilly, Charles. 1978. "Migration in Modern European History." Pages 48–72 in William H. McNeil and Ruth S. Adams, eds. *Human Migration.* Bloomington: Indiana University Press.

Tilly, Charles, and C. H. Brown. 1967. "On Uprooting, Kinship, and the Auspices of Migration." *International Journal of Comparative Sociology* 8: 139–164.

Todaro, Michael P. 1976. *Internal Migration in Developing Countries.* Geneva: International Labour Office.

Trebous, M. 1970. *Migration and Development: The Case of Algeria*. Paris: Organization for Economic Cooperation and Development.

Treiman, Donald J. 1975. "Problems of Concept and Measurement in the Comparative Study of Occupational Mobility." *Social Science Research* 4: 183–230.

———. 1977. *Occupational Prestige in Comparative Perspective*. New York: Academic Press.

United Nations. 1980. *Patterns of Urban and Rural Population Growth*. Population Studies No. 68. New York: United Nations.

———. 1983. *Manual X: Indirect Techniques for Demographic Estimation*. Population Studies No. 81. New York: United Nations.

Van Arsdol, Maurice D., Jr., Joan W. Moore, David M. Heer, and Susan P. Haynie. 1979. *Non-apprehended and Apprehended Undocumented Residents in the Los Angeles Labor Market: An Exploratory Study*. Washington, D.C.: U.S. Department of Labor, Manpower Administration.

Vázquez, Daniel. 1985. "La Ciudad en Perspectiva." Pages 57–76 in Patricia Arias, ed. *Guadalajara: La Gran Ciudad de la Pequeña Industria*. Zamora, Michoacoán: El Colegio de Michoacán.

Veerkamp, Verónika K. K. 1981. *La Comercialización y Distribución de Productos Agrícolas a Partir de un Mercado Semanario: El Tianguis de Ciudad Guzmán. Sur de Jalisco*. Tésis de Maestría, Universidad Iberoamericana, Mexico City.

Verduzco, Gustavo. 1984. "Crecimiento Urbano y Desarrollo Regional: El Caso de Zamora, Michoacán." *Relaciones: Estudios de Historia y Sociedad* 5(17): 9–40.

Verduzco, Gustavo, and Margarita Calleja. 1982. "La Pobreza de una Economía Rica: El Caso del Bajío Zamorano." *Cuadernos de Trabajo del Colegio de Michoacán 1*. Zamora: El Colegio de Michoacán.

Villalpando, M. Vic. 1977. *A Study of the Socioeconomic Impact of Illegal Aliens on the County of San Diego*. San Diego: Human Resources Agency, County of San Diego.

Walton, John. 1978. "Guadalajara: Creating the Divided City." Pages 25–50 in Wayne A. Cornelius and Robert V. Kemper, eds. *Metropolitan Latin America: The Challenge and the Response*. Latin American Urban Research, Vol. 6. Beverly Hills and London: Sage.

Wiest, Raymond E. 1973. "Wage-labor Migration and the Household in a Mexican Town." *Journal of Anthropological Research* 29: 180–209.

———. 1979. "Implications of International Labor Migration for Mexican Rural Development." Pages 85–97 in Fernando Camara and Robert Van Kemper, eds. *Migration Across Frontiers: Mexico and the United States*. Albany, N.Y.: Institute for Mesoamerican Studies, State University of New York.

———. 1984. "External Dependency and the Perpetuation of Temporary Migration to the United States." Pages 110–135 in Richard C. Jones, ed. *Patterns of Undocumented Migration: Mexico and the United States*. Totowa, N.J.: Rowman and Allanheld.

Wolf, Eric R. 1959. *Sons of the Shaking Earth*. Chicago: University of Chicago Press.

———. 1966. *Peasants*. Englewood Cliffs, N.J.: Prentice-Hall.

Wood, Charles C. 1981. "Structural Changes and Household Strategies: A Conceptual Framework for the Study of Rural Migration." *Human Organization* 40: 338–344.

Zazueta, Carlos H., and R. Corona. 1979. *Los Trabajadores Mexicanos en los Estados Unidos: Primeros Resultados de la Encuesta Nacional de Emigración*. Mexico City: Centro Nacional de Información y Estadísticas del Trabajo.

Zorbaugh, Harvey W. 1929. *The Gold Coast and the Slum*. Chicago: University of Chicago Press.

Index